Ethics

in

Higher Education

A Reader for Writers

edited by:

Nancy Henke

Lisa Langstraat

Adam Mackie

Emily Morgan

FOUNTAINHEAD
PRESS

Our green initiatives include:

Electronic Products
We deliver products in non-paper form whenever possible. This includes pdf down-loadables, flash drives, & CDs.

Electronic Samples
We use Xample, a new electronic sampling system. Instructor samples are sent via a personalized web page that links to pdf downloads.

FSC
FSC Certified Printers
All of our printers are certified by the Forest Service Council which promotes environmentally and socially responsible management of the world's forests. This program allows consumer groups, individual consumers, and businesses to work together hand-in-hand to promote responsible use of the world's forests as a re-newable and sustainable resource.

Recycled Paper
Most of our products are printed on a minimum of 30% post-consumer waste recycled paper.

Support of Green Causes
When we do print, we donate a portion of our revenue to green causes. Listed below are a few of the organizations that have received donations from Fountain-head Press. We welcome your feedback and suggestions for contributions, as we are always searching for worthy initiatives.
Rainforest 2 Reef
Environmental Working Group

Cover Photo: CSU Media Relations

Books may be purchased for educational purposes.

For information, please call or write:

1-800-586-0330
Fountainhead Press
Southlake, TX 76092
Web Site: www.fountainheadpress.com
E-mail: customerservice@fountainheadpress.com

First Edition

ISBN: 978-1-59871-723-5

Printed in the United States of America

Acknowledgements

We would like to thank the CSU English department, especially our colleagues who, with dedication, creativity, and integrity, make our Composition Program stellar. Special thanks to Vani Kannan and Sam Iacovetto, whose early work on this project shaped its direction. Your enthusiasm, critical acumen, and sense of humor have sustained us. Thanks to the world's best copyeditor, Tiffany Myers. Our appreciation also goes out to Fountainhead Press for their support of this project.

We wish to acknowledge the talents and dedication of former CSU composition director Sarah Sloane, who first forged a relationship with Fountainhead Press and modeled the intellectual energy and curiosity vital for projects like this one.

Nancy Henke thanks her husband, Kyle, for always reminding her of the benefits of projects like this—especially when the workload casts a wide shadow and makes them hard to see; her mother, Sheila, who instilled respect for the written word in thousands of kids (including five of her own); and her colleagues who energize, inspire, and entertain her.

Emily Morgan thanks Chad Morgan, the most devoted father and encouraging husband; her little leprechauns, Addie and Matt, whose antics make her smile even when the hours are long and the projects seem never-ending; and her parents, who once told her to follow her heart and never look back. Emily sends a final thanks to her colleagues for making this project so enjoyable.

Adam Mackie expresses his gratitude to his wife Margaret, his son Noah, and his daughter Hazel for their continuous love and support. He also gives special thanks to his mother Tennie, his sister Amy, and his colleagues for walking with him through the writing process.

Lisa Langstraat is deeply grateful for the opportunity to work with colleagues of Emily, Nancy, and Adam's caliber. They have taught her much and well. To put it simply, they rock!

Finally, special thanks to our composition students, whose willingness to converse and write about these important issues solidifies our faith in the next generation of college graduates.

Please note that the copyright of this reader is not granted to any individual but is instead held by the CSU Composition Program as a whole. All funds earned through the sales of this book are allocated to individuals and projects that enhance CSU students' educational experiences.

The content of this book does not necessarily represent the views of the CSU English Department. These readings are offered as examples of different rhetorical strategies, intended audiences, purposes, genres, and rhetorical contexts. They are included here not to promote any single point-of-view, but to present a wide range of views and rhetorical possibilities available for writers.

Table of Contents

CHAPTER 1

Ethical Education: Changes in Mission, People, and Places 3

Changes in Mission and Vision

Changes in People and Places

CHAPTER 2

Ethical Values: Economic Costs 105

Costs and Student Loans

For-Profit Education

CHAPTER 3

Ethical Actions: Academic Integrity 191

Honor and Integrity

Plagiarism and Cheating

CHAPTER 4

Introduction:
Ethics in Higher Education

> "Above all things I hope the education of the common people will be attended to; convinced that on their good sense we may·rely with the most security for the preservation of a due degree of liberty."
>
> —Thomas Jefferson, Letter to James Madison, 1787

Thomas Jefferson and his fellow revolutionaries were adamant: an educated citizenry was indispensable if the democracy they envisioned would be successful. Certainly, voters in this new democracy needed basic literacy skills to read about important concerns of the day. They also, however, needed *critical* literacy skills—the ability not only to comprehend, but also to evaluate, question, and develop multiple courses of action. Without that critical literacy, without the power of citizens to make ethical decisions and challenge those in power through their votes, Jefferson maintained that the principles of democracy and liberty would be jeopardized.

The Jeffersonian ideal of an educated, critical public resulted in our system of public schools (the first in any country), as well as the programs of study at U.S. universities of the time. In fact, if you were an 18th century college student at, say, Harvard, public debate about the political and social problems of the day would constitute the majority of your studies. As historian S. Michael Halloran explains, in order to graduate from Harvard, you wouldn't have been required to take final exams in, for example, the medical, legal, or clerical subject areas. Instead, your "final exam" would have been a public debate about a current civic issue. Your audience—your professors, fellow students, and other eminent citizens (politicians, authors, etc.)—would evaluate your performance. To earn your diploma, you would have to present a persuasive, well-reasoned, well-supported argument worthy of communal action. In other words, you would have to be a great rhetorician.

Today, the term "rhetoric" has rather negative connotations. We think of a bloated, insincere politician or radio host, willing to say anything to get the votes or to increase a fan base. But rhetoric was at the center of university curricula for centuries. It was necessary to have good rhetorical skills if you were to fully participate in public life, whether as a doctor or a merchant. Only by expressing your knowledge well could you render that knowledge of *use* in a democracy. Halloran refers to this university curriculum as the "rhetoric of citizenship" because, rather than focusing primarily on personal growth or vocational training, it focuses on each student's right and responsibility to actively participate in a democracy, to develop habits of mind and action that further the common good (252).

Ethics in Higher Education is intended to tap into and revive that "rhetoric of citizenship." This isn't to say that we propose a nostalgic return to the antiquated ways of 18th century universities. After all, despite their democratic motivations, universities were quite exclusive back then: only the sons of very wealthy, white families were admitted to U.S. universities like Harvard. Women were not admitted to universities until the 1830's, and even then, they were generally shepherded toward the "domestic" studies considered appropriate for the female mind. African Americans were segregated; only after the civil war were historically black colleges, such as Howard University, inaugurated. And until very recently, only the wealthiest could attend college—federal financial aid and student loans were nonexistent. It's quite a contradiction; universities devoted to democratic principles excluded great numbers of Americans, many of whom were also denied the right to vote.

The very tenets of that rhetoric of citizenship, however, eventually resulted in challenges to many exclusionary college admission policies. And that is where *Ethics in Higher Education* steps in. We invite you to develop your understanding of powerful rhetorical strategies and to use your rhetorical skills to address and act upon issues that are genuinely important for all students and communities in our contemporary democracy. This collection provides an entry point into conversations that are timely and sometimes heated. We hope that learning to recognize how writers employ successful rhetorical strategies will empower you to do the same: to listen to various perspectives in a conversation, to expand the conversation and gather various perspectives about it, and to contribute to that conversation.

At the heart of critical literacy is the ability to carefully listen, analyze, communicate, and act. While this book focuses on the subject of higher education, the habits of mind and rhetorical strategies these essays embody are transferable to any subject, any issue that demands understanding, analysis, and action. As a college student, you have probably been mulling over many of the subjects addressed in *Ethics in Higher Education*. If you haven't considered the ways in which your own higher-education experiences are linked to democratic principles, ethical decisions, and rhetorical strategies, we hope these essays illustrate that these issues are deeply intertwined.

We have organized *Ethics in Higher Education* into four chapters, but you'll find that the essays, articles, and images are relevant across all chapter topics. Chapter One, "Ethical Education: Changes in Mission, People, and Places" (developed by Lisa Langstraat), provides an introduction to the changing landscape of higher education. It features mission statements from various colleges and universities, each of which has diverse views about their roles in our society and students' needs; an exploration of changing academic labor practices, particularly given the significant increase of part-time, non-tenure-track faculty who teach the great majority of college courses today; and a range of discussions about the changing place of learning—in particular, the meteoric increase in on-line courses and degrees. Each of these issues is greatly affected by new economic challenges facing colleges and universities in our nation, and this chapter invites you to explore the connections between missions, the people who teach you, and the places where learning happens.

Chapter Two, "Ethical Values: Economic Costs" (developed by Nancy Henke), more overtly explores the changing economics of higher education. In 2010, many Americans were stunned to learn that 67 percent of college graduates had accrued student loan debt, and that, for the first time in history, Americans owed more on their student loans than they did on their credit cards (Cohn). Chapter Two invites you to consider the causes and effects of this turn of events, as well as the ethical challenges inspired by a new sector of higher education: for-profit colleges and universities.

Chapter Three, "Ethical Actions: Academic Integrity" (developed by Adam Mackie), engages an issue more overtly associated with ethical questions— plagiarism and academic integrity. According to the Educational Testing Service, academic dishonesty is at an all-time high: between 75 and 98 percent of college students admit to cheating in high school, compared to 20% in the 1940's. Colleges and universities are scrambling to address the problem by developing Honor Codes and Academic Integrity contracts. Plagiarism, a focus of this chapter, is linked to changes in technology, especially the Internet, as well as changing perceptions of intellectual property.

Chapter Four, "Ethical Engagement: Campus Communities" (developed by Emily Morgan), spotlights students' relationships with one another and with the faculty and administrators whose policies shape attitudes about campus life. Narrowing the discussion to college athletics programs, the dynamics of fraternities and sororities, and the problems of sexual assault and harassment on college campuses, Chapter Four offers a provocative view of the connections between campus communities and the ethical challenges facing all citizens in a democracy.

Ethics in Higher Education is by no means an exhaustive overview of the ethical quandaries facing college students, faculty, and administrators today. It does, however, illustrate how our daily actions and relationships demand careful ethical consideration. By exploring these issues and the rhetorical dynamics of communication, by reading, researching, and writing in principled ways, you will be engaging the democratic foundation of our institutions of higher education. We hope this collection challenges you to enhance your critical literacy skills and to understand writing as an integral feature of life in a democracy.

Works Cited

Cohn, Scott. "The Debt That Won't Go Away." *CNBC.* NBC Universal. 20 Dec 2010. Web. 10 July 2013. <http://www.cnbc.com/id/40680905>.

Educational Testing Service. "Cheating Is a Personal Foul." *Glass Castle*, n.d. Web. 10 July 2013. <http://www.glass-castle.com/clients/www-nocheating-org/adcouncil/research/ cheatingfactsheet. html>.

Halloran, S. Michael. "Rhetoric in the American College Curriculum: The Decline of Public Discourse." *PRE/TEXT* 3 (Fall 1983): 245-69.

Jefferson, Thomas. "Letter to James Madison Paris, Dec 20, 1787." *American History From Revolution to Reconstruction.* University of Groningen. 2012. Web. 17 July 2013. <http://www.let.rug.nl/ usa/presidents/thomas-jefferson/letters-of-thomas-jefferson/jefl66.php>.

Chapter 1

Ethical Education: Changes in Mission, People, and Places

Changes in Mission and
Vision

Changes in People and
Places

1

Ethical Education: Changes in Mission, People, and Places

> "Intelligence plus character—that is the goal of true education."
>
> —Martin Luther King Jr.

Few could dispute the spirit of Martin Luther King's sentiment. A formal education should provide you with the fundamental information necessary for critical understanding and professional proficiency. A formal education should also help you cultivate an ethical compass, an informed and compassionate character that inspires informed and compassionate action. The question, however, is *how* colleges should reach these aspirations, especially given new economic realities, extraordinary technological developments, and changing cultural expectations. What should a college *do* for its students? For you? How can a college practice ethical conduct, so that you learn not only through direct instruction, but also by example? How should institutions of higher learning negotiate a changing technological landscape and still maintain the sense of community and personal relationships so important to learning? These are tough questions, and this chapter invites you to consider them in light of three specific issues facing higher education today: how colleges and universities should articulate their missions; whether colleges have an ethical obligation to ensure fair labor practices and academic freedom; and whether something—some quality of exchange and inspiration—might be sacrificed in online courses as they proliferate and supplant traditional brick-and-mortar places of learning.

We begin with mission statements from five quite different colleges: Howard University, a historically black university; University of Phoenix, a for-profit institution; Front Range Community College, a two-year college; Michigan State University, a land-grant research university; and Wake Forest University, a private liberal arts school. Historically, the mission statement (like the vision statement or the strategic plan) was the purview of the corporate realm; a company's mission statement was designed to induce customer and stakeholder "buy in." Perhaps institutions of higher learning have found that a business model is necessary in the current economic climate? And is it possible that, as both Mark Edmundson ("Who Are You and What Are You Doing Here?") and Nels Granholm ("Global Imperatives of the 21st Century: The Academy's Response") argue, that contemporary universities suffer from conflicting goals and expectations, making it difficult to foster the kind of knowledge-making that leads to humane, ethical action?

Another recent development in higher education that has important ethical ramifications is the increasing number of non-tenure-track faculty on campus. If you've ever examined a course catalog and noticed that the word "STAFF" appears multiple times where the professor's name should be listed, you're seeing evidence of a dramatic transformation in colleges' hiring practices. "STAFF" usually refers to a "contingent" (sometimes called "adjunct") faculty member—a non-tenure-track, part-time instructor who might be hired at the last minute to teach a course, depending on enrollment needs. Reports from the American Association of University Professors and the National Council of Teachers of English, as well as articles by contingent faculty and activists Maria Maistos, Steven Street, and Karen Thompson, provide a nuanced perspective about the growing number of non-tenure-track faculty whom colleges are hiring. As Maistos and Street note in "Confronting Contingency: Faculty Equity and the Goals of Academic Democracy," more than 50% of all college faculty today are contingent. This, they contend, creates unethical work conditions in the very institutions of higher learning where such ethics are imperative.

Is the increased reliance on contingent faculty born out of economic necessity, or is it simply a way for universities to take advantage of low-cost labor? And what are the consequences of the university's heavy reliance on contingent faculty who are ineligible for tenure? Historically, colleges primarily appointed faculty who, upon establishing a good publication record, teaching effectively, and contributing to the governance of their college, would be eligible for tenure after a seven-year probation period. Tenure has long been instituted not simply to provide job security, but to ensure academic freedom: without tenure, professors who investigate highly controversial issues—from human stem cell research to systemic racism—may face dismissal, simply because their ideas or findings are unpopular. Since careful, unbiased research can lead to unpopular results, tenure protects not only professors, but the pursuit of truth and reliable information.

These ethical concerns apply not only to the hiring and retention of faculty on campus, but also to the role of technology in higher education. As colleges rush to institute more online courses and online degree programs, we all face the challenge of ensuring that new technologies are implemented ethically. In Doug Lederman's "Growth in Online Learning" and The Sloane Consortium's report in this chapter, you'll see that online courses already have a strong foothold in the academy, and that there are conflicting perspectives about the efficacy and value of online instruction. The Sloane Consortium's report, for example, notes that many university faculty and students consider online courses and online degree programs evidence of an institution's desire to generate revenue at the sacrifice of genuine, rigorous learning. Others, such as Todd Gilman, argue that online classes can surpass traditional face-to-face instruction if, and only if, instructors employ creative teaching strategies and recognize that the place of learning—whether in virtual or brick-and-mortar settings—affects how we learn. In "Veterans Weigh Pros, Cons of Online Education," Devon Haynie discusses both the value and challenges of online education for a specific student population, post-9/11 veterans.

As the title of this chapter, "Ethical Education: Changes in Mission, People, and Places," suggests, institutions of higher learning are facing dramatic, long-term changes in their missions, faculty, and places of learning. Each of these changes raises crucial ethical questions. We invite you to join the conversation about these issues and, as a student and writer, take the action that your ethical compass, hopefully enhanced by reading the texts in this chapter, guides you toward.

Collected Mission and Vision Statements

Howard University, University of Phoenix, Front Range Community College, Michigan State University, and Wake Forest University

The following mission statements (also called "vision statements" or "strategic plan objectives") represent an array of colleges and universities. Howard University is a historically black university, established in 1867, soon after the Civil War, to provide higher education opportunities to African Americans; University of Phoenix is a for-profit, mostly online institution that advertises primarily to business professionals; Front Range Community College offers two-year degrees, and a large percentage of its student population is "non-traditional" (over 24 years old, working 30 or more hours a week, etc.); Michigan State University is a public "land-grant" university which focuses on research and offers PhD programs; and Wake Forest College is a private liberal arts school, historically intended to focus on open inquiry, rather than primarily on vocational objectives. Each of these mission statements is published on the college or university's website. As you review these statements, consider how each is appealing to multiple audiences: prospective students, parents of students, alumni donors, university trustees, and stakeholders.

1. Which of these mission statements is most consistent with your ideal of a college education? Why?

2. Locate and review your own college's mission statement. What would you add to that statement to ensure that it meets your educational goals?

3. Compare the visual rhetoric (the layout, font choices, image choices, etc.) of two mission statements. Which statement uses visual strategies most persuasively? Why?

Office of the President

Mission

Howard University, a culturally diverse, comprehensive, research intensive and historically Black private university, provides an educational experience of exceptional quality at the undergraduate, graduate, and professional levels to students of high academic standing and potential, with particular emphasis upon educational opportunities for Black students. Moreover, the University is dedicated to attracting and sustaining a cadre of faculty who are, through their teaching, research and service, committed to the development of distinguished, historically aware, and compassionate graduates and to the discovery of solutions to human problems in the United States and throughout the world. With an abiding interest in both domestic and international affairs, the University is committed to continuing to produce leaders for America and the global community.

Vision Priorities

Vision: Through its programs of exemplary quality, Howard University will be the first HBCU to become a top-50 research university, while it continues its traditions of leadership and service to underserved communities nationally and abroad.

- Enhance status as a major comprehensive metropolitan research university (with competitive undergraduate, graduate, and professional programs)
- Increase excellence in teaching and learning
- Expand the international footprint and role in world affairs
- Provide environment of open discourse (*Think Tank* for the Nation)
- Extend public service role through expanded engagement with local, national and international communities

 **University of Phoenix®**

Locations › Continuing Education › Military ›

Degrees ▾ | Admissions ▾ | Aca

Home › About University of Phoenix › Mission and Purpose

Mission and Purpose

University of Phoenix provides access to higher education opportunities that enable students to develop knowledge and skills necessary to achieve their professional goals, improve the productivity of their organizations and provide leadership and service to their communities.

Purposes

- To facilitate cognitive and affective student learning—knowledge, skills, and values—and to promote use of that knowledge in the student's work place.
- To develop competence in communication, critical thinking, collaboration, and information utilization, together with a commitment to lifelong learning for enhancement of students' opportunities for career success.
- To provide instruction that bridges the gap between theory and practice through faculty members who bring to their classroom not only advanced academic preparation, but also the skills that come from the current practice of their professions.
- To provide General Education and foundational instruction and services that prepare students to engage in a variety of university curricula.
- To use technology to create effective modes and means of instruction that expand access to learning resources and that enhance collaboration and communication for improved student learning.
- To assess student learning and use assessment data to improve the teaching/learning system, curriculum, instruction, learning resources, counseling and student services.
- To be organized as a for-profit institution in order to foster a spirit of innovation that focuses on providing academic quality, service, excellence, and convenience to the working student.
- To generate the financial resources necessary to support the University's mission.

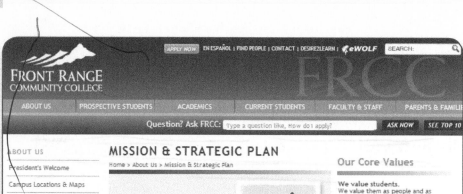

APPLY NOW | EN ESPAÑOL | FIND PEOPLE | CONTACT | DESIRE2LEARN | eWOLF   SEARCH:

FRONT RANGE
COMMUNITY COLLEGE

FRCC

ABOUT US   PROSPECTIVE STUDENTS   ACADEMICS   CURRENT STUDENTS   FACULTY & STAFF   PARENTS & FAMILIE

Question? Ask FRCC: Type a question like, How do I apply?   ASK NOW   SEE TOP 10

ABOUT US

President's Welcome

Campus Locations & Maps

Online Learning

Continuing Education

Corporate Solutions & Small Business Development

Foundation

Institutional Research

Accreditation

Mission & Strategic Plan

Administration

Area Advisory Council

Job Opportunities

SMART MOVE

FRONT RANGE COMMUNITY COLLEGE

START HERE

MISSION & STRATEGIC PLAN

Home > About Us > Mission & Strategic Plan

Our Mission

At Front Range Community College, we enrich lives through learning.

Download Phase I of our Strategic Plan.

FRONT RANGE
COMMUNITY COLLEGE
VISION 2015

Our Vision

Our vision is that all students at Front Range Community College will accomplish their educational and career goals. We will be recognized for our singular focus on student success, our exceptional teaching, our strong commitment to diverse learners and communities, and our effective business and community partnerships.

Our Strategic Priorities

Student Success

FRCC supports and improves student persistence and completion through instructional excellence, exceptional student support services, and a commitment to the understanding that learning happens everywhere. Faculty, instructors, and staff are well-versed in the scholarship of teaching and learning as it relates to their area of expertise, and receive meaningful professional development and training to enhance their respective practices and support innovation. We improve student success with careful assessment and measurement and a commitment to using data to make effective decisions.

Opportunities for Diverse Learners and Communities

Our student body reflects the diversity of our communities because we create learning environments that welcome diversity in all its forms and actively engage the growing minority communities in our service area. All students benefit from our college services, which are welcoming, easy to navigate, and focused on the learning, growth, and development of the whole student.

Strong Partnerships

We are the first-choice educational partner for industry, K-12 education, and community organizations. Local businesses value us for our high-quality instructional services that respond to immediate and long-term industry needs. We work closely with our business and community partners to educate and train highly qualified employees, develop a strong regional workforce, and identify opportunities for appropriate and responsible program development; consequently, the state of Colorado views us as a vital component of building a robust workforce.

Culture of Collaboration, Innovation, and Pride

We recognize that the success of this plan rests on the success of our employees and their ability to be responsive, dynamic, and creative. We are committed to a culture that supports innovation, creativity, collaboration, healthy work-life balance, and excellence in all that we do. We support and encourage additional staff training and professional development. We invest appropriately in additional staff whenever possible and necessary to provide quality service to students and work-life balance for our employees.

Resource Development and Sustainability

We are mindful of the importance of holding our institution in trust for future generations. To that end, we invest in safe, appealing facilities that meet student and staff needs and are viable in the long-term on all campuses. We also continue to be committed to fiscal responsibility and efficiency in all operations. With state funding uncertain, we invest in successful grant development and fundraising to broaden our funding sources.

Our Core Values

We value students.
We value them as people and as learners and for the diverse perspectives that they contribute.

We value teaching and learning.
We value exceptional teaching in a dynamic and varied learning environment.

We value community.
We value a sense of community and collaboration in partnerships.

We value employees.
We value the commitment, knowledge, diversity, and uniqueness of our employees. We value the strengths of our employees, as well as their potential.

Download Phase I of our Strategic Plan.

MICHIGAN STATE UNIVERSITY | Office of the President
Lou Anna K. Simon

Home

From the President's Desk

Presidential Initiatives

Communications

- President's Reports
- Speeches
- Podcasts
- Academic Publications

Presidential Statements

- Core Values
- Diversity and Inclusion
- Free Speech

President's Biography

Leadership Planning
Meetings

Advancing our Campus

History of the MSU
Presidency

MSU Mission Statement

MSU Mission Statement

The following statement was approved by the Board of Trustees on April 18, 2008.

Michigan State University, a member of the Association of American Universities and one of the top 100 research universities in the world, was founded in 1855. We are an inclusive, academic community known for our traditionally strong academic disciplines and professional programs, and our liberal arts foundation. Our cross- and interdisciplinary enterprises connect the sciences , humanities, and professions in practical, sustainable, and innovative ways to address society's rapidly changing needs.

As a public, research-intensive, land-grant university funded in part by the state of Michigan, our mission is to advance knowledge and transform lives by:

- providing outstanding undergraduate, graduate, and professional education to promising, qualified students in order to prepare them to contribute fully to society as globally engaged citizen leaders

- conducting research of the highest caliber that seeks to answer questions and create solutions in order to expand human understanding and make a positive difference, both locally and globally

- advancing outreach, engagement, and economic development activities that are innovative, research-driven, and lead to a better quality of life for individuals and communities, at home and around the world

Wake Forest:
The Collegiate University

Vision and Mission Statements

Vision

Wake Forest University aspires to:

- Emphasize exceptional teaching, discovery, and student engagement within a dynamic academic community;

- Integrate the intimacy of an undergraduate liberal arts college with the academic vitality of a research university;

- Become a crossroads of discussion on the important national and international issues of our time;

- Attract a diverse community of the brightest educators and students from throughout the country and the world;

- Link intellectual curiosity, moral reflection and a commitment to service, shaping ethically informed leaders to serve humanity.

Mission

Wake Forest is a distinctive university that combines a liberal arts core with graduate and professional schools and innovative research programs. The University embraces the teacher-scholar ideal, prizing personal interaction between students and faculty. It is a place where exceptional teaching, fundamental research and discovery, and the engagement of faculty and students in the classroom and the laboratory are paramount.

The University continues to fulfill its ideal of a more diverse learning community, providing students an example of the world they will be called upon to lead. The University sustains a vibrant residential community with a broad-based program of service and extracurricular activities. The University recognizes the benefits of intercollegiate athletics conducted with integrity and at the highest level.

Central to its mission, the University believes in the development of the whole person – intellectual, moral, spiritual and physical. From its rich religious heritage, Wake Forest is committed to sustaining an environment where vital beliefs and faith traditions can engage secular thought in a climate of academic freedom and an unfettered search for truth. The University embraces the challenges of religious pluralism.

While national in scope, the university has been shaped by a culture that is distinctively North Carolinian. This history provides it with a sense of place and community responsibility. In extending its reach, the University has made a priority of international study and international understanding. Wake Forest seeks to be a place where a vibrant and diverse learning community weds knowledge, experiences and service that lift the human spirit.

Who Are You and What Are You Doing Here?

Mark Edmundson

Oxford American

August 2011

Mark Edmundson is a tenured Professor of English at the University of Virginia. He has published widely, in both scholarly and popular venues, about literature, higher education, and popular culture. This article was originally published in the *Oxford American*, a non-profit literary magazine "dedicated to featuring the best in Southern writing while documenting the complexity and vitality of the American South." This article appeared in a special issue of the magazine dedicated to educational issues.

1. Edmundson claims that ours is a culture in which "the major and determining values are monetary." How do these values, according to Edmundson, shape higher education for students, teachers and administrators?

2. Consider the subtitle of this article, "A message in a bottle to the incoming class." It operates metaphorically to suggest that students and higher education may be lost at sea or stranded on a desert island. What other metaphors does Edmundson rhetorically employ in this essay? Do you agree with his claim that, as you earn your college degree, "you'll be looking into the reach of every metaphor that every discipline offers, and you'll be trying to see around their corners"?

3. Compare Edmundson's characterization of college faculty to Karen Thompson's portrayal of herself and her colleagues, later in this chapter. How might Thompson respond to Edmundson's depiction of university faculty?

Welcome and congratulations: Getting to the first day of college is a major achievement. You're to be commended, and not just you, but the parents, grandparents, uncles, and aunts who helped get you here.

It's been said that raising a child effectively takes a village: Well, as you may have noticed, our American village is not in very good shape. We've got guns, drugs, two wars, fanatical religions, a slime-based popular culture, and some politicians who—a little restraint here—aren't what they might be. To merely survive in this American village and to win a place in the entering class has taken a lot of grit on your part. So, yes, congratulations to all.

You now may think that you've about got it made. Amidst the impressive college buildings, in company with a high-powered faculty, surrounded by the best of your generation, all you need is to keep doing what you've done before: Work hard, get good grades, listen to your teachers, get along with the people around you, and you'll emerge in four years as an educated young man or woman. Ready for life.

Do not believe it. It is not true. If you want to get a real education in America you're going to have to fight—and I don't mean just fight against the drugs and the violence and against the slime-based culture that is still going to surround you. I mean something a little more disturbing. To get an education, you're probably going to have to fight against the institution that you find yourself in—no matter how prestigious it may be. (In fact, the more prestigious the school, the more you'll probably have to push.) You can get a terrific education in America now—there are astonishing opportunities at almost every college—but the education will not be presented to you wrapped and bowed. To get it, you'll need to struggle and strive, to be strong, and occasionally even to piss off some admirable people.

I came to college with few resources, but one of them was an understanding, however crude, of how I might use my opportunities there. This I began to develop because of my father, who had never been to college—in fact, he'd barely gotten out of high school. One night after dinner, he and I were sitting in our kitchen at 58 Clewley Road in Medford, Massachusetts, hatching plans about the rest of my life. I was about to go off to college, a feat no one in my family had accomplished in living memory. "I think I might want to be pre-law," I told my father. I had no idea what being pre-law was. My father compressed his brow and blew twin streams of smoke, dragon-like, from his magnificent nose. "Do you want to be a lawyer?" he asked. My father had some experience with lawyers, and with policemen, too; he was not well-disposed toward either. "I'm not really sure," I told him, "but lawyers make pretty good money, right?"

My father detonated. (That was not uncommon. My father detonated a lot.) He told me that I was going to go to college only once, and that while I was there I had better study what I wanted. He said that when rich kids went to school, they majored in the subjects that interested them, and that my younger brother Philip and I were as good as any rich kids. (We were rich kids minus the money.) Wasn't I interested in literature? I confessed that I was. Then I had better study literature, unless I had inside information to the effect that reincarnation wasn't just hype, and I'd be able to attend college thirty or forty times. If I had such info, pre-law would be fine, and maybe even a tour through invertebrate biology could also be tossed in. But until I had the reincarnation stuff from a solid source, I better get to work and pick out some English classes from the course catalog. "How about the science requirements?"

"Take 'em later," he said, "you never know."

My father, Wright Aukenhead Edmundson, Malden High School Class of 1948 (by a hair), knew the score. What he told me that evening at the Clewley Road kitchen table was true in itself, and it also contains the germ of an idea about what a university education should be. But apparently almost everyone else—students, teachers, and trustees and parents—sees the matter much differently. They have it wrong.

Education has one salient enemy in present-day America, and that enemy is education—university education in particular. To almost everyone, university education is a means to an end. For students, that end is a good job. Students want the credentials that will help them get ahead. They want the certificate that will give them access to Wall Street, or entrance into law or medical or business school. And how can we blame them? America values power and money, big players with big bucks. When we raise our children, we tell them in multiple ways that what we want most for them is success—material success. To be poor in America is to be a failure—it's to be without decent health care, without basic necessities, often without dignity. Then there are those back-breaking student loans—people leave school as servants, indentured to pay massive bills, so that first job better be a good one. Students come to college with the goal of a diploma in mind— what happens in between, especially in classrooms, is often of no deep and determining interest to them.

In college, life is elsewhere. Life is at parties, at clubs, in music, with friends, in sports. Life is what celebrities have. The idea that the courses you take should be the primary objective of going to college is tacitly considered absurd. In terms of their work, students live in the future and not the present; they live with their prospects for success. If universities stopped issuing credentials, half of the clients would be gone by tomorrow morning, with the remainder following fast behind.

The faculty, too, is often absent: Their real lives are also elsewhere. Like most of their students, they aim to get on. The work they are compelled to do to advance—get tenure, promotion, raises, outside offers—is, broadly speaking, scholarly work. No matter what anyone says, this work has precious little to do with the fundamentals of teaching. The proof is that virtually no undergraduate students can read and understand their professors' scholarly publications. The public senses this disparity and so thinks of the professors' work as being silly or beside the point. Some of it is. But the public also senses that because professors don't pay full-bore attention to teaching they don't have to work very hard—they've created a massive feather bed for themselves and called it a university.

This is radically false. Ambitious professors, the ones who, like their students, want to get ahead in America, work furiously. Scholarship, even if pretentious and almost unreadable, is nonetheless labor-intense. One can slave for a year or two on a single article for publication in this or that refereed journal. These essays are honest: Their footnotes reflect real reading, real assimilation, and real dedication. Shoddy work—in which the author cheats, cuts corners, copies from others—is quickly detected. The people who do this work have highly developed intellectual powers, and they push themselves hard to reach a certain standard: That the results have almost no practical relevance to the students, the public, or even, frequently, to other scholars is a central element in the tragicomedy that is often academia.

The students and the professors have made a deal: Neither of them has to throw himself heart and soul into what happens in the classroom. The students write their abstract, over-intellectualized essays; the professors grade the students for their capacity to be abstract and over-intellectual—and often genuinely smart. For their essays can be brilliant, in a chilly way; they can also be clipped off the Internet, and often are. Whatever the case, no one wants to invest too much in them—for life is elsewhere. The professor saves his energies for the profession, while the student saves his for friends, social life, volunteer work, making connections, and getting in position to clasp hands on the true grail, the first job.

No one in this picture is evil; no one is criminally irresponsible. It's just that smart people are prone to look into matters to see how they might go about buttering their toast. Then they butter their toast.

As for the administrators, their relation to the students often seems based not on love but fear. Administrators fear bad publicity, scandal, and dissatisfaction on the part of their customers. More than anything else, though, they fear lawsuits. Throwing a student out of college, for this or that piece of bad behavior, is very difficult, almost impossible. The student will sue your eyes out. One kid I knew (and rather liked) threatened on his blog to mince his dear and esteemed professor (me) with a samurai sword for the crime of having taught a boring class. (The class was *a little* boring—I had a damned cold—but the punishment seemed a bit severe.) The dean of students laughed lightly when I suggested that this behavior might be grounds for sending the student on a brief vacation. I was, you might say, discomfited, and showed up to class for a while with my cellphone jiggered to dial 911 with one touch.

Still, this was small potatoes. Colleges are even leery of disciplining guys who have committed sexual assault, or assault plain and simple. Instead of being punished, these guys frequently stay around, strolling the quad and swilling the libations, an affront (and sometimes a terror) to their victims.

You'll find that cheating is common as well. As far as I can discern, the student ethos goes like this: If the professor is so lazy that he gives the same test every year, it's okay to go ahead and take advantage—you've both got better things to do. The Internet is amok with services selling term papers and those services exist, capitalism being what it is, because people purchase the papers—lots of them. Fraternity files bulge with old tests from a variety of courses.

Periodically the public gets exercised about this situation, and there are articles in the national news. But then interest dwindles and matters go back to normal.

One of the reasons professors sometimes look the other way when they sense cheating is that it sends them into a world of sorrow. A friend of mine had the temerity to detect cheating on the part of a kid who was the nephew of a well-placed official in an Arab government complexly aligned with the U.S. Black limousines pulled up in front of his office and disgorged decorously suited negotiators. Did my pal fold? Nope, he's not the type. But he did not enjoy the process.

What colleges generally want are well-rounded students, civic leaders, people who know what the system demands, how to keep matters light, not push too hard for an education or anything else; people who get their credentials and leave the professors alone to do their brilliant work, so they may rise and enhance the rankings of the university. Such students leave and become donors and so, in their own turn, contribute immeasurably to the university's standing. They've done a fine job skating on surfaces in high school—the best way to get an across-the-board outstanding record—and now they're on campus to cut a few more figure eights.

In a culture where the major and determining values are monetary, what else could you do? How else would you live if not by getting all you can, succeeding all you can, making all you can?

The idea that a university education really should have no substantial content, should not be about what John Keats was disposed to call Soul-making, is one that you might think professors and university presidents would be discreet about. Not so. This view informed an address that Richard Brodhead gave to the senior class at Yale before he departed to become president of Duke. Brodhead, an impressive, articulate man, seems to take as his educational touchstone the Duke of Wellington's precept that the Battle of Waterloo was won on the playing fields of Eton. Brodhead suggests that the content of the courses isn't really what matters. In five years (or five months, or minutes), the student is likely to have forgotten how to do the problem sets and will only hazily recollect what happens in the ninth book of *Paradise Lost*. The legacy of their college years will be a legacy of difficulties overcome. When they face equally arduous tasks later in life, students will tap their old resources of determination, and they'll win.

All right, there's nothing wrong with this as far as it goes—after all, the student who writes a brilliant forty-page thesis in a hard week has learned more than a little about her inner resources. Maybe it will give her needed confidence in the future. But doesn't the content of the courses matter at all?

On the evidence of this talk, no. Trying to figure out whether the stuff you're reading is true or false and being open to having your life changed is a fraught, controversial activity. Doing so requires energy from the professor—which is better spent on other matters. This kind of perspective-altering teaching and learning can cause the things which administrators fear above all else: trouble, arguments, bad press, etc. After the kid-samurai episode, the chair of my department not unsympathetically suggested that this was the sort of incident that could happen when you brought a certain intensity to teaching. At the time I found his remark a tad detached, but maybe he was right.

So, if you want an education, the odds aren't with you: The professors are off doing what they call their own work; the other students, who've doped out the way the place runs, are busy leaving the professors alone and getting themselves in position for bright and shining futures; the student-services people are trying to keep everyone content, offering plenty of entertainment and building another state-of-the-art workout facility every few months. The development office is already scanning you for future donations. The primary function of Yale University, it's recently been said, is to create prosperous alumni so as to enrich Yale University.

So why make trouble? Why not just go along? Let the profs roam free in the realms of pure thought, let yourselves party in the realms of impure pleasure, and let the student-services gang assert fewer prohibitions and newer delights for you. You'll get a good job, you'll have plenty of friends, you'll have a driveway of your own.

You'll also, if my father and I are right, be truly and righteously screwed. The reason for this is simple. The quest at the center of a liberal-arts education is not a luxury quest; it's a necessity quest. If you do not undertake it, you risk leading a life of desperation—maybe quiet, maybe, in time, very loud—and I am not exaggerating. For you risk trying to be someone other than who you are, which, in the long run, is killing.

By the time you come to college, you will have been told who you are numberless times. Your parents and friends, your teachers, your counselors, your priests and rabbis and ministers and imams have all had their say. They've let you know how they size you up, and they've let you know what they think you should value. They've given you a sharp and protracted taste of what they feel is good and bad, right and wrong. Much is on their side. They have confronted you with scriptures—holy books that, whatever their actual provenance, have given people what they feel to be wisdom for thousands of years. They've given you family traditions—you've learned the ways of your tribe and your community. And, too, you've been tested, probed, looked at up and down and through. The coach knows what your athletic prospects are, the guidance office has a sheaf of test scores that relegate you to this or that ability quadrant, and your teachers have got you pegged. You are, as Foucault might say, the intersection of many evaluative and potentially determining discourses: you boy, you girl, have been made.

And—contra Foucault—that's not so bad. Embedded in all of the major religions are profound truths. Schopenhauer, who despised belief in transcendent things, nonetheless thought Christianity to be of inexpressible worth. He couldn't believe in the divinity of Jesus, or in the afterlife, but to Schopenhauer, a deep pessimist, a religion that had as its central emblem the figure of a man being tortured on a cross couldn't be entirely misleading. To the Christian, Schopenhauer said, pain was at the center of the understanding of life, and that was just as it should be.

One does not need to be as harsh as Schopenhauer to understand the use of religion, even if one does not believe in an otherworldly god. And all of those teachers and counselors and friends—and the prognosticating uncles, the dithering aunts, the fathers and mothers with their hopes for your fulfillment—or their fulfillment in you—should not necessarily be cast aside or ignored. Families have their wisdom. The question "Who do they think you are at home?" is never an idle one.

The major conservative thinkers have always been very serious about what goes by the name of common sense. Edmund Burke saw common sense as a loosely made, but often profound, collective work, in which humanity has deposited its hard-earned wisdom—the precipitate of joy and tears— over time. You have been raised in proximity to common sense, if you've been raised at all, and common sense is something to respect, though not quite—peace unto the formidable Burke—to revere.

You may be all that the good people who raised you say you are; you may want all they have shown you is worth wanting; you may be someone who is truly your father's son or your mother's daughter. But then again, you may not be.

For the power that is in you, as Emerson suggested, may be new in nature. You may not be the person that your parents take you to be. And—this thought is both more exciting and more dangerous—you may not be the person that you take yourself to be, either. You may not have read yourself aright, and college is the place where you can find out whether you have or not. The reason to read Blake and Dickinson and Freud and Dickens is not to become more cultivated, or more articulate, or to be someone who, at a cocktail party, is never embarrassed (or who can embarrass others). The best reason to read them is to see if they may know you better than you know yourself. You may find your own suppressed and rejected thoughts flowing back to you with an "alienated majesty." Reading the great writers, you may have the experience that Longinus associated with the sublime: You feel that you have actually created the text yourself. For somehow your predecessors are more yourself than you are.

This was my own experience reading the two writers who have influenced me the most, Sigmund Freud and Ralph Waldo Emerson. They gave words to thoughts and feelings that I had never been able to render myself.

They shone a light onto the world and what they saw, suddenly I saw, too. From Emerson I learned to trust my own thoughts, to trust them even when every voice seems to be on the other side. I need the wherewithal, as Emerson did, to say what's on my mind and to take the inevitable hits. Much more I learned from the sage—about character, about loss, about joy, about writing and its secret sources, but Emerson most centrally preaches the gospel of self-reliance and that is what I have tried most to take from him. I continue to hold in mind one of Emerson's most memorable passages: "Society is a joint-stock company, in which the members agree, for the better securing of his bread to each shareholder, to surrender the liberty and culture of the eater. The virtue in most request is conformity. Self-reliance is its aversion. It loves not realities and creators, but names and customs."

Emerson's greatness lies not only in showing you how powerful names and customs can be, but also in demonstrating how exhilarating it is to buck them. When he came to Harvard to talk about religion, he shocked the professors and students by challenging the divinity of Jesus and the truth of his miracles. He wasn't invited back for decades.

From Freud I found a great deal to ponder as well. I don't mean Freud the aspiring scientist, but the Freud who was a speculative essayist and interpreter of the human condition like Emerson. Freud challenges nearly every significant human ideal. He goes after religion. He says that it comes down to the longing for the father. He goes after love. He calls it "the overestimation of the erotic object." He attacks our desire for charismatic popular leaders. We're drawn to them because we hunger for absolute authority. He declares that dreams don't predict the future and that there's nothing benevolent about them. They're disguised fulfillments of repressed wishes.

Freud has something challenging and provoking to say about virtually every human aspiration. I learned that if I wanted to affirm any consequential ideal, I had to talk my way past Freud. He was—and is—a perpetual challenge and goad.

Never has there been a more shrewd and imaginative cartographer of the psyche. His separation of the self into three parts, and his sense of the fraught, anxious, but often negotiable relations among them (negotiable when you come to the game with a Freudian knowledge), does a great deal to help one navigate experience. (Though sometimes—and this I owe to Emerson—it seems right to let the psyche fall into civil war, accepting barrages of anxiety and grief for this or that good reason.)

The battle is to make such writers one's own, to winnow them out and to find their essential truths. We need to see where they fall short and where they exceed the mark, and then to develop them a little, as the ideas themselves, one comes to see, actually developed others. (Both Emerson and Freud live out of Shakespeare—but only a giant can be truly influenced by Shakespeare.) In reading, I continue to look for one thing—to be influenced, to learn something new, to be thrown off my course and onto another, better way.

My father knew that he was dissatisfied with life. He knew that none of the descriptions people had for him quite fit. He understood that he was always out-of-joint with life as it was. He had talent: My brother and I each got about half the raw ability he possessed and that's taken us through life well enough. But what to do with that talent—there was the rub for my father. He used to stroll through the house intoning his favorite line from Groucho Marx's ditty "Whatever it is, I'm against it." (I recently asked my son, now twenty-one, if he thought I was mistaken in teaching him this particular song when he was six years old. "No!" he said, filling the air with an invisible forest of exclamation points.) But what my father never managed to get was a sense of who he might become. He never had a world of possibilities spread before him, never made sustained contact with the best that had been thought and said. He didn't get to revise his understanding of himself, figure out what he'd do best that might give the world some profit.

My father was a gruff man, but also a generous one, so that night at the kitchen table at 58 Clewley Road he made an effort to let me have the chance that had been denied to him by both fate and character. He gave me the chance to see what I was all about, and if it proved to be different from him, proved even to be something he didn't like or entirely comprehend, then he'd deal with it.

Right now, if you're going to get a real education, you may have to be aggressive and assertive.

Your professors will give you some fine books to read, and they'll probably help you understand them. What they won't do, for reasons that perplex me, is to ask you if the books contain truths you could live your lives by. When you read Plato, you'll probably learn about his metaphysics and his politics and his way of conceiving the soul. But no one will ask you if his ideas are good enough to believe in. No one will ask you, in the words of Emerson's disciple William James, what their "cash value" might be. No one will suggest that you might use Plato as your bible for a week or a year or longer. No one, in short, will ask you to use Plato to help you change your life.

That will be up to you. You must put the question of Plato to yourself. You must ask whether reason should always rule the passions, philosophers should always rule the state, and poets should inevitably be banished from a just commonwealth. You have to ask yourself if wildly expressive music (rock and rap and the rest) deranges the soul in ways that are destructive to its health. You must inquire of yourself if balanced calm is the most desirable human state.

Occasionally—for you will need some help in fleshing-out the answers—you may have to prod your professors to see if they take the text at hand—in this case the divine and disturbing Plato—to be true. And you will have to be tough if the professor mocks you for uttering a sincere question instead of keeping matters easy for all concerned by staying detached and analytical. (Detached analysis has a place—but, in the end, you've got to speak from the heart and pose the question of truth.) You'll be the one who pesters his teachers. You'll ask your history teacher about whether there is a design to our history, whether we're progressing or declining, or whether, in the words of a fine recent play, The History Boys, history's "just one fuckin' thing after another." You'll be the one who challenges your biology teacher about the intellectual conflict between evolution and creationist thinking. You'll not only question the statistics teacher about what numbers can explain but what they can't.

Because every subject you study is a language and since you may adopt one of these languages as your own, you'll want to know how to speak it expertly and also how it fails to deal with those concerns for which it has no adequate words. You'll be looking into the reach of every metaphor that every discipline offers, and you'll be trying to see around their corners.

The whole business is scary, of course. What if you arrive at college devoted to pre-med, sure that nothing will make you and your family happier than a life as a physician, only to discover that elementary-school teaching is where your heart is?

You might learn that you're not meant to be a doctor at all. Of course, given your intellect and discipline, you can still probably be one. You can pound your round peg through the very square hole of medical school, then go off into the profession. And society will help you. Society has a cornucopia of resources to encourage you in doing what society needs done but that you don't much like doing and are not cut out to do. To ease your grief, society offers alcohol, television, drugs, divorce, and buying, buying, buying what you don't need. But all those too have their costs.

Education is about finding out what form of work for you is close to being play—work you do so easily that it restores you as you go. Randall Jarrell once said that if he were a rich man, he would pay money to teach poetry to students. (I would, too, for what it's worth.) In saying that, he (like my father) hinted in the direction of a profound and true theory of learning.

Having found what's best for you to do, you may be surprised how far you rise, how prosperous, even against your own projections, you become. The student who eschews medical school to follow his gift for teaching small children spends his twenties in low-paying but pleasurable and soul-rewarding toil. He's always behind on his student-loan payments; he still lives in a house with four other guys (not all of whom got proper instructions on how to clean a bathroom). He buys shirts from the Salvation Army, has intermittent Internet, and vacations where he can. But lo—he has a gift for teaching. He writes an essay about how to teach, then a book—which no one buys. But he writes another—in part out of a feeling of injured merit, maybe—and that one they do buy.

Money is still a problem, but in a new sense. The world wants him to write more, lecture, travel more, and will pay him for his efforts, and he likes this a good deal. But he also likes staying around and showing up at school and figuring out how to get this or that little runny-nosed specimen to begin learning how to read. These are the kinds of problems that are worth having and if you advance, as Thoreau said, in the general direction of your dreams, you may have them. If you advance in the direction of someone else's dreams—if you want to live someone else's life rather than yours—then get a TV for every room, buy yourself a lifetime supply of your favorite quaff, crank up the porn channel, and groove away. But when we expend our energies in rightful ways, Robert Frost observed, we stay whole and vigorous and we don't weary. "Strongly spent," the poet says, "is synonymous with kept."

Global Imperatives of the 21st Century: The Academy's Response

Nels H. Granholm

Perspectives on Global Development and Technologies

January 2013

Nels H. Granholm is a Professor Emeritus of Global Studies and Biology at South Dakota State University, where he coordinated the Honors Program and the Global Studies Program. He has written extensively about global and environmental issues, and for twelve years he taught "The Two Cultures—Bridging the Sciences and the Humanities,"a course designated for Honors students. Granholm's report appears in a peer reviewed, scholarly journal, *Perspectives on Global Development and Technologies*, which provides social scientists a forum to discuss climate, technological, and economic change.

1. Granholm claims that, "Our 21st century world deteriorates socially, biologically, and physically while we in the Academy blindly pursue our 'disciplinary truths.'" What does he mean by "disciplinary truths"?

2. In this report, Granholm argues that the primary aim of the university should be to foster "interculturally competent and authentic global citizens." Do you agree with his position? Why or why not?

3. Compare Granholm's discussion of the aims of education to Mark Edmundson's thoughts earlier in this chapter. How do these professors' positions differ? How are they similar?

Introduction

Our 21st century world is rapidly declining while we in the Ivory Tower bury our collective ostrich heads in the sand while continuing to pursue our disciplinary truths. The purpose of this paper is to make the case that we in the Academy have to "step up," become authentic members of our proud tradition and profession in the Academy, and take an active role in resolving global problems. We need to "get out of our parent's basements," "smell the coffee," and get a life—a real 21st century life. It is both reckless and unethical for us to ignore the world around us. We would prefer not to leave our comfortable disciplinary homes; we are warm and secure. Or, so we think. Perhaps we are paralyzed in academia because we don't know "how to get out," how to grapple with 21st century global imperatives. The parakeet when liberated from its cage flies back to the security of its "home". We academic parakeets need to break out, engage the world, and make a difference. We need to lead by example! Hopefully this paper will provide some of that impetus.

"The sky is falling" opined Chicken Little in the traditional fairy tale. Well, the sky is not falling, but it is accumulating CO_2 at the highest concentrations (reaching 400 ppm) known to science over the last 800,000 years as revealed in deep drilled Antarctic ice cores (Pachauri and Reisinger 2007).

In addition to atmospheric CO_2 our Eden, our home, our world has other problems as well—social, biological, and physical—unprecedented natural resource depletion; stark evidence of incipient global environmental change disasters (flooding of coastal cities, displacement of agricultural zones, melting of Himalayan glaciers that provide significant annual flows to major rivers in China, India, and southeast Asia), pollution and dead zones in our oceans; crushing losses of biodiversity affecting the health of global ecosystems, food insecurity for millions of people; serious poverty and lack of fundamental resources (a.k.a. Maslow's hierarchy) for one to two billion people; political unrest, terrorism, war, "WikiLeaks," and various conflicts; failing, and failed states like Somalia and the DRC; absence of decent schooling for millions of children; child soldiers, violations of basic women's rights, abhorrent health conditions in developing countries, and others. I have dubbed these horrendously comprehensive problems our *21st century global imperatives.*

Academia's Responsibility

Are we in the Academy responding in any way to these global challenges? For the most part, no. Most of the time we academics act as if we have no clue. We, the time-honored and cherished professoriate, are doing virtually nothing in the way of addressing and resolving global problems. However, as members of one of society's "special institutions"—the Academy, we should. After all we, at least in principle, represent society's intellectual vanguard, a cadre presumably of public intellectuals. Because of academic freedom, our presumed desire to seek truths, and our unconstrained ability to probe deeply into all manner of societal activity, we have the power to expose wrongs, injustices, and damaging human behaviors no matter how well-concealed, shielded, and protected they may be. Collectively, we are one of society's most valuable and capable institutional means to seek the truth, to engage the world, and ultimately to redress the wrongs of the world. I would like to argue that in this early 21st century, the Academy's primary and most essential responsibility entails informing our students, colleagues, administrators, and others about our global crises in compelling ways. But most importantly, our job largely involves instilling a sense of passion and desire to work in teams to provide solutions to resolve these seemingly intractable global issues.

In short, what the world needs most is a cadre of authentic global citizens who communicate well, have a passion for solving problems, and are willing and able to work in teams. We desperately need lawyers, businesspeople, CEOs, CFOs, global financiers, governmental agencies at all levels, NGOs, supra-national groups (like UN, IMF, WTO, WLO, WB, and others) who dedicate a good part of their time and efforts to effective global problem solving. What we no longer need is university graduates, socially blasé egomaniacal hyper-individuals, and others hell-bent on a materially-addicted, self-centered, and highly resource-extractive Western lifestyles and who show little regard for community interests and the public good. We in the professoriate have an iron-clad responsibility, a duty or obligation, to produce globally competent student-citizens, i.e., passionate and competent authentic global citizens who just happen to be majoring in electrical engineering, dairy science, nursing, agriculture, business, accounting, marketing, advertising, modern languages, global studies, biology, sociology, history, political science, and others and who just happen to have a passion to remedy the wrongs of this seriously troubled and severely compromised 21st century Earth.

OK you say. "This is classic 'pie in the sky Pollyannaish stuff'!" And I can hear you say, "All of this is probably impossible". However, there really is no alternative. Given the present state of our Earth, we have no other rational choice. In the end, it is "the only game in town". And, shouldn't we "give it our best shot"? Perhaps "for openers," we could remember the lines of the Edgar Albert Guest poem of 1916 entitled "It Couldn't Be Done"—"He started to sing as he tackled the thing that couldn't be done and he did it" (Guest 1916).

Ignorance of the World is No Excuse

We in the Academy can no longer afford to ignore 21st century global realities. Because of our economically integrated, highly interdependent, profoundly troubled, resource depleted, conflict-ridden, and thoroughly interconnected 21st century world, we in the Academy can ill afford the luxury of exclusively pursing our own individual disciplines, our own careers, and our own personal interests while ignoring pervasive global resource problems and fundamental social inequities. We cannot, in good faith, stand by and passively watch the slow disintegration of our physical, biological, and social world. Somehow, we need to act. And, somehow, we need to get this action message across to not only our students, our hope for tomorrow, but also to our faculty colleagues and our university administrators, our hope for today. Neglecting our 21st century global imperatives is simply not a choice—not for our professoriate, one of society's presumed intellectual elites.

Neglecting global imperatives presents two fundamental problems: 1) Quite simply, as ethical human beings, it is incumbent upon us to engage with and attempt to resolve global imperatives—to do the right thing! We ought to act for our fellow human beings (as well as the rest of the global biota) from a Rawlsian ("Justice as Fairness") and Kantian (each and every person has equal worth) kind of universally accepted principled approach and 2) If we are ill-inclined to "buy" the purely ethical approach, then perhaps the brutally pragmatic approach may "cut the mustard," i.e., unless there is at least a basal level of social, political, biological, and environmental stability in the world, those of us with wealth (members of the G20, OECD, rapidly-developing countries, and others) may be unable to enjoy a high quality of life. In the absence of global stability, our lives may be greatly diminished, perhaps even impoverished. Thus for purely selfish, egoistic reasons we ought to have the good sense to promote fairness, justice, and freedom for all people of the world. Also, we should be clever enough to understand that our well being on planet Earth is a direct reflection of the overall health and welfare of our biotic brethren. Accordingly, a rational species would work to ensure the bounty and flourishing of the global biota. I prefer the principled Kantian approach as opposed to the starkly practical and utilitarian modus, but we can and should do both!

My Hope for this Article

It is my fervent hope that you will gain an understating of why it is incumbent upon those of us in Academia to respond in highly active and significant measure to current global imperatives. And hopefully, I can convince you that we in the Academy have a special role to play in this process. By introducing ourselves, our students, colleagues and administrators to these 21st century global dilemmas in our various course curricula and other academic forums (faculty senate; all-campus colloquia; year of the book [read Lester Brown or Bill McKibben]; distinguished lecture series; department/college meetings; community-university programs; and others) we can become major change agents in this process. The situation is so dire that we really have no alternative. I wish I could convince you of this! Academia must get "on board!" This is one train the professoriate can't afford to miss. Let us begin.

Section One—Framing the Problem: Institutional Indifference to Global Imperatives

Colleges, universities, related institutions, and other professional organizations have been at best unresponsive and at worst, derelict in their societal obligations to confront and resolve global imperatives.

Our college and university education, although highly specialized, rigorous, and of excellent academic quality has been fragmented, overly discipline-specific, and has generally "missed the mark" of a comprehensive global education. Our graduating seniors are simply not globally competent. They possess little "worldliness". *It is not their fault, it is ours!* Our colleges and universities have failed to deliver the necessary strategies, methodologies, and requisite information for students "to connect the interdisciplinary dots" in ways that address fundamental global problems.

In defense of our current system of higher education, the quality of the overall system should not be faulted. It is simply "misguided". In a sense, we may have done it right over the course of human history or at least until the 20th century. But in the last century the world has changed; we have drastically altered our Earth biologically, physically, socially, and politically. Because of our incredible "Earth extraction efficiencies," we have laid bare the mantel of the Earth. As Aldo Leopold stated in his essay "The Land Ethic" (Leopold 1949), "We are remodeling the Alhambra with a steam-shovel, and we are proud of our yardage". Because of our greatly increasing human social problems as well as our drastic global extirpation of our natural resource base, our current Earth is qualitatively distinctive from our early twentieth century Earth (McKibben 2010). Accordingly, we desperately require fresh ways to view our Earth as well as new global regulatory and governing paradigms if we are to, and I'd rather not say this, survive in some kind of stable and peaceful 21st century world.

Academic Deception?

Because of the devastating effects of our disruptive activities on the surface of the Earth, especially the biosphere, the 21st century is qualitatively different from all previous centuries. It's hard to imagine that one species could have such a devastating effect. But we have! *Homo sapiens* is such an enigma—so creative, imaginative, sublime on one hand and so uninformed, violent, destructive, unthinking, blasé, and devastating on the other. We in the Academy need to address what we, as a global community, have done to our Earth, attempt to rectify, and to the maximum extent possible, work to remediate our past actions. But, this is a tall order. How should we go about this?

Quite simply, we in 21st century professoriate are called not only to teach disciplinary truths but also international and global studies truths. Students desperately need to know what is truly going on in our world. The Academy's 21st century primary responsibility is to provide students with real and ongoing global truth, the authentic global situation, and then to provide the tools and training to engage productively with that world. It is deceptive if not dishonest for the professoriate not to inform students about our 21st century world. Such behavior is akin to our physician telling us that everything is fine when in reality, we are suffering from a serious and life-threatening systemic disorder.

We possess scientific clarity regarding phenomena like global environmental change, impact of the global population on the world's natural resources (horrendously detrimental collective ecological footprint), pervasive social problems of poverty, poor health, food insecurity, failed/fragile states, global terrorism and others, we now (21st century) live in a drastically and qualitatively different world than humans have heretofore experienced. Bill McKibben has dubbed this qualitatively different, ecologically-compromised world, *Eaarth*—the title of his new book (McKibben 2010). And yes, *Eaarth* with a new spelling to signify a new, significantly degraded earth, not the Eden we inherited. This is a sad business indeed.

To continue with academic business as usual in the 21st century would deceive ourselves, our stakeholders, and compromise our academic mission. We need to address ourselves to the critical business at hand—the clear understanding and then, resolution of global imperatives. Accordingly, we ought to devote a significant portion of the academic enterprise to analyzing and developing methodologies for resolving global imperatives. In short, we ought to keep our focus on academic excellence but shift the subject from disciplinary pursuit to interdisciplinary, international endeavors, i.e., pursuit of interdisciplinary problem–solving including service learning—especially in the resolution of global dilemmas. In short, to be effective, we need to work at all institutional levels. An institution's mission statement is a good place to begin; we might as well start at the top!

If You Know You Are in Trouble, it is Generally a Good Idea to Take Corrective Action

We know in our bones that our world is hurting. If we know we're in global jeopardy, it would seem that the proper role for the Academy would be to "take action". It seems we should, as a globally informed academic community, take corrective action. We have no other reasonable alternative than to attend to these global challenges. Could we not vigorously embrace a new and heightened urgency leading to action on behalf of the world's deteriorating sociopolitical as well as physical and biological conditions including devastating poverty of the world's poor and disenfranchised

Mission & Vision

peoples? Philosophically, academia's response to 21ˢᵗ century global imperatives is nothing less than a bona fide categorical imperative in and of itself.

Yet, for a number of very curious reasons, we continue to be "held hostage" (an extraordinary self-imposed hostage) in our Ivory Towers (disciplinary specialties). We academics just don't seem to get it! We don't seem to recognize that the world's plight is our plight. We are all in this together. And for those who may recognize the future consequences of our 21ˢᵗ century global imperatives, they can't seem to muster the energy, motivation, or persuasive and compelling arguments to convince others (or ourselves) to embrace the kinds of significant academic adjustments and incentives to address these global realities. It's a most curious business, but all so human!

Moot at Best

The Academy needs to act. It is our societal obligation. We need to clearly, graphically, and starkly outline the undeniable and pervasive global challenges we face in the 21ˢᵗ century. We need to "grab" ourselves and our students. Our college and university colleagues do not truly sense the precariousness of our current global status. Unless we can bring them "on board," the whole idea of energizing colleges and universities to engage productively in 21ˢᵗ century global imperatives will be moot at best!

Section Two—Principles, Tools, and Modus Operandi to Address the Problem

University courses that focus on interdisciplinary global interrelationships and global interdependence, the kinds of education we require in the 21ˢᵗ century, are simply not being taught. Few if any university courses allow students to connect the dots between what goes on in one country and how those apparently isolated national events can drastically affect millions of people in scores of other countries around the world. University students receiving training in global citizenship and intercultural competence may be equipped to connect the dots. We must work to train students in all disciplines to become authentic global citizens. Our world needs civil engineers trained in global studies as well as in the design of sewage treatment plants, highways, and bridges. We need nursing majors who advocate for global health, and education majors willing to go abroad and teach in developing countries. In short, we need students of all disciplines who, by virtue of their specialty training (economics, history, pharmacy, English, dairy science, theatre, speech, etc.) as well as their education in global citizenry and intercultural competence, will engage and inform the world in the 21ˢᵗ century!

The World Needs Legions of Authentic Global Citizens

By definition, well-trained global citizens possess the wherewithal to understand the complex relationships between the events of one country and the consequences of those events on others. This ability to draw compelling connections, sometimes

referred to as "connecting the dots," remains the *sine qua non* of true global citizens. Let me provide two examples to affirm the power of connecting the dots—the phenomenon of quantitative easing and underground water supplies (aquifers) in fertile agricultural zones.

Take the concept of "quantitative easing" as a case in point. In November 2010, the U.S. Federal Reserve ("The Fed") decided to conduct an experiment called "quantitative easing" to stimulate the American economy. It purchased six billion dollars worth of U.S. bonds to increase the supply of money, lower long-term interest rates, and hopefully, stimulate the economy by expanding businesses and creating new jobs. However, what may be good for the American economy may not be advantageous for other countries. In short, the U.S.'s attempts to improve our economy could have negative effects in the global economy. Quantitative easing could also cause inflation lowering the value of the dollar causing serious ripple effects throughout the global economy. Did decision-makers at the Fed carefully consider the potential global consequences of quantitative easing? Did they connect the dots between U.S. quantitative easing and the possibility of currency devaluation, inflation, and potentially drastic economic dislocations in the global economy? The upshot—a holistic understanding of the global economy, the motivation of individual countries, a true conversation between representatives of many countries, transparency, and an ability to connect the fiscal and monetary dots—represents the *sine qua non* of an educated, interculturally competent, global citizen. In our 21st century world we need legions of such authentic global citizens. Let's look next at agricultural aquifers.

We excel at collecting data but lack the political will to connect the dots and formulate beneficial policy based on those data. With respect to aquifers (underground water supplies under prime agricultural land), we acquire data describing in comprehensive, "excruciatingly quantitative" detail how we are drawing down or depleting the world's most critical aquifers beneath fertile agricultural land (i.e., data galore on annual drawdown levels, recharge rates, number of years until depletion, liters per day of drawdown, and so on *ad nauseam*). Armed with knowledge of sociology (human nature), economics, soils/geology, agriculture, history, local culture, and others, global citizens may be able to connect all of these dots. Following this analysis, we may recognize that specific incentives must be provided for people in order to: 1) Increase efficiency of irrigation via new methods like drip irrigation; 2) Create private watershed or irrigation districts where local people with vested interests have pricing control of the water rather than larger, indifferent governmental or distant private agencies; 3) Devise pricing incentives—by charging more for each unit of water, the total water usage will decline; and 4) Other creative and highly sustainable incentives that embrace the aboriginal "Seventh Generation" principle, i.e., act in such a way that the resource will be available seven generations into the future (140-175 years hence)!

Intercultural Competence and Global Citizenship

Two critically fundamental foci for engaging in 21st century dilemmas include intercultural competence—seeing the world through the eyes of "the other" and authentic global citizenship—connecting the dots and devising policies most optimal for multiple nations or the global community rather than simply one nation (Adams and Carfagna 2006; Tetreault and Lipschutz 2009). One could say that intercultural competence and global citizenship are fundamental if not the *sine qua non* for engagement with and resolution of 21st century global imperatives. But there are others.

Other intellectual tools and educational approaches for productive 21st century engagement include:

a. Intercultural communication;

b. Language training;

c. Knowledge of global governance (e.g., role of the United Nations and other governing structures like the World Trade Association, World Bank, International Monetary Fund, and others);

d. Knowledge of the physical and biological conditions of our world;

e. Critical need for education of young women in developing sub-Saharan and other desperately poor countries:

f. How the global economy really works along with basic training in international economics (e.g., role of subsidies and trade barriers, structural adjustment programs of the IMF and WB, economic factors hostile to developing countries like escalating tariffs, and others);

g. Role of international treaties like human rights treaties, the International Campaign to Ban Landmines, the International Criminal Court, the Kyoto Protocol;

h. Why the number of "failed" and "fragile" States is increasing (Brown 2009) and

i. Others deemed to be central to the discussion.

In essence, faculty colleagues and students alike need to learn "how the world works" and how to connect the dots. Such training requires multidisciplinary approaches; serious, deliberate, and exhaustive case study analyses; rigorous service work abroad; learning of foreign languages; knowledge of international governing agencies, and many others. Because of our traditional and ingrained disciplinary bias, we have failed to create the kinds of interdisciplinary international studies and other globally-defined interdisciplinary programs to provide that critical background sorely needed to productively engage in the analysis and resolution of global imperatives. But, the good news—we still have time. Not much, but enough if we can get on board.

Lessons from Aldo Leopold

During his early forestry career, Aldo Leopold (1887–1948) was an unabashed advocate for intense utilization of forestry and agricultural resources of America's vast and rich lands. However, as he observed the devastating ecological effects of such all-encompassing utilitarian practices on the health and vigor of the land, he underwent a profound sea change as comprehensively described in his seminal work, *A Sand County Almanac* (Leopold 1949). In short, Leopold evolved from a strictly utilitarian, economic approach (harvest lumber and trees at all costs) to a profoundly deep and rational ecological approach (preserve forest ecosystems well into the future via strict adherence to ecological principles including sustainable harvests). The simple but profound lesson that Leopold learned is that the economy is a subset of the ecology and not, as most of us assume, the other way around. In short, ecology is primary while economy is secondary! In order to sustainably maintain reasonable yields of lumber, agricultural products, oceanic fisheries, and other natural resources over time, one must be attuned to and operate in concert with the ecology of the various resources.

Leopold could not understand why professionals in resource management did not share this fundamental view of the necessity to operate by the basic ecological rules. He reasoned that part of the problem lies in the absence of holistic ecological training in our universities and professional schools. Leopold wrote about the "fragmentation" that occurs within the university. The quote below provides striking and thoughtful metaphors (a single *"instrument of the great orchestra"* for each discipline, research as *"dismemberment,"* and the concept of *"the place for dismemberment"* as the university):

> There are men charged with the duty of examining the construction of plants, animals, and soils which are the instruments of the great orchestra. Each selects one instrument and spends his life taking it apart and describing its strings and sounding boards. This process of dismemberment is called research. The place for dismemberment is called a university. A professor may pluck the strings of his own instrument, but never that of another, and if he listens for music he must never admit it to his fellows or his students. For all are restrained by an iron-bound taboo which decrees that the construction of instruments is the domain of science while the detection of harmony is the domain of poets. (Leopold 1949).

Somehow, we in the Academy must get to the point where we can simultaneously "construct the instruments of the great orchestra and listen to the harmony" with our peers in a truly collective enterprise! We are in need of Leopold's message. If somehow we could get on board with a truly holistic education at our universities, one which unifies disciplines as opposed to our current pattern of fragmentation, then we may possess not only the basic understanding but also the mental courage and the political backbone to engage with 21st century global imperatives.

A Paradigm Shift: New Programs, Majors, Courses—Our Academic Imperative

Addressing 21st century global imperatives will require higher education to shift or refocus the fundamental role of the Academy and of its practitioners—the professoriate to one of interdisciplinarity and global focus as opposed to single discipline study and local or national focus. Creation of a new model, a new paradigm in academia—one that is fundamentally interdisciplinary and one that is capable of rigorous and enthusiastic engagement in our 21st century world—is fundamental. We have very little to lose and everything to gain from this paradigm shift. We need this large-scale restructuring in order to act and make progress on behalf of the world's basic social restoration goals and earth restoration goals clearly delineated by Lester Brown (Brown 2009). Essential tools include the overarching fundamental principles of global citizenship, intercultural competence, and fundamental knowledge of how the world really works politically, economically, socially, biologically, and others. Along with these tools, we in the professoriate need somehow to gain the desire and confidence to engage in the 21st century world—to have the courage to make a difference.

One approach may be to develop a number of uniquely new and comprehensively structured interdisciplinary university programs. Examples of such new programs include: Global Ethics; Global Studies; Political History of Global Resources; Global Languages; International Development; Global Agriculture; Global Governance; Global Regulatory and Governing Paradigms; Global Resource Sustainability; National Sovereignty, Global Literature (Literature of Humanity); or how about just plain Sustainability; and others. Think of the fun and reinvigoration we could have developing these novel, overlapping, interdisciplinary, and fascinating programs! Think of the new, productive, and exciting contacts we could make with our university colleagues in different departments, maybe even different colleges no less! And think of the wonderful opportunities to work abroad!

Another approach could be development of new interdisciplinary courses that stress international themes and concepts in each of our current academic majors. For example, math majors could enroll in a course on "Global Mathematicians: How Language and Culture Shape Mathematics". Biology majors could analyze "Indigenous Biology: Lessons from the Oral Tradition," and others. Failing this, at the very least, each of us can introduce themes and texts of internationalization in our ongoing courses; this individual course development stressing broader international concepts and views should become another one of our academic imperatives.

Interdisciplinary Course Content and 21st Century Global Imperatives: The Case for Great Literature

To achieve an international understanding, there is simply no substitute for living abroad and working with the people. However, the critical analysis of great books that comprehensively, with great sensitivity depict the very soul of humanity from different cultural perspectives may also be constructive. Fundamentals of the human condition including human rights issues can be productively evaluated by deliberative and serious analysis of fiction as well as nonfiction. For example, poignant and compelling texts include:

a. Wangari Maathai—*Unbowed.* As a Nobel Peace Prize recipient, parliamentarian, and human rights advocate of Kenya (Dr. Maathai died in December, 2011), Dr. Maathai's life represents an exquisite model of the profound value of one individual in improving the world;

b. Ellen Johnson Sirleaf, now in her second term as head of state of Liberia in West Africa. Her autobiography—*This Child will be Great: Memoir of a Remarkable Life by Africa's First Woman President* is a serious and honest recounting of her life and times in Liberia, a stunningly magnificent life. Can you imagine what it must have been like for Ms. Sirleaf to deal with the likes of Samuel Doe and Charles Taylor?;

c. Chinua Achebe's *Things Fall Apart*—all was well and in balance in this 19th century Nigerian community until the British colonized the Ibo; then, things degenerated and fell totally apart;

d. Alan Paton's *Cry the Beloved Country*. One of the few white citizens of South Africa attempting to help the Blacks during apartheid was ruthlessly murdered in a random act of violence by a gang of Black youths (total irony);

e. Kamala Markandaya—*Nectar in a Sieve*. A poor Indian woman overcomes insurmountable odds of poverty, political adversity, rapidly changing societal rules, and disaster testifying to the unyielding "fiber of the human spirit";

f. Arundhati Roy—*God of Small Things*—"History's Henchmen" or the established order, come and "clean things up" no matter how insidiously heinous the social disruption;

g. Louis DeBernieres' *Birds Without Wings* is a text of extraordinary depth and feeling allowing the reader to gain an appreciation of how the plight of Turkey itself and the destinies of many of Turkey's ethnic groups were tragically controlled by the Great Powers and other forces external to Turkey; and

h. Readings by and of Mohandas K. Gandhi (Mahatma Gandhi) and other models, heroes, or exemplars. Who are your heroes? "Be the change"—Mahatma Gandhi.

Finally, Antoine de Saint-Exupery's *The Little Prince* is nothing short of a beautiful, lyrical text embedded within a simple story with a huge message. Not unlike the characters in Voltaire's *Micromegas*, the Little Prince wanders around the earth and solar system looking for "truths" of one sort or another. The desert fox explains two truths to the Little Prince:

a. When you "tame" something like getting married, having children, or living in and reaping the benefits of a globalized world, you have a responsibility to the things you tame! The fox laments that we may have forgotten that fundamental lesson and

b. If you succumb to living in our current era of "numbers envy," hyper-individualistic lifestyles, material addiction, and pursuit of numerous false gods without concern for community and the public good, you too may also have forgotten the desert fox's "lesson of responsibility."

Productive Models and Issues to Address 21ˢᵗ Century Global Imperatives

Our global population could be around nine billion people by 2050; unfortunately the collective "global footprint" of nine billion people requires vast global resource requirements and, at the same time, inhibits resolution of global problems like poverty, hunger, illiteracy, health, and many others. Lester Brown (2009) quotes economist Gene Sperling who states, "Expansion of female secondary education may be the single best lever for achieving reductions in fertility." Young girls in developing countries who stay in school marry later, have fewer children, and because of their education, are better able to care for their children nutritionally and with respect to health. Connecting these dots should be highly instructive for our students. We would also learn the value in taking positive action to keep young women in school. A university course entitled "Keeping Girls in School" could become a national and international model—one in which virtually all concerned global citizens could participate. Would that our higher education institutions could offer an exciting course entitled "Keeping Girls in School"; it could be offered as an optional institutional requirement. By exploring the many dimensions of education, poverty, malnutrition, adverse health conditions, and diminishment of human dignity suffered by one to two billion poor people daily, such a course could serve as a unique frame of reference comparing our world of plenty and opportunity versus their world of abject poverty. It may even encourage us to act.

Promotion and Tenure Requirements at the University

As outlined in Childress (2010), there exist ways to incentivize universities to encourage faculty members to address global imperatives and a range of other international issues in their respective courses. Tenure and promotion criteria could reward faculty who:

a. Serve as members of cross- disciplinary campus internationalization committees;

b. Internationalize their individual courses;

c. Develop foreign language proficiency (seems like an ideal win-win situation for nine-month faculty to receive pay for learning a foreign language during the summer);

d. Take students abroad;

e. Conduct service work either abroad or at home as one component of course requirements;

f. Join and participate in international organizations,

g. Serve on various departmental or college internationalization, committees;

h. Publish papers on international themes;

i. Develop interdisciplinary research and teaching teams with foreign faculty members across departments and colleges, and others.

The Direct Approach: Changing the Mission of the University to Address 21st Century Global Imperatives

Those of us concerned with addressing global problems including issues of global justice should all be proud of Fairleigh Dickenson University (FDU). The FDU mission statement is presented below:

> Fairleigh Dickinson University is a center of academic excellence dedicated to the preparation of world citizens through global education. The University strives to provide students with the multi-disciplinary, intercultural, and ethical understandings necessary to participate, lead, and prosper in the global marketplace of ideas, commerce and culture. (Adams and Carfagna 2006).

This mission statement sets the tone for an extensive reorganization and restructuring of academic programs at FDU. Fortunately, we have a wonderful opportunity, in fact a detailed "Operator's Manual," to evaluate philosophical rationale and practical aspects of this FDU global competency initiative in the published book of FDU President, Dr. J. Michael Adams (Adams and Carfagna 2006). This text details the kinds of academic experiences and training at FDU that led to the fulfillment of the goals and objectives in the mission statement above. An excellent source of fundamental principles, tools, and recipes for reshaping one's institution, this text provides the necessary tools and rationale to enable us to engage productively in the resolution of our 21st century global imperatives.

A second compelling text (Tetreault and Lipschutz 2009) provides additional "hands on" approaches to tackle global problems; the last chapter (Chapter 10—People Matter) provides a superb analysis of how everyday people like you, me, our faculty colleagues, and our college and university students can "get into the action" in highly productive ways to become agents of change for global imperatives. Finally, Lisa K. Childress (2010) has recently published *The 21st Century University: Developing Faculty Engagement in Internationalization*. This excellent "nuts and bolts" text delineates both historical contexts and critical analyses of "how-to-do-it" internationalization instructions plus compelling descriptions of heuristic models of internationalization employed at Duke University and the University of Richmond. In short, these three above-mentioned texts provide bedrock directions and highly practical methods of strategically organizing our universities to enable us to get on with the business of confronting and engaging productively with our 21st century global imperatives.

Summary

We (our world and its people) find ourselves at a critical turning point, perhaps even a "point of no return"; we can continue on with business as usual (Plan A) or we can accept the fact that our 20th century global modus operandi will simply not work in the 21st century and therefore adopt Plan B (Brown 2009). With "business as usual," we have little to gain and much to lose including our credibility as academics not to mention the inexorable degradation and decline of our social, political, biological, and physical worlds.

Recognizing the precariousness of our current situation, we are then required to act. How then can we carry out "Plan B"? As academics, we return to our base, our foundation, our well of pure "truth-pursuit"—our research, curricula, academic programs, instructors, and our entire academic armamentarium—the panoply of the noble Academy going back to one of our very first Western mentors—Socrates and his analysis of fundamental truths. We have all the necessary tools; we simply need the political will to get into the thick of the action!

We have sufficient human energy, intellectual curiosity, academic zeal, and history of learning communities of the ages dating back to Plato's noble academy. We even have Socrates' admonition in Plato's "Apology"—"The unexamined life is not worth living". We simply need to redirect that academic zeal from our individual disciplinary pursuits to the collective, frightful, and horrific imperatives of the 21st century—to very real and sobering global imperatives instead of our individual academic domains, however exciting, compelling, and rewarding our disciplinary academic truths may be. We need to recognize anew that we are all in the global business (life on this planet) together. We will survive together or perish together. Just as all nations of the world need to shift from carbon- based energy to renewable energy, we in higher education need to redirect our energies from pure disciplinary pursuit to interdisciplinary, connect-the-dots type projects directed toward the understanding and resolution of specific global imperatives.

We can, like Fairleigh Dickenson University, revamp our institutional missions, either comprehensively all at once or in a non-threatening, incremental fashion while creating the kinds of academic programs to productively and successfully confront our 21st century demons. We just need some boldness and daring. We may need a little old-fashioned "backbone". We can do this. We just need some impetus. This "academic redirection" could turn out to be one of the most significant turning points in the history of higher education and the noble Academy! I'm convinced this redirection is going to happen sooner or later (if and when global conditions become so apparently dire that we will be forced to finally acknowledge our grim situation and the need for action). We would all be better off if the Academy could act now. And our initiatives might as well occur at any one of a number of private universities (like Fairleigh Dickenson University) as well as public institutions including our noble land-grant institutions.

Conclusion: Lewis Thomas' Admonition

In his classic text "Late Night Thoughts on Listening to Mahler's Ninth Symphony," mid-twentieth century physician/scientist Lewis Thomas (1983) asserted that our species, *Homo sapiens*, is an immature species. The late Dr. Thomas worried that we, by virtue of our immaturity, would blow ourselves to smithereens in a nuclear holocaust. He hoped that our immature species could survive for a couple more millennia, or at least for a sufficient duration of time for us to become a mature species. Then *H. sapiens*, along with non-human biota of the world's global ecosystems as well as our physical global environment would have a real chance at longevity.

We are now confronted with a series of profoundly serious, unprecedented, and life-threatening global problems—our 21st century global imperatives. Can we mature as a species and confront our ominous global imperatives? We are a highly resilient species. That's proven! We can rise to the occasion, engage the world, design new curricula, programs, majors, colleges, endowed chairs, get excited and have a lot of fun in this energizing process. We have the tools to understand how we arrived at this precipice of global jeopardy. And the good news—we possess the creativity, artistry, sufficient cerebral "gray cells," and resilience to work together to resolve our current 21st century global dilemmas. Our future's in the balance!

References

Achebe, Chinua. 1994. *Things Fall Apart*. New York. Knoph Doubleday Publishers.

Adams, J. Michael and Angelo Carfagna. 2006. *Coming of Age in a Globalized World: The Next Generation*. Bloomfield, CT: Kumarian Press, Inc.

Brown, Lester. 2009. *Plan B 4.0: Mobilizing to Save Civilization*. Earth Policy Institute. New York. W.W. Norton & Company.

Childress, Lisa K. 2010. *The 21st Century University: Developing Faculty Engagement in Internationalization*. New York. Peter Lang Publishing Inc.

DeBernieres, Louis. 2007. *Birds Without Wings*. New York. Knoph Doubleday Publishers.

De Saint-Exupery, Antoine. 2000. *The Little Prince*. New York. Houghton Mifflin Harcourt.

Guest, Edgar A. 2007. *Collected Works of Edgar A. Guest*. Charleston, South Carolina. BiblioBazar Press.

Leopold, Aldo. 1949. *A Sand County Almanac: Sketches Here and There*. New York. Oxford University Press.

Maathai, Wangari. 2007. *Unbowed: A Memoir*. New York: Anchor Books.

Markandaya, Kamala. 2010. *Nectar in a Sieve*. New York: Penguin Group.

McKibben, Bill. 2010. *Eaarth: Making a Life on a Tough New Planet*. New York: Times Books.

Pachauri, R.K. and A. Resiinger. (Eds). 2007. "Intergovernmental Panel on Climate Change (IPCC) Fourth Assessment Report." Geneva, Switzerland. *Climate Change 2007: Synthesis Report*. IPCC.

Paton, Alan. 1996. *Cry, The Beloved Country*. New York. Scribner Publishing.

Roy, Arundhati. 1998. *The God of Small Things*. New York: Random House.

Sirleaf, Ellen Johnson. 2009. *This Child Will Be Great: Memoir of a Remarkable Life by Africa's First Woman President*. New York: Harper Collins Publishers.

Tetreault, Mary Ann and Lipschutz, Ronnie D. 2009. *Global Politics as if People Mattered*. New York. Rowman & Littlefield Publishers, Inc.

Thomas, Lewis. 1983. *Late Night Thoughts on Listening to Mahler's Ninth Symphony*. New York: Bantam Books.

(1) This paper was originally published as:

Granholm, Nels H. 2013. "Global Imperatives of the 21st Century; The Academy's Response." In: *Perspectives on Global Development and Technology*. Special Issue - Dystopia and Global Rebellion, Harris, Jerry. Ed. BRILL. Leiden, The Netherlands.

Higher Education Trends to Watch for in 2013

Emily Driscoll

Fox Business

January 2013

Emily Driscoll is a staff reporter for the "Money 101" feature of the *Fox Business* news website, which is often associated with more conservative fiscal values. Driscoll often writes about education issues, including employment-related recommendations for newly-graduated college students. In this article, she identifies two trends in colleges and universities, both associated with the changing economic status of institutions of higher education in the U.S.

1. What does it mean to "flip the classroom" in online course settings?

2. Driscoll is careful to avoid editorializing—offering her opinion directly—in her article. Driscoll, however, makes a clear rhetorical choice to end the article with a reference to the lower cost of hiring part-time faculty and the greater "practical" experience that part-time faculty may bring to the classroom. How does this rhetorical choice affect reader's perceptions of the issue?

3. Driscoll links both online trends and the rise in part-time faculty with economic challenges that higher education faces today. What other trends might evolve from those challenges?

Despite years of steady growth, college enrollment dropped by 0.2% in the fall of 2011, the first decline in 15 years, according to the U.S. Education Department's National Center for Education Statistics.

The number of undergraduates enrolled dropped to 18.62 million in 2011 from 18.65 million in 2010, but that doesn't necessarily mean less people are pursuing a four-year degree. The number of college students enrolled in at least one online course increased for the ninth straight year, according to the Babson Survey Research Group.

The 2011 study reports that the number of students taking at least one online course has now surpassed six million and nearly one-third of all students in higher education are taking at least one online course.

The college experience is slowly shifting off campus and into the internet as students seek out multiple sources for their educational experience, says Adam Newman, managing partner at Education Growth Advisors.

"Colleges that fail to focus on supporting, and frankly exceeding, the academic needs and expectations of students will do so at their peril given the increasing number of plausible alternatives emerging," he says.

Especially considering the increasing costs of a college education, students are expecting a return on investment more than ever before, says Brian Kibby, president of McGraw-Hill Higher Education. "Students want a good experience but ultimately what they want is a great job, a great opportunity," he says. "Everything that colleges and universities do should be focused on what is the student's result—if the students don't have results, it's just harder for them to get that return on investment and then ultimately contribute to the global economy."

For traditional colleges and universities evolving to meet the needs of their students, here are three trends the experts predict will have a significant role in shaping higher education in 2013.

More Online Programs

While many colleges and universities have increased their online learning opportunities, experts predict that schools will continue to bolster these courses and degree programs.

Mission & Vision

"They're looking to accelerate that, not only because of the school's initiatives, but as for assigning a stigma to online learning— it's gone," says Kibby. "There are too

many good studies that exist now that show students do better in online programs."

The introduction of Massive Open Online Courses (MOOCs) means that every university now needs an online strategy, with the more progressive institutions figuring how they can provide meaningful credentials online, says Ryan Craig, managing director at University Ventures.

"Add to this the increased number of 'online enablers' or 'service providers'—companies that partner with universities to help them develop online degree programs—and 2013 should see the greatest ever annual increase (on an absolute basis) in online courses and degree programs."

More Emphasis on 'Self-Directed' Learning

With a large number of adult learners over age 25 in higher education programs, there are already an increasing number of self-paced and competency-based programs, which will become more common with traditional college students in a trend dubbed "flipping the classroom," predicts Craig.

"Flipping the classroom involves requiring students to view lectures online prior to class, which is then reserved for focused learning, problem solving and group work—students in a flipped classroom environment need to be much more self-directed," he says.

While there will continue to be a rise of self-directed learning options, a key issue will be how institutions and employers value these experiences, as the quality and caliber of self-directed learning programs vary widely, says Newman.

"For those students pursing them with the context of personal enrichment, that may be fine," he says. "As it relates to employability and demonstrated competencies, it's an entirely different matter in which the value of these self-directed options remains unproven."

Shift in Faculty Hiring Processes

As schools continue to experience decreased endowments and tight budgets, fewer faculty members will be hired on a full-time basis, say the experts.

"One of the hardest jobs to get anywhere is full-time, tenured faculty positions, whether they're at a community college or more elite colleges," says Kibby. "Having said that, the need for passionate master teachers, whether you're a fourth grade teacher or at the highest level, that will never change and in fact, it will accelerate."

In order to offer the same number of classes, maintain class size, and serve the same number of students with fewer full-time faculty members, universities will be hiring more part-time faculty in 2013, says Jon Lenrow, Associate Dean, Academic Operations and Faculty Support at Peirce College in Philadelphia.

"The direct cost to the institution is much lower to hire part-time faculty over full-time faculty," he says. "Part-time faculty members also frequently bring more practical experience to the classroom."

Trends in Instructional Staff Employment Status, 1975-2009

American Association of University Professors

aaup.org

March 2011

According to their website, the American Association of University Professors (AAUP) safeguards academic freedom for university faculty, works with policy and law makers to support effective higher-education legislation, and develops procedural guidelines (regarding work and family policies, distance education, and intellectual property, etc.) for colleges to follow. The chart here, published in 2009, cites information from the U.S. Department of Education to illustrate the significant rise in part-time and non-tenure-track faculty in U.S. colleges.

1.   This chart refers to tenured, tenure-track, and non-tenured faculty. What is the difference between these positions?

2.   Review Driscoll's article, as well as Maistos and Street's essay (also in this chapter). What accounts for the significant increase in part-time, non-tenure-track faculty since 1975?

FIGURE 1
Trends in Instructional Staff Employment Status, 1975–2009
All Institutions, National Totals

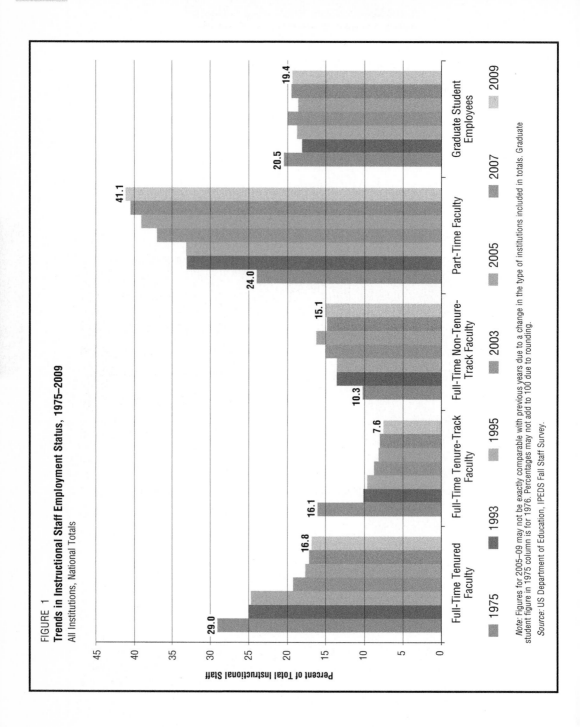

Note: Figures for 2005–09 may not be exactly comparable with previous years due to a change in the type of institutions included in totals. Graduate student figure in 1975 column is for 1976. Percentages may not add to 100 due to rounding.

Source: US Department of Education, IPEDS Fall Staff Survey.

Confronting Contingency: Faculty Equity and the Goals of Academic Democracy

Maria Maistos and Steve Street

Liberal Education

January 2011

A non-tenure-track English instructor at Cuyahoga Community College and the University of Akron, Maria Maistos is president of New Faculty Majority: The National Coalition for Adjunct and Contingent Equity (NFM). Steve Street was an adjunct professor of composition and literature at several colleges, including the State University of New York. Street was an activist for fair labor practices in U.S. colleges, and also a member of NFM, which advocates for improved working conditions for non-tenure-track faculty. This article argues that the democratic values of U.S. higher education are compromised when universities employ unfair labor practices, and the authors are careful to emphasize that non-tenure-track faculty are not lesser teachers than tenure-track faculty; instead, their working conditions may compromise the quality of higher education.

1. What are three features of "academic democracy," according to Maistos and Street?

2. The peer-reviewed journal in which this article originally appeared, *Liberal Education*, is intended for an audience of university professors and administrators. What rhetorical strategies do Maistos and Street employ to convince this audience that they should participate in efforts to address labor inequities in the university?

3. Research the working conditions for non-tenure-track faculty at your university. Which of Maistos and Street's recommendations for improving working conditions for contingent faculty might be most effective at your college? Why?

People & Places

Much has been written about higher education's increasing reliance on contingent academic labor over the last few decades. The narrative, which includes differing accounts of what, or who, is most to blame, has been well rehearsed: the increase came in slow and steady waves tied to significant political and economic events, including postwar enrollment surges, economic downturns, and the shift to a corporate management model; it came with the knowing or unknowing complicity of administrators; it was caused by the complacency of the tenured, the fear of the untenured, or is simply collateral damage in a war against tenure.

It is not our purpose here to analyze the causes of contingency; in this essay we focus on the efforts of those who have worked to reform or eliminate it. However, because the decades-old struggle to mitigate or reverse the trend has, in spite of a variety of efforts, seen the percentage of postsecondary faculty on contingent appointments actually rise from 43 percent in 1975 to almost 75 percent in 2010, and because troubling new developments include brazen union busting by the administration at East-West University in Chicago and the proposals by two community colleges in Michigan to outsource the hiring and administration of contingent faculty to new "academic temporary agencies," it is impossible not to return to questions of cause—and effect. For whether one believes that the reliance on contingent employment is a positive development, a simple fact of life of contemporary higher education, or (as we believe) one of the biggest threats yet to its integrity, it is imperative that we consider the implications for the health of the profession, for the future of institutional leadership, and for the state of liberal education. Such consideration will allow us to (re)write the narrative going forward, rather than to allow the narrative simply to repeat in an endless and ever-expanding loop, as it seems to have done since the American Association of University Professors issued its first official policy statement on contingency in 1980.

We suggest that the growth of contingency reflects a gradual distancing of the practice of higher education from its purpose as trustee of the ideals of liberal education and democracy. Contingency persists for the following four reasons.

1. The solutions that have been offered by unions, activists, and progressive administrations on individual campuses have been too few and too isolated (if not too localized), and organizing efforts

have been too difficult to coordinate effectively on a larger scale. Additionally, in some—particularly nonunionized—locations, contingency has become so much a part of the institutional culture that reform has been scarce and the pessimism or fear of would-be reformers difficult to overcome.

2. These same reform efforts, though isolated and sporadic, have also been substantial enough to lead far too many individual administrative, faculty, and union leaders into thinking that problems with contingency have been sufficiently addressed—or into shielding them from realizing that the problem was ever truly there to begin with.

3. The heterogeneity of the contingent faculty population, long recognized but inadequately documented, researched, or addressed, has encouraged the various stakeholders in the debate over contingency to extrapolate the experiences of one sector—usually the sector whose characteristics are most compatible with those stakeholders' interests—to the whole. This leads many adjunct faculty advocates to suggest that the "satisfied adjunct" is an anomaly and many administrators (and satisfied adjuncts) to deny that there are any contingent faculty members who qualify for food stamps. Such attitudes create a stubborn myopia that impedes conversation and cooperation.

4. The debates that have raged within and about higher education over vocational versus liberal education, tenure, the "corporatization" of higher education, governmental oversight and accreditation, and funding models and sources have obscured, deferred, or overridden the need for action on the fundamental ethical and practical concerns that attend the professional and personal needs of faculty on contingent appointments. Yet, ironically, attending to those concerns—ensuring a living wage, access to health care, professional development, and the protections of academic freedom—would exercise the very values of academic democracy that these debates are really all about.

While the roots of contingent academic employment go back many decades, and surged in the early 1970s (Berry 2005), it was not until

People & Places

the 1980s that the higher education community really began to notice that contingency had exploded to a level of concern. Marked by radically reduced wages, frequent lack of access to benefits, limited access to professional support and opportunities for advancement, and institutional disrespect, contingency is one of higher education's darker secrets. In the last twenty-five years, however, and particularly in the last decade, there have been sincere, if belated, efforts to respond. These include a proliferation of studies, articles, and books; resolutions, statements, guidelines, and best-practice publications by unions, institutions, and associations; and most effectively, both union- and nonunion-affiliated organizing efforts leading to successful collective bargaining, cooperative negotiations with receptive administrations, and groundbreaking litigation and legislation. All of these efforts have resulted, practically speaking, in some improved working conditions for many adjunct faculty members.

Yet, paradoxically, even as these accomplishments have signaled a huge step forward, they have not succeeded in substantially alleviating the sense of foreboding over the status and future of the professoriate, or the ramifications for education that the higher education community began to recognize a generation ago. In fact, that sense of crisis has been heightened as the federal government, allied with major corporations, seeks greater influence over college curricula, particularly at the community college level, with the danger of minimal—or token—consultation with higher education faculty (Wilson 2010).

Several years ago, activists in the contingent faculty movement recognized the impasse at which the movement found itself in the face of this lack of progress (Hoeller 2007), and initiated discussion about the need for a structured national organization. In 2009, such an organization was founded. New Faculty Majority: The National Coalition for Adjunct and Contingent Equity (NFM) is the only national organization exclusively devoted to improving the quality of higher education by improving the working conditions of the majority of its faculty.

NFM came into existence because we believe that higher education needs to move into a new phase of coordinated, intentional, and ethically grounded activity to confront contingency. The goal of such efforts should be to repair the damaging effects on students, faculty, and the country of the haphazard and shortsighted decisions that led to the spread of contingency in the first place, and to bring to fruition the valiant but uncoordinated and all too often superficial reforms that a generation of educators has tried to implement. And, while incremental change may continue to be the only way forward, we believe that what is needed is a new sense of urgency and a defined goal that acknowledges the need for a transformation of academic culture from its current hierarchical, stratified structure into real academic democracy rooted in the values of liberal education.

The current lay of the land: One step forward, two steps back

The first decade of the new century began with many advocates for contingent faculty feeling hopeful. The previous two decades had seen a gradual intensification of awareness of the severity of the contingent faculty problem, along with efforts that culminated in the formation of two important groups: the Coalition on Contingent Academic Labor (COCAL), a loose coalition of unions and activists, and the Coalition on the Academic Workforce (CAW), notable because it brought disciplinary associations, higher education associations, and unions together with a wide range of representation in its membership. COCAL was instrumental in creating a national community of adjunct activists where none had existed before, which aided tremendously in organizing efforts and in the ability of unions to consult with contingent faculty members in the development of many union positions and policy statements. CAW encouraged its member organizations to focus attention on contingent faculty issues.

Several milestones from the 2000s deserve special mention, not least because they represented concerted efforts by contingent faculty to effect change themselves: two Washington State part-time faculty class-action lawsuits related to retirement and health care, which cost the state $25 million (Ruiz 2007); the efforts in California to work legislatively to eliminate caps on part-time faculty workloads (Yoshioka 2007); Barbara Wolf's documentary *A Simple Matter of Justice* (2002), a follow-up to *Degrees of Shame* (1999); and the 2005 publication of Joe Berry's *Reclaiming the Ivory Tower* and his later guide, along with Helena Worthen and Beverly Stewart, for contingent faculty applying for unemployment insurance.

Even as many conscientized faculty, higher education associations, and unions were mobilizing to resist the new trend toward contingency— albeit with different motives, levels of urgency, and conceptions of the crisis—institutions themselves were also beginning to recognize that the cost savings of contingency come with educational and human costs that require reform. While much of the literature dealing with contingency from managerial perspectives is marked by paternalism or rhetorical distancing from contingency's real-life effects (some of the more disconcerting titles include "Making Adjuncts Part of the 'Family,'" "A Systems Approach to Strategic Success with Adjunct Faculty," and incredibly, "Managing a Department's Adjunct Faculty: Let Them Eat Sweet Rolls"), more tenure-stream faculty and administrators began to confront the contradiction between institutional and professional ideals, on the one hand, and the day-to-day reality of life on contingent appointments, on the other. Outspoken professors like Dan Maguire at Marquette University (2009) and administrators like A. G. Monaco (see Jaschik 2008) made moral and ethical cases for reform, and quantitative studies (Jaeger 2008; Eagan and Jaeger 2009; Umbach 2007; Bettinger and Long 2010) debated the effectiveness for student outcomes of so-called "exposure" to contingent faculty.

The effect of this heightened awareness has been undeniable: concrete improvements in contingent faculty working conditions in many places, from mailboxes and parking passes to faculty senate representation and access to professional development funds. Some unions have even obtained access to due process, benefits, and increases in pay for adjuncts, while nonunionized adjuncts are occasionally able to work with administrators to address working conditions (McGrew and Untener 2010).

It has become increasingly clear, however, that cumulatively, these improvements have been the equivalent of faint praise, and are equally damning (or at least confusing). A recurring theme over the last ten years has been the periodic impulse to restudy and resurvey the issue or to issue guidelines and recommendations that are promptly ignored or that lack any enforceability.[1] These studies and guidelines, along with limited improvements, may allow tenured faculty, administrators, and presidents to remain ignorant of the reality of life for many contingent faculty and of the effects on education. At the 2009 Chronicle Leadership Forum session on "The Road Scholar," for example, an administrator responded with incredulity to the session presenters' descriptions of the typical hardships faced by many adjuncts, claiming that she had "never heard" of any such thing, and a significant number of her fellow attendees indicated a similar perspective. If contingent faculty members remain silent, either by choice or out of fear (because they have no union—or, worse, a union that replicates the divide between the two tracks), then campus leaders must have the interest and ability to seek out the truth, which is certainly more complicated than the administrator above understood.

Complicating matters further is the release of studies and surveys that identify a percentage of contingent faculty as "satisfied" with variously described working conditions (Gappa 2000; American Federation of Teachers 2010), blurring a crucial distinction between the gratifying nature of teaching and satisfactory working conditions. Seldom adequately parsed, such studies challenge administrators and faculty activists alike to confront the complicated reality that the contingent faculty population is not homogeneous. The response to that challenge, all too often, has been entrenchment rather than engagement.

Entrenchment persists in matters of finance, as well. While attempts to "integrate" faculty more effectively into the life of the institution have become more commonplace, institutions making these efforts have largely ignored bread-and-butter issues like salary, benefits, access to due process, academic freedom, job security, and professional advancement. These institutions cite financial hardship and resist inquiry into the questionable prioritizing suggested by recent studies that show massive increases in spending on such items as presidential and administrative salaries, facilities, athletics, and public relations along with sharp decreases in spending on direct instruction (Desrochers, Lenihan, and Wellman 2010; Schneider 2009).

In short, solutions meant to alleviate the worst aspects of contingency have had the paradoxical effect of promoting it. For example, institutions often cite with approval the rapid growth of the category of the full-time, non-tenure-track instructor. However, this trend has made the divisive academic class system even more so, and more firmly entrenched; with three classes of faculty rather than two, the "division and conquering" of faculty solidarity is more pronounced. Part-time faculty who see a possible promotion to

People & Places

full-time status have incentive not to speak out, and those who get such a contract, maybe after years of part-time service, are so relieved that they may not dare express concern about their own position and prospects, much less that of their colleagues on the often inaccurately named "part-time" track. Similarly, workload caps imposed on contingent faculty members by their unions are proclaimed to be in the interest of contingent faculty themselves, but, without real progress on per-course compensation or an ultimate goal of equity, caps force many contingent faculty members to teach on multiple campuses in order to earn a living wage.

From incrementalism to goal-oriented structural reform

In practical terms, these examples point to the short-sightedness of many of the solutions to the contingent faculty crisis that have been enacted over the last twenty-five years. The problem has been that, to date, there is no common goal toward which to work and no benchmarks by which to assess the changes that have been made. Like the growth of contingency itself, the response to contingency has been haphazard, localized, self-interested, arbitrary, and defined by the very institutional structures that created it. (Indeed, the claim that "many part-timers don't want to be full time" is a common objection in discussions of inequity, as if the notion of equivalent compensation for equivalent work can only be addressed in terms of the very two-tiered system that needs to change.) Many of the advances that have been made have been short-term gains and long-term losses, treatment of symptoms rather than causes: a new orientation program here, a $100-per-credit-hour gain there.

Incremental or piecemeal change that brings occasional, by no means comprehensive progress on some fronts while lacking a clear understanding of why change is necessary or what kind of change must ultimately be achieved, we contend, is not deep enough change. Treating symptoms does not necessarily lead to the correct diagnosis or treatment of the underlying disease, and in fact it can further mask the real root disorder. The danger of incrementalism, in other words, is not that it makes small changes over time; it is that without a clear view of the ultimate destination, small changes over time can actually obstruct progress toward a definable goal.

But of course the question becomes, what is the definable goal? If the problem is that no consensus exists on how to define that goal, then addressing that problem becomes the first step. At NFM, we propose adapting the thriving example of the Vancouver Community College model, where, among other things, there is a single salary schedule and where all faculty have equal access to permanent status. We have articulated the goals of equity in compensation, job security, academic freedom, faculty governance, professional advancement, benefits, and unemployment insurance. We contend that each of these goals is rooted in a larger goal that has long been defined in the foundational principles of the idea of the university and in the purpose and functioning of our democracy: the protection and refinement of academic, or campus, democracy for the purpose of ensuring quality education and safeguarding and advancing our national democracy. As Rich Moser (2004, 5) explains, "the concept of campus democracy implies that the campus is a distinctive but integral part of the broader society serving the public good. If we take a step further and define the public interest as the defense of core values, then the campus should become an exemplar of freedom, democracy, equality, and justice. The constitution of the campus could be considered its most important pedagogy and the efforts to shape that constitution our best classroom." There are few more compelling definitions of the purpose and process of education. As every parent and every educator knows, there is no better— or more unforgiving—pedagogical tool than the power of example. The next step forward, then, involves a look inward.

From ivory tower to academic democracy

To many observers, the formation of NFM was puzzling and counterintuitive; hadn't unionization efforts among contingent faculty increased and hadn't advances been made through collective bargaining? And weren't many institutions now paying attention to and implementing the types of reforms and strategies that for years had been recommended for the purpose of "integrating" contingent faculty more effectively into the life of the college and university and showing them respect?

If the concerns of contingent faculty had only to do with working conditions, then the progress made over the last generation might not have required NFM's formation. Contingent faculty would have continued to support local organizing efforts and internal reform efforts, celebrating advances as they have occurred and fighting for change where necessary.

People & Places

But NFM is not just about improving working conditions. It is about improving working conditions for an ultimate purpose: to ensure the quality of education and the integrity of the profession. NFM aims to remind the academy that it exists not for itself, and not simply to preserve itself, but for the common good—and that the operative definition of "common" in that expression should not evoke the unfortunate connotation of "second rate," but rather its root, communis, or community.

Clearly, the contingent faculty crisis is simply the most obvious manifestation of the steady erosion of community in higher education. The faculty (in part, through its own doing) has moved, or been pushed, away from its role as a full partner in higher education to a literally "adjunct" position—peripheral, disempowered—in terms of either numbers or function. Tenure-stream faculty, who have authority over the curriculum and at least a nominal role in governance, are now too small in number or too cowed to initiate or resist change effectively, while faculty off the tenure track, though the majority in number, must risk their livelihoods to do so. To fight against this trend is to "reclaim" the ivory tower, as Joe Berry (2005) has put it, by transforming it into the academic democracy that it is really supposed to be.

If the marginalization of the faculty as a whole is the disease whose most obvious symptom is the mistreatment of those with the lowest status, then what is needed is a cure that builds on the body's natural strengths. What is needed is a revitalization of the concept of academic democracy, one rooted in the social contract that has traditionally defined faculty work and that embodies the values of liberal education. Again, as Moser (2004, 2) explains, "as students, faculty, and campus workers make common cause to secure workplace rights and basic economic security, we must also articulate new ideals and mobilize alternative forms of community. We could organize such a project under the rubric of 'campus democracy, community and academic citizenship': ideals of service that revisit classical conceptions of the university, are grounded in existing economic and political conditions, rooted in democratic traditions of freedom, and already legible in the many struggles for justice on today's campuses." It is those ideals and traditions—along with sheer willpower—that will be needed to combat the pessimistic notion that "once the university budget has absorbed their [non-tenure-track faculty] lower cost . . . it becomes almost impossible to retreat" (Cross and Goldenberg 2002, 27–28).

Confronting contingency is not an impossible task, though it is a formidable one. As Caryn McTighe Musil has pointed out, it is "radical"—but only because it is so necessary: "Of course, treating the contingent faculty like 'real' faculty, especially women and women with children, is a radical act. It requires considerable shifts in attitude, in economic remuneration, and in job security. It means incorporating these faculty members as equal partners in departments, welcoming them as academic colleagues, and nurturing their professional growth" (Musil 2009). As daunting as this task is, however, Musil reminds us that we can do it—because we've done it before. "The academy figured out how to rethink entire fields when DNA was discovered and mapped, when technology changed everything about our lives and work, and when women's studies and ethnic studies forever altered the foundations of knowledge. The academy should be able to make this other change too" (Musil 2009).

We could not agree more. It will take leadership, courage, trust, and a willingness to reject the ignorance and cynicism that always plague efforts to effect such massive but necessary change in institutional culture. NFM exists, and will do whatever is necessary, to facilitate that change.

References

American Association of University Professors. 1980. *The Status of Part-Time Faculty*. Washington, DC: American Association of University Professors.

American Federation of Teachers. 2010. *American Academic: A National Survey of Part-time/Adjunct Faculty*. Washington, DC: American Federation of Teachers.

Berry, Joe. 2005. Reclaiming the Ivory Tower: Organizing Adjuncts to Change Higher Education. New York: *Monthly Review Press*.

Bettinger, Eric P., and Bridget Terry Long. 2010. "Does Cheaper Mean Better? The Impact of Using Adjunct Instructors on Student Outcomes." *Review of Economics and Statistics* 92 (3): 598–613.

Biliczky, Carol. 2010. "UA OKs Raises for Instructors." *Beacon Journal* (Akron, Ohio), November 2, http://www.ohio.com/news/106501343.html.

Cross, John G., and Edie N. Goldenberg. 2002. "Why Hire Non-Tenure-Track Faculty?" Peer Review 5 (1): 25–28.

Desrochers, Donna M., Colleen M. Lenihan, and Jane V. Wellman. 2010. *Trends in College Spending 1998-2008: Where Does the Money Come From? Where Does It Go? What Does It Buy?* Washington, DC: Delta Cost Project.

People & Places

Eagan, M. Kevin, Jr, and Audrey J. Jaeger. 2009. "Effects of Exposure to Part-time Faculty on Community College Transfer." *Research in Higher Education* 50: 168–88.

Gappa, Judith M. 2000. "The New Faculty Majority: Somewhat Satisfied but Not Eligible for Tenure." *New Directions for Institutional Research* 105: 77.

Hoeller, Keith. 2007. "The Future of the Contingent Faculty Movement." *Inside Higher Ed*, November 13, http://www.insidehighered.com/views/2007/11/13/hoeller.

Jaeger, Audrey J. 2008. "Contingent Faculty and Student Outcomes." *Academe* 94 (6): 42–43.

Jaschik, Scott. 2008. "Call to Arms for Adjuncts . . . From an Administrator." *Inside Higher Ed*, October 14, http://www.insidehighered.com/news/2008/10/14/adjunct.

Maguire, Daniel C. "Seeking the Path to Adjunct Justice at Marquette University." *Thought & Action* (Fall): 47–55.

McGrew, Heidi, and Joe Untener. 2010. "A Primer on Improving Contingent Faculty Conditions." *Academe* 96 (4): 43–45.

Moser, Richard. 2004. "Campus Democracy, Community, and Academic Citizenship." Paper presented at the Conference on Contingent Academic Labor VI, Chicago, IL, August.

Musil, Caryn McTighe. 2009. "Red Blood Cells on Reserve." *On Campus with Women* 37 (3), http://www.aacu.org/ocww/volume37_3/director.cfm.

Ruiz, Eddy A. 2007. "The Stone that Struck Goliath: The Part-Time Faculty Association, Washington State Community and Technical Colleges, and Class-Action Lawsuits." *New Directions for Community Colleges* 140: 49–54.

Schneider, Mark. 2009. "Where Does All That Tuition Go?" *Education Outlook* 12, http://www.aei.org/docLib/09-EduO-Dec-g.pdf.

Umbach, Paul D. 2007. "How Effective Are They? Exploring the Impact of Contingent Faculty on Undergraduate Education." *The Review of Higher Education* 30 (2): 91–123.

Wilson, David McKay. 2010. "The Casualties of the Twenty-First-Century Community College." *Academe* 96 (3): 12–18.

Yoshioka, Robert B. 2007. "Part-Time Faculty in California: Successes, Challenges, and Future Issues." *New Directions for Community Colleges* 140: 41–47.

Note

1. A notable exception is Phi Beta Kappa's denial of a chapter to the University of Akron thanks to high numbers of adjunct faculty at that institution (Biliczky 2010).

Contingent Faculty and Student Learning: Welcome to the Strativersity

Karen Thompson

New Directions for Higher Education

September 2003

When Karen Thompson published this article, she was a part-time lecturer at Rutgers University, as well as a member of the AAUP Committee on Part-Time and Non-Tenure-Track Appointments. *New Directions for Higher Education* is a peer-reviewed academic journal that addresses major issues in post-secondary education. In this essay she draws from her experiences as both a non-tenure-track faculty member and an advocate for contingent faculty at Rutgers to predict the long-term effects of current labor practices on universities and student learning.

1. What does Thompson mean by the word "strativersity"?

2. Usually, peer-reviewed academic journal articles synthesize a significant number of researched sources to provide support for their claims. Thompson's article, however, relies on her personal experience for evidence. Does Thompson employ her ethos to effectively persuade the reader? Why or why not?

3. Both Thompson and Maistros and Street discuss the importance of academic freedom for non-tenure-track faculty. How do these authors define academic freedom? Do you agree with their claims that academic freedom must be protected, even if it results in higher costs for colleges?

People & Places

I intend to present the perspective of adjunct and part-time faculty in the academy, but I think the questions raised by contingent faculty have resonance for every sector of the university today.

Part-Time Faculty Issues

Let me begin with some of the hard realities that I recently presented to the New Jersey legislature, linking the ways that typical contingent working conditions may undermine student learning conditions.

Accessibility. Faculty accessibility is the first and most frequently cited problem associated with contingent faculty when they become the primary teaching force in undergraduate education. Adjunct and part-time lecturers in particular most often face heavy teaching loads, commute between multiple positions, and lack basic support facilities like offices, mailboxes, telephones, Web sites, and e-mail accounts. These conditions, to say nothing of the grading workload, diminish and fragment their time—and directly undermine their ability to meet with students. Tenure-track faculty themselves are also increasingly unavailable, as their ranks are eroded by contingent appointments and as their responsibilities are increasingly centered on graduate students and research.

The previous chapters put numbers to this trend. More anecdotally, a recent Rutgers graduate wrote to the student newspaper that only 18 of her 120 credits for graduation were in courses taught by tenure-track faculty— all the rest were led by part-time lecturers or teaching assistants. So if we consider student access to faculty beyond the immediate classroom to be a condition that enhances student engagement and learning, the growing contingency of university teachers is a negative trend with no remedy in sight.

Even collective bargaining, which can be an effective tool to address inadequate salaries and working conditions, may be impotent when it comes to the circumstances of teacher accessibility. Collective bargaining law differs from state to state, but in New Jersey we have found that mirrors in the bathroom are a more protected topic of bargaining than offices, phones, and mailboxes—the latter are only necessary if educational managers judge them to be, whereas the mirror is an option of desire or convenience that educational workers are free to request. Evidently, the importance of offices, phones, and mailboxes to teachers' accessibility is not even debatable sometimes.

Student Advising. A clear consequence of inaccessibility is inadequate student advising. Undergraduates, particularly those in their first two years of study, are more likely to be in introductory and core courses taught by contingent faculty, which also tend to be the classes with better student/teacher ratios. These lower-division undergraduate students are the students most in need of advising, and this is the best moment to reach them. But contingent faculty may not be familiar with the range of academic programs, requirements, and possibilities available to students. They are certainly not paid to advise or become mentors beyond their classroom hours of work. That responsibility presumably falls on the tenure-track faculty, yet there are fewer of them and especially fewer of them teaching undergraduates in small classes.

At the Rutgers Writing Program, we try to bridge the gap first by distributing standardized "registration" handouts in class, then by sending students to the department Web page. But is effective advising a matter of isolated reading and independent Web browsing? Students miss the chance to develop real relationships with faculty, a factor some say is the single most important contributor to an outstanding education. In the direction we are heading, it is fair for students to ask their college: Who will be there to help us select the right major, sponsor an independent study, call in an incomplete, suggest an alternative reading, cut through some bureaucratically scrambled credits, or just write a reference that is taken seriously? We have tried to negotiate compensation for extra duties at Rutgers where some part-timers write recommendations, cover incompletes, and advise regularly without pay, but it remains to be seen when these crucial aspects of the college teachers' role will become fully acknowledged.

Classroom Issues. Accessibility and advising are at risk outside the classroom, but contingency increases the ways students can be shortchanged inside the classroom as well. Let me recast this more positively— if students are not going to be shortchanged, they need courses taught by faculty who know ahead of time that they

People & Places

are teaching, what they are teaching, and when they are teaching. For the teacher this means advance notice of reappointment; for the student, it means courses will more likely be well planned and well organized. In my work for the American Association of University Professors (AAUP), at Rutgers and nationally, I see dozens of excellent, qualified, and committed instructors leave academia because they are tired of not being able to plan ahead. Through collective bargaining, we have gradually pushed notice of assignment and appointment so that now departments are encouraged to make decisions one term ahead of time. But as often occurs with bargaining, the key word is "encouraged"; we still have work to do if teachers and students are to get the advance planning they deserve.

Professional Development. But better notice of reappointment is not enough. Support for professional development should be available to anyone in front of a college classroom. Students need instructors who are in tune with the continual transformations taking place in higher education. Students benefit from teachers who are aware of developing pedagogies, changing disciplines, and new classroom practices and technologies—and teachers in tune with the mission of their institution. Students suffer when instructors stagnate—and although this certainly can happen to full-timers, it is built into the structure of contingent appointments.

Professional development means being able to attend conferences in your field, give papers at such meetings, participate in discipline associations and departments. At the Rutgers Writing Program, royalties from the composition textbook are used to fund professional travel for part-time lecturers and full-time non-tenure-track instructors. But in a sense, this funding is then coming out of tenured faculty pockets rather than institutional budgets. The Rutgers Writing Program also encourages us all to build Web pages, but even teaching assistants and non-tenure-track instructors can take Web page design courses for free; in contrast, part-time lecturers must pay their own way. This is another topic we have been struggling with at the bargaining table.

Collegial Involvement. Professional development and student advising depend on collegial involvement. Instructors who keep up in their fields, are abreast of developments in their institutions, and are in touch with other faculty members make the best student mentors and advisers. There can be no collegial interchange if faculty are operating in rigid tiers with no contact between contingent instructors and the tenure-track faculty.

Students will not necessarily see these invisible dividers, but the results will affect their educations. Students need to talk with faculty who are up-to-date, well-connected, and encouraging; they need to see faculty who are positive examples of where advanced education can take you; and they need to interact with faculty who can steer them most effectively through their institutions.

The need for collegial involvement extends beyond the departmental level. At Rutgers last year, the university senate added three representatives for part-time lecturers and annual appointees for the first time ever. This is an opportunity for contingent faculty to participate in the governance forum in which administrators, tenure-track faculty, and students were already involved. This may be just another occasion to collect unpaid service from those already exploited, but it may also be another step toward revealing the invisible faculty. It is an important opportunity for the university community to hear contingent faculty voices, to hear a perspective that might not otherwise be heard.

A Stable Workforce.   You can see that I am on a slippery slope here but trying to roll the stone up the slope. If universities invest in the professional development and collegial involvement of contingent faculty, then clearly the payoff can only be realized by having a long-term and stable workforce. This brings us back to the issue of tenure, or at very least, longer-term and full-time non-tenure-track appointments. But to secure such stability, even in an adjunct workforce, the pay and benefits would have to match comparable jobs in other sectors. This implies salary and health care coverage. And these are areas where collective bargaining has made its greatest inroads: seniority, security, salary, and health insurance.

Decent Pay and Benefits.   Decent pay and benefits are necessary to the conditions of student learning because students need committed instructors, who have the necessary time and are not distracted by extra employment responsibilities and schedules required to supplement their incomes and live decent lives. Most adjuncts are not Nobel laureates or retired CEOs wanting to give back to the next generation, although a few may be. Believe it or not, a fair number of part-time faculty get menial full-time jobs just so they can continue teaching and using their advanced degrees. I was on a panel once with a fellow who grudgingly gave up his part-time teaching position to do warehouse work that would better support his family. Then he realized he could go back to teaching as a second job. Something seems backwards when the blue-collar position ensures the academic one. All those years of education turn out to be not such a good investment. I wonder if the warehouse position had collective bargaining protections.

Academic Freedom. And now we come to the heart of the matter. Would the young fellow in this example have dared to tell his story (there was more to it, of course, involving union organizing, I believe) on a panel if he did not feel secure in his basic employment? Academic freedom cannot really be obtained for those appointed by the term or year. Even making the slightest waves could lead to "nonreappointment." In most cases, without collective bargaining, nonreappointment requires no explanation. Surely, contingent faculty can seldom advocate curriculum reform, support unpopular causes, or take risks in the classroom in an atmosphere like this.

At Rutgers, when we have tried to negotiate an academic freedom clause in our contract, we have been told that "everyone" has academic freedom. Yet how can that be if part-timers have to be reappointed each term? And if that were the case why would those of us in the writing program have to note "All Grades Subject to Department Review" on our syllabi? Good teachers must be able to experiment and take risks, they must demand and display critical thinking skills. Students suffer when an instructor's innovative impulse is constrained, and full-time tenure-track faculty feel the chilling effects of a department or institution populated with teachers (and perhaps students) watching their backs.

Faculty Governance. When so many teaching faculty are insecure and

without academic freedom, it is difficult for faculty governance to flourish even among the elite minority. Tenure-track faculty often resist governance participation by part-time faculty, whom they perceive as too dependent on administration to exercise independent judgment. And as governance bodies become moribund and peer decision-making mechanisms disappear, academic freedom diminishes for everyone. When academic freedom is weak, quality education becomes threatened by conformity, mediocrity, and the safest approaches, including "objective" multiple choice or true-false tests rather than essay evaluation, grade inflation, and choosing to protect one's position rather than extend students' horizons.

Due Process Protections.   Generally we speak of protecting academic freedom with tenure, but the extent that probationary tenure-track faculty and non-tenure-track faculty have any assurance of academic freedom is the extent to which their appointments are associated with due process protections. These may be based on collective bargaining or institutional regulations, but the key feature of due process is usually an opportunity for a hearing before a neutral adjudicator. Contingent faculty appointments are defined specifically to preclude such procedures not only by omitting any regular review and hearing procedures but by explicitly disavowing any standards or expectation of reappointment.

 When a part-time lecturer of twenty years at Rutgers was not renewed this year for supposedly abandoning her classroom, even with a collective bargaining agreement there was little we could do to save her job. How many of us think that canceling a class will lead to the end of a career? Without an opportunity to defend her behavior before a neutral third party, the department was able to represent this part-time lecturer as negligent. Due process protections are probably the most important items in a collective bargaining agreement, yet grievance procedure language seldom gets the attention it needs to function fairly. As long as instructors can be denied reappointment at will, they will lack academic freedom and students will lack the opportunity to study with faculty who are working under the minimal conditions necessary to protect the opportunity to exercise professional integrity.

What sort of example does this set for that special class of student learners: the bright students who might consider becoming teachers in higher education themselves—the students we should be attracting as majors in our departments, as prospective graduate students, and as future members of our faculties? What are they observing in these trends and scenarios that will encourage them to invest years of income, sacrifice, and intellectual endeavor—a shrinking shot at positions of integrity and security in the

People & Places

university or a growing chance of becoming the academic braceros of the 21st century?

Conditions of Employment That Will Contribute to Improved Student Learning

Our part-time and full-time non-tenure-track faculty need stable appointments, decent pay and benefits, and due process protections of employment and academic freedom, as well as a voice in course development and pedagogy, peer consultation with tenured faculty, resources for professional development, paid time for office hours and extra-classroom mentoring—oh yes, and an office for those hours, along with access to a copy machine, a computer, and a Web site. And let us throw in a little clerical help from the department too.

How many institutions today present this scene? Pretty well none, even though the trends are plain as day and the costs to student learning palpable. The answer, we are told, is threefold. First, harsh economic realities dictate cost-cutting measures; economizing has meant limiting the core of tenure-track faculty while the lower tiers of part-time and nontenure-track faculty grow. At the same time, administrative expansion takes up more space at the top. So now the university has an hourglass employment structure—wide at the top and bottom, pinched in the middle—exactly parallel to the workforce picture in the larger society, and just as perilous in terms of mobility, skill transmission, and collegiality. We want to reverse this trend—restore the bulge in the middle—to a faculty that is stable and committed.

The second justification for contingent faculty is flexibility. There are real contingencies, such as fluctuations in enrollment, faculty members on leave, and so on, but not on the scale of two contingents for every tenured faculty member. What appears at first to be attractive flexibility becomes in reality a faculty where the majority are unrepresented and without peer review. And again, a huge gap opens between the administrator and the classroom, with little accountability or communication on either side. We want that gap to close through representation and investment. And if we close that gap, flexibility would not continue to circumvent accountability.

Finally, there is a new argument that contingent faculty actually provide a better educational environment—they have a teaching focus and bring real-world expertise into the classroom. But for all the reasons I have detailed—precarious working conditions, heavy workloads, time constraints, stunted professional development—these potential assets cannot be captured in the current structure. Even if the occasional adjunct hero (or, more likely, heroine) surmounts all obstacles, or wins the lottery, this is not a sustainable recruitment strategy. We want a strategy that rewards, not consumes, intellectual capital.

Concerns

The distance between what is happening and what needs to happen leaves me with a set of big questions. Can high-quality higher education, especially at public universities, be sustained with exploitative conditions and the work of a second-class citizenry? If the ranks of tenure-track faculty continue to erode, who will be the arbitrators of quality? Who will have the academic freedom to make those decisions? How will administrators know what is being taught and who is really teaching? And what happens when administration gets outsourced along with teaching?

If we deconstruct the university—and set aside the trendy rhetoric of a multiversity—are we not actually approaching a "strativersity," a hierarchy of teaching that more strictly imposes a hierarchy of learning than anything we have seen in three generations? As higher education structures teachers into narrowly tiered channels, students' opportunities go that way as well. We need a more secure and rewarded faculty who are held accountable for their teaching quality and who can also hold our institutions accountable in supporting the learning process.

People & Places

Position Statement on the Status and Working Conditions of Contingent Faculty

National Council of Teachers of English

National Council of Teachers of English

September 2010

A disproportionate number of non-tenure-track faculty teach in the liberal arts, including English departments. The National Council of Teachers of English, an influential organization which advocates for language arts teachers' and students' rights, adopted this position statement in 2010. Intended to set standards for all colleges employing contingent faculty in composition and literature courses, this statement suggests very concrete actions for university employers.

1. Of the four "conditions of employment" outlined in this position statement, which do you consider most important for *any* job? Why?

2. While this position statement is aimed at an audience of college administrators and faculty, consider this issue from *your* perspective, the perspective of a student. Given that perspective, what would you add to this list of recommendations for employing contingent faculty?

3. How do the recommended actions in this position statement compare to the actions suggested in Maistros and Street's essay (also in this chapter)?

Conditions of Employment

1. Fair Working Conditions

- Appointment/offer letters should clearly describe the position and identify workload distributions.

- Appointments should be made in a timely manner (as opposed, for example, to two weeks before the start of an academic term).

- Annual evaluations should be provided to all faculty members, and should be based on the workload distribution defined in the appointment/offer letter.

- New appointments should receive an appropriate and timely orientation that informs and ensures access to institutional resources, such as access to parking passes, library privileges, computer access, ID cards, assistance with scholarly work, and so on.

- Class size limitations consistent with the recommendations of NCTE and CCCC should be placed on courses taught by faculty members serving in contingent positions.

- Faculty members in contingent positions who have served for three or more years in a program should not be terminated without at least a full term's notice.

2. Fair Compensation

- Faculty members serving in contingent positions should receive a salary that reflects their teaching duties and any duties outside the classroom they are asked to assume. Compensation, per course, for part-time faculty should never be lower than the per-course compensation for tenure-line faculty with comparable experience, duties, and credentials.

- Faculty members serving in contingent positions should receive annual pay increases consistent with those awarded to tenure-line faculty.

- Faculty members serving in contingent positions should have access to the same benefits packages provided to tenure-line faculty.

- Mechanisms should be developed to allow faculty members serving in contingent positions who are not employed during one or more academic terms (for example, for reasons of childbirth, illness, or other exigencies) to maintain benefits and leave accrual until their return to the institution.

PART-TIME   ASSOCIATE   TENURED

- Faculty members serving in contingent positions should receive support, in the form of office space, secretarial support, access to computers and telephones, access to copying, and so on, comparable to that afforded to tenure-line faculty.

3. Involvement in Shared Governance

- Faculty members serving in contingent positions should be invited to faculty meetings and asked to serve (and, if they agree, compensated for their service) on relevant department, college, and university committees.

- Faculty members serving in contingent positions should be involved in the development of evaluation procedures and instruments.

- The rights and responsibilities of faculty in contingent positions should be identified in relevant department, college, and university governing codes.

- Efforts should be made to ensure appropriate and reasonable communication with faculty in contingent positions, so as to more fully involve them in department, college, and university activities and initiatives.

4. Respect and Recognition

- Faculty members serving in contingent positions should be viewed and treated as a valued and integral part of the academic faculty.

People & Places

- Faculty members serving in contingent positions should have access to most, if not all, of the resources and services that are available to tenure-line faculty, including mentoring programs, support for scholarly work, support for travel, and so on.

- In the event of the conversion of contingent faculty lines to tenure lines, faculty members in those positions should be afforded the opportunity to participate in professional development activities that will prepare them to compete for the tenure-line positions. This might also include the creation of a probationary period in which the current holder of the line is allowed to work toward the fulfillment of the requirements of the new tenure-line position.

Security of Employment

- Instructors should be afforded the opportunity to earn tenure or, in the alternative, "long-term security of employment" as teaching specialists. Their position descriptions should recognize the specialized nature of their appointments, and evaluations should be tied to those position descriptions and conducted at intervals comparable to those of faculty in traditional tenure-line positions.

Growth for Online Learning

Doug Lederman

Inside Higher Ed

January 2013

Doug Lederman is editor and one of the founders of *Inside Higher Ed*, the online companion to the newspaper *Chronicle of Higher Education*. Lederman is a leading figure in higher education; he is often interviewed on C-Span and National Public Radio, and he has won multiple National Awards for Education Reporting from the Education Writers Association. Here he discusses the results of a national survey about the growth of online courses in higher education today.

1. What is a MOOC and how does it differ from a "regular" online college course?

2. If you or someone you know has enrolled in a college course online, consider the course from a student's perspective. What were the benefits of that experience? The drawbacks?

3. According to the survey that Lederman discusses, while the number of college administrators now consider online courses integral to their educational offerings, the vast majority of college faculty are skeptical about the educational value of these courses. Why might this gap between faculty and administrators' perceptions exist?

MOOCs may have snared most of the headlines, but traditional, credit-based online learning continued to chug along just fine last year, thank you very much.

More than 6.7 million, or roughly a third, of all students enrolled in postsecondary education took an online course for credit in fall 2011, according to the 2012 iteration of the Babson Survey Research Group's annual Survey of Online Learning. While the upturn in the number of online enrollees (9.3 percent) represented the smallest percentage increase in the 10 years that Babson has conducted this study, overall enrollment in American colleges and universities fell in 2011 for the first time in 15 years, to put the slowing of online growth in some context.

And speaking of said MOOCs—the massive open online courses that have captured the imagination of the public and turbocharged the discussion about digitally delivered instruction in many quarters—the Babson survey for the first time queried institutional officials about their views about the courses.

Given their relative newness, the answers are probably unsurprising: lots of uncertainty about whether to embrace them, and significant skepticism about whether the free open courses (at least as of the time when the survey was conducted) present a "sustainable method for offering online courses."

Slowing But No Plateau

With college enrollments flattening overall, driven by the end of the baby boom echo and the incremental improvement of the job market, online enrollments might be expected to flatten. But as the following table shows, while the rate of growth fell to its lowest level in at least a decade, the survey shows that enrollment in distance courses and programs continues to be more than healthy. (This being the survey's 10th year, the report's authors, I. Elaine Allen and Jeff Seaman, the Babson group's co-directors, included data on changes over the decade they've been conducting it.)

Online Enrollments, 2002-2011			
	Students Taking at Least 1 Online Course	Increase Over Previous Year	% Increase
2002	1,602,970	n/a	n/a
2003	1,971,397	368,427	23.0%
2004	2,329,783	358,386	18.2
2005	3,180,050	850,267	36.5
2006	3,488,381	308,331	9.7
2007	3,938,111	449,730	12.9
2008	4,606,353	668,242	16.9
2009	5,579,022	972,669	21.1
2010	6,142,280	563,258	10.1
2011	6,714,792	572,512	9.3

Perhaps most strikingly, online enrollments continue to make up an increasing proportion of all enrollments in higher education, as seen in the chart below.

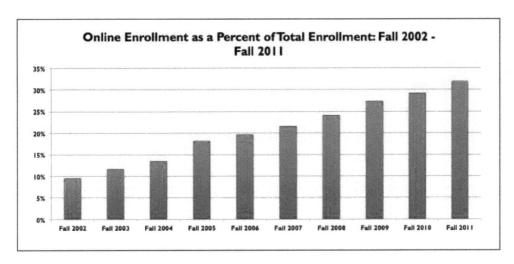

And as seen in this chart, more than 7 in 10 public and for-profit colleges are now offering full academic programs (as opposed to merely freestanding courses) online, far more than were doing so a decade ago. Nearly half of

People & Places

private nonprofit colleges are offering fully online programs, about double the number that were doing so in 2002.

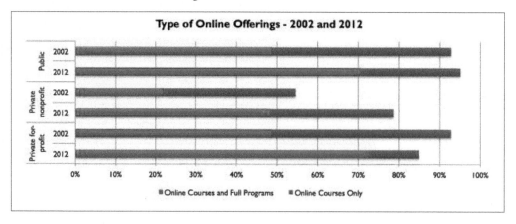

Type of Online Offerings - 2002 and 2012

Measuring MOOCs

The Babson researchers asked a series of questions about institutions' usage of and plans for MOOCs.

A small fraction (2.6 percent) of the roughly 2,500 responding colleges said they currently have massive open courses, and another 9.4 percent said they are planning one.

Chief academic officers queried about the sustainability of MOOCs as a way of offering courses were deeply divided. Nearly half were neutral, with the rest evenly split between yes and no. There was much more widespread support for the idea that MOOCs could help institutions learn about online pedagogy, with nearly three in five respondents agreeing that they would serve that purpose.

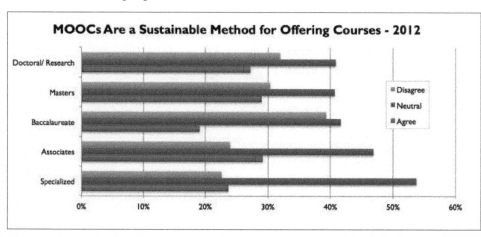

MOOCs Are a Sustainable Method for Offering Courses - 2012

Among other highlights of the survey:

- Nearly 7 in 10 chief academic leaders (69.1 percent) now say that online learning is critical to their long-term strategy. And just 11.2 percent say it is not.

- More than three-quarters (77.0 percent) of chief academic officers rate the learning outcomes in online education as the same or superior to those in face-to-face courses, up from 57.2 percent when Babson first asked the question in 2003.

- Fewer than a third (30.2 percent) of CAOs believe that faculty members on their campuses accept the value and legitimacy of online education—lower than the rate in 2004.

Changing Course: Ten Years of Tracking Online Education in the United States

The Sloan Consortium

sloanconsortium.org

The Sloan Consortium is a nonprofit organization providing educators with information about trends in online instruction, as well as strategies for effective online teaching and course administration. The charts in this report refer to the same survey that Lederman discusses: the Babson Survey Research Group and the College Board's "Changing Course: Ten Years of Tracking Online Education in the United States."

1. What piece of information was most surprising or interesting to you? Why?

2. The graphics and charts in this report are intended to provide readers with a quick visual overview of key issues regarding online education. Review each visual carefully. Which do you think is most effective? What rhetorical strategies make it so?

3. While this report does not discuss the connection between the growth of online course offerings and the increase of part-time, non-tenured faculty in colleges, can you offer a theory about why *both* are expanding at this time?

Changing Course:

TEN YEARS OF TRACKING ONLINE EDUCATION IN THE UNITED STATES

Survey by I. Elaine Allen and Jeff Seaman, Babson Survey Research Group; based
on responses from over 2,800 Chief Academic Officers (CAOs) and academic leaders

Infographic by Pearson Learning Solutions

What are Chief Academic Officers planning for MOOCs in 2012?

32.7%	55.4%	12%
No plans	Not decided	Have or planning a MOOC

What percent are working with others on a MOOC?

Planning to add a MOOC:	Currently have a MOOC:
50%	37%
0% 100%	0% 100%

Current academic leader opinions of MOOCs

	Agree	Neutral	Disagree
MOOCs are a sustainable method for offering courses	28%	45%	27%
MOOCs are important for institutions to learn about online pedagogy	49%	32%	19%
MOOCs can be used to attract potential students	44%	35%	22%
MOOCs are good for students to determine if online instruction is appropriate	51%	31%	19%
MOOC instruction will not be accepted in the workplace	19%	45%	36%
Credentials for MOOC completion will cause confusion about higher education degrees	55%	26%	19%

Is online learning strategic?

CAOs perceive online education to be critical to the long-term strategy of their institution

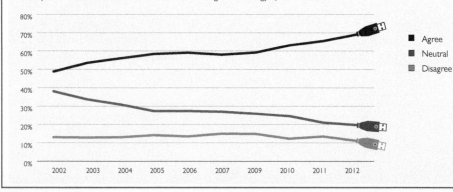

- Agree
- Neutral
- Disagree

How many students are learning online?

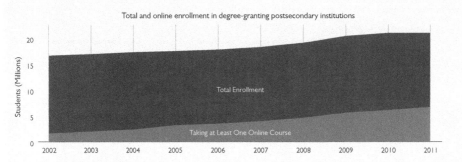

Total and online enrollment in degree-granting postsecondary institutions

Year after year the number of online enrollments steadily increases its proportion of total enrollments starting at 11.7% in 2003 and increasing to 32% in 2011.

■———■ Online enrollment as a percent of total enrollment

■———■ Annual growth rate of online enrollment

■———■ Annual growth rate of total enrollment

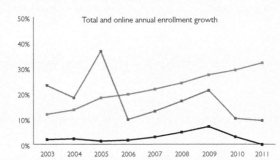

Total and online annual enrollment growth

Does it take more faculty time and effort to teach online?

45% of CAOs agree that it takes more faculty time and effort to teach an online course than a face-to-face course

▨ Agree   ☐ Neutral   ▦ Disagree

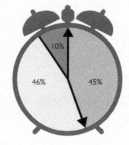

Are student learning outcomes comparable?

77%

Of academic leaders surveyed reported online learning outcomes to be the same, somewhat superior or superior to face-to-face in 2012.

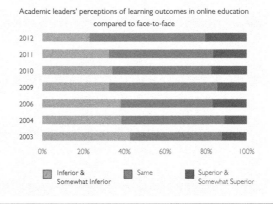

Academic leaders' perceptions of learning outcomes in online education compared to face-to-face

| | 2012 | 2011 | 2010 | 2009 | 2006 | 2004 | 2003 |

0%   20%   40%   60%   80%   100%

▨ Inferior & Somewhat Inferior   ▦ Same   ▦ Superior & Somewhat Superior

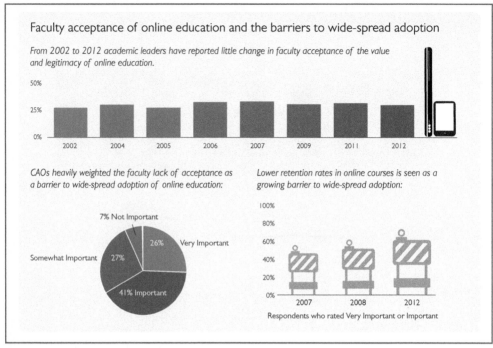

Faculty acceptance of online education and the barriers to wide-spread adoption

From 2002 to 2012 academic leaders have reported little change in faculty acceptance of the value and legitimacy of online education.

CAOs heavily weighted the faculty lack of acceptance as a barrier to wide-spread adoption of online education:

Lower retention rates in online courses is seen as a growing barrier to wide-spread adoption:

Respondents who rated Very Important or Important

Key report findings include:

- Over 6.7 million students were taking at least one online course during the fall 2011 term, an increase of 570,000 students over the previous year.

- Thirty-two percent of higher education students now take at least one course online.

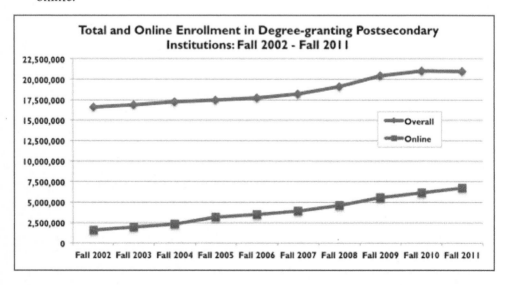

Total and Online Enrollment in Degree-granting Postsecondary Institutions: Fall 2002 - Fall 2011

- Only 2.6 percent of higher education institutions currently have a MOOC (Massive Open Online Course), another 9.4 percent report MOOCs are in the planning stages.

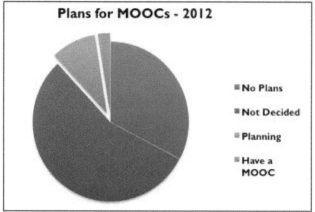

- Academic leaders remain unconvinced that MOOCs represent a sustainable method for offering online courses, but do believe that they provide an important means for institutions to learn about online pedagogy.

- Seventy-seven percent of academic leaders rate the learning outcomes in online education as the same or superior to those in face-to-face.

- Only 30.2 percent of chief academic officers believe that their faculty accept the value and legitimacy of online education—a rate lower than recorded in 2004.

- The proportion of chief academic leaders that say that online learning is critical to their long-term strategy is at a new high of 69.1 percent.

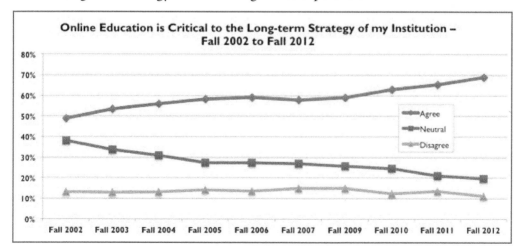

- A majority of chief academic officers at all types of institutions continue to believe that lower retention rates for online courses are a barrier to the widespread adoption of online education.

People & Places

Veterans Weigh Pros, Cons of Online Education

Devon Haynie

U.S .News and World Report: Online Education

May 2013

Reporter Devon Haynie covers online education issues for *U.S. News and World Report,* a news source well-known for compiling annual "Top 100" lists of colleges and universities. In this article, Haynie focuses on a very specific student population: Post-9/11 veterans. Recipients of generous GI Bill benefits for education, veterans represent a new student demographic for whom online courses offer both benefits and drawbacks.

1. What are two advantages and two disadvantages of online education for today's veterans?

2. How would you characterize Haynie's depiction of Post-9/11 veterans? Do you consider her portrayal accurate? Why or why not?

3. Review Chris Kirkham's article (included in Chapter 2 of this book) about some for-profit colleges' predatory recruiting practices. In your opinion, do online courses increase the possibility that veterans may be exploited in some educational settings?

Online programs can provide flexibility for veterans but may also have drawbacks.

Online degrees are good options for veterans who aren't ready for on-campus programs.

For Joe Bayron, 42, the choice to pursue an online degree was an obvious one.

As a part-time flight instructor for the Air Force Reserve, he regularly bounces between his home in Florida and his military base in North Carolina. With that schedule, he felt an on-campus program wasn't an option.

"It's just a convenience issue," says Bayron, who is in the graduate nursing program at Indiana's Ball State University. "I can study at my own pace."

Bayron is one of the thousands of service members and veterans taking advantage of the GI Bill this year. Those cashing in their federal dollars have a choice to make: pursue an online degree, or attend a brick-and-mortar school.

Online programs can offer a variety of benefits to veterans, including flexibility and a gentler transition back to civilian life. But they can also pose challenges in the form of a heavy workload and a lack of face-to-face interaction.

"If you're going to be a student, you need to recognize where you are in life," says Michael Dakduk, executive director of Student Veterans of America, an advocacy group for veterans in higher education. "Choose programs wisely."

Online programs are convenient for nontraditional students juggling work, school, and family, but they may have specific benefits for former and current military members.

Service members are particularly transient, often moving from base to base. Distance learning programs allow troops to study anywhere, be it Kentucky or Afghanistan. Online programs also allow students to study at any time of day—a perk for veterans accustomed to working unconventional hours.

"The flexibility is huge," says Raymond Lee, an Army veteran who served in the first Gulf War. He says he wakes up at 3 a.m.—a holdover from his military days. Still, he says his schedule doesn't get in the way of his online MBA program at Kaplan University.

Distance learning programs can also be good options for veterans who aren't quite ready for the traditional on-campus experience.

Beck Hannaford, Ball State's veterans benefits and financial assistant coordinator, says it's common for veterans on campus to field insensitive questions—including what roles they played in current conflicts—from classmates with little understanding of what it's like to serve in the military.

"A lot of veterans are very uncomfortable when they return to a traditional campus," he says. "They'll come in and say to me, 'What are these stupid questions the 18-year-olds ask me?' It's a problem."

Adding to their challenges, veterans returning to school must navigate a bureaucracy that is very different from the highly structured one they encountered in the military. Tasks such as ordering books or registering for classes can seem daunting without guidance.

Matthew Barth, a 29-year-old Navy veteran, says he took his first on-campus college courses about a year ago.

"I was worried about where my classes were and how everything works," says Barth, who is now enrolled in an online bachelor's program at Excelsior College. "There is less to worry about and more familiarity when you're just taking online classes."

Veterans dealing with physical or invisible wounds can have an even harder time adjusting to life on campus.

"Many veterans are coming back with transition issues, whether it comes from traumatic brain injury or PTSD," says Ball State's Hannaford. "Those cause problems in the classroom and make you feel uncomfortable."

People & Places

Hannaford says he's worked with veterans with post-traumatic stress disorder who face a range of challenges. Some, recalling explosions, refuse to sit in classrooms with or without windows. He says one of his students ran out of a class when the government tested tornado sirens because they reminded him of Scud missiles.

Despite the various benefits of online degree programs, veterans and service members should also be aware of their potential drawbacks.

Some veterans, for example, say they learn better when they have face-to-face interaction with peers and instructors. Others want the camaraderie and networking that come with student veterans groups.

Some online programs, such as Excelsior, do have discussion groups and mentor programs for current and former service members seeking advice and assistance—but those tend to be the exception rather than the rule.

Finally, an online degree program might not be a wise choice for a veteran who doesn't have strong time management skills.

Online courses tend to be more work than traditional courses, experts say, and students need to be motivated and capable of developing their own work schedules. That could be challenging for some veterans used to the military's regimented approach.

"Everything in the military is very structured," says Barth, the Navy veteran enrolled at Excelsior College. "This is just 'you're on your own.'"

Combating Myths About Distance Education

Todd Gilman

Chronicle of Higher Education

February 2010

Todd Gilman is an academic librarian at Yale University, and he also teaches online courses as a non-tenure-track faculty member. In this article, Gilman addresses many of the concerns that fellow faculty have expressed about the value and effectiveness of online classes. This article, one of a series on this subject for the *Chronicle of Higher Education*, recommends effective pedagogical strategies for teachers of online courses.

1. Why does Gilman sometimes feel like "Pinocchio, not a 'real boy'" when he tells fellow university faculty that he teaches online courses?

2. Gilman suggests that online instruction not only demands that faculty change the way they deliver knowledge, but that it changes the ways students learn. He explains that faculty can no longer act as a "sage on the stage," but must instead become "the guide on the side." Do you agree that online learning is dramatically different from learning in brick-and-mortar settings? Why or why not?

3. As Gilman explains, this is one of several articles about effective strategies for online instruction. Locate one of Gilman's other articles about this topic. Do you agree with his recommendations about assignments and pedagogical approaches that are more constructive in online settings? What additional advice would you, as a student, offer Gilman?

People & Places

In addition to my day job as an academic librarian at Yale University, I have been teaching online courses for several library schools since 2002. I have taught courses on reference, online searching, children's literature, U.S. government documents (finding them, that is, not creating them), and book and library history—all on a part-time, adjunct basis. I've even taught a few online courses on writing or research skills for undergraduates.

I enjoy the work and feel confident that I have helped students become better readers, writers, future librarians, curators, and researchers. Yet every time I speak with faculty colleagues who have only taught what distance educators call "face to face" or "on ground" courses, I get the same bewildered responses: "I've never understood this whole online teaching thing" or "So do you teach via e-mail?" or "Is that like a correspondence course?"

Hidden beneath the surface of such seemingly innocuous comments and questions is a little jab, which, if put into words, would go something like this: "You're not a real college teacher, are you? If you were, you'd be interacting with students in a bricks-and-mortar classroom like I do."

No doubt that attitude owes, in part, to the bad press emanating from investigations into certain online "colleges" that have turned out to be little more than diploma mills. But the attitude also seems to be connected to the very idea of online teaching, as though no real college-level content could be delivered or absorbed without face-to-face interaction between teacher and students. That myopic notion even extends, in some cases, to administrators of the programs themselves: One department I have taught for at a big state university does not even acknowledge its online instructors as members of the faculty on its Web page. In the department's eyes, I am, like Pinocchio, not a "real boy."

I'll be the first to admit that online delivery of undergraduate or graduate course work is not always a wonderful teaching and learning experience for everyone. But then, neither is face-to-face delivery. The method of delivery itself is not ipso facto a blessing or a curse. That's because any classroom, whether it's the face-to-face, online-only, or hybrid variety, is only as good as the people in it. If both teachers and students are prepared, responsive, and engaged, things run remarkably well. But if the instructor is teaching at too low or too high a level, or if the students are underprepared for the work—or, heaven forbid, if both are the case—problems will arise whether the course is face-to-face or online.

That said, online education does have its particular challenges. That's why there's no guarantee that a great classroom instructor will make an equally great (or even adequate) online instructor. By contrast, in my experience, good students in a traditional classroom also make good online students because the key to online learning is initiative and a strong sense of responsibility, qualities that all really good students seem to have. I would also guess that many instructors who are good online are also good in a traditional classroom. That's because part of what makes instructors good in the first place is their sensitivity to how different learning environments can affect the quality of the course, and a concomitant ability to make adjustments based on that sensitivity.

Why might a good classroom instructor have trouble making the transition to online instruction?

Any number of possible factors could affect the quality of instruction online, including skills as seemingly trivial as speed and accuracy in typing and a good proofreader's eye. But the crucial factors in online instruction are organization and, related to that, course design or presentation of material.

Organization and course design. What student hasn't sat in a face-to-face course in which the syllabus gets adjusted on a daily basis as the professor, realizing that he was overly ambitious, is forced to acknowledge that he is not covering the material according to the original plan?

That's all well and good in a traditional classroom: Most students come to class, so the instructor can just announce any adjustments to the next day's schedule. He or she might also grant a deadline extension on the spot, since students can't be expected to hand in their essays on Shakespeare if the instructor is still back on Chaucer.

But online, changing the schedule of what is to be covered and altering assignment deadlines can cause chaos. Say you get behind in the content and decide to extend the deadline for a paper assignment. Inevitably, some students will overlook the announcement you post on the course Web site. They will go ahead and write the paper without the benefit of the instructor's lectures or class discussions and hand it in on the original deadline. When they get it back with a less-than-stellar grade and a note from the instructor explaining that many of their errors could have been avoided by reading the lecture and participating in discussion, they will complain that they didn't know they could have had more time because you, the instructor, didn't stick to the original posted schedule. And you didn't go back through your course Web site and change all the deadlines affected because you knew you risked creating another problem: Would everyone understand that they were now looking at the new due dates and not the old?

The online learning environment can be much less forgiving, for instructors as well as students. That's why it is crucial to be organized when you teach online.

That's also why you need good course design. Without it, your students can easily overlook important components of the course like the schedule of readings and assignment due dates. Because students are mostly silent online (unless you hold real-time meetings, as some instructors do), neither of you may know what they've missed until it's too late.

My advice on course design is to keep it clean, simple, and straightforward. Most of all, post deadlines in as many places as possible on your course Web site: on the syllabus, on the schedule, on the calendar, in the grade book, and under the assignments and readings tabs if you have them.

Best practices. Beyond those basics, what makes for good online courses? Surely the answer varies from discipline to discipline.

But let me begin with two crucial distinctions. The first is that undergraduate courses should be run differently from graduate courses, just as they are in a traditional classroom. While many face-to-face undergraduate courses involve lots of lecturing, many graduate courses do not. The same should hold true for online courses.

The second distinction is that students have to be up to the challenge of learning online, meaning that there is a level of maturity required that is less necessary in a physical classroom.

When undergraduates take courses in a traditional classroom, they can skip class or the reading (or both), and sit passively like baby birds awaiting a worm from Mother, thereby forcing the instructor to do the heavy lifting required to make the course engaging. And as long as students show up at least some of the time, take and pass the tests and quizzes, and turn in their papers, they usually do fine. Trust me, I was a face-to-face instructor (and before that, a student) for long enough to be thoroughly familiar with the panoply of tricks that can be used to thwart full participation in class, or anything like mastery of the course material while still receiving a decent grade.

By contrast, when undergraduates take good courses online, they are required to be full partners in their learning process. That's because "attendance and participation" means not simply warming a seat in a classroom but logging on to the course site, posting a thoughtful and informed comment to the current discussion on the discussion board within a specified time frame, and getting graded on the quality of that comment.

Can you imagine a course in a traditional classroom in which every student participates in every discussion and gets graded specifically for his or her comments? I can't.

Another feature of quality online courses—both undergraduate and graduate—is good course-management software that instructors use to design highly functional, easy-to-navigate virtual classrooms. (It helps if instructors have expert and responsive support from information-technology administrators at their college or university.)

Over the years I have had to use much of the available courseware out there: eCollege, WebCT, WebCT Vista, Blackboard, Blackboard Vista, Angel, Sakai, and a host of programs developed in house by various universities. As much as they have evolved, they are still not all created equal.

Some are easy to use for both instructors and students; others not so much. To cite just one typical problem: The fewer clicks required to reach the course content you're after, the better; that saves time and frustration. Yet much of the software out there is not built to minimize clicks but to ensure that the instructor has maximum flexibility when designing a course.

I guess it's a trade-off, because courseware built that way inevitably adds clicks and headaches for all users. In some courseware these days, after you log on, you may have to click seven times before you reach the grade book and are actually reading a student's paper. Ditto with reading students' comments posted to the discussion board. That's too many clicks. So if you have a choice, use good courseware.

Finally, be friendly and welcoming, just as you would in a traditional classroom. Make yourself available to students as much as possible via cellphone, e-mail, or even instant messaging. That does not mean 24/7, even if some students will hope it does. But if students think you are unavailable to them or unapproachable, they will like you and your course much less.

As you begin to imagine yourself becoming an online instructor, it might be helpful to think of your new role, not as that of the sage on the stage, but the guide on the side.

Chapter 2

Ethical Values: Economic Costs

Costs and Student Loans

For-Profit Education

2 Ethical Values: Economic Costs

> "The price of anything is the amount of life you exchange for it."
>
> —Henry David Thoreau

You've done it. You've made the decision to seek higher education. It's a big choice and, as we all know, isn't right for everyone. Now that you're enrolled and taking classes, it might be easy to forget the many questions and choices that led to your decision to seek higher education. You had to ask yourself, will I go full time or part-time? To a two-year institution or a four-year school? Will a community college best fit my needs? A public university? What about these for-profit schools I've been hearing about? And how will I afford it? Inundated with so many questions and confused about the long-term consequences of the answers, it's not surprising that many students find themselves overwhelmed.

One of the most difficult questions you may be facing is how you will finance your education. For those not lucky enough to have a full scholarship or families who can foot the bill, a student loan can be the "golden ticket" that allows you to pursue your degree. But escalating costs and increasing student debt are making that "golden ticket" less desirable. In Jennifer Ludden's NPR podcast and Mandi Woodruff's Business Insider article, we hear from college graduates who are struggling to keep their heads above water with their student loan payments – and from others who are drowning. Ludden profiles one student who has $100,000 in student loans and Woodruff features another whose initial $80,000 loan is now $135,000 due to variable rates and capitalized interest. The long-term consequences of such debts and the high tuition costs that generally prompt the debt in the first place are causing tense conversations among students, their families, and the institutions they attend.

Some students, though, are tackling these contentious issues head-on. In his "Open Letter to Chancellor Linda P.B. Katehi," Nathan Brown explains the violence that ensued in 2011 when students at the University of California at Davis protested increasing tuition and budget cuts that they felt decreased the quality of their education. "The UC Student Investment Proposal" describes an innovative plan crafted by University of California students to radically re-structure the way students pay for their education, with no up-front costs and tuition bills that come after you have graduated. Whether or not you find such actions ethical or even feasible to implement, these examples demonstrate some of the ways students are speaking out and working actively to shape the conversation about the cost of higher education.

Another question you may have been faced with which was less common a generation ago is whether or not to attend a for-profit college—a group of institutions whose numbers have increased 225% in the past decade (Marklein). For-profit schools are owned by private companies who, like other businesses, hope to make money from the operation of the school. Some only offer classes online and others have physical campuses in addition to online options, but nearly all focus on helping their students obtain jobs upon graduation. Despite their focus on student employment, for-profits have stirred criticism on many fronts. Some, such as David

Halperin in "Taming the For-Profit College Monster," point out that for-profit education is "a $40 billion industry whose big players get more than 85% of their revenue from US taxpayers." Others are frustrated by for-profits' accreditation practices which can leave students with credits that are not transferable to other institutions (Marklein). Some critics have damned for-profits for heavily recruiting veterans, which, they say, is not an altruistic endeavor to help former service members expand their education, but is instead an effort to get access to the federal GI benefits which many veterans use to pay for college (Kirkham).

The for-profit schools themselves, though, have repeatedly argued that they fill a niche in the market by having highly diverse student bodies and providing flexibility in programs, class schedules, and student services, especially for students who have families and work full time. In fact, some argue that other types of institutions can take a page from for-profits. Joanna Schilling contends that "There may be lessons to be learned from the for-profit model that would enhance the student learning experience at community colleges," such as making the admission and enrollment process less cumbersome and updating course curricula more frequently. These debates about for-profit schools could have consequences for you, even if you don't attend one, as administrators at non-profit schools make changes to compete with their increasingly popular (and expensive) for-profit cousins.

As you read the following texts, you'll probably discover they generate as many questions as they help answer: Should for-profit schools be more highly regulated? Do their high costs and student loan default rates necessitate reform? Or could other types of institutions seek to learn from them and, consequently, better serve their own students? Are large student loans simply an economic reality for those who must finance their education? Or are there ways to make college more affordable and keep students from accruing crippling debt?

Henry David Thoreau did not have to face the many questions you do about your higher education, but thinking about these questions in the context of Thoreau's epigraph at the beginning of this chapter may help you discover the true price of the education for which you're exchanging several years of your life.

Higher Education: Not What It Used to Be

The Economist

December 2012

This article, like all articles from *The Economist*, is unsigned. According to the publication's website the reasoning is that "What is written is more important than who writes it." In some contexts, having no clear author weakens the credibility of the text and should make the reader skeptical about the information within it. In the case of *The Economist*, though, other factors ensure the reader of its credibility: its long history of covering business and politics, its well-researched articles, and its praise from scholars, businesspeople, and world leaders. The authors of this publication target a well-educated audience and thus assume the readers have working knowledge of terms such as "securitization" and what "risk" and "value" mean in economic contexts. The author of this article provides the reader with many statistics and figures, so as you read consider how they contribute to the overall argument presented in the article.

1. Explain some of the evidence the author uses to support the assertion that "a degree may now mean less than it once did."

2. If "nearly 30% of college students who took out loans eventually dropped out" leaving these students "saddled with a debt they have no realistic means of paying off," is it ethical for our society to continue encouraging so many students to go to college? Why or why not?

3. Consider this article alongside the article by William M. Chace (in chapter 3) about cheating at universities. How might the issue *The Economist* discusses about the value of a college education be linked with the argument Chace makes about plagiarism and academic honesty?

American universities represent declining value for money to their students.

On the face of it, American higher education is still in rude health. In worldwide rankings more than half of the top 100 universities, and eight of the top ten, are American. The scientific output of American institutions is unparalleled. They produce most of the world's Nobel laureates and scientific papers. Moreover college graduates, on average, still earn far more and receive better benefits than those who do not have a degree.

Nonetheless, there is growing anxiety in America about higher education. A degree has always been considered the key to a good job. But rising fees and increasing student debt, combined with shrinking financial and educational returns, are undermining at least the perception that university is a good investment.

Concern springs from a number of things: steep rises in fees, increases in the levels of debt of both students and universities, and the declining quality of graduates. Start with the fees. The cost of university per student has risen by almost five times the rate of inflation since 1983 (see chart 1), making it less affordable and increasing the amount of debt a student must take on. Between 2001 and 2010 the cost of a university education soared from 23% of median annual earnings to 38%; in consequence, debt per student has doubled in the past 15 years. Two-thirds of graduates now take out loans. Those who earned bachelor's degrees in 2011 graduated with an average of $26,000 in debt, according to the Project on Student Debt, a non-profit group.

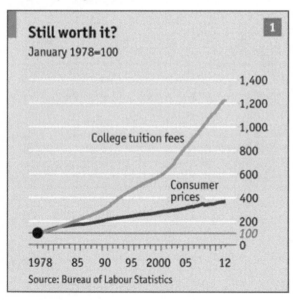

Still worth it?
January 1978=100

College tuition fees

Consumer prices

1,400
1,200
1,000
800
600
400
200
100
0

1978   85   90   95   2000   05   12

Source: Bureau of Labour Statistics

More debt means more risk, and graduation is far from certain; the chances of an American student completing a four-year degree within six years stand at only around 57%. This is poor by international standards: Australia and Britain, for instance, both do much better.

At the same time, universities have been spending beyond their means. Many have taken on too much debt and have seen a decline in the health of their balance-sheets. Moreover, the securitisation of student loans led to a rush of unwise private lending. This, at least, has now been curbed by regulation. In 2008 private lenders disbursed $20 billion; last year they shelled out only $6 billion.

Despite so many fat years, universities have done little until recently to improve the courses they offer. University spending is driven by the need to compete in university league tables that tend to rank almost everything about a university except the (hard-to-measure) quality of the graduates it produces. Roger Geiger of Pennsylvania State University and Donald Heller of Michigan State University say that since 1990, in both public and private colleges, expenditures on instruction have risen more slowly than in any other category of spending, even as student numbers have risen.

Plenty of padding

Non-faculty professional employees per 100 faculty members

1976   1999   2009

Sources: Department of Education; National Centre for Education Statistics

Universities are, however, spending plenty more on administration and support services (see chart 2).

Universities cannot look to government to come to the rescue. States have already cut back dramatically on the amount of financial aid they give universities. Barack Obama has made it clear that he is unhappy about rising tuition fees, and threatens universities with aid cuts if they rise any further. Roger Brinner from the Parthenon Group, a consultancy, predicts that enrolment rates will stay flat for the next five to seven years even as the economy picks up. The party may be well and truly over.

Balloon debate

In 1962 one cent of every dollar spent in America went on higher education; today this figure has tripled. Yet despite spending a greater proportion of its GDP on universities than any other country, America has only the 15th-largest proportion of young people with a university education. Wherever the money is coming from, and however it is being spent, the root of the crisis in higher education (and the evidence that investment in universities may amount to a bubble) comes down to the fact that additional value has not been created to match this extra spending. Indeed, evidence from declines in the quality of students and graduates suggests that a degree may now mean less than it once did.

For example, a federal survey showed that the literacy of college-educated citizens declined between 1992 and 2003. Only a quarter were deemed proficient, defined as "using printed and written information to function in society, to achieve one's goals and to develop one's knowledge and potential". Almost a third of students these days do not take any courses that involve more than 40 pages of reading over an entire term. Moreover, students are spending measurably less time studying and more on recreation. "Workload management", however, is studied with enthusiasm—students share online tips about "blow off" classes (those which can be avoided with no damage to grades) and which teachers are the easiest-going.

Yet neither the lack of investment in teaching nor the deficit of attention appears to have had a negative impact on grades. A remarkable 43% of all grades at four-year universities are As, an increase of 28 percentage points since 1960. Grade point averages rose from about 2.52 in the 1950s to 3.11 in 2006.

At this point a skeptic could argue that none of this matters much, since students are paid a handsome premium for their degree and on the whole earn back their investment over a lifetime. While this is still broadly true, there are a number of important caveats. One is that it is easily possible to overspend on one's education: just ask the hundreds of thousands of law graduates who have not found work as lawyers. And this premium is of little comfort to the 9.1% of borrowers who in 2011 had defaulted on their federal student loans within two years of graduating. There are 200 colleges and universities where the three-year default rate is 30% or more.

Another issue is that the salary gap between those with only a high-school diploma and those with a university degree is created by the plummeting value of the diploma, rather than by soaring graduate salaries. After adjusting for inflation, graduates earned no more in 2007 than they did in 1979. Young graduates facing a decline in earnings over the past decade (16% for women, 19% for men), and a lot more debt, are unlikely to feel particularly cheered by the argument that, over a lifetime, they would be even worse off without a degree than with one.

Moreover, the promise that an expensive degree at a traditional university will pay off rests on some questionable assumptions; for example, that no cheaper way of attaining this educational premium will emerge. Yet there is a tornado of change in education that might challenge this, either through technology or through attempts to improve the two-year community college degree and render it more economically valuable. Another assumption, which is proved wrong in the case of 40% of students, is that they will graduate at all. Indeed, nearly 30% of college students who took out loans eventually dropped out (up from 25% a decade ago). These students are saddled with a debt they have no realistic means of paying off.

Some argue that universities are clinging to a medieval concept of education in an age of mass enrolment. In a recent book, "Reinventing Higher Education", Ben Wildavsky and his colleagues at the Kauffman Foundation, which focuses on entrepreneurship, add that there has been a failure to innovate. Declining productivity and stiff economic headwinds mean that change is coming in a trickle of online learning inside universities, and a rush of "massive open online courses" (MOOCs) outside them. Some universities see online learning as a way of continuing to grow while facing harsh budget cuts. The University of California borrowed $6.9m to do this in the midst of a budget crisis. In 2011 about 6m American students took at least one online course in the autumn term. Around 30% of all college students are learning online—up from less than 10% in 2002.

Digital dilemmas

To see how efficient higher education can be, look at the new online Western Governors University (WGU). Tuition costs less than $6,000 a year, compared with around $54,000 at Harvard. Students can study and take their exams when they want, not when the sabbaticals, holidays and scheduling of teaching staff allow. The average time to completion is just two-and-a-half years.

MOOCs have also now arrived with great fanfare. These offer free college-level classes taught by renowned lecturers to all-comers. Two companies, Coursera and Udacity, and one non-profit enterprise, edX, are leading the charge. At some point these outfits will need to generate some revenue, probably through certification.

The broader significance of MOOCs is that they are part of a trend towards the unbundling of higher education. This will shake many institutions whose business model is based on a set fee for a four-year campus-based degree course. As online education spreads, universities will come under pressure to move to something more like a "buffet" arrangement, under which they will accept credits from each other—and from students who take courses at home or even at high school, spending much less time on campus. StraighterLine, a start-up based in Baltimore, is already selling courses that gain students credits for a few hundred dollars.

Some signs suggest that universities are facing up to their inefficiencies. Indiana University has just announced innovations aimed at lowering the cost and reducing the time it takes to earn a degree. More of this is needed. Universities owe it to the students who have racked up $1 trillion in debt, and to the graduate students who are taking second degrees because their first one was so worthless. They also bear some responsibility for the 17m who are overqualified for their jobs, and for the 3m unfilled positions for which skilled workers cannot be found. They even owe it to the 37m who went to college, dropped out and ended up with nothing: many left for economic reasons.

Universities may counter that the value of a degree cannot be reduced to a simple economic number. That, though, sounds increasingly cynical, when the main reason universities have been able to increase their revenue so much is because of loans given to students on the basis of what they are told they will one day earn.

UC Student Investment Proposal

Fix UC

FixUC.org

March 2012

This text represents a very different genre than the others in this chapter. It is a formal proposal written by students attempting to solve the problem of high tuition at the University of California by asking the UC regents to re-think how the university collects fees. The proposal was prompted by large budget cuts from the State of California which, in turn, caused the UC system to raise student tuition to make up for the difference in funds lost from the state. As you read the proposal, think about the ways in which the authors consider their audience (regents of the UC system), as well as the historical and social context that surrounds the text.

1. Summarize the plan proposed by Fix UC. How does the plan differ from a traditional university funding structure?

2. What are the potential objections or counterarguments the audience might have about the proposal?

3. Both this text and the one that follows, "Open Letter to Chancellor Linda P.B. Katehi," are attempting to persuade the audience to take specific action on the issue discussed. How might the genre of each of these texts influence the way the author addresses the audience?

Preface

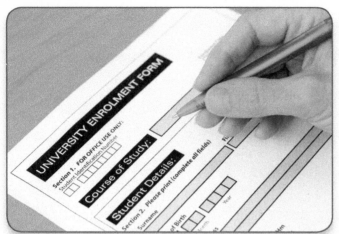

An education from the University of California offers students an array of skills and opportunities that lead toward both a career and the overall enrichment of one's life.

While the latter is an intangible and priceless benefit of graduating from UC, the path it sets individuals on toward a career can be measured by the income one earns from employment. The Student Investment Proposal aims to remedy this discrepancy by allowing students to attend UC with no up-front costs while maximizing revenue for the UC.

The University of California system represents the pinnacle of public higher education. But as it stands, the UC cannot sustain itself through another massive budget cut from the State of California. In order to meet the budget shortfall, students have been asked repeatedly to pay more to attend a UC suffering the loss of resources and faculty members, essentially raising the cost on an education of lessening quality. The UC's dependency on the state leaves it at the will of financial ebbs and flows. Another budget cut like that of 2011 could fatally cripple the University of California.

In order to ensure a promising future, the University of California needs to reevaluate its current revenue system and pursue options that can support it indefinitely while still working to the advantage of students. This proposal outlines a stable and predictable plan toward growth and sustainability for the distant future.

Beyond its practical application as a real long-term solution to the University of California's current revenue system, one of the goals of the UC Student Investment Proposal is to encourage a shift in thought about the education students receive by attending the university, and their relationship with that university after graduation.

Students will begin to think about the value of their education and its significance in the trajectory of their life from graduation to retirement. Therefore, the University of California will invest in the success of its students by providing the up-front costs for attending the university with the expectation that the investment will return once a student graduates and enters a career.

This proposal presents, in detail, a potential solution for the University of California. It is intended for consideration by UC regents as the groundwork for a new long-term funding plan.

Outline

Under the proposed UC Student Investment Plan–Models A and B, graduates of the University of California pay a small percentage of their income, based on 5%, interest free, to the UC upon entering a career after graduation for twenty years of employment. Therefore, undergraduate students pay no fees up-front to the university, and attend school without the financial burden and risk of increased fees.

The current system of prepaid student fees will be dismantled in favor of the new investment plan. The Financial Aid system, including the Blue and Gold Plan, will also cease to exist, its funds being dedicated elsewhere.

Graduates of the University of California, as they begin participation in the new financial contribution program, will have access to extended alumni programs and benefits that help them stay involved with their campus into the future.

The amount of revenue entering the UC compounds annually with an additional graduating class paying into the system. Over time, the UC's annual revenue will exceed that which it currently receives from student tuition.

UC Student Investment Plan - Model B includes all provisions of Model A, but also incorporates caps on minimum and maximum income thresholds for contribution. Graduates will not begin contributing to the UC until their income exceeds $30,000 annually. A high-income ceiling is also in place, so no income beyond $200,000 annually would be subject to percentage contribution.

Implementation

In order to implement the new UC Student Investment Plan, the UC will change its current Blue and Gold program to incorporate the UC Student Investment Plan. A group of students on the Blue and Gold program whose entire cost of attending is covered by Blue and Gold (UC Return to Aid Funds) will serve as the initial population to enter the plan. These students will attend UC with no up-front costs, just as they would have before the UC Student Investment Plan, but would pay a percentage of their income to the UC upon graduating and entering a career. The revenue the UC would have otherwise not received is then used as capital to put more and more students on the plan, until the entire UC student body is attending with no up-front cost.

Details

Contribution will be enforced by a new department of the United States Internal Revenue Service in charge of collecting contributions from graduates of American universities, beginning with the University of California. This department, in conjunction with the UC, would maintain a database of graduates and arrange the regular contributions of graduates in-state, out-of-state and abroad. Other institutions could then use the infrastructure to implement their own similar funding systems.

Students who transfer into the UC system will pay 1% less of their income.

Students who drop out/transfer out of the system will pay a set amount upon leaving equivalent to the would-be annual tuition rate for their time spent in the system.

Contributions from students who die while attending the UC will be absorbed by UC Student Investment Plan.

Extended alumni benefits for UC graduates paying into the UC will include full career center and employment support. Because the UC will depend on the earnings of its graduates, it is in its best interest to ensure that graduates are in stable, high-paying jobs. The UC will use its tremendous network of graduate and private industry contacts to provide its graduates with job opportunities both upon graduating and afterwards.

Incentives, in the form of decreased percentages of contributions to the UC, will be in place for those who live and work within the state of

California after graduation (0.5%), as well as for those who seek careers in the public sector (1%). Individual campuses may also offer incentives to academic and athletic high achievers as a means of recruiting, but with a cap on the amount of students who can receive these incentives per campus.

Out-of-state and international students pay an increase of 1%, with the same incentive option to stay and work in California.

Contribution waivers for emergency situations will be available.

Contribution rate at the time a student enters UC must remain unchanged for that individual's total contribution period. Changes in contribution percentage can only be applied to incoming students.

State of California investment in UC must not fall below 2% of the total state budget at any time. A decrease in state investment cannot go into effect until 10 years after UC Student Investment Plan is initiated, and can only be done in 0.2% annual increments.

Federal and state aid will continue to go directly to students for educational expenses.

The revenue collected from students of each campus will first cover that campus' budget. Additional funds enter a UC savings account, with some of those funds being saved for emergencies, and some being used for investing in bolstered K-12 programs.

Campuses will be encouraged to refrain from giving preferential treatment to departments and majors that lead students to more traditionally lucrative careers.

Campus fees will be covered by graduate contribution percentage. Each new referendum voted on by a student body will be reflected in a small increase in percentage for future incoming classes.

Student on-campus housing will be covered by UC Student Investment Plan, with a 0.65% increase in contribution percentage per year of housing, paid for the first ten years of the twenty-year contribution period.

Studying abroad through campus programs will be covered, as long as it is done during the academic year and units taken fulfill full-time student status requirements.

Benefits

To students: No financial burden on parents or students upon entering system and during college. Students will also not incur any debt upon graduation. Students financially contribute to the UC at a time when they are making money, as opposed to when they are not. The annual amount collected by the UC will always be within means, because amount is set on percentage of income earned. The UC's extended alumni benefits will provide graduates with robust employment support.

To UC: Compounded revenue over time, increasing annually with each new class paying into system. Plan puts UC on path towards growth, stability and decreased dependency on fluctuating investment by state of California.

Open Letter to
Chancellor Linda P.B. Katehi

Nathan Brown

UC Davis Bicycle Brigade

November 2011

Nathan Brown's open letter demonstrates what happened in 2011 when the issue of rising student fees collided with the Occupy Movement. Consider the context: due to state budget cuts prompted by the poor economy, UC regents approved large tuition hikes for students. In the fall of 2011 as part of the Occupy Movement, UC students (including those at Davis, Berkeley, and other campuses) gathered in support of education and to protest tuition increases, lay-offs, furloughs, and other money-saving actions that were taking place at UC schools. Brown's letter explains what happens next and voices the outrage he and many others felt at these actions. Brown uses frequent questions and repetition as he crafts his letter, so while reading consider the impact these stylistic devices have on his message.

1. Why does Brown hold Chancellor Katehi responsible for what happened at UC Davis?

2. Brown writes in the genre of an open letter, a letter that is directed at a particular individual or a small group but published in such a way so that a wide audience can read it. Why do you think Brown chose this genre to make his argument?

3. As Brown himself might ask, what happened next? Upon publication, Brown's letter spread widely across the Internet. Did Chancellor Katehi resign? Why might this letter still be worth reading within the context of ethics in higher education?

Linda P.B. Katehi,

I am a junior faculty member at UC Davis. I am an Assistant Professor in the Department of English, and I teach in the Program in Critical Theory and in Science & Technology Studies. I have a strong record of research, teaching, and service. I am currently a Board Member of the Davis Faculty Association. I have also taken an active role in supporting the student movement to defend public education on our campus and throughout the UC system. In a word: I am the sort of young faculty member, like many of my colleagues, this campus needs. I am an asset to the University of California at Davis.

You are not.

I write to you and to my colleagues for three reasons:

1. to express my outrage at the police brutality which occurred against students engaged in peaceful protest on the UC Davis campus today

2. to hold you accountable for this police brutality

3. to demand your immediate resignation

Today you ordered police onto our campus to clear student protesters from the quad. These were protesters who participated in a rally speaking out against tuition increases and police brutality on UC campuses on Tuesday—a rally that I organized, and which was endorsed by the Davis Faculty Association. These students attended that rally in response to a call for solidarity from students and faculty who were bludgeoned with batons, hospitalized, and arrested at UC Berkeley last week. In the highest tradition of non-violent civil disobedience, those protesters had linked arms

and held their ground in defense of tents they set up beside Sproul Hall. In a gesture of solidarity with those students and faculty, and in solidarity with the national Occupy movement, students at UC Davis set up tents on the main quad. When you ordered police outfitted with riot helmets, brandishing batons and teargas guns to remove their tents today, those students sat down on the ground in a circle and linked arms to protect them.

What happened next?

Without any provocation whatsoever, other than the bodies of these students sitting where they were on the ground, with their arms linked, police pepper-sprayed students. Students remained on the ground, now writhing in pain, with their arms linked.

What happened next?

Police used batons to try to push the students apart. Those they could separate, they arrested, kneeling on their bodies and pushing their heads into the ground. Those they could not separate, they pepper-sprayed directly in the face, holding these students as they did so. When students covered their eyes with their clothing, police forced open their mouths and pepper-sprayed down their throats. Several of these students were hospitalized. Others are seriously injured. One of them, forty-five minutes after being pepper-sprayed down his throat, was still coughing up blood.

This is what happened. You are responsible for it.

You are responsible for it because this is what happens when UC Chancellors order police onto our campuses to disperse peaceful protesters through the use of force: students get hurt. Faculty get hurt. One of the most inspiring things (inspiring for those of us who care about students who assert their rights to free speech and peaceful assembly) about the demonstration in Berkeley on November 9 is that UC Berkeley faculty stood together with students, their arms linked together. Associate Professor of English Celeste Langan was grabbed by her hair, thrown on the ground, and arrested. Associate Professor Geoffrey O'Brien was injured by baton blows. Professor Robert Hass, former Poet Laureate of the United States, National Book Award and Pulitzer Prize winner, was also struck with a baton. These faculty stood together with students in solidarity, and they too were beaten and arrested by the police. In writing this letter, I stand together with those faculty and with the students they supported.

One week after this happened at UC Berkeley, you ordered police to clear tents from the quad at UC Davis. When students responded in the same way—linking arms and holding their ground—police also responded in the same way: with violent force. The fact is: the administration of UC campuses systematically uses police brutality to terrorize students and faculty, to crush political dissent on our campuses, and to suppress free speech and peaceful assembly. Many people know this. Many more people are learning it very quickly.

You are responsible for the police violence directed against students on the UC Davis quad on November 18, 2011. As I said, I am writing to hold you responsible and to demand your immediate resignation on these grounds.

On Wednesday, November 16, you issued a letter by email to the campus community. In this letter, you discussed a hate crime which occurred at UC Davis on Sunday, November 13. In this letter, you express concern about the safety of our students. You write, "it is particularly disturbing that such an act of intolerance should occur at a time when the campus community is working to create a safe and inviting space for all our students." You write, "while these are turbulent economic times, as a campus community, we must all be committed to a safe, welcoming environment that advances our efforts to diversity and excellence at UC Davis."

I will leave it to my colleagues and every reader of this letter to decide what poses a greater threat to "a safe and inviting space for all our students" or "a safe, welcoming environment" at UC Davis: 1) Setting up tents on the quad in solidarity with faculty and students brutalized by police at UC Berkeley? or 2) Sending in riot police to disperse students with batons, pepper-spray, and tear-gas guns, while those students sit peacefully on the ground with their arms linked? Is this what you have in mind when you refer to creating "a safe and inviting space?" Is this what you have in mind when you express commitment to "a safe, welcoming environment?"

I am writing to tell you in no uncertain terms that there must be space for protest on our campus. There must be space for political dissent on our campus. There must be space for civil disobedience on our campus. There must be space for students to assert their right to decide on the form of their protest, their dissent, and their civil disobedience—including the simple act of setting up tents in solidarity with other students who have done so. There must be space for protest and dissent, especially, when the object of protest and dissent is police brutality itself. *You may not* order police to forcefully disperse student protesters peacefully protesting police brutality. You may not do so. It is not an option available to you as the Chancellor of a UC campus. That is why I am calling for your immediate resignation.

Your *words* express concern for the safety of our students. Your *actions* express no concern whatsoever for the safety of our students. I deduce from this discrepancy that you are not, in fact, concerned about the safety of our students. Your actions directly threaten the safety of our students. And I want you to know that this is clear. It is clear to anyone who reads your campus emails concerning our "Principles of Community" and who also takes the time to inform themselves about your actions. You should bear in mind that when you send emails to the UC Davis community, you address a body of faculty and students who are well trained to see through rhetoric that evinces care for students while implicitly threatening them. I see through your rhetoric very clearly. You also write to a campus community that knows how to speak truth to power. That is what I am doing.

I call for your resignation because you are unfit to do your job. You are unfit to ensure the safety of students at UC Davis. In fact: you are the primary threat to the safety of students at UC Davis. As such, I call upon you to resign immediately.

Sincerely,

Nathan Brown
Assistant Professor
Department of English
Program in Critical Theory
University of California at Davis

College Grads Struggle to Gain Financial Footing

Jennifer Ludden

National Public Radio

May 2012

The correspondent for this piece, Jennifer Ludden, has been reporting for National Public Radio (NPR) since 1995. This podcast is an example of an aural text – that is, a sound-based text that asks the listeners to "read" with their ears. Aural texts offer the listener things that print texts cannot: the ability to hear the voices of the reporter and the people being interviewed and the opportunity to use music to enhance the text, among others. On the other hand, hearing an aural text without a printed transcript can make it difficult to identify people's names or nail down particular statistics or numbers for future reference. Consider whether hearing a text rather than reading it affects your understanding of the information within the piece.

1. Why has a college graduate "living rent-free with her parents . . . . come to symbolize graduating post-recession"?

2. In her report, Ludden lets you hear a person's voice before she tells you that person's name and credentials. Why might Ludden have chosen this technique for a radio report?

3. How does the issue of student loan debt connect with the argument made by the author of "Higher Education: Not What It Used to Be," from *The Economist*? How are student loans and the value of higher education linked?

DAVID GREENE, HOST:

It's MORNING EDITION from NPR News. Good morning, I'm David Greene.

STEVE INSKEEP, HOST:

And I'm Steve Inskeep.

This spring, about one and half million people across the United States are graduating from a four-year college. Most will be looking for a job.

GREENE: And they have reason to expect one. Experts have said countless times, including on this program, that a college education tremendously improves your odds in the job market. But if the experiences of recent graduates are any guide, many will be disappointed.

INSKEEP: A new survey out today tracks college grads since 2006. Just half of them are working full-time.

NPR's Jennifer Ludden reports.

JENNIFER LUDDEN, BYLINE: The recession started in Caitlin Lacour's freshman year at Columbia College, Chicago. By graduation last year...

CAITLIN LACOUR: I thought that I wasn't going to get a job...

(SOUNDBITE OF LAUGHTER)

LACOUR: ...like many people. But I was happy to, you know, have one part-time job.

LUDDEN: And Lacour feels lucky that it's related to her major in radio production. She does promotions at a radio station. But she earns just $10 an hour. And by the time she had to start payments on her $100,000 in student loans, she realized it would not be nearly enough.

Lacour took on a second part-time job, at a shoe store, then a third, also at the radio station.

LACOUR: Like I got addicted to working, pretty much, to where I kind of just like burned myself out. 'Cause I didn't want to have to worry about not being able to pay my loans.

LUDDEN: Those student loans are more than $700 a month. And the only way she can pay them, living rent-free with her parents - a situation that's come to symbolize graduating post-recession.

CLIFF ZUKIN: More come out with debt than come out with jobs.

LUDDEN: Cliff Zukin is with the Heldrich Center for Workforce Development at Rutgers University. His new study finds six in 10 students take on debt - more than $20,000 on average - even as a lack of jobs leaves them less able to pay it back.

ZUKIN: In the data, there's certainly a suggestion that the American Dream has stopped at these guys' doorstep.

LUDDEN: Zukin says nearly half those with full-time work are in jobs that don't actually require a college degree. And as for a career, very few say their first job would lead to that. In fact, a third of recent college grads say they no longer believe education plus hard work will necessarily lead to success.

ZUKIN: They don't even see in the foreseeable future a secure job, a comfortable income, starting a family, and even more - 45 percent - do not see owning a home at any point in the near future.

LUDDEN: And Zukin notes these are the cream of the crop. Unemployment is far higher among the majority of young Americans who don't go to college. The Rutgers study finds a fifth of recent grads have gone back to school, where many are accumulating more debt. Meantime, those getting jobs since the recession have seen a hit on their paychecks.

TILL VON WACHTER: About 10 percent lower earnings. And that earnings effect fades in about 10 years.

LUDDEN: Although it varies, says Columbia University economist Till von Wachter. If you're, say, an engineering grad from a top school, his research shows you can job-hop and get back to what you would have been earning in three or four years. But...

WACHTER: Students who come from smaller, less well-known schools and have majors such as humanities or arts, they tend to have depressed career paths lasting for a very long time.

LUDDEN: And in fact, many grads in the Rutgers survey say they wished they'd majored in something else.

Researcher Cliff Zukin wonders if it's the end of the happy, self-confident millennials, as we've come to know them. Then again, it can be more depressing to read the study's numbers than to speak with some recent grads.

TIFFANY CONNER: I love the people I work with. I love my customers. I'm a people person.

LUDDEN: Tiffany Conner's working two part-time retail jobs in Wisconsin, by choice. After graduating in 2009, she actually landed a full-time job in her field of marketing. But it didn't make her happy. So she quit and moved back in with her parents to figure out something new. Conner's focus now is paying down student loan and credit card debt.

CONNER: You know, debt is just one of those pieces of life, and being miserable about it isn't good either. So keep my head up high, I guess. Keep plugging away and I have nothing to be ashamed of.

(SOUNDBITE OF LAUGHTER)

LUDDEN: After all, she knows she has plenty of company.

Jennifer Ludden, NPR News.

Students are Already Workers

Marc Bousquet

*How the University Works: Higher Education
and the Low-Wage Nation*

2008

Marc Bousquet is a tenured professor at Santa Clara University who earned his bachelor's degree at Yale University and his PhD at the City University of New York. He has been an active figure in the academic labor movement and has worked to draw attention to burgeoning labor problems at the modern university. The following excerpts are from his 2008 book *How the University Works: Higher Education and the Low Wage Nation*, and are specifically drawn from the chapter that aims to demonstrate what lengths students go to in order to pay for their education. As you read, compare these issues with those discussed in "Higher Education: Not What It Used to Be" and in the texts about student loan debt.

1. What is "Metropolitan College" and why, according to the article, was it created?

2. Why, especially in the latter part of the text, does Bousquet ask his reader so many questions? What role do they play in advancing his argument?

3. Why does Bousquet spend the first few paragraphs describing Prof. Susan Erdmann's home, commute, and arrival at the airport? How might this be similar to the strategy Mary Beth Marklein uses in her article when she uses the example of Chelsi Miller?

I know that I haven't updated in about two and a half weeks, but I have an excuse. UPS is just a tiring job. You see, before, I had an extra 31 hours to play games, draw things, compose music . . . do homework. But now, 31+ hours of my life is devoted to UPS. I hate working there. But I need the money for college, so I don't have the option of quitting. My job at UPS is a loader. I check the zip codes on the box, I scan them into the database, and then I load them into the truck, making a brick wall out of boxes.

—"Kody" (pseud.), high-school blogger
in a UPS "school-to-work" program, 2005

The alarm sounds at 2:00 a.m. Together with half a dozen of her colleagues, the workday has begun for Prof. Susan Erdmann, a tenure-track assistant professor of English at Jefferson Community College in Louisville, Kentucky. She rises carefully to avoid waking her infant son and husband, who commutes forty miles each way to his own tenure-track community college job in the neighboring rural county. She makes coffee, showers, dresses for work. With their combined income of around $60,000 and substantial education debt, they have a thirty-year mortgage on a tiny home of about 1,000 square feet: galley kitchen, dining alcove, one bedroom for them and another for their two sons to share. The front door opens onto a "living room" of a hundred square feet; entering or leaving the house means passing in between the couch and television. They feel fortunate to be able to afford any mortgage at all in this historically Catholic neighborhood that was originally populated by Louisville factory workers. It is winter; the sun will not rise for hours. She drives to the airport. Overhead, air-freight 747s barrel into the sky, about one plane every minute or so. Surrounded by the empty school buildings, boarded storefronts, and dilapidated underclass homes of south-central Louisville, the jets launch in post-midnight required of air traffic in middle-class communities. Every twelve or eighteen months, the city agrees to buy a handful of the valueless residences within earshot.

Turning into the airport complex, Susan never comes near the shuttered passenger terminals. She follows a four-lane private roadway toward the rising jets. After parking, a shuttle bus weaves among blindingly lit aircraft hangars and drops her by the immense corrugated sorting facility that is the United Parcel Service main air hub, where she will begin her faculty duties at 3:00 am, greeting UPS's undergraduate workforce directly as they come off the sort. "You would have a sense that you were there, lifting packages," Erdmann recalls. "They would come off sweaty, and hot, directly off the line into the class. It was very immediate, and sort of awkward. They'd had no moment of downtime. They hadn't had their cigarette. They had no time to pull themselves together as student-person rather than package-thrower." Unlike her students, Susan and other faculty teaching and advising at the hub are not issued a plastic ID card and door pass. She waits on the windy tarmac for one of her students or colleagues to hear her knocking at the door. Inside, the noise of the sorting facility is, literally, deafening: the shouts, forklift alarms, whistles, and rumble of the sorting machinery actually drown out the noise of the jets rising overhead. "Teaching in the hub was horrible," recalled one of Erdmann's colleagues. "Being in the hub was just hell. I'd work at McDonald's before I'd teach there again. The noise level was just incredible. The classroom was just as noisy as if it didn't have any walls." In addition to the sorting machinery, UPS floor supervisors were constantly "screaming, yelling back and forth, 'Get this done, get that done, where's so and so.'"

Susan is just one of a dozen faculty arriving at the hub after midnight. Some are colleagues from Jefferson Community College and the associated technical institution; others are from the University of Louisville. Their task tonight is to provide on-site advising and registration for some of the nearly 6,000 undergraduate students working for UPS at this facility. About 3,000 of those students work a midnight shift that ends at UPS's convenience—typically 3:00 or 4:00 a.m., although the shift is longer during the holiday and other peak shipping seasons.

Nearly all of the third-shift workers are undergraduate students who have signed employment contracts with something called the "Metropolitan College." The name is misleading, since it's not a college at all. An "enterprise" partnership between UPS, the city of Louisville, and the campuses that employ Susan and her colleagues, Metropolitan College is, in fact, little more than a labor contractor. Supported by public funds, this "college" offers no degrees and does no educating. Its sole function is to entice students to sign contracts that commit them to provide cheap labor in exchange for education benefits at the partner institutions. The arrangement has provided UPS with over 10,000 ultralow-cost student workers since 1997, the same year that the Teamsters launched a crippling strike against the carrier. The Louisville arrangement is the vanguard of UPS's efforts to convert its part-time payroll, as far as possible, to a "financial aid" package for student workers in partnership with campuses near its sorting and loading facilities. Other low wage Louisville employers, such as Norton and ResCare have joined on a trial basis.

As a result of carefully planned corporate strategy, between 1997 and 2003, UPS hired undergraduate students to staff more than half of its 130,000 part-time positions. Students are currently the majority of all part-timers, and the overwhelming majority on the least desirable shifts. Part of UPS's strategy is that only some student employees receive education benefits. By reserving the education benefits of its "earn and learn" programs to workers who are willing to work undesirable hours, UPS has over the past decade recruited approximately 50,000 part-time workers to its least desirable shifts without raising the pay (in fact, while pushing them to work harder for continually lower pay against inflation) ("Earn and Learn Factsheet"). The largest benefit promises are reserved for students who think they can handle working after midnight every night of the school week.

Between 1998 and 2005, UPS claims to have "assisted" 10,000 students through the Metropolitan College arrangement. Of the 7,500 part-time employees at UPS's Louisville hub in May 2006, some were welfare-to-work recipients picked up in company buses from the city and even surrounding rural counties. A few hundred were Louisville-area high school students in school-to-work programs. Three-quarters of the part-timers—5,600—were college students (Howington). More than half of the students—about 3,000—were enrolled in Metropolitan College, which, with few exceptions, accepts only those willing to work the night shift. Metropolitan College "enrollment" and "recruitment" activities are entirely driven by UPS's staffing needs. Ditto for scheduling: all of the benefits enjoyed by Metro College students are contingent on showing up at the facility every weeknight of the school year at midnight and performing physically strenuous labor for as long as they are needed.

The consequences of night-shift work are well documented, and the preponderance of available evidence suggests markedly negative effects for the Louisville students. Every instructor to whom I spoke reported excessive fatigue and absenteeism (due to fatigue, but also an extraordinarily high physical injury rate: "They all got hurt," Erdmann reports). Students who signed employment contracts with Metro College showed substantial failure to persist academically. "I would lose students midterm, or they would never complete final assignments," Erdmann said.

"They would just stop coming at some point." Erdmann served as chair of a faculty committee that attempted to improve the academic success of students employed by UPS at her institution. The group scheduled special UPS-only sections between 5:00 and 11:00 p.m., both on campus and at the hub, and began the ritual of 3:00 am advising. Since nearly all of the faculty involved taught and served on committees five days a week, their efforts to keep students from dropping out by teaching evenings and advising before dawn resulted in a bizarre twenty-four-hour cycle of work for themselves. The institutions even experimented with ending the fall semester before Thanksgiving for the thousands of UPS employees, in order to keep their finals from conflicting with the holiday shipping rush (and the one season a year when the students could be assured of a shift lasting longer than four hours). Even in the specially scheduled classes and shortened terms, Erdmann recalls classes with dropout rates of 30 to 40 percent. "It was most definitely worse for those with children," she concluded:

> It was a disaster for those with children. Students who had family obligations tended to do poorly. When you had younger, more traditional age students with a very clear and limited goal—and they were often men—if they had a limited goal, such as "I am going to get Microsoft certified," and if they were healthy and young, and physically active, those individuals might be okay. Whenever you had people with children— you know, people who can't sleep all day, they would get tremendously stressed out. I feel like very few of them actually did well with the program, the ones with family.

Pressed to offer instances of individual students who indisputably benefited from the program, Erdmann described just two individuals, both at the extreme margins of economic and social life. One was a single mother who worked multiple jobs and saved some of her wages toward a down payment on a residential trailer, thus escaping an abusive domestic life. The other was a young man coping with severe mental illness.

Rather than relieving economic pressure, Metropolitan College appears to have increased the economic distress of the majority of participants. According to the company's own fact sheet, those student workers who give up five nights' sleep are typically paid for just fifteen to twenty hours a week. Since the wage ranges from just $8.50 at the start to no more than

$9.50 for the majority of the most experienced, this can mean net pay *below* $100 in a week, and averaging out to a little over $120. The rate of pay bears emphasizing: because the students must report five nights a week and are commonly let go after just three hours each night, their take-home pay for sleep deprivation and physically hazardous toil will commonly be less than $25 per shift.

In fact, most UPS part-timers earn little more than $6,000 in a year. Most have at least one other job, because their typical earnings from UPS in 2006–2007 would generally have covered little more than the worker's car payment, insurance, gasoline, and other transportation related expenses. "Everyone had another job," Erdmann says. "Even the high school students had another job. The high school students were working two jobs. For some people, that meant working Saturday nights as a waitress, but for others, it was much more extensive. For a lot of people, it meant that they got up every day and went to work in the afternoon before going in to classes and UPS in the evening." Every instructor to whom I spoke confirmed the pressure that the ultralow wage added to the unreasonable working hours and physical hazards as a detriment to students' chances for academic persistence. "That was when they skipped class," affirmed another instructor, "when they were going to another job. I was just amazed how many of them were going to another job."

UPS presents a triple threat to students' prospects for academic persistence: sleep deprivation and family-unfriendly scheduling; ultralow compensation, resulting in secondary and tertiary part-time employment; and a high injury rate. Student employees report being pressured to skip class. Especially at the end of the fall term, the night sorts can run four or five hours beyond the anticipated 4:00 a.m. completion: "Each time I said I was unwilling to miss class for an extended sort, the supe would tell me to 'think long and hard about my priorities,'" reports one student employee. "I got the message."

UPS refuses to provide standard statistics that would permit evaluation of the impact that this triple threat is actually having on the students it employs. None of its partner institutions appears to have responsibly studied the consequences of the program for its students in terms of such major measures as persistence to degree, dropout rate, and so on.

Amazingly, all of the press coverage of the UPS earn and learn programs in general, and the Louisville Metropolitan College arrangement in particular, has been positive. In fact, most of the coverage appears to have been drawn closely from UPS press releases themselves or conducted with students selected for their success stories. Acknowledging that the night shift "took some getting used to," one local newspaper's coverage is typical in quoting a student shrugging off the challenges, "I just schedule my classes for the afternoon" (Howington). Other stories are more meretricious, suggesting that the UPS jobs keep students from partying too much. One quotes a UPS supervisor who suggests that college students "are staying up until dawn anyway" (Karman).

Ironically, UPS has received numerous awards for "corporate citizenship" and was named one of the "best companies for minorities" in connection with the program. It emphasizes recruitment among Latino students, and numerous Hispanic organizations have either endorsed the program or published unedited UPS press releases marketing the program to "nontraditional students, such as retirees and moms re-entering the workforce" (LatinoLA).

. . .

The Social Meaning of Student Labor

According to one observer, in 1964, all of the expenses associated with a public university education, including food, clothing, and housing could be had by working a minimum-wage job an average of twenty-two hours a week throughout the year. (This might mean working fifteen hours a week while studying and forty hours a week during summers.) Today, the same expenses from a low-wage job require fifty-five hours a week fifty-two weeks a year.

At a private university, those figures in 1964 were thirty-six minimum-wage hours per week, which was relatively manageable for a married couple or a family of modest means and would have been possible even for a single person working the lowest possible wage for twenty hours a week during the school year and some overtime on vacations. Today, it would cost 136 hours per week for fifty-two weeks a year to "work your way through" a private university (Mortenson). In 2006, each year of private education amounted to the annual after-tax earnings of nearly four lowest-wage workers working overtime.

Employing misleading accounting that separates budgets for building, fixed capital expenses, sports programs, and the like from "instructional unit" budgets, higher education administration often suggests that faculty wages are the cause of rising tuition, rather than irresponsible investment in technology, failed commercial ventures, lavish new buildings, corporate welfare, and so on. The plain fact is that many college administrations are on fixed-capital spending sprees with dollars squeezed from cheap faculty and student labor: over the past thirty years, the price of student and faculty labor has been driven downward massively at exactly the same time that costs have soared.

For the 80 percent of students who are trying to work their way through, higher education and its promise of a future is increasingly a form of indenture, involving some combination of debt, overwork, and underinsurance. It means the pervasive shortchanging of health, family obligations, and, ironically, the curtailment even of learning and self culture. More and more students are reaching the limits of endurance with the work that they do while enrolled. One major consequence of this shift of the costs of education away from society to students, including especially the costs of education as direct training for the workforce, is a regime of indebtedness, producing docile financialized subjectivities (Martin, *Financialization of Daily Life*) in what Jeff Williams has dubbed "the pedagogy of debt." The horizon of the work regime fully contains the possibilities of student ambition and activity, including the conception of the future.

Overstressed student workers commonly approach their position from a consumer frame of analysis. They are socialized and even legally obliged to do so, while being disabled by various means, including employment law, from thinking otherwise. To a certain extent, the issue is that student workers are underpaid and ripped off as consumers. In terms of their college "purchase," they are paying much more, about triple, and not getting more: the wage of the average person with a four-year degree or better is about the same today as in 1970, though for a far greater percentage, it takes the additional effort of graduate school to get that wage. From the consumer perspective, the bargain has gotten worse for purchasers of credit hours, because there are many more years at low wages and fewer years at higher wages, plus there are reductions in benefits, a debt load, and historically unprecedented insecurity in those working "full-time" jobs.

But the systematically fascinating, and from the perspective of social justice far more significant, difference is that the U.S. worker with only a high school education or "some college" is paid astonishingly less than they were in 1970, when the "college bonus" was only 30 to 40 percent of the average high-school-educated worker's salary. Now, the "going to college" bonus is more than 100 percent of the high-school educated worker's salary, except that this "bonus" represents exclusively a massive reduction in the wage of the high school educated and is in no part an actual "raise" in the wages of the college educated.

So while it is true and important that higher education is much less of a good deal than it used to be, we also have to think about the role higher education plays in justifying the working circumstances of those who can't make the college bargain. Whether one is inclined to accept higher education as an unspecial and seamless path—school to work—or alternatively as something "special," without any necessary or obvious relation to work, it can be considered straightforwardly as a distribution issue. That is: Who should enjoy the "specialness," whether that specialness is college as self-culture or college as a relatively larger and safer paycheck? On what terms? Who pays for it? What kinds and just how much specialness should the campus distribute? Why should the public fund a second-class and third-class specialness for some working lives, and provide the majority of working lives none at all? Wouldn't it be a straighter—not to mention far more just—path to dignity, security, health, and a meaningful degree of self-determination, even for the most highly educated, if we simply agreed to provide these things for everyone, regardless of their degree of education? Why should education be a competitive scramble to provide yourself with health care?

And here we've run up against the classic question of education and democracy: Can we really expect right education to create equality? Or do we need to *make equality* in order to have right education? With Dick Ohmann, Stanley Aronowitz, Cary Nelson, and others, I think the "crisis of higher education" asks us to do more than think about education, educators, and the educated. It challenges us to make equality a reality. It asks us to identify the agencies of inequality in our lives (including the ideologies and institutions of professionalism), to find a basis for solidarity with inequality's antagonists, and to have hope for a better world on that basis.

For me, the basis of solidarity and hope will always be the collective experience of workplace exploitation and the widespread desire to be productive for society rather than for capital. So when we ask, "Why has higher education gotten more expensive?" we need to bypass the technocratic and "necessitarian" account of events, in which all answers at least implicitly bring the concept of necessity beyond human agency to bear ("costs 'had to' rise because . . ."). Instead, we need to identify the agencies of inequality and ask, "To whom is the arrangement of student debt and student labor most useful?" The "small narratives" of technocracy function to obscure the fundamental questions of distribution. Not just: Who pays for education? But: Who pays for low wages?

The employer doesn't pay. By putting students to work, UPS accumulates more than it would otherwise accumulate if it put nonstudents to work, because of the different material costs represented by persons who claim citizenship in the present, not citizenship in the future. These low wages aren't cheap to society; they're just cheap to employers. Students themselves subsidize this cheapness: by doubling the number of life hours worked, by giving up self-culture and taking on debt. The families of adult students subsidize the cheapness, both in direct labor time and in sacrificed leisure, in time lived together, and other emotional costs. Other service workers subsidize the cheapness, as the huge pool of cheap working students helps to keep down the price of nonstudent labor. And student workers, located, as I've said, in a kind of semiformal regulation environment, are themselves inevitably patrons of the larger informal economy of babysitters, handymen, and the cheap-work system of global manufacturing and agribusiness.

So, on the one hand, the labor time of the low-wage student worker creates an inevitable, embodied awareness that the whole system of our cheap wages is really a gift to the employer. Throwing cartons at 3:00 a.m. every night of one's college education, it becomes impossible not to see that UPS is the beneficiary of our financial aid, and not the other way around. As Dick Ohmann has commented of another group of campus flex-timers, the contingent faculty, there's some potential in this experience for militancy—for new kinds of self-organization for workplace security—and even a quest for new alliances with other hyper-exploited and insecure workers. And in the United States, there are always more than 10 million people who are simultaneously workers and students at any given time, for many of whom the prospects of an "escape" from contingency are dim at best. Even under present conditions of extreme labor repression, the transformative agency of the millions of student employees is evident in the anti-sweatshop movement and in graduate-employee union movements, which have allied themselves with other insecure workers and not with the tenured faculty. "Professional" workers increasingly have interests and experiences in common with other workers.

On the other hand, especially for those for whom schooling does indeed provide an escape from contingency, these long terms of student work can also serve to reinforce commitments to inequality. The university creates professional workers who understand the work that everyone else does in a very particular way: they see manual work and service work through the lens of their own past, through their own sense of their past selves as students, likely comprising all of the feelings of the non-adult, of the temporary, of the mobile, of the single person. As one contributor to Bartlett's *Working Lives* site put it, it's "something I did once upon a time just to get through college." For the professional workers created by the university, these "other" workers, no matter their age or circumstances, are always doing the work of someone who isn't really a full citizen and who doesn't make the full claims of social welfare—just like themselves when they were not (yet) full adults and citizens. Their feeling is that these other workers, like the students who aped them for a few years, really ought to be moving on—out of the sphere of entitlement, out of "our" schools and hospitals, out of "our" public. The view of globalization from above is assisted by the voice of the beat cop to the guest worker loitering around the health-care system: move along, move along.

From here, we could go on to explore the meaning of contingency: not just part-time work but the insecurity and vulnerability of full-time workers. We could ask, for whom is this contingency a field of possibility? And for whom is contingency, in fact, a field of constraint? It takes a village to pay for education and to pay for low wages and to pick up the cost for life injuries sustained by the absence of security and dignity. So perhaps the village should decide what education and wages should be, and the sort of dignity and security that everyone should enjoy, very much apart from the work they do.

9 Unbelievable Student Loan Horror Stories

Mandi Woodruff

Yahoo! Finance Business Insider

November 2012

Mandi Woodruff, an editor and reporter for *Business Insider*, is the stated author of this article, but as you read you'll notice that the majority of the article is composed of personal stories about people's struggles with paying their student loans. Woodruff pulls these narratives from the Consumer Financial Protection Bureau's message board which the CFPB began in 2011 to get information on how private student loans affect students, lenders, and schools. As you read the testimonials, consider how hearing the stories from the students themselves, rather than having them summarized or paraphrased by a reporter, affects the way you understand and react to them.

1. How are private student loans different than federal student loans?

2. In the article, Michael Speck points out that his student loan debt is so extensive he is "unable to assist [his] son with his education expenses (thereby effectively making the debt trans-generational)." What does he mean by this? In what other ways might student loan debt affect more people than just those who took out the loans?

3. Given the anonymity of many of the people who share their stories, should we be skeptical about their authenticity? Why or why not? How might knowing the full names of those who share their stories influence the reader's response to the text?

With the cost of college continuing to rise and the economy still stagnating, the student debt burden has swollen to a record $1 trillion.

Mark Kantrowitz, publisher of Fastweb.com and FinAid.org, believes that one of the main culprits behind the student debt crisis is the private student loan sector.

"Students are following their dreams and don't pay attention to their debt," Kantrowitz says. "They sign whatever piece of paper is put in front of them, figuring they'll pay it back when they graduate."

Unlike federal loans, private loans usually come with variable interest rates that seem low at first glance but can skyrocket by 5 points over the loan's lifetime. They also offer far fewer options for cash-strapped graduates struggling with payments, such as deferment, lengthy forbearance periods and income-based relief.

And since it's next to impossible to discharge student loan debt in bankruptcy, millions of students are left drowning in private debt they have no hopes of ever paying off.

Last year, the Consumer Financial Protection Bureau (CFPB) put out a call for consumers to share their student loan stories on its message board and get the ball rolling on lending reform.

But for these nine commenters, it may already be too little, too late.

Steve Macintyre: $100,000 in debt and out of a job

"I used to work in the entertainment industry but have been unemployed for a few years and I needed to desperately update my skillset if I could hope to find a job in the highly competitive field of games and animation.

Searching for various schools, I kept seeing advertisements for the Art Institute and talked with one of their recruiters and was told wonderful stories about how the school was accredited, how students went on to successful careers, etc.

I told them I wanted to get a degree in Game Art and Design but was told I could but needed to take the Graphic Design course first. I didn't think much of it at first, but I agreed. I was dismayed at the quality of the classes...(Now) I'm stuck with over $100,000 dollars in debt, which qualifies as theft as I received nothing substantive in return.

I actually had to sign up for other courses outside the school in order to successfully complete assignments! Courses that offered REAL *VIDEO* Instruction at a fraction of the cost ($35 dollars per month as opposed to $2000+ dollars!) and by a company that trains people in the industry.

It's now 8 months since loans have run out and I couldn't complete my degree and I'm still looking for work."

Socialworkmary: Paid $350+ per month on her loans for 14 years to no avail

"I admit I did not understand capitalized interest until recently. I consolidated my loans in 1997 when the interest rate was 8 percent. My student loan office at Tulane University led me to believe that I 'had' to consolidate and Sallie Mae was the only option offered to me.

I have repaid them over $61,000 (over 14 years). I think I should be done now, but according to Sallie Mae I still owe $25,000. A Sallie Mae employee directed me to write the legal department and ask to have my loan written off and to appeal if they denied. They denied, stating that federal government regulation prevents them from writing off the balance of the loan.

When I talked to the Sallie Mae employee and said I was confused about why on most months more of my payment goes to interest than principal... she chuckled and said 'We certainly don't go out of our way to put that in big bright red letters across the front page.'"

Dgoeck: Stuck with a clunker—indefinitely

"I'm not really sure what to do at this point. I am a victim of a for-profit school that definitely seemed in cohorts with Sallie Mae. My original loan was $80,000 but has grown to $135,000 and all I can pay is interest only, which is already $700 a month.

It's ridiculous how sad this market has become. No one offers consolidation anymore or those that do will pin you at a ridiculous interest rate.

I am definitely in this for life… It looks like I will be stuck living in a low-rate apartment for the rest of my life and drive a 15-year-old car. I'm at least glad I found a really good job in the industry I was hoping for, but these loans are a real burden. Just thinking about them hurts my overall outcome each and every day."

Michael Speck: Passing on a generation of debt

"I have three degrees, including an MA and a JD. When I graduated from law school in '99 all of the offers—with the exception of those from the upper echelon firms that essentially own you—were for little money, leaving next to nothing for living expenses.

Now I am making a decent living and can pay my loans under the (Income-based repayment) program, but repayment is a distant dream. As a result, I am unable to assist my son with his education expenses (thereby effectively making the debt trans-generational), or buy a home, start my own practice, etc.

As a macro-economic problem, those of us saddled with this debt are unable to fully participate in the economy."

KDF11: Dogged by debt collectors

"I am a graduate (doctoral) student with a 2005 loan from Bank of America which was passed to American Education Services. AES passed my loan to their subsidiary National Collegiate Trust…

They cited that my (notice to them) was over 60 days late and the loan was in repayment and refused to negotiate. Then, when I called/wrote/emailed NCT to negotiate, they sent my loan to another subsidiary— their collection agency MRS.

These companies are working together and when students are full-time in school, they bombard them with calls and deadlines and capitalize by taking punitive measures such as outlined above, from which they no doubt profit.

... I believe that a lot of students have had loans placed at (a) collection agency while they are full-time in school. This should be amended to allow students wiggle room to complete their studies stress-free. If students graduate, find employment and refuse to pay, only then collections should be appropriate."

Debttired: Needs to hit the lotto to pay off loan debt

"I am the first in my family to go to college. Without family support, I self-financed three college degrees (BA, MA and PhD) at state colleges between 1988 and 2005 using Pell Grants, multiple jobs, scholarships and $90,000 in subsidized and unsubsidized student loans.

My loans have been bought and sold so many times it is impossible to keep track of changes in rates, balances and terms of service since I have never had to resign any promissory notes. Eventually, I was able to consolidate the loans with Sallie Mae at a 7% interest rate. My loan payments have ranged from $400-600/mo. depending on the loan provider and lowest possible payment option available.

... I am currently a public school teacher with an income of $50,000, barely enough income to pay the interest-only payments. I have never missed a payment in over ten years ... and my loan balance stands at $105,000. To date, I have paid over $40,000 in loan payments and because my income restricts me to interest-only payments, and the 7% daily capitalized interest rate, I now owe $15,000 more than I borrowed....

My student loan situation has nothing to do with a lack of financial responsibility.

I have never missed a student loan payment and I have paid off $20,000 in credit card debt and a $10,000 car loan since graduation. I have no mortgage or any other outstanding debt, just my student loans. I have a credit score of 820. However, because of the usurious interest rates, capitalization of interest and the sole option of interest-only payments, I will never be able to pay off my student loan. It's just not possible, unless I win the lottery."

Jnsmith553: Drowning in daughter's debt

"Unfortunately, (my daughter) picked a very expensive private school . . . We ended up going with CUstudentLoan. The interest rate was slightly higher (than Sallie Mae).

We pay $25 per month while in school. I can get off the note 24 months after graduation and there is an 18% cap on interest, which is extremely high but the lowest I found. Many were 25%.

These interest rates are extremely ridiculous and do not encourage higher education. My daughter will graduate in 2015 with about $80,000 in debt. Worse case scenario for me (is) two years of payments.

(The loan payments are) going to be more than my mortgage."

Laws65: Single mother can't find humanity in lenders

"Being a single mom with three children and two disabilities, I have found the unworkability or flexibility, depending on how you look at it, with (private) student loans to be impossible bureaucracy at it's finest.

If you consolidate (your loans), you're stuck and the interest rates are high. If you can't afford them, regardless of the documentation you show, it doesn't matter. When you call Sallie Mae, they claim to be workable, but in reality are not.

If you default, it is nothing short of a harassment nightmare that needs legal representation to assist in the matter—(like) having to prove a closed school, nothing short of another nightmare in which the individual does all the work—even when you've gone to your (state) congressmen twice.

. . . Why are student loans, in this economy, not being looked at like mortgages-as some are as much as mortgage payments?

Where is the humanity in any workability with student loans? There, simply put, isn't any."

Nick Keith: Collects cans and squeaks by on disability benefits

"I am a victim of a for-profit school that sold me a private student loan that I cannot afford to repay. I borrowed $60,000 to attend a culinary school—a school that has settled a class action lawsuit admitting that it lied to students about the value of the program and the statistics of the number of graduates getting employment in the culinary field.

I was lied to about the terms of the private student loan. After completing the program, my first job in the culinary field paid $10 per hour. It took me three months to save enough money to make the first student loan payment of $1,300. I spoke to Sallie Mae. I wrote to Sallie Mae. But Sallie Mae would not refinance my debt with a reasonable interest rate or reasonable payments.

They maintained my private loan balance at 19% variable interest rate and monthly payments of over $1,000 per month. I never made another payment. I could not afford to make a student loan payment because my choice each month was to either pay my rent or make a student loan payment.

I spoke to a bankruptcy attorney as well as a CPA, and they both gave me the same answer: don't make any payments.

. . . That was in 2005. My private student loan, held by Sallie Mae, has been in default for sometime, and the balance due is nearly three times the amount that I borrowed. After working in the culinary field for almost two years, I was injured at work and became permanently disabled in 2007.

I have not been able to work since that time. I have no means to pay my student loans . . .

Today, my credit rating is below poor and all of my debts from student loans to credit cards are in default, but I cannot file bankruptcy until Congress restores the ability to discharge student loan debt.

Right now, there is no hope for me to achieve the American dream. I will never be able to own a home. I will not be able to save for retirement. I cannot go back to school for a real education. My total defaulted debt right now is more debt than I have ever borrowed and repaid in my lifetime . . .

Today, I am living on my social security disability income and have less than $4 left in my checking account until the next check arrives in about two weeks. Every day, I walk around the public areas of town collecting cans and bottles. I get groceries at the local food bank.

I have sold or lost 99% of everything I ever owned. I need debt relief in order to even begin a path to becoming a productive American. PLEASE HELP. Please help me start over by giving me an opportunity to get rid of my bad debt that I cannot repay. Please stop companies like Sallie Mae from victimizing helpless students who have been lied to by their schools and were given loans they could never afford."

Graduating in Debt

John Batchelor

The Bagpipe

February 2013

This photo was taken by John Batchelor and appeared in a post on the website *The Bagpipe* in February of 2013. As you look at this image, try to "read" the photograph like you would a written text. Think about the many choices Batchelor made in creating this image—composition, setting, and focus all work together to support a clear theme.

1. Student debt is a serious issue, yet in some ways the choice to put debt amounts on mortar boards seems playful. Do you think the students in this picture meant their act to be tongue-in-cheek? Serious? Somewhere in between? Why?

2. How does the context (i.e., the pomp and circumstance of a college graduation ceremony) affect the way in which the audience understands the message on the mortar boards?

3. How does a visual text about student debt such as this compare with the stories we hear from students in the pieces by Ludden and Woodruff? Which is most effective? Why?

The Path to Student Debt

Virginia Tech
The Collegiate Times
December 2011

This infographic originally appeared in *The Collegiate Times*, the student-run newspaper from Virginia Polytechnic Institute (Virginia Tech). *The Collegiate Times* has been in print for more than 100 years and has an estimated 26,000 readers during the school year. This image was part of a series of articles about debt and the effects of debt on students' lives. As you examine the image, consider both the content (i.e., the information it's presenting) and the way in which the author chose to convey the message.

1. What is EFC and why is it relevant to discussions of student debt?

2. Why did the author choose to make the image look like a board game? How might this choice affect the intended audience?

3. Why might a visual text with written words be a more effective genre for explaining how students accrue debt than an article, such as Woodruff's, or a podcast, such as Ludden's?

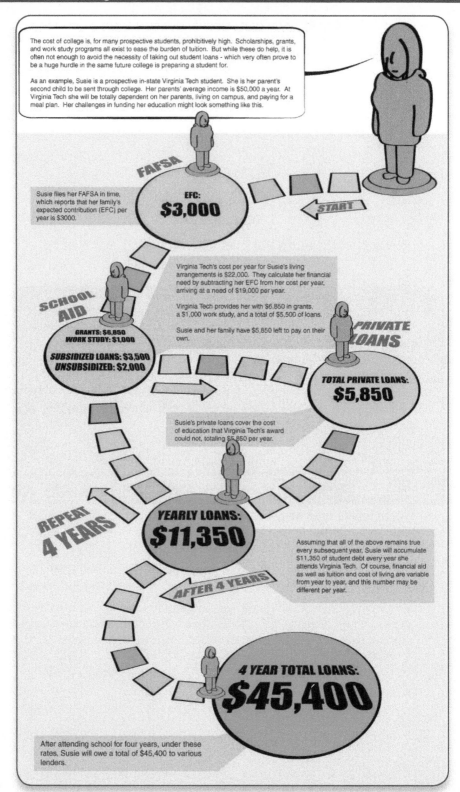

The cost of college is, for many prospective students, prohibitively high. Scholarships, grants, and work study programs all exist to ease the burden of tuition. But while these do help, it is often not enough to avoid the necessity of taking out student loans - which very often prove to be a huge hurdle in the same future college is preparing a student for.

As an example, Susie is a prospective in-state Virginia Tech student. She is her parent's second child to be sent through college. Her parents' average income is $50,000 a year. At Virginia Tech she will be totally dependent on her parents, living on campus, and paying for a meal plan. Her challenges in funding her education might look something like this.

FAFSA

Susie files her FAFSA in time, which reports that her family's expected contribution (EFC) per year is $3000.

EFC: **$3,000**

START

Virginia Tech's cost per year for Susie's living arrangements is $22,000. They calculate her financial need by subtracting her EFC from her cost per year, arriving at a need of $19,000 per year.

Virginia Tech provides her with $6,850 in grants, a $1,000 work study, and a total of $5,500 of loans.

Susie and her family have $5,850 left to pay on their own.

SCHOOL AID

GRANTS: $6,850
WORK STUDY: $1,000

SUBSIDIZED LOANS: $3,500
UNSUBSIDIZED: $2,000

PRIVATE LOANS

TOTAL PRIVATE LOANS: **$5,850**

Susie's private loans cover the cost of education that Virginia Tech's award could not, totaling $5,850 per year.

REPEAT 4 YEARS

YEARLY LOANS: **$11,350**

AFTER 4 YEARS

Assuming that all of the above remains true every subsequent year, Susie will accumulate $11,350 of student debt every year she attends Virginia Tech. Of course, financial aid as well as tuition and cost of living are variable from year to year, and this number may be different per year.

4 YEAR TOTAL LOANS: **$45,400**

After attending school for four years, under these rates, Susie will owe a total of $45,400 to various lenders.

For-Profit Colleges Under Fire Over Value, Accreditation

Mary Beth Marklein

USA Today

September 2010

Mary Beth Marklein has been reporting on higher education for *USA Today* since 1997 and has both undergraduate and graduate degrees in journalism. In this article she works to untangle some of the controversies of for-profit colleges and universities, especially with regard to accreditation practices, and provides background and contextual information to help the audience understand the significant increase in the number of students enrolled at for-profit schools. While reading the article, consider the way Marklein organizes her piece—that is, how she opens and closes it, what background information she chooses to include, and where she puts it—and think about the rhetorical strategies she uses to help her readers understand this potentially complex issue.

1. Why is regional accreditation considered superior to national accreditation? Why do these differences especially impact for-profit schools?

2. Why do you think Marklein begins and ends her article with Chelsi Miller's story? How might this rhetorical strategy affect the reader?

3. How does Marklein's purpose with this article compare with the purpose of the piece from *The Economist* about the value of higher education? How might her purpose change the way she writes her article?

For Chelsi Miller, the wake-up call came when University of Utah officials said her credits wouldn't transfer from her old school.

Utah's flagship public university accepted her to its pre-med program last fall but said her courses at Everest College, a national for-profit institution with a campus in Salt Lake City, wouldn't count toward her bachelor's degree. That left Miller with a 3.9 grade-point average for an associate's degree that she says did nothing to advance her education and career goals. And, she has more than $30,000 in student-loan debt.

She says Everest misled her when it suggested her credits would transfer and misrepresented what it would cost her.

"I feel as if I had been sold a college experience from a used-car salesman," says Miller, 26, of Midvale, Utah, who last week filed a class-action lawsuit in state court with two other students accusing Corinthian Colleges, Everest's owner, of fraud.

Miller's claim—which Corinthian disputes—is the latest in a string of actions raising questions about for-profit colleges, whose enrollments are soaring as many Americans beef up their education as a hedge in a tough job market.

In 2008, about 2,000 for-profit colleges eligible for federal student aid enrolled nearly 1.8 million students—an increase of 225% in 10 years. About 9% of all college students now attend for-profits; most attend schools owned by one of 15 large, publicly traded companies that each enroll tens of thousands of students. Last year, federal student loans and grants made up an average 77% of revenue at the five largest for-profits.

Advocates of for-profit colleges say their programs, which often operate online or in rented office space, serve a key role in educating students who juggle work and family demands. But the U.S. government has stepped up its scrutiny amid growing

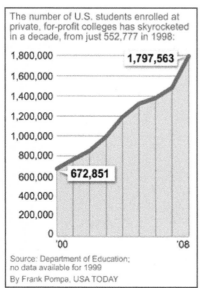

The number of U.S. students enrolled at private, for-profit colleges has skyrocketed in a decade, from just 552,777 in 1998:

1,800,000   **1,797,563**
1,600,000
1,400,000
1,200,000
1,000,000
800,000
600,000   **672,851**
400,000
200,000
0
    '00   '08

Source: Department of Education; no data available for 1999
By Frank Pompa, USA TODAY

concern that for-profits are reeling in billions of dollars in federal aid by using aggressive—some say deceptive—practices to lure students to programs that might not yield a useful education.

The Education Department has proposed penalizing for-profits whose students graduate with more debt than they can afford, and Congress began a series of hearings this summer on whether federal aid to for-profit colleges—more than $24 billion in 2008–09—is being put to good use.

"It is our responsibility to ensure that for-profit colleges are putting the needs of students before the needs of shareholders," says Sen. Tom Harkin, D-Iowa, chairman of a Senate education committee whose hearing Thursday aims to explore the magnitude of the federal investment in for-profits. "We need to learn more about whether students are succeeding at these schools and whether the taxpayer investment is actually benefiting students."

A question of standards

As the topic heats up in Washington, more than 1,000 students are expected to converge on Capitol Hill today in support of for-profit colleges. But for others, including Miller, the problems with for-profits start with concern about accreditation, a coveted assurance of educational quality.

Accreditation, a sort of third-party seal of approval designed to protect consumers and taxpayers from diploma mills, is important to colleges because the Education Department relies on it to determine which schools may get federal student aid. It's important to students because it can help them transfer credits from one college to another and can signal that a candidate's academic training has met certain standards.

It's also confusing because there is more than one type of accreditation.

Miller says she was "a naive single mother from a small farm town" when she responded to an ad for Everest's surgical technology program. When she asked if her credits would transfer to the University of Utah, she says, an Everest admissions official "assured me that the college was going through an accreditation change and would have full accreditation by the time I graduated."

In fact, Everest College is accredited by the Accrediting Council for Independent Colleges and Schools, one of the more than 70 organizations recognized by the Education Department.

The problem: The organization is a national body.

Historically, for-profit colleges have been accredited mostly by national groups, which traditionally have focused on short-term college programs in fields such as the culinary arts, medical billing or business administration.

In contrast, most non-profit, degree-granting public and private institutions are accredited by one of six regional bodies. (To complicate matters more, some professional associations accredit academic programs in fields such as pharmacy or nursing at both regionally and nationally accredited institutions.)

Those historic distinctions are blurring as more for-profits offer degree programs, which make them eligible for regional accreditation. Types of accreditation differ because institutional missions differ, but most specialists in higher ed accreditation agree that regional accreditation, which takes at least two years for a college to earn and must be renewed every 10 years, is considered the most rigorous and most prestigious.

Kevin Kinser, an education professor at the State University of New York at Albany who studies the for-profit higher education industry, estimates that close to half of all for-profit enrollments today are in schools that have been regionally accredited. The credential serves "a legitimizing function," he says.

Colleges "promote that about themselves, often in terms (such as), 'We have the same accreditation as the University of Chicago.'"

It's up to institutions to decide whether to accept or deny transfer credits, but many use accreditation status as a guideline. The University of Utah, for example, requires students who want to transfer from nationally accredited schools such as Everest to seek permission from its faculty to get credit for courses already taken at a different institution.

"Often those courses are found lacking in some way or another," says Suzanne Wayment, associate director of admissions at the University of Utah. For example, she says, an algebra textbook used by a nationally accredited school may be for an introductory course, while the university requires that students complete a higher-level course.

On the other hand, she says, the university tweaked its policy this summer, when it began allowing coursework from the regionally accredited University of Phoenix, the USA's largest for-profit college, to count as elective credits. Wayment says officials from the University of Phoenix—which enrolls about 476,000 students nationwide, either online or at one of more than 200 locations—recently requested a review because the original policy, in place since the 1980s, was outdated.

Manny Rivera, spokesman for the Apollo Group, which owns the University of Phoenix, says "it is the student's responsibility to confirm whether credits earned at University of Phoenix will be accepted by another institution."

But Harris Miller, president of the Association of Private Sector Colleges and Universities, which represents about 1,800 for-profit institutions, suggests that many more non-profit schools follow blanket policies that waste students'—and taxpayers'—time and money because students have to retake a course "over and over."

"Even when a school does become regionally accredited, other schools will often take a discriminatory attitude simply because they're for-profit," he says. "The stratification of the higher-ed system is incredibly elite."

Confused students

Recent lawsuits, and a probe by the Government Accountability Office, suggest that some nationally accredited colleges may be exploiting confusion about accreditation by omitting or glossing over relevant details.

The GAO report, for example, said a representative for the nationally accredited Kaplan College in Florida told an undercover government investigator who was pursuing an associate's degree in criminal justice that the college was accredited by "the top accrediting agency—Harvard, the University of Florida, they all use that accrediting agency." But that was not true.

A class-action lawsuit filed in August against the for-profit Westwood College in California noted that the college's website said the school was a candidate for regional accreditation but failed "to disclose that it has been a candidate for two years and was passed over for accreditation during its first evaluation."

And Chelsi Miller's lawsuit argues that Corinthian is "aware of prospective students' ignorance of, or confusion about, this important distinction."

Kent Jenkins, vice president of public affairs communications at Corinthian Colleges, declined to comment on Miller's case. But, he said, "we are very straightforward and direct with our students and prospective students about what they can expect from their diploma or degree. We have detailed processes and procedures that require our admissions counselors to disclose whether credits are or are not likely to transfer to other institutions.

"We work very hard to treat our students honestly and fairly, and we don't tolerate deception, period."

In a development that has captured the interest of the Education Department, a growing number of for-profits have taken a shortcut to regional accreditation: buying an already accredited non-profit college. At least 11 non-profits have been converted to for-profits that way in recent years, Kinser says.

In 2004, for example, investors purchased Grand Canyon University, then a small, financially struggling Christian college in Phoenix that has been accredited since 1968 by the Higher Learning Commission of the North Central Association of Colleges and Schools, which accredits more than 1,000 institutions in 19 states. Today, Grand Canyon enrolls 40,000 students, most of them in its online program.

Regional accrediting associations, facing a policy development that didn't exist until for-profit colleges began to proliferate, have since tightened their reins or are re-examining rules regarding ownership changes. In February, the Higher Learning Commission told Chancellor University in Cleveland, which was acquired in 2008 by a for-profit company, that it would withdraw accreditation unless the school could show that it met certain criteria. In June, it denied re-accreditation for Dana College in Blair, Neb., which was in the process of being purchased by a for-profit company. The college has since closed.

"This is the type of thing we want to keep a close eye on," says James Kvaal, a deputy undersecretary of education.

But federal officials and lawmakers are not just watching for-profit colleges.

The Education Department's inspector general, who investigates compliance problems, threatened in December to strip the Higher Learning Commission's authority because it approved accreditation of the for-profit American InterContinental University despite an agreement among commission members that the school had an "egregious" policy of giving more credit for certain graduate and undergraduate courses than was "common practice in higher education."

This summer, lawmakers grilled officials of regional and national accreditors during hearings about whether colleges found to engage in questionable practices—such as encouraging students to lie on their financial aid forms or pressuring students to sign legally binding contracts—should be allowed to keep their accreditation. Sen. Michael Enzi, R-Wyo., ranking member of the Senate's education committee, has said he wants any investigation of problems in the for-profit higher education industry "to also include a review of all institutions of higher education."

Those developments worry many leaders of traditional college and universities, who comply with a host of federal regulations but for decades have fought to keep federal regulators out of classroom matters. Accreditors say they're taking the government's concerns seriously.

"The absence of credibility for accreditation means the absence of credibility for our colleges, universities and programs," says Judith Eaton, president of the Council for Higher Education Accreditation, a membership organization of degree-granting colleges that advocates for self-regulation of academic quality.

Harris Miller, head of the association of for-profit schools, says he would welcome wider federal oversight to ensure quality. He says his schools, and particularly their completion rates, would stack up favorably when compared with community college systems, the for-profit sector's main competitors.

But Chelsi Miller, who has put more schooling on hold until she can save more money, says something has to change so more students aren't duped.

"I received misleading guidance and answers that led me to sign my life away," she says. "I can't speak to other colleges, but as far as Everest goes, they really have taken advantage of people that cannot afford to be taken advantage of."

Taming the For-Profit College Monster

David Halperin

Politico

August 2012

The author, David Halperin, is a lawyer and policy analyst who frequently writes about higher education issues. In addition to writing for *Politico*, where this article was published, he has had pieces published in *The Huffington Post*, *The New York Times*, and the website RepublicReport.org. *Politico* focuses much of its coverage on Congress and the President, and as you'll see in the piece, Senator Tom Harkin's report on for-profit institutions prompted Halperin to write his article. As you read the article, consider how Halperin's genre, an opinion column, influences how he crafts the text.

1. What is Halperin's plan for solving the problems with "the for-profit college monster"?

2. The author cites several statistics and stories from Senator Tom Harkin's report on for-profit schools. How does Halperin's use of this source affect his credibility as an author?

3. Compare the tone of this piece with that of Marklein (in the previous article) or Schilling (in the article that follows). How might the tone of each author relate to his/her specific purpose, audience, and genre?

With for-profit colleges, the government has created a monster: a $40 billion industry whose big players get more than 85 percent of their revenue from U.S. taxpayers - and use their riches to buy influence and avoid accountability. We need a new approach to end this cycle and ensure that federal aid goes to schools that benefit students, rather than ruin their lives.

The recent report from Senator Tom Harkin (D-Iowa), tells two stories that underscore the need for action.

The first story is about how some for-profit colleges deceive and abuse their students. It's about boiler room salespeople facing constant pressure to sign up new "starts," aka students, and using coercive scripts to "poke the pain" of low-income people. It's about a recruiter who went to Camp Lejeune and enrolled a wounded warrior so impaired he couldn't remember what he signed up for.

It's about Rashidah Smallwood, fired as a financial aid administrator at ITT Tech in Texas after refusing to cooperate in what she considered systematic fraud to maximize federal dollars. It's about students in a Kaplan College dental assistant program in North Carolina who learned after a year of classes and $18,000 in costs that school officials misled them about credentials the program provided.

While some for-profit colleges are honest and work to educate their students, others charge sky-high prices, spend more on advertising than on teaching, have high dropout rates, and leave many students with worthless credits. A number of these schools have been caught lying to regulators to hide dismal job placement rates.

Fueled by permissive federal policies, the sector grew three-fold over the last decade, reaching 2.4 million students in 2010. For-profit colleges now have 10 percent of all college students, but their financial footprint is much larger: 25 percent of federal student aid—$32 billion a year—and nearly half of student loan defaults. They are the leading edge of a student debt crisis that recalls the harrowing subprime mortgage disaster.

But the second story referenced by Harkin's report is just as disturbing. It's about how this sector has waged a relentless campaign to weaken, overturn, and evade common-sense rules aimed at denying taxpayer money to schools that engage in rampant fraud and abuse.

Senator Dick Durbin (D-Ill.), recently said that reforms are almost impossible because for-profit colleges "own every lobbyist in town." Last year, the industry spent $10.2 million on lobbying, and more on public relations. They hire big names like former Senate Majority Leader Trent Lott (R-Miss.), former House Majority Leader Dick Gephardt (D-Mo.), and former Obama Communications Director Anita Dunn.

The lobbying is backed with campaign contributions: In the 2012 election cycle, the industry has given $2.4 million to federal candidates. More than $500,000 has gone to Mitt Romney or the pro-Romney super PAC. (Romney has praised the sector, pointing to Florida's Full Sail University, whose owners are among his big donors, as a place that uses innovation to "hold down the cost of their education," when in fact it may be the third most expensive college in America.)

Despite their stated commitment to smaller, more efficient government, nearly every Republican in the House of Representatives has voted to overturn efforts by the Obama administration to stop the flow of federal money to predatory schools. They've been joined by a significant number of House Democrats who, like Republicans, receive contributions from the industry.

This pressure has led the administration to weaken its reforms. The rules that it has issued have been gutted further in the courts, where for-profit colleges retain the highest-priced lawyers. Other industry attorneys use confidential settlements to conceal lawsuits demonstrating fraudulent conduct. And the for-profits use their resources to dominate accrediting bodies and state licensing agencies.

It gets worse. When the government has adopted significant rules, for-profit colleges devise schemes to systematically evade them. Harkin's report details how companies like Corinthian and EDMC circumvent a rule that cuts off aid to schools whose students frequently default on loans. Schools

For-Profit Education

relentlessly pursue financially-imperiled students with round-the-clock call centers, even private investigators, to convince students to put their loans in "forbearance" and delay default. Interest keeps accruing, and students may be no better off, but it hides failures from government auditors.

In short, the for-profits have used our taxes to finance a race to the bottom: the more you abuse students, the more money you make. Their wealth may doom to failure the current approach to regulation, which has created benchmark after benchmark that schools must flunk to lose federal aid. Not only has the industry schemed to weaken and evade such tests, but also it has exploited opportunities to gain sympathy and support from non-profit and state colleges, when new rules add greater compliance burdens for those schools as well.

Although greater public awareness of for-profit college abuses has recently reduced student enrollments—and the share prices—for some for-profit colleges, these companies still can and do devote enormous resources to blocking accountability measures.

It's time for a new approach to overseeing this taxpayer-dependent industry, one that starts by asserting that the evidence warrants treating for-profit colleges differently. For-profit education can be an important part of the landscape, but the tension between pleasing shareholders and serving students is now patently obvious.

The second tenet is that federal aid is, for a school, a privilege, not a right. Instead of new measures to determine whether aid should be taken away, for-profits should be required to apply anew for eligibility.

The U.S. Department of Education should house a nonpartisan board that establishes broad criteria for eligibility. The board, comprised of members without prior financial ties to for-profit education, would hold public proceedings and use expert judgment to make decisions. Approval would require a unanimous vote every two years. As much as possible, eligibility decisions should be insulated from legal maneuvering and court processes.

Citizens should demand real reforms. Honest and effective for-profit colleges would benefit, as would the rest of us, from a system that stops enabling abusive, predatory businesses and instead targets funding to schools that help students learn and build careers.

What's Money Got to Do with It: The Appeal of the For-Profit Education Model

Joanna Schilling

Community College Journal of Research and Practice

January 2013

"What's Money Got to Do with It" is an academic (also known as peer-reviewed or scholarly) article published in *Community College Journal of Research and Practice*, a journal whose audience is researchers, faculty, and administrative professionals at community colleges. As you read, you'll notice certain characteristics of scholarly articles: an initial abstract that briefly outlines the article, frequent in-text citations, and a list of references at the end. The authors of academic articles are generally researchers and faculty members at colleges and universities and usually hold graduate degrees. In this case, author Joanna Schilling is the Vice President for Academic Affairs at Cerritos College in California, and has a B.A. in English, an M.F.A in Playwriting, and a Ph.D. in Education.

1. What are some of the "lessons to be learned from the for-profit model" that Schilling encourages community colleges to adopt?

2. Schilling cites a quote from Persell and Wenglinsky which notes that the view of higher education has gone from "'a social institution toward a view of higher education as an industry.'" What is the difference between the two? What might be the consequences of such a shift?

3. Mary Beth Marklein's article (earlier in this chapter) notes that community colleges are the main competitor of for-profit institutions. How might that competition influence Schilling's article—both the way she as an author writes it and the way her audience reads it?

For-profit colleges have been dismissed by community college administrators and faculty as imperfect institutions that focus too heavily on skills-based training, to the detriment of a well-rounded academic experience. Although there are many appropriate criticisms of an educational model that relies on federal funding to

make a profit—while enticing the lowest income group of students to take on huge debt—there may also be practices and resource efficiencies that can be exported to the community college. This paper seeks to examine what aspects of the for-profit model might be positively applied to the community college learning experience.

For-profit higher education has existed in the United States since the 19th century, but it is only in the last decades of the 20th century that career colleges have been acknowledged as part of the higher educational system. Although accounting for only 5% of the total higher education enrollment in the United States (Hoyle, 2009), this "third sector" (Kinser, 2006, p. 1) joins public and private institutions as a potential educational choice for students seeking "need, speed, and ease" (Howard-Vital, 2006, p. 69).

Clowes (1995) noted that proprietary schools tend to be silent partners in higher education, but they are becoming more like community colleges because of regional accreditation, federal financial aid, and the programs offered. A 1995 study on proprietary schools and community colleges concluded that the differences in student demographic characteristics at both institutions are diminishing (Cheng & Levin, 1995, as cited in Outcalt & Schirmer, 2003). Yet, few community college leaders see career colleges as competition, mostly due to the disparity in tuition charged (Bailey & Morest, 2006). As Kinser (2006) noted, more attention to proprietary schools does not equate to a better understanding of these institutions.

Few studies have been done at for-profit institutions, and the research that has been completed is conflicting (Kinser, 2006; Outcalt & Schirmer, 2003; Persell & Wenglinsky, 2004). Faculty at for-profit institutions tend to be practitioners, not researchers, which may allow the misconceptions about this sector to continue. For example, Hassler (2006) noted the majority of faculty in research institutions believed that for-profit schools are delivered strictly online.

What is known about this third sector is that almost 90% of the profit is derived from tuition and fees (Alfred, 2006; Hassler, 2006; Kinser, 2006) and there are no donations, state support, or endowments (Alfred, 2006). Since the 1980s there has been a heavy reliance on Title IV funding, which critics maintain is a misuse of federal funding (Persell & Wenglinsky, 2004).

By focusing on what for-profits are not, however, many critics cannot acknowledge the reality of a more efficient system of education (Hassler, 2006). There may be lessons to be learned from the for-profit model that would enhance the student learning experience at community colleges.

Historical Background

Although for-profit education has gained attention in recent years with the rise of the "super-system colleges" (Hoyle, 2009, p. 186) composed of large publicly-traded corporations, the history of the proprietary institution dates back to the 16th century. Bookkeeping schools in England and courses for handwriting, commercial arithmetic, and business courses in France were the first "commercial colleges" (Kinser, 2006, p. 13). The first bookkeeping textbook was published in 1543, and by the 1700s English grammar schools began to include "practical education courses for students who had no interest in the classical training common in schools of the day" (Kinser, 2006, p. 14).

Nonacademic programs began to find a place in the educational system. By the end of 19th century, there were 81,000 students enrolled in trade schools in contrast to 157,000 undergraduates enrolled in universities. These programs continued to find favor into the 20th century with the Smith-Hughes Act of 1917, which incorporated a mandate for vocational education in public schools (Berg, 2005). Enrollments held steady until after World War II when vocational schools were included in the GI bill. Initially, funding did not include for-profit institutions, but large numbers of returning servicemen requested enrollment at proprietary trade schools.

This signaled the beginning of federal funding of for-profit institutions, a trend that was further enhanced by the expansion of the Higher Education Act in 1972 that allowed students in vocational programs to apply for student loans (Kinser, 2006; Morey, 2004).

By the late 1980s, there were more than 4,000 proprietary schools operating in the United States with more than 1.8 million students enrolled (Morey, 2004). The 1990s witnessed the rise of more than 650 degree-granting schools in a 3.5 billion dollar industry. In 1994, with the initial public offering of the Apollo Group, the Wall Street era officially began through large publically traded companies looking to solicit substantial profits for their shareholders (Kinser, 2006).

Students at For-Profit Institutions

Morey (2004) argued that for-profit schools have gained hold in the modern era due to two factors: the demise of the apprenticeship programs in the trades, and the inability of traditional education to reform its curriculum to include more practical studies. Prior to the 1980s, the student profile for a vocational student was "younger than 25 years of age, preferred a quick education, was eligible to attend other higher education institutions but preferred the vocational path, borrowed to pay for school and desired a training-related job" (Kinser, 2006, p. 69). After the 1990s, however, this demographic group changed. In the current corporate-driven era students tend to (a) be from a minority background; (b) have a weak academic background; (c) have low income; (d) be older than 25; (e) be financially self-sufficient; (f) be first-generation college students; (g) demonstrate low civic engagement; and (h) be less likely to vote or participate in political or community activities (Persell & Wenglinksy, 2004).

Critics often note that the disproportional number of minorities, especially Black students, at proprietary schools underscores the exploitive nature of educational profit (Hassler, 2006). But Berg (2005) argued that, "proprietary schools are making significant in-roads among minority students who are turned off by traditional educational institutions who put up barriers to entrance" (p. 36). Minority students also tend to be unaware of the financial aid programs available at other institutions, information the for-profit schools make readily accessible to their prospective students (Howard-Vital, 2006).

Regardless of what the critics say, few dispute the fact that the for-profit model is rewarded for being student centered and offers options that traditional educational institutions have either misunderstood, cannot afford, or do not see as part of their mission (Alfred, 2006; Hassler, 2006; Howard-Vital, 2006). Beginning with an expanded students services support system, cohort curriculum model, focused training, and job placement assistance, the for-profit colleges have done their homework regarding what their student needs to be successful (Bailey & Morest, 2006). As Persell and Wenglinsky (2004) noted, "the dominating legitimating idea of public higher education has moved away from the idea of higher education as a social institution toward a view of higher education as an industry" (p. 337).

The Customer Service Model

Proprietary institutions treat their employers and students as customers, and everything these institutions do is "dedicated to identifying and serving customer needs" (Alfred, 2006, p. 189). In a study of enrollees at for-profit institutions in North Carolina, Howard-Vital (2006) discovered that students were initially attracted by the opportunity to complete their degrees quickly at proprietary institutions. The author further identified a general disenchantment with the services provided at other higher education institutions. Students stated they (a) didn't care about licensure or accreditation; (b) liked that their education led to something concrete; (c) didn't like the large anonymous classes associated with traditional colleges; (d) preferred hands-on teaching and activities rather than text-oriented coursework; (e) appreciated that registration, financial aid, book ordering, access to computers and technology, and placement services were facilitated by staff; (f) believed teachers took a practical approach to instruction; and (g) desired good parking, convenience to start courses immediately, and could complete courses quickly (Howard-Vital, 2006, p. 69). Morey (2004) found that the students attracted to for-profit schools wanted the same relationship with their school as with the bank or supermarket. The proprietary industry understands this market and aims its services directly for this audience.

So what exactly is a customer service model? "Using a business model, the organization thrives when exceptional products are delivered and the customer is satisfied" (Alfred, 2006, p. 190). Hassler (2006) defined the customer service model as a fiscal chain of responsibility where all departments must run in an accountable way. This efficiency is enhanced by, and leads to, better customer service that increases revenue, student retention and, in turn, more revenue, resulting in better stock value for shareholders.

This kind of mercenary approach to education sets off all sorts of alarm bells for academics who believe a business model is at odds with the philosophical purpose of higher education. As Morey (2004) noted, "for-profits provide education to make money; traditional institutions accept money to provide education" (p. 143). This approach contradicts the idea of the university as a place of teaching universal knowledge (Newman, 1907). Potts (2005) argued that "the fundamental end of the college or university is to impart knowledge, including particular intellectual virtues such as free inquiry, intellectual honesty, and academic excellence" (p. 62), and that a customer service model leads to the logical conclusion that education is a commodity to be bought. If the customer is always right, high grades should be awarded to keep the customer satisfied (Potts, 2005).

But is a business model the antithesis of how education should be run? Labland and Lentz (2004) studied the true costs of an education at 1,450 public, 1,316 private not-for profit, and 176 private for-profit higher education institutions. They found a "greater difference between private not-for-profit and public institutions than they did at for-profit institutions" (Labland & Lentz, 2004, p. 429). Due to the saturation of more business and science-related programs offered at for-profit-colleges, these institutions spent more per student than did public not-for-profit institutions. Labland and Lentz (2004) concluded that the higher tuition charged at both for-profit institutions and private not-for-profit colleges were spent proportionally on students and could "fatally damage the theory of positional competition" (p. 438) between for-profits and traditional higher education.

Morey (2004) further argued that globalization has fueled changes in higher education, and the technology revolution has driven the need for more flexibility, skilled workers, and jobs shared by the global community.

Levine (2001) argued that although over 65% of students are seeking postsecondary degrees, the government does not see higher education as a growth industry but as a mature one. This leads to more regulations and control, decreases in autonomy, and increases in accountability. This move away from the teaching process in higher education places more emphasis on learning outcomes, further inhibiting institutions' ability to act quickly, efficiently, and with students' needs in mind.

The ideal that higher education was formed for the public good is a relatively late addition to educational philosophy (Kinser, 2006). But the claim that "education is indispensable to the maintenance and growth of freedom, thought, faith, enterprise, and association" (Zook, 1947, p. 5) runs deep in the academy and probably forms the greatest resistance to the for-profit model. As government support for traditional education wanes and tuition rises at public institutions, however, all colleges are compensating and sacrificing more for the bottom line (Persell & Wenglinsky, 2004). Is it possible that education can also be profitable and still maintain the mission of serving the public good?

Are Good Business Practices at Odds with Higher Education?

Levine (2001) argued that higher education is at a crossroads, and much of this is due to misinterpreting the value of good business practices in education:

There is an underlying belief that colleges and universities are making precisely the same mistake that the railroads made. The railroads believed they were in the railroad business; they focused on making bigger and better railroads. The problem is that they were actually in the transportation industry and, as a result, were derailed by the airlines. Similarly, it can

be said that higher education is making the same mistake of thinking it is in the campus business, when in reality it is in the very lucrative education business. High technology and entertainment companies are viewing non campus-based education as an opportunity. (p. 17)

Outcalt and Schirmer (2003) argue that student services are highly fragmented at community colleges. But in the for-profit sector, generating revenue allows proprietary institutions a singularity of mission that provides focused individual attention to each student. The emphasis on packaging admissions, financial aid, and career placement means student services are better integrated into the learning experience.

Research indicates that although career colleges are successful at reaching the singular goal of helping students find a job, it may do so at the expense of the greater goals of higher education (Hassler, 2006). Gumport (2000) noted that "applying the logic of economic rationality to higher education may prove detrimental to the longer-term educational legacies and democratic interests that have long characterized American public education" (p. 1).

The lack of academic presence at the top of a for-profit organization means that too often academic standards may be forsaken for "business principles such as growth and profit" (Alfred, 2006, p. 193). But the same author also admitted that by "using a business model, the organization thrives when exceptional products are delivered and the customer is satisfied" (p. 190).

Much has been made of completion and placement rates at career colleges (Bailey & Morest, 2006) but Persell and Wenglinsky (2006) cautioned that when a job is the only institutional goal, students may complete more often but are not encouraged to go further in education. The cooling out function identified by Clark (1960), which encourages students to aim lower in order to achieve a more attainable goal, is even more prevalent in for-profit institutions who have little vested interest in what happens to their students after they obtain that first job. The job placement services offered at career colleges mean students are likely to find employment (Farrell, 2003), but lower income students, the mainstay of these institutions, tend to stay on the same low economic rung after completing their education. Studies show that few students who have received their certificate or degree at a career college increase their earning potential beyond their first entry-level position (Grubb, 1993; Kinser, 2006).

Implications for Practice

Although there are major philosophical differences between publicly supported two-year institutions and for-profit colleges, Hoyle (2009) emphasized that community colleges should not be so quick to dismiss the proprietary school model. "These two sectors have more to learn from each other than they have to fear" (Hoyle, 2009, p. 185). The author identifies nine key ways community colleges could benefit from the for-profit model:

1. Update curriculum continuously
2. Streamline the admissions process
3. Enhance management practices through entrepreneurial practices
4. Emphasize academic excellence by employing focused academic curricula
5. Activate employer advisory boards
6. Diversify delivery models
7. Audit all programs annually
8. Leverage strategic partnerships
9. Instill a culture of accountability

Adaptability is the most important element public institutions could adopt from the for-profit colleges (Berg, 2005). As traditional institutions are threatened by reduced budgets, demand for technology, and increased pressure from community and legislative stakeholders, the ability to change quickly and efficiently is not something that higher education does well. The most successful institutions, public or for-profit, are those that balance academic values with economic realities; "too often community colleges, in their attempt to serve many constituencies, drift far afield of their core mission" (Berg, 2005, p. 182).

Community colleges began as high school extensions with an academic infrastructure modeled much on the liberal arts traditions of the university (Alfred, 2006; Cohen & Brawer, 2008), but they have evolved to take on a broad mission that is varied and diverse. Alfred (2006) noted that

For-Profit Education

comprehensive institutions are usually stable because "faculty, curricula, and students change little from year to year, and reflect the makeup of the communities they serve" (p. 187). But this attempt to maintain multiple, and often competing, missions has also resulted in an institution that cannot easily distinguish one priority from another.

For-profit institutions' singularity of scope demonstrates a clarity of mission that could serve the community college—not by emulating the proprietary model wholesale—but by clarifying its mission and, therefore, streamlining its processes based on clear values. That does not mean community colleges should become revenue-generating institutions or abandon the mission of serving those who are educationally underserved. But Berg (2005) maintains that for-profit schools do a more thorough job at blending their mission of generating revenue with a continual reassessment process that has positive outcome for students:

Higher education institutions should consider their own organizational goals as a mix of socio-political agendas with attention to the marketplace, understand how customer focus leads to increased diversity, align clear pedagogical objectives with the institutional mission, continually test the relevance of the missions, and use distinctive missions to test the limits of the domain. (p. 184)

The literature supports the claim that for-profit institutions are not losing sleep wondering about how to compete with traditional higher education institutions. They have identified their clients and spend time and money serving this audience. Neither are community colleges worrying about losing their students to proprietary schools. But competition among colleges and universities contributes to a series of checks and balances that can be healthy because it does not allow for any one system of education to be dominant (Clark, 1976, as cited in Morey, 2004). If higher education recognized the viability of the for-profit sector and established a more open exchange of ideas and operating procedures with the institutions who are successfully managing their revenues, there may be lessons to be learned that could benefit community colleges without sacrificing their educational mission.

References

Alfred, R. L. (2006). Managing the big picture in colleges and universities: From tactics to strategy. Westport, CT: Praeger.

Bailey, T., & Morest, V. S. (2006). Defending the community college equity agenda. Baltimore, MD: Johns Hopkins University.

Berg, G. A. (2005). Lessons from the edge: For-profit and nontraditional higher education in America. Westport, CT: Praeger.

Clark, B. R. (1960). The "cooling-out" function in higher education. The American Journal of Sociology, 65(6), 569–576.

Clowes, D. (1995). Community colleges and proprietary schools: Conflict or convergence? New Directions for Community Colleges, 91, 5–15.

Cohen, A. M., & Brawer, F. B. (2008). The American community college (5th ed.). San Francisco, CA: Jossey-Bass.

Farrell, E. F. (2003, May 30). For-profit colleges see rising minority enrollment. The Chronicle of Higher Education, A35–A36.

Grubb, W. N. (1993). The varied economic returns to postsecondary education: New evidence from the class of 1972. Journal of Human Resources, 28(2), 365–382.

Gumport, P. J. (2000). Academic restructuring: Organizational change and institutional imperatives. Higher Education, 39, 67–91.

Hassler, R. (2006). The flogging of for-profit colleges. Academic Questions, 19(3), 63–74. doi:10.1007/s12129-006-1005-9

Howard-Vital, M. (2006). The appeal of for-profit institutions. Change: The Magazine of Higher Learning, 38(1), 68–71.

Hoyle, M. (2009). For-profit higher education and stressed colleges: A strategic opportunity. In J. Martin & J. E. Samels (Eds.), Turnaround: Leading stressed colleges and universities to excellence (pp. 185–193). Baltimore, MD: Johns Hopkins University.

Kinser, K. (2006). From Main Street to Wall Street: The transformation of for-profit higher education. San Francisco, CA: Jossey-Bass.

Labland, D. N., & Lentz, B. F. (2004). Do costs differ between for-profit and not-for-profit producers of higher education? Research in Higher Education, 45(4), 429–441. doi:10.1023/B:RIHE.0000027394.33115.71

Levine, A. (2001). The remaking of the American university. Innovative Higher Education, 25(4), 253–268.

Morey, A. I. (2004). Globalization and the emergence of for-profit higher education. Higher Education, 48(1), 131–150.

Newman, J. H. (1907). The idea of a university: Defined and illustrated. New York, NY: Longmans Green.

Outcalt, C., & Schirmer, J. E. (2003). Understanding the relationships between proprietary schools and community colleges: Findings from recent literature. Community College Review, 31(1), 56–73. doi:10.1177/009155210303100104

Persell, C. H., & Wenglinsky, H. (2004). For-profit post-secondary education and civic engagement. Higher Education, 47(3), 337–359.

Potts, M. (2005). The consumerist subversion of education. Academic Questions, 18(3), 54–64. doi:10.1007/s12129-005-1018-9

Zook, G. F. (1947). Higher education for American democracy: A report of the president's commission on higher education. New York, NY: Harper & Brothers.

For-Profit Education

Senate Legislation Targets Aggressive Recruiting of Veterans by For-Profit Colleges

Chris Kirkham

The Huffington Post

January 2012

The author of this article, Chris Kirkham, earned his bachelor's and master's degrees in journalism from Northwestern University and currently reports on business issues for *The Huffington Post*. *The Huffington Post* is a left-leaning, online-only news outlet which provides commentary and analysis on politics, media, business, entertainment, and lifestyle issues. *The Huffington Post* broke journalistic ground in 2012 by being the first online-only news organization to win a Pulitzer Prize, awarded in the National Reporting category. Note as you read the article that two of the senators referenced in the article, Richard Durbin and Tom Harkin, are also referenced in Mary Beth Marklein's article for *USA Today* and David Halperin's piece for *Politico*.

1. What is the 90/10 rule and why is it relevant to veterans?

2. Why do Senators Durbin and Harkin object to for-profits counting military assistance as private funding? Why is this controversial?

3. Given that "for-profit colleges have higher graduation rates than public community colleges for short-term programs of two years and less" (a statistic confirmed by the graph from the National Center for Education Statistics), should we be skeptical about the schools' intentions in recruiting veterans for their programs? Why or why not?

Over the past two years, for-profit colleges have been aggressively recruiting returning veterans in an effort to tap into billions of dollars in federal benefits available for soldiers to pay for college.

Not only have the schools been eager to capture a new source of revenues, but former soldiers represent an added benefit for the industry: a way to secure more federal student loan and grant money.

By law, for-profit colleges must come up with at least 10 percent of their revenue from sources other than federal student aid programs in order to keep that money flowing.

The 90 percent threshold, known as the 90/10 rule, was put in place to ensure that at least 10 percent of the revenues at for-profit schools would come from the private sector, according to congressional testimony and reports from the early 1990s.

Yet many schools are complying with the requirement for private funds by dipping into a separate government revenue stream: educational benefits given to former military personnel.

The military subsidies, part of the new GI bill passed by Congress in 2008, aren't technically considered federal student aid funds, which gives corporations an incentive to actively pursue veteran enrollments.

Sen. Richard Durbin (D-Ill.) on Monday said he will propose legislation that would prevent for-profit colleges from counting the military assistance money as private funding. He, along with Sen. Tom Harkin (D-Iowa), plans to introduce the measure this week.

Durbin's legislation would, for the purpose of for-profit colleges, consider any benefits from the GI bill and the Department of Defense tuition-assistance program to be federal student aid revenues. The bill would also lower from 90 percent to 85 percent the amount of money that schools can receive from the federal government.

Lawmakers and advocacy groups say current practices have resulted in many returning veterans being steered into high-cost programs of dubious value.

Since the GI bill went into effect in 2009, it has "inadvertently created a federal bonus for the for-profit schools," Durbin told HuffPost.

"For-profit college companies have created aggressive marketing plans and a sales force specifically designed to target and enroll as many veterans, service members and family members as possible," Durbin said at a Monday forum on for-profit colleges and veteran enrollment in Chicago.

Questions about Outcomes

Trade groups representing for-profit colleges say that their schools are providing flexible course offerings and crucial career training for veterans returning from duty.

"Career colleges are proud to offer members of the military and veterans access to higher education and job training for in-demand careers," Penny Lee, managing director of the Coalition for Educational Success, an industry lobbying group, said in a statement.

Yet veterans advocates argue that the GI bill has created perverse incentives for the industry to prey on soldiers. Holly Petraeus, who handles military affairs issues at the Consumer Financial Protection Bureau, appeared with Durbin at Monday's forum and has raised concerns at past Senate hearings.

"Unfortunately, I think military folks at this point are seen like a dollar sign wearing a uniform for many recruiters in a for-profit model," she said at a hearing in July. "They're seen as cash that enables them to sell more of their product, and that's unfortunate," added Petraeus, who is married to CIA director and former Army General David Petraeus.

For-profit colleges are, on average, nearly twice as expensive as public four-year universities and cost nearly five times as much as public community colleges. But the expense of obtaining a college degree at a for-profit institution isn't necessarily translating into success in the workplace. A recent report by Harvard researchers found that students exiting for-profit colleges are more likely to be unemployed in the years after graduation than are those finishing traditional universities.

For-profit schools have higher graduation rates than public community colleges for short-term programs of two years and less but have significantly lower graduation rates for bachelor's degree programs.

While questions have been raised about whether these schools truly serve former military personnel, the institutions themselves have much to benefit from obtaining military subsidies.

Public Funds Fuel For-Profit Schools

The stakes involved are enormous for the for-profit college industry. For-profit institutions have struggled to find students willing to put up their own money for their programs but have ended up attracting mostly lower-income students who require federal aid. In order to create a private stream of revenue to comply with the 90/10 law, some schools have even gone so far as to increase tuition for some of their programs so that students must find outside private loans beyond what they receive from the government.

Complying with the law has become a central concern of higher-education companies and their shareholders. On quarterly earnings calls, executives at for-profit college companies are constantly quizzed about compliance with the law, and many have referenced the veteran-recruiting strategy in public filings with the Securities and Exchange Commission.

Internal documents from Kaplan University provided to Senator Harkin's staff showed a list of objectives related to recruiting of military, including "Grow our military enrollments to 9K per year by 2011" and "Improve 90/10 by 5 %." Among the strategies to achieve these goals were "Drive awareness via print advertising in key military publications and targeting key military installations."

As things stand today, many of the largest for-profit colleges receive more than 85 percent of their revenues from federal student aid programs, not counting military benefits. The Apollo Group, which owns the University of Phoenix, noted in a recent filing that 86 percent of its cash revenues came from federal student aid subsidies.

The Washington Post Co., which owns Kaplan University, another major industry player, said in a quarterly filing that a number of its schools could be in violation of the 90/10 rule this year, based on recent enrollment trends. Because of this, several Kaplan-run schools could be at risk of losing access to their federal funds, according to the filing.

In general, for-profit college corporations are enormous beneficiaries of government aid, relying almost entirely on the federal government for revenues and profits. In 2010, the industry took in more than $30 billion in federal student loan and Pell Grant dollars. And the eight largest for-profit college corporations received more than a half-billion dollars in veterans' assistance money from the Post-9/11 GI Bill during the 2010-11 school year.

Overall, for-profit colleges received nearly 40 percent of the $4.4 billion money given out under the GI bill program since 2009, despite educating only a quarter of the veterans using those benefits. By contrast, public colleges instructed 59 percent of the veterans and took in 40 percent of the GI bill money.

Prospects for Reform

Durbin will find that obtaining support for his bill will be a tough task, as most Republicans in Congress have traditionally been strong backers of for-profit colleges. The current House speaker, John Boehner, was a strong supporter of eliminating the 90/10 rule when he chaired the House Education and Workforce Committee from 2001 to 2006.

The for-profit college industry has also hired many Democratic lobbyists in recent years, including former House Speaker Dick Gephardt, and lawmakers on the left have increasingly come to the aid of the industry. Lee, who heads the industry trade group, was a former top adviser to Senate Majority Leader Harry Reid and a senior staff member on the Democratic National Committee.

"The industry is going to fight tooth and nail," Durbin said. "There's so much money at stake here—millions if not billions of dollars."

Retention and Graduation Rates for 2011

National Center for Education Statistics

nces.ed.gov

2011

The following graph from the National Center for Education Statistics compares retention rates and graduation rates at three different types of higher education institutions: public colleges and universities, private non-profit schools, and private for-profit schools. Public colleges and universities are largely funded through state taxes and, because they are non-profit, do not pay taxes. Private not-for-profit schools are also tax-exempt but are funded through the tuition students pay, donations (often from alumni), and money from endowments. Private for-profit schools are run by privately-owned companies and, because they seek to make money from operation of the school, pay taxes to the government on their earnings.

1. What conclusions can you draw about retention rates and graduation rates for two-year for-profit schools versus four-year for-profit schools?

2. What stakeholder in this issue would find the information in this graph most valuable? Who would find it least valuable? Why?

3. Compare the information from this graph to the criticisms leveled against for-profit schools by authors like David Halperin. Would the information in this graph ultimately help or hurt the reputation of for-profit schools?

Figure CL-7. Overall annual retention rates and graduation rates within 150 percent of normal time at degree-granting institutions, by level and control of institution and student attendance status: Fall 2009

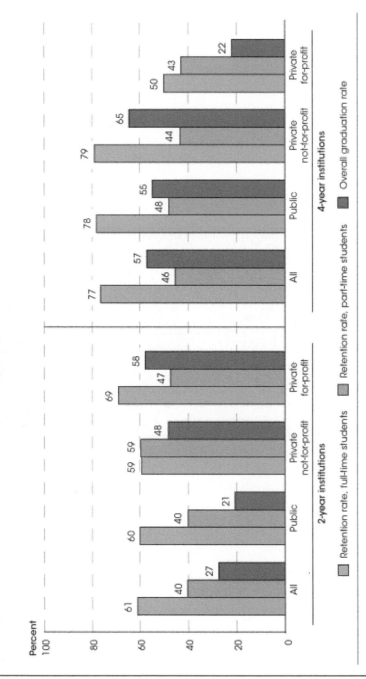

NOTE: Degree-granting institutions grant associate's or higher degrees and participate in Title IV federal financial aid programs. The retention rate is the percentage of first-time, bachelor's degree-seeking students who return to the institution to continue their studies the following year, in this case Fall 2009. The overall graduation rate is the percentage of full-time, first-time students who graduated within 150 percent of normal program completion time, in this case by Fall 2008 for the cohort that enrolled in 4-year institutions in Fall 2002 and for the students that enrolled in 2-year institutions in Fall 2005. For more information on IPEDS, see supplemental note 3. Institutions in this indicator are based on the highest degree offered. For more information on the classification of postsecondary institutions, see supplemental note 8.
SOURCE: U.S. Department of Education, National Center for Education Statistics, 2009 Integrated Postsecondary Education Data System (IPEDS), Spring 2010.

For-Profit Colleges—Are They Only After Your Money?

Ready for Zero

visual.ly

2012

This infographic was put together by Ready for Zero, a company who provides services for helping people (including students) manage and reduce their debt. This image compares price of attendance, amount spent on instruction, and average loan amount per student for three different types of institutions.

1. Why does the author include the information about how much each school spends on instruction? How is that information relevant to our understanding of this issue?

2. What argument do you think the author is making with this image? How persuasive is that argument?

3. What strategies does the author of this text use to establish credibility? How do those strategies compare with authors who use written text to achieve their purpose, such as Halperin or Schilling?

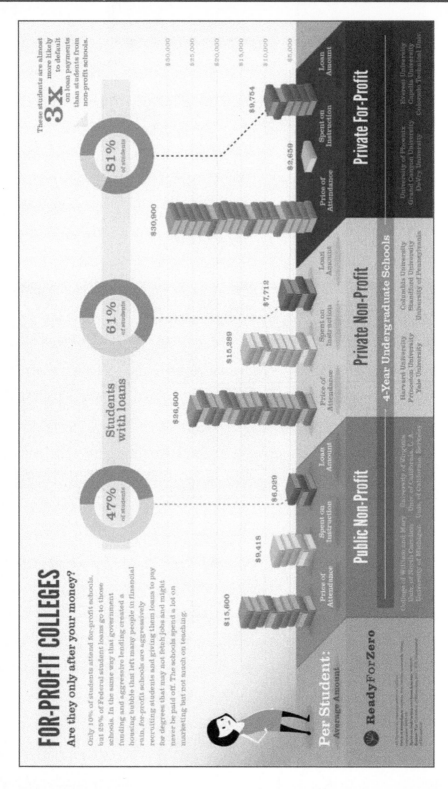

FOR-PROFIT COLLEGES
Are they only after your money?

Only 10% of students attend for-profit schools, but 25% of Federal student loans go to those schools. In the same way that government funding and aggressive lending created a housing bubble that left many people in financial ruin, for-profit schools are aggressively recruiting students and giving them loans to pay for degrees that may not fetch jobs and might never be paid off. The schools spend a lot on marketing but not much on teaching.

Per Student: Average Amount

ReadyForZero

These students are almost **3X** more likely to default on loan payments than students from non-profit schools.

Students with loans

47% of students

61% of students

81% of students

Public Non-Profit

Price of Attendance — $15,600
Spent on Instruction — $9,418
Loan Amount — $6,029

College of William and Mary
Univ. of North Carolina
University of Michigan
University of Georgia
Univ. of California, L.A.
Univ. of California, Berkeley

Private Non-Profit

Price of Attendance — $26,600
Spent on Instruction — $15,289
Loan Amount — $7,712

Harvard University
Princeton University
Yale University
Columbia University
Stanford University
University of Pennsylvania

4-Year Undergraduate Schools

Private For-Profit

Price of Attendance — $30,900
Spent on Instruction — $2,659
Loan Amount — $9,754

$30,000
$25,000
$20,000
$15,000
$10,000
$5,000

University of Phoenix
Grand Canyon University
DeVry University
Everest University
Capella University
Colorado Technical Univ.

Chapter 3

Ethical Actions:
Academic Integrity

Honor and Integrity

Plagiarism and Cheating

3 Ethical Actions: Academic Integrity

> "Why, simpleton, do you mix your verses with mine? What have you to do, foolish man, with writings that convict you of theft? Why do you attempt to associate foxes with lions, and make owls pass for eagles? Though you had one of Ladas's legs, you would not be able, blockhead, to run with the other leg of wood."
>
> -Marcus Valerius Martial

Plagiarism is by no means a new problem. In an epigram addressed "to a plagiarist" nearly two thousand years ago, the poet Martial raises ethical concerns about taking someone else's work and passing it off as your own. As Martial says, a fox may be cunning, but he's no lion. In other words, you might think you're being clever by putting your name on one of Shakespeare's sonnets, but you're no Shakespeare. Taking credit for the work of another might seem like a good idea in the moment, but if you try to build on plagiarized ideas, it's like trying to run a sprint with one good leg and the other made of a tree trunk.

When we talk about academic integrity, then, what do we mean? Academic integrity refers to approaching your scholarly endeavors with honesty, and striving to create an atmosphere where both faculty and students can trust that the work being produced is original, thoughtful, and professional. When standards of academic integrity are being upheld in an institution of higher education, the entire campus community benefits; when academic integrity isn't practiced, true scholarly discourse becomes impossible.

Students can't grow and thrive when the work submitted is not fully their own. After all, how can you build on skills and ideas that were never yours in the first place?

Maintaining academic integrity is indispensable in writing because it allows your audience to trust you. *The Harvard Guide for Using Sources* says "taking credit for anyone else's work is stealing, and it is unacceptable in all academic situations, whether you do it intentionally or by accident." However, despite a near-universal agreement among students and faculty that plagiarism is unacceptable, a 2001 study published in *Ethics and Behavior* shows that cheating in one form or another has been prevalent in higher education for decades (McCabe, Butterfield, and Treviño 219).

Unfortunately, modern advances in technology have helped the problem of plagiarism in academia grow to new heights. The Internet, as discussed by many of the authors in this chapter, has opened up a wide frontier for cheating. In a *Denver Post* piece titled "Rise in Student Plagiarism Cases Attributed to Blurred Lines of Digital World," Kevin Simpson quotes Colorado State University English professor Sarah Sloane who speaks about the rise of "blatant cut-and-paste copying from the Internet." Sloane's experience testifies to how technology allows for students to easily copy and plagiarize information with the simple click of a mouse.

We're not just talking about students and straightforward cases of direct plagiarism, either. The corruption of academic integrity has been seen in teachers, too. Earlier this year, *The Atlantic* published "It's Time for a Real Code of Ethics in Teaching," which exposed teachers who allegedly changed student scores on standardized tests in public schools in Atlanta, Georgia. An incident such as this calls the character of even trusted public servants into question.

The issue of academic integrity remains fraught with complication. Plagiarism, cheating, honor, intellectual property rights, and copyright are all aspects of this problem worthy of discussion. As long as the pressure to succeed academically and professionally exists, the temptation to bend the boundaries of ethical behavior will remain. How we approach and frame the issue can make all the difference in understanding the causes, consequences, and strategies for preventing dishonest academic behavior.

Works Cited

Harvard Guide for Citing Sources. Harvard Collage Writing Program, 2013. Web. 07 July 2013.

<http://usingsources.fas.harvard.edu/icb/icb.do>.

It's Time for a Real Code of Ethics in Teaching

Noah Berlatsky

The Atlantic

September 2010

Noah Berlatsky is the editor of *The Hooded Utilitarian*, an online comics and culture website. Berlatsky's article, "It's Time for a Real Code of Ethics in Teaching," was published in *The Atlantic* in April of 2013 immediately following a cheating scandal in public schools in Atlanta, Georgia. Berlatsky reports how teachers were accused of changing answers on their students' high-stakes tests. As you read Berlatksy's discussion on cheating, consider more than just the ethics of teachers cheating on student exams. Consider, too, the causes and conditions that may have led these teachers to cheat.

1. What kind of ethics does Berlatsky think teachers need?

2. What argument does Berlatsky make about the way teachers are perceived and what is expected of them? How does Berlatsky relate the public perception of teachers to cheating?

3. What connections can be made between the student conditions surrounding the scandal discussed in "Harvard Cheating Scandal: Can an Honor Code Prevent Cheating at Harvard?" and this scandal involving teachers in Atlanta public schools?

Earlier this week at *The Atlantic*, Emily Richmond asked whether high-stakes testing *caused the Atlanta schools cheating scandal*. The answer, I would argue, is yes... just not in the way you might think. Tests don't cause unethical behavior. But they did cause the Atlanta cheating scandal, and they are doing damage to the teaching profession.

The argument that tests do *not* cause unethical behavior is fairly straightforward, and has been articulated by a number of writers. Jonathan Chait quite correctly points out that unethical behavior occurs in virtually all professions—and that it occurs particularly when there are clear incentives to succeed.

Incentivizing any field increases the impetus to cheat. Suppose journalism worked the way teaching traditionally had. You get hired at a newspaper, and your advancement and pay are dictated almost entirely by your years on the job, with almost no chance of either becoming a star or of getting fired for incompetence. Then imagine journalists changed that and instituted the current system, where you can get really successful if your bosses like you or be fired if they don't. You could look around and see scandal after scandal—*phone hacking! Jayson Blair! NBC's exploding truck! Janet Cooke! Stephen Glass!*—that could plausibly be attributed to this frightening new world in which journalists had an incentive to cheat in order to get ahead.

It holds true of any field. If Major League Baseball instituted tenure, and maybe used tee-ball rules where you can't keep score and everybody gets a chance to hit, it could stamp out steroid use. *Students* have been cheating on tests forever—massive, systematic cheating, you could say. Why? Because they have an incentive to do well. Give teachers and administrators an incentive for their students to do well, and more of them will cheat.

For Chait, then, teaching has just been made more like journalism or baseball; it has gone from an incentiveless occupation to one with incentives.

There's an interesting slippage here, though. Chait refers to violations of journalistic ethics—like the phone-hacking scandal—and suggests they are analogous to Major-League steroid use, and that both are similar to teachers (or students) cheating on tests. But is phone hacking "cheating"? Chait says it is, but I doubt that that's the first term that would leap to mind for most people. Journalism isn't a game like basketball, where the goal is to win or rack up the most points or the highest test scores. It's an (arguably debased, but still) profession. Phone hacking was, then, not an example of cheating. It was a violation of professional ethics. And those ethics are not arbitrarily imposed, but are intrinsic to the practice of journalism as a profession committed to public service and to truth. If journalism were incentivized like teaching, Chait might be paid based on how many people link to his stories—which might lead him to go around the web linking to himself on random comments threads. *That* would, arguably, be "cheating"—but it also would have little to do with journalistic ethics as we usually understand them.

This is an important distinction. Behaving ethically matters, but how it matters, and what it means, depends strongly on the context in which it occurs. Thus, the fact that teachers in the Atlanta schools were "cheating" on tests tells you a lot about how teachers are perceived and what is expected of them. Ethics for teachers is not, apparently, first and foremost about educating their students, or broadening their minds. Rather, ethics for teachers in our current system consists in following the rules. The implicit, linguistic signal being given is that teachers are not like journalists or doctors, committed to a profession and to the moral code needed to achieve their professional goals. Instead, they are like athletes playing games, or (as Chait says) like children taking tests.

Using "cheating" as an ethical lens tends to both trivialize and infantilize teacher's work. Professions with social respect and social capital, like doctors and lawyers, collaborate in the creation of their own standards. The assumption is that those standards are intrinsic to the profession's goals, and that, therefore, professionals themselves are best equipped to establish and monitor them. Teachers' standards, though, are imposed from outside—as if teachers are children, or as if teaching is a game.

High-stakes testing, then, does lead to cheating. It does not create unethical behavior—but it does create the particular unethical behavior of "cheating."

And while it's true that unethical behavior in itself is not a reason to get rid of incentives for excellence, it seems like this scandal might be a good moment to think about what incentives we actually are creating, and why.

For example, would we want to tie oncologist salaries to patient outcomes, so that their pay was docked if too many patients died? You would then have a case where doctors would probably start cheating the system by falsifying patient records. That cheating would, surely, be a sign of something wrong—not because it caused unethical behavior, but because it created a system in which bureaucratic record-keeping had replaced meaningful moral commitment.

This is what has happened with teaching. We have reached a point where we can only talk about the ethics of the profession in terms of cheating or not cheating, as if teachers' main ethical duty is to make sure that scantron bubbles get filled in correctly. Teachers, like journalists, should have a commitment to truth; like doctors, they have a duty of care. Translating those commitments and duties into a bureaucratized measure of cheating-or-not-cheating diminishes ethics; it turns it into a game. For teachers it is, literally, demoralizing. It severs the moral experience of teaching from the moral evaluation of teaching, which makes it almost impossible for good teachers (in all the senses of "good") to stay in the system.

It's a bad thing for teachers to cheat on tests. But the fact that badness for teachers has come to be defined in large part as cheating on tests is even worse. If we want better schools, we don't just need more ethical teachers. We need better ethics *for* teachers—ethics that treat them as adults and professionals, not like children playing games.

A Question of Honor

William Chace

American Scholar

Spring 2012

Throughout his long career in academia, William Chace has served as the Vice-Provost for Academic Planning and Development at Stanford University, the president of Wesleyan University, and the president of Emory University. An outspoken advocate for institutional reform in higher education, Chace is perhaps best known as the author of *100 Semesters: My Adventures as Student, Professor, and University President and What I Learned Along the Way*. In "A Question of Honor," Chace examines student responsibility in maintaining academic honesty and integrity on college campuses and universities. While reading Chace, consider the ways in which his experience may have shaped his perspective on this issue.

1. How does Chace discuss originality within his conversation of plagiarism?

2. Why does Chace argue that, "At its core, cheating is self-destructive?"

3. Chace asks, "What would it take to transform classrooms throughout the United States into arenas of moral practice? How would American higher education look then?" How would you respond to these questions?

One of the gloomiest recent reports about the nation's colleges and universities reinforces the suspicion that students are studying less, reading less, and learning less all the time: "American higher education is characterized," sociologists Richard Arum and Josipa Roksa said last year, "by limited or no learning for a large proportion of students." Their book, *Academically Adrift*, joins a widening, and often negative, reassessment of what universities contribute to American life. Even President Obama has gotten into the act, turning one problem with higher education into an applause line in his latest State of the Union address. "So let me put colleges and universities on notice," he said, "If you can't stop tuition from going up, the funding you get from taxpayers will go down. Higher education can't be a luxury—it is an economic imperative that every family in America should be able to afford."

Where should we lay the blame for the worsening state of one of the foundations of American civilization, one that has long filled us with justifiable pride? The big public universities are already bogged down by diminishing financial support from the states; private education is imperiled by tuition costs that discourage hundreds of thousands of middle-class and poorer students from applying. Some schools have made heroic attempts to diversify their student bodies, but too little financial aid is available to make access possible for all the applicants with academic promise.

What is happening inside the classroom for those who do get in? Who is teaching the students? Less and less often it is a member of an institution's permanent faculty, and rarer still one of its distinguished professors. More and more of the teaching has been parceled out to part-time instructors who have no hope of landing a full-time position. Because of this, their loyalty to the school that hired them, and to the students they will probably meet in just one course and never again, has diminished.

Amid such melancholy reports from the front, campus amusements that have nothing to do with education—intercollegiate athletics leads the festivities—sop up money, keep coaches in the headlines, and divert public attention from the essential mission of education: to strengthen the minds of young people and to prepare them to cope with the demands of life.

Perhaps that is why, when the public is asked about colleges and universities, the response is increasingly negative with each passing year.

According to the Pew Research Center, most American citizens (57 percent) say that higher education "fails to provide good value for the money students and their families spend." Within the innermost sanctum of the academy the view is almost the same: "About four-in-ten college presidents say the system is headed in the wrong direction," according to Pew. If university presidents, who by profession and temperament routinely find every glass more than half-full, are so disconsolate, the public can't be expected to be optimistic.

Were this situation to get any worse, it could legitimately be called a crisis. But American colleges and universities are not going under anytime soon. Despite their problems, they employ hundreds of thousands of people, keep towns and even cities financially afloat, and offer cultural resources and, yes, athletic and other entertainments. They adorn the nation with their well-kept campuses. The research done on those campuses makes us safer, improves our health, and inspires our nobler human impulses. Along the way, colleges and universities provide multiyear habitat for millions of postadolescents who, more often than not, are bewilderingly short of ideas about what to do after leaving secondary school. And they continue to offer a haven to those who finish their undergraduate years and do not or cannot enter the present bleak job market. Most of these students are happy to find themselves—for four, five, or even six years—with other people their age, with whom they can develop social skills while entertaining each other and themselves and exposing their minds to selected academic topics. For all these reasons, the college experience in this country long ago became one of its most acceptable rites of passage. The schools are there because they serve a variety of needs. The challenge is to make them better.

But now they are up against a spectrum of problems whose magnitude they have never faced before. What can they do—amid financial pressures, dwindling public esteem, pre-professional anxieties on the part of their students, and eroded faculty loyalty—to recover the prestige they once enjoyed?

One answer, I believe, rests in what they can do, and must do, about a large and ugly presence on almost every campus: academic dishonesty. Cheating now hurts American higher education; it might well be cheating that can begin to save it.

In college and university classrooms across the country, every student sooner or later faces the apparently simple task of writing an essay. The essay might focus on a philosophical topic (the argumentative structure of John Stuart Mill's *On Liberty*, for example), or the student's interpretation of a play (Harold Pinter's *The Homecoming*, say), or a political issue (the likely shape of demographic changes in the United States in the next 20 years). The topics are endless, but the ground rules are not: be clear, employ the rules of logic, and most pointedly, be original.

The last requirement is where the system gets confused. No teacher really expects any student essay to revolutionize our understanding of the world, to be so original that the firmament begins to wobble. The opportunity to be truly original has gotten rarer through the eons. As Mark Twain put it, "What a good thing Adam had. When he said a good thing he knew nobody had said it before." No, originality means something more modest: that the student, after much reflection and weighing of the assembled evidence, has written in a way that reflects the particular contours of his or her thinking. The turns and twists of the prose, the things emphasized and the things neglected, the way the essay opens and closes, and how errors, some small and some large, inevitably infiltrate the prose—these features, constituting the essay's fingerprint, are evidence that the student has written something original. But truth to tell, it's not working that way. Today, lots of students cheat. They use the work of others. They buy essays. They plagiarize. Still, even though the Web makes cheating easier than ever before, and thus more prevalent, the phenomenon of cheating is nothing new. Students have been at it for a long time.

Eighty years ago, Dean Clarence W. Mendell of Yale University declared that the problem of cheating at his school was widespread enough to require instant reform: "It is altogether imperative that the growing disregard of this traditional standard on the part of many unthinking undergraduates should be wiped out." He sternly added, "the faculty has but one attitude toward cheating, an attitude shared, we believe, by the undergraduate body." But 45 years later, in 1976, another Yale dean, Eva Balogh, described cheating at the school as "rampant." New Haven hadn't changed much, and Yale was no isolated case. That same year, on the other side of the country, the student newspaper at the University of Southern California reported that as many as 40 percent of students there were plagiarizing their written work.

The first comprehensive study of cheating at colleges and universities (5,000 students at almost 100 institutions) was completed in 1964. It found that 75 percent of the students had engaged in one form or another of academic dishonesty. A generation later, in 2001, an authoritative survey conducted by Donald L. McCabe of Rutgers and his colleagues concluded that cheating was now "prevalent" across the country and that "some forms of cheating have increased dramatically in the last 30 years."

Indeed, every study over the decades has concluded that cheating at American colleges and universities is rampant. Despite Dean Mendell's desire long ago to wipe it out, grim admonitions from college presidents year after year, and any number of cheating eruptions around the nation, dishonesty, indigenous to almost every campus, flourishes. A recent survey by the online journal *Inside Higher Ed* of more than a thousand chief academic officers at schools nationwide revealed that more than two-thirds of them believe that cheating has become a much worse problem than it once was. But, interestingly enough, fewer than a quarter of them thought it was on the rise on their own campuses.

Students cheat for many reasons, some of them even doing so without malign intent, either because they don't understand the rules of academic honesty or are confused about the assignment. Some students cheat because of pressures to succeed in a competitive world. Some cheat because they are lazy, tired, or indifferent. Some, overwhelmed by the oceanic wash of information pouring in upon them as they open their computers to the Web, conclude that there is nothing new to say. And some cheat because they look at all academic tasks as exciting opportunities to fool the system as well as the teacher.

They learn early. The Josephson Institute of Ethics sampled more than 40,000 public and private high school students and found that three-fifths of them admitted to having cheated on a test. Nearly half of these were honors students; a third had cheated twice or more in the previous year. In high school, every applicant to college is given an open invitation to cheat—the personal essay that college admissions offices require. How many students write these essays without help? How many parents write them? How many friends, counselors, and commercial agencies write them? No one knows, but the pressure to get such help must be precisely as strong as the pressure to write the kind of essay that will win respect from an admissions dean. The temptation to cross the line shows up early in a young person's life.

As with any transgressive cultural activity both scorned and widespread (running red lights, using recreational drugs, evading taxes), some cheaters are exposed while others go untouched. For every cheating student who is nabbed, another slips under the radar. Nor is the radar kept in good working order. Some teachers know when a student's work is fraudulent but elect to do nothing. It takes time, and time is expensive; bringing a student before a campus judicial council is also labor intensive, and the outcome is unpredictable; students or their parents can retain attorneys to fight the charges and endlessly complicate the procedure; administrators cannot be counted on to back up professors making accusations. Professors like the elevation of teaching but not the grubby business of prosecuting. For the increasing number of adjunct instructors, vigilance about cheating could put their professional futures at risk. They could earn an unappealing tag: "high maintenance." And some teachers have concluded that the only person hurt by cheating is the cheater, and so they wash their hands of the entire business.

On many campuses, dishonesty is simply accepted as an unwelcome but ubiquitous feature of teaching and learning, the equivalent of friction in the pedagogical machine. Reflect on what Dean Mendell said, but perhaps only dimly understood, all those decades ago. The "unthinking undergraduates" at Yale who were cheating made up part of the undergraduate body at Yale as a whole that presumably shared the faculty's revulsion toward cheating. Denouncing a wrong does not necessarily mean being innocent of committing it. Most students know that cheating surrounds them, but few see ways to do anything about it, even when they hold it in contempt. Some of those who cheat are morally offended by others who cheat, but they too are, for obvious reasons, disinclined to complain. In every cultural domain, we grow accustomed to breaches that, with time and repetition, we wind up believing are normal.

But how does cheating become tolerated, assimilated, and ultimately absorbed into our understanding of normality? The answer partly resides in the peculiar kind of wrong it is. Compared with the violation of copyright, a crime punishable in a court of law, cheating at school is "only" a moral and ethical wrong. Plagiarism, one of the most common forms of cheating, often leaves behind no apparent victim; the author from whose body of work the plagiarist extracts a useful portion might never know anything has happened; and the work, despite the theft, remains in the author's possession (lawyers call this "usufruct"). The downloading without attribution of finished essays from the Internet, another immensely popular way of completing classroom assignments, harms no honest author, as copying them for publication would. And if several students conspire to compose an essay in the name of one, who is the exploited party? Any outrage can seem tolerable if it looks victimless.

Consider, moreover, with what emollients any feeling of guilt about cheating can be soothed in a student's mind. To begin, the culture outside the campus gates seems long ago to have accepted dishonesty when it comes to the writings of certain important people. Just how much of *Profiles in Courage* did John F. Kennedy write and how much did Theodore Sorensen write? How strongly do we care? What should we say about the Rev. Martin Luther King Jr.'s doctoral dissertation at Boston University, once we know that it is filled with the writings of others, copied down paragraph after paragraph, in vast profusion? Think also of Roger Clemens, Barry Bonds, and almost everyone involved in international cycling—sports figures about whom allegations of cheating are now featured in every newspaper in the land. What of the plagiarism of prize-winning historians Doris Kearns Goodwin and Stephen E. Ambrose, not to mention the elaborate transfer, generations ago, of the ideas of German philosophers into the "philosophy" of Samuel Taylor Coleridge? Don't we just note such derelictions and then generously move on to matters more pressing?

The much-quoted aphorism by T. S. Eliot that "immature poets imitate; mature poets steal" can give license enough to a student faced with the chore of writing an original senior thesis on, say, Eliot himself. That immature student, emboldened by fantasies, can think himself into maturity by doing no more than what Eliot said the great customarily do: steal.

Yet another social reality erodes the moral offensiveness of cheating, a reality that universities and colleges find themselves ill equipped to cope with. Given that so much professional life—the legal and medical systems, entrepreneurial capitalism, the operations of established companies and the public sector, the very working life that many college graduates will enter—

is based on the pooling of ideas and the energy of teamwork, how is it that the academic world can demand wholly independent work and originality? Indeed, students can wonder why colleges observe the principles of solitary labor when they will soon work in offices where ideas are meant to be merged and where the inspiration of one person achieves value only when coupled with the inspiration of many others.

Nowhere is this tension between the ethical code of the campus and that of the working world more awkwardly felt than in the discipline of computer science. On campuses, students taking courses in this fertile area of study are urged to work independently to develop their skills, but if they are fortunate enough upon graduation to get a job with a firm making use of such skills, they will join highly ambitious teams of men and women who, to succeed, will merge their talent and their scientific knowledge to create something—a new piece of money-making software, for instance—that not one of them, working alone, could have come up with.

On campus, solitary independence; off campus, collective energy. The contradiction between these two methods partially explains why the greatest incidence of cheating at high-powered universities like Stanford and others occurs among students enrolled in computer science courses. Those students must hold in their minds that a wrong in one place is highly prized in another. Nor is it irrelevant, as one imagines the incentives to cheat, to consider the attractive beginning salaries offered to successful computer-science graduates of schools such as Stanford. The urge to succeed can yield to the temptation to cheat if a good job awaits just beyond the campus gates.

Few students are ignorant of the prevailing ethical standards of their home institutions. Should those standards be strong and consistently enforced, and should those institutions provide example after example of moral courage, students who cheat do so with the knowledge that they are violating a code of honor that has substance. But if the institutions themselves exhibit questionable ethical standards—leaving a trail of shoddy compromise, corner cutting, and breaches of trust—those students come to understand that honor is only a word and not a practice. Since nothing more quickly leaps into a young person's mind than the recognition of hypocrisy, cheating becomes easier once institutional duplicity is detected.

In colleges and universities, then, where primary teaching duties are given over to part-time instructors so that well-paid professors can devote themselves to research projects; where tuition is very high but certain classes are large and crowded; where extra tutorial help is lavishly provided to students on athletic scholarships (many of whom never would be admitted on academic grounds) and only rarely to students who play no intercollegiate sports; where the values seem to be corporate rather than academic; where, as at Claremont McKenna College, an administrator submits false SAT scores to publications like *U.S. News & World Report* in order to boost the school's "selective" reputation; and where, as a consequence, campus morale is low, some students can and will respond as one would to any organization proclaiming one set of values while practicing another. Students entering colleges and universities are told that these places are, and have been, "special." When they turn out to be commonplace, commonplace standards will triumph.

Students are under personal, parental, and pre-professional pressures that have never been more intense. Getting into the right school, and achieving in such a way that one can then proceed to the next right station in life, makes the college experience for many young people more a matter of getting ahead—acquiring the proper credential—than undergoing a unique ritual devoted to self-knowledge and intellectual growth. If resources beyond oneself are needed to get ahead—even illicit resources such as the writings of others, all easily acquired by a few keyboard strokes in the privacy of one's room, and all gained with no apparent sense of injury to anyone else—so be it. Nothing seems lost; forward motion has been sustained.

The most appalling aspect of the rise of cheating on campus in recent times is that some professors themselves have offered sophisticated defenses of plagiarism. An ambitious student can now turn to the writings of teachers who have made ingenious theoretical defenses for the very cheating practices proscribed by the universities at which they teach. If a student faces the accusation that his work is not original, that student can respond: Don't you know that the idea of "originality" has been hammered into nothingness by thinkers such as Michel Foucault? After all, he proclaimed four decades ago that the very idea of an author, any author, is dead, and hence there is no one around to claim originality. Instead, wrote Foucault, in *What Is an Author?*, we should welcome a new world in which the inhibiting codes of authorship have been cast to the winds:

> All discourses, whatever their status, form, value, and whatever the treatment to which they will be subjected, would then develop in the anonymity of a murmur. We would no longer hear the questions that have been rehashed for so long: Who really spoke? Is it really he and not someone else? With what authenticity or originality? … And behind all these questions, we would hear hardly anything but the stirring of an indifference: What difference does it make who is speaking?

Once a student adopts, under so impressive an aegis as Foucault, an indifference about authorship, the coast is clear and all noisome ethical restrictions can be jettisoned. *Perspectives on Plagiarism* (1999), edited by Lise Buranen and Alice Myers Roy, brings together essays demonstrating the problem. Gilbert Larochelle, who teaches political philosophy at the University of Quebec and who is a professorial devotee of the celebrated philosopher, puts it this way: "Can plagiarism still exist in an intellectual universe where it has become impossible to differentiate the representation from the referent, the copy from the original, and the copyist from the author?" Another teacher, Debora Halbert of Otterbein College, inspired by both Foucault and feminism, ups the ante and provides students who might be thinking of plagiarizing with dreams of anti-establishment revolution: "Appropriation or plagiarism are acts of sedition against an already established mode of knowing, a way of knowing indebted to male creation and property rights. … No concept of intellectual property should exist in a feminist future." Yet another professor, Marilyn Randall of the University of Western Ontario, writes that "later critical discourse whole-heartedly adopts the notion of plagiarism as an intentional political act" and, perhaps sensitive to the unattractive connotations of the word itself, repackages plagiarism as "discursive repetition." Buoyed up by such sophisticated arguments, and keen to be part of a bright new future, students might well be ashamed if they did *not* cheat.

A less theoretical defense of cheating comes by way of something called "patchwriting." It combines low-level Foucauldian thinking ("no such thing as originality") with American confessionalism ("folks, let's be honest, everybody cheats all the time"). It argues that whatever we write is no more than proof that we are forever standing on the shoulders of giants. We're fooling ourselves if we believe that we are writing something that has not, in so many words, been written before. Human beings can't be original. As a species, we endlessly use and reuse what has been used and reused before, forever recycling the logic, the words, the turns of phrase, and all the rest. So why not, says a chief apologist for patchwriting, go easy on the students? Teach them, says Rebecca Moore Howard of Syracuse University, that it's okay to download essays from the Internet, to pluck useful phrases or even paragraphs from Wikipedia, and to cobble whatever seems to fit together into the semblance of an essay ready for grading. "[Patchwriting] is a form of verbal sculpture, molding new shapes from preexisting materials," Howard writes. "It is something that all academic writers do. Patchwriting belongs not in a category with cheating on exams and purchasing term papers but in a category with the ancient tradition of learning through apprenticeship and mimicry." It's really how we all write anyway, if only we had the courage as patchwriters to say so.

What explains this peculiar defense of plagiarism? Pedagogical and professional anxiety may be one cause: if we go after cheaters, pursuing them all the way to the judicial councils, we will have done nothing, say the defenders, but reinforce the barriers between teachers and students, the invidious social hierarchies separating those possessing the standards (even if they are ill-paid teachers of composition) and those supplying the tuition (even if they are freshmen and sophomores). In the interests of both candor and classroom egalitarianism, why not let everyone in on the secret about writing: plagiarism is at the heart of prose; it's how it gets done. Once that forbidden truth is out in the open, genuine teaching can begin. Neither students nor teacher will feel inferior any longer. They will hold in common the abiding truth of writing: it's all patched together.

And yet. As I have written these words, one by one, knowing all the while that none of them is original with me, all of them (except "usufruct") drawn from the common well of English diction, and recognizing that neither my sentence construction nor my way of organizing paragraphs is unique to me, and while I have gone to many sources to find the information I've needed to write, I believe this essay is mine, mine alone, and would not exist had I not written it. I don't believe I have patched, or that I've plagiarized. As it is with me, so it has always been with writers, and so it will always be. The arguments protecting or even championing plagiarism fall before the palpable evidence of originality, modest and grand, ephemeral and enduring, as it has existed in writing everywhere.

Almost every reader of this essay began, I assume, with the presumption that plagiarism is a serious wrong. Most readers will find its assorted defenders more ridiculous than credible, whether they are disciples of postmodern theory or teachers warning students away from the allegedly phony attractions of originality. Such readers can find kinship, then, with the students who do not cheat. To them we must turn our attention. Both groups have a stake in a clean system. For the students, it means grades honestly earned; for the readers, it means the hope that this country's educational enterprise is ethically sound. Together the two groups can find much to respect in what another kind of composition teacher, Augustus M. Kolich, expressed a generation ago:

> [P]lagiarism cuts deeply into the integrity and morality of what I teach my students, and it sullies my notions about the sanctity of my relationship to students. It is a lie, and although lies are often private matters between two people, plagiarism is never merely private because it breaches a code of behavior that encompasses my classroom, my teaching, my university, and my society.

Here, then, is the situation: abundant evidence that something is wrong, coupled with an abiding sense that the wrong is pernicious and widespread, and highly resistant to remedies. So, to quote Vladimir Lenin's famous pamphlet (whose title was plagiarized from a novel by Nikolai Chernyshevsky): *What Is to Be Done?*

Assuming that something should be done, one response could be to stiffen the apparatus of policing. Internet sites such as "Turnitin," to which students and teachers can submit student work to see if it contains material from essays already on electronic file, could be employed by more and more teachers to track down those who misuse the material. Penalties could be increased; the pursuers could try to become more clever than the pursued; teaching could take on an even more suspicious and hostile attitude. But this plan of attack might well underestimate the resourceful talents of young people—versed as they are in every aspect of the digital world—to outwit even vigilant professorial hawks.

But another strategy already exists. Some institutions, rare but sturdily resolute in spirit, have fought the infection of cheating for decades. Many of them, but hardly all, are small liberal arts colleges. They have had history and tradition at their back. All of them have expended both time and social capital in encouraging honesty and trust. Instead of a campus culture in which adversarial tensions between administrators and students are a given and where cheating is presumed, these institutions convey to the students themselves the authority to monitor the ethical behavior of their classmates. Every student on these campuses is informed, directly and formally, what honor means and why it is important. Every student is presumed to want every classmate to observe the principles of honor. This puts everyone at the same moral starting line. Then students are expected to act as if the work of one is in fact the responsibility of all. Nothing about this is perfunctory. Indeed, at these schools, academic honor is a dominating concern.

Which are these colleges and universities, few in number and proud of their traditions? Washington and Lee, Haverford, Rice, Cal Tech, and the University of Virginia are among them. At some of them, the students themselves hear cases of alleged honor violations and render the judgments with no members of the faculty joining them. Professors note the violation; students then take charge. At such schools, when students cheat, students mete out the justice, which can be swift and uncompromising. At a few of these schools, there exists what is called the "single sanction": any violation of the honor code means permanent expulsion. At all these places, honor has been enshrined as fundamental to the history and the life of the institution. Known to every student who enrolls, the code of honor is already in practice while they matriculate; it is remembered with respect after they graduate. By maintaining such systems, these campuses are less likely to be collections of individuals than, at their best, small societies of truthful men and women. They see the dangers of cheating for what they are: practices in which many students can be hurt by the dishonesty of a few. And not just students but, in the words of Professor Kolich, the university as a whole, and the larger society beyond the gates.

Can the number of such campuses increase? More than 100 American campuses have some form of honor code already, even if many of them give only lip service to the concept. What would it take to transform classrooms throughout the United States into arenas of moral practice? How would American higher education look then? Might it have in hand one small but powerful argument to turn aside the criticisms hurled against it by those who think that it has lost its ethical bearings and who see it as given over to misplaced values such as pre-professional practicalities or simple-minded political correctness? Such critics—noisy and passionate—might be brought to attention with the news that moral instruction, at the foundation of some of the nation's best schools, had been given a central position at other schools across the country.

If such a reconsideration of one of the essential purposes of higher education were to take place, things on American campuses could begin to seem quite different. Instead of training a suspicious eye on students, professors could turn to them with an understanding of how much they have at stake, and how much they fear they can lose, as long as cheating thrives. In those students who do not cheat resides a core of strength, a habit of mind and morality, thus far employed at too few schools. Those schools should remind themselves of one central fact: at their best, students are dedicated to learning. Students who cheat undermine who they are. At its core, cheating is self-destructive.

The lesson is about students and what they alone can do, not about schools and what they have failed to do. The institutions, after all, can always find ways to walk away from the problem. Although no school welcomes negative publicity about academic dishonesty, administrators can always point the finger downward at those who break the rules. And professors can always distance themselves in the same way. So it is the students who stand at the center of this drama.

Doubters might say that what works at small schools couldn't work at larger ones. Big universities, sprawling with students, promote anonymity, and with anonymity comes blamelessness. At such places, no one is responsible for anything and honor codes are bound to fail. But even big places are composed of individual classes, each taught by one teacher, often in small rooms where, once again, principles of individual honor and personal responsibility can be secured and, once again, those with the most to lose can act to bring honesty to bear. Keep in mind that though universities might be large or small, the average student-teacher ratio today is excellent, according to a 2010 survey by *U.S. News & World Report*: slightly less than 15-to-one, with liberal arts colleges averaging 12.2 students per faculty member, and national universities averaging 15.5 students per faculty member. The numbers are small enough to permit, if not to encourage, local and intimate moral responsibility.

To do nothing is not an answer. Once the emptiness of such a response to so serious a problem is recognized, a form of education beneficial to all can come. To encourage moral awareness is to appreciate what rests at the heart of what it means to teach. In the end, it also rests at the heart of what it means to learn.

Should such a pattern of student responsibility spread more widely across the nation, classroom after classroom will benefit. Students will more fully understand how legitimate societies are established and how they survive—by a consensual agreement that they will govern themselves by rule, by mutual respect, and by vigilance. At that point, universities and colleges will be able to recover some of the trust and respect they have lost. They will be able to say, with authority, that the essential virtue of honorable behavior is both promoted and protected on campus.

Honor and Integrity

Harvard Cheating Scandal: Can an Honor Code Prevent Cheating at Harvard?

Justin Pope and Lindsey Anderson

Huffington Post

August 2012

Justin Pope and Lindsey Anderson are Associated Press reporters that covered a cheating scandal at Harvard University where 125 students inappropriately assisted each other on a take-home final exam. The piece criticizes Harvard for not having an honor code established. The AP story was picked up by *The Huffington Post* and coupled on its website with a short video covering the event. The resulting multi-genre web page shows how information can be communicated not only with words, but also with images and sound. You can find the page by inputting the title of Pope and Anderson's article into the search box on *The Huffington Post*'s website.

1. According to the article, what percentage of college students cheat and what is the traditional response of a university?

2. After watching the video on *The Huffington Post*'s website, consider the differences in genre between reading the article and watching the video. How does a differing genre shape the effectiveness of the authors' purpose with their audience?

3. How does Pope and Anderson's argument align with your reading of "Cheating in Academic Institutions: A Decade of Research"?

Harvard University, whose motto "Veritas" means "truth," has never had a student honor code in its nearly 400-year history—as far as it knows. But allegations against 125 students for improperly collaborating on a take-home final in the spring are leading to renewed consideration of the idea.

Though widely associated with college life, formal honor codes are hard to implement and fairly rare on American campuses. But some would argue they're especially important at places like Harvard that are wellsprings of so many future leaders in government and business.

Cheating and plagiarism are serious rule violations at Harvard, just like anywhere else. But Donald McCabe of Rutgers University, an expert on academic cheating, puts the number of schools that go beyond such rules with some sort of formal honor code at no more than about 100. Details vary, but the commonalities are a pledge signed—and largely enforced—by students not to cheat. Some require students also to report any cheating they witness.

At a few places, such as the military academies, the University of Virginia and some tradition-bound liberal arts colleges, honor codes extend far beyond academic misconduct and cover any lying and cheating. Many such schools are clustered in the South. William & Mary, in Virginia, claims to have had the first student honor code, dating to 1779, at the behest of Thomas Jefferson, an alumnus and the state governor at the time.

"You have surveys showing between two-thirds and three-quarters of college students cheat, and higher ed leaders don't care, or at least not enough to do anything about it," said David Callahan, senior fellow at Demos, a think tank, and author of the book *The Cheating Culture: Why More Americans Are Doing Wrong to Get Ahead*.

If cheating cost schools points in the *U.S. News & World Report* college rankings, he joked, "then you'd see more action."

Research dating back 40 years shows lower rates of cheating on campuses with honor codes—in McCabe's data, the rate is about a quarter lower.

Still, such numbers show codes aren't a panacea, and he says they won't work everywhere.

For schools that have them, honor codes are a point of pride, with visible effects on campus. At tiny all-male Hampden-Sydney in Virginia, students leave their backpacks in hallways and other public places without fear of theft. At schools like Wellesley and Davidson, the whole feel of final exam season is different. Students typically schedule exams themselves, or take them home, signing a pledge to follow the rules and not to share the questions with other students.

At Davidson, outside Charlotte, N.C., the student-run honor council, which can impose punishments up to indefinite suspension, hears about 12 to 15 cases per year. Taylor White, a senior who leads the honor council, said that's a remarkably small number for a school of 1,950 students.

But the code does more than instill a socially beneficial fear of getting caught, she said. It also imbues the whole campus with an atmosphere of trust, and gives students values they carry after graduation.

"It's liberating," White said, for students not to worry others are cheating. "We all sort of feel that there's an instant respect when you meet any student in any class, and also a trust." The code, she said, "works for students here every single day. It works against students 12 to 15 times a year."

But that culture can take decades, even centuries, to develop. McCabe's research found that while honor code schools have less cheating overall, there are exceptions.

His research shows that what appears to prevent cheating is a culture of taking academic integrity seriously. Often that correlates with a code, but not always. Also required are buy-in from students and faculty, and constant renewal for incoming students. That usually only works on a manageably sized residential campus with a strong identity.

McCabe said the honor code was a defining experience for him and virtually all his classmates as an undergraduate at Princeton. But he doubts it could work at an enormous university like Rutgers. In the Ivy League, undergraduate-focused Princeton and Dartmouth have prominent honor codes, but schools with bigger graduate and professional programs such as Yale, Columbia, Cornell and—for now—Harvard do not.

While the size and high-achieving ethos are a challenge, Harvard has the kind of culture where a code should work, McCabe said.

"The more selective the school, the better chance it'll work because students will be more responsive to the danger of being thrown out," he said.

Harvard officials said Thursday they discovered roughly half the students in a class of about 250 people may have shared answers or plagiarized on a final. The Harvard *Crimson* student newspaper and *Wall Street Journal* reported the cheating allegations concerned a government course called "Introduction to Congress."

"These allegations, if proven, represent totally unacceptable behavior that betrays the trust upon which intellectual inquiry at Harvard depends," President Drew Faust said.

In Harvard Yard on Friday, several students said that even without a formal code, Harvard does send the message academic honesty is important. They doubted a code would help.

"'Veritas,' it's honesty," said Anna Maguire, a freshman from Westfield, N.J. "I think you come to an institution like that and it's a shame that not everybody can handle the motto of the school. But if people want to cheat, they're going to cheat. A code isn't going to change that."

Joseph Lanzillo, a freshman from Glen Ellyn, Ill., said he thought a code was a good idea, though it can't be something "you just make people sign," he said. "It has to be really engrained in the place, and I kind of expected it would be, until I heard about this."

A few schools have implemented honor codes in recent years, such as Georgetown in 1996, but others have dropped them or continued without.

Another hesitation for colleges is that putting potentially career-altering punishments in the hands of students is getting riskier, with students more likely to sue.

Discussions about a possible honor code at Harvard have been underway since at least 2010, the *Crimson* has reported, but the university said this episode would lead to a campus-wide conversation about academic honesty, which could include starting an honor code.

Callahan, the author of the book on cheating, said that as a place grooming so many future global leaders, Harvard should demand more of itself.

"I find it shocking that a place like Harvard doesn't have an honor code," he said. "This is a major failure of leadership in higher education. If a school like Harvard doesn't have an honor code, without all of its leadership responsibilities, somebody's not paying attention."

Honor and Integrity

Cheating in College

Scott Jaschik

Inside Higher Ed

September 2012

In Scott Jaschik's interview with professors Donald L. McCabe, Kenneth D. Butterfield, and Linda K. Treviño, the authors discuss their collaborative book titled *Cheating in College: Why Students Do It and What Educators Can Do About It*. Jaschik's question-and-answer email interview explores the morality of cheating in the wake of the Harvard University cheating scandal. McCabe, Butterfield, and Treviño consider preventative measures that colleges and universities, large or small, can take to avoid academic dishonesty. The conversation also positions itself within the ever-changing context of the digital age, raising questions that reference the authors' decade-long research on cheating.

1. What does Jaschik ask about sanctions and punishments against cheating and how do the authors respond?

2. Instead of being seen as a means to facilitate plagiarism, how might the Internet instead be used to educate students about plagiarism and serve as a preventative measure against cheating?

3. According to Jaschik, "experts say that many students arrive in college already skilled at and not morally troubled by cheating." In what ways does this statement and the scandal that happened at Harvard speak about integrity and honor in colleges and universities in the United States?

A scandal at Harvard University has many educators talking about cheating and whether anything can be done about it. Experts say that many students arrive in college already skilled at and not morally troubled by cheating, and scandals at top high schools back up this point of view. What, if anything, can professors and colleges do? These issues are explored in a new book, *Cheating at College: Why Students Do It and What Educators Can Do About It* (Johns Hopkins University Press). The authors are Donald L. McCabe, professor of management and global business at the Rutgers University Business School; Kenneth D. Butterfield, associate professor of management, information systems and entrepreneurship at Washington State University; and Linda K. Treviño, professor of organizational behavior at Pennsylvania State University. They responded via e-mail to questions about the book.

Q: Is cheating getting worse? Or do those who say that only imagine a golden age when academic honesty prevailed?

A: Interestingly, the hard data we present in our book suggest cheating may now be on the decline. Similar results have been obtained by the Josephson Institute in their work with high schools. After a period of steep increases, some moderation in cheating was reported in their 2010 report. They will issue a new report in October 2012 and it will be most interesting to see what's happening now. But, it is important to keep in mind that the data are self-reported and, in our studies, we have moved from print surveys to online surveys. That move may have affected the numbers we are seeing, possibly making the picture look rosier than it really is.

In our college work, we have observed a kind of ebb and flow in our data—some types of cheating seem to have increased (surprisingly not necessarily those related to the Internet) and others seem to be on the wane. However, there seems to be little question, based on various comments offered by students, that changes in student attitudes can't be ignored. Many students have indicated that they have had no involvement in certain types of cheating, but in open-ended questions near the end of our survey, they say that they actually have engaged in these actions, but when they did it, it was not cheating because…. Of course, this may simply be a rationalization process so students don't have to admit, maybe even to themselves, that they've actually cheated.

Q: Did the Internet fundamentally change the nature of cheating, or did it just provide new tools to do what previous generations did offline?

A: The role of the Internet raises some fascinating questions. Many students have a difficult time understanding why they can't use information they find on the Internet to a greater degree in doing assignments. Many reason that if they were smart enough to be able to find this information, they should be able to take advantage of their superior search skills. Some note that when they are in the "real" world they will be asked to do this all the time—i.e., to put together reports that are as factual as possible, not necessarily original. In fact, they probably won't be given enough time by their employers to do in-depth original searches. They are only acquiring skills now that will serve them well as they enter the real world. As educators, we need to do a better job of teaching students that they can use this information, but they must quote it and reference it as they would if the source material were in print.

Of course, there are also students who use the Internet to complete assignments simply because they are too lazy to do the work themselves and/or because they want to ensure they get a good grade on the assignment. This is especially true of students who may have time management problems and neglect assignments until the last minute. More than one student has suggested to us that they have used the Internet to copy information because it's the only way they can get a particular assignment done when it is due the next day.

Q: Compared to previous generations, are today's college students less aware of the moral issues associated with cheating? Are they aware that they are cheating?

A: Today's students do not appear to be any less aware of the moral implications associated with "cheating," but many have convinced themselves that what they are doing is not cheating. They have rationalized their choices, leaving no moral implications left to consider. While they have a sense that some of the activities they are engaging in are morally questionable in the abstract, for any number of reasons (parental pressure, others are doing it and they are being unfairly disadvantaged, etc.) they have convinced themselves that they have no choice.

Another issue that may be more pertinent to today's college students than previous generations is collaborative cheating (cheating on written assignments when the instructor explicitly asked for individual work). This is one type of cheating that appears to be on the rise. Some students believe that what many professors consider cheating more accurately falls into an ethical "gray area." They reason that if professors teach the virtues of collaboration and collaboration will be expected in the workplace, it should be acceptable for students to collaborate on assignments even when the professor requires individual work. By appealing to gray areas, students can justify or deny wrongdoing.

Q: How can colleges better educate new students so they won't cheat?

A: This, of course, is the big question. In our book, our final chapter advances a model that we believe is the only approach that is likely to succeed. Rooted in a model originally designed by Linda Treviño and Kate Nelson (in their book *Managing Business Ethics*, 2011, Wiley) to address creating ethical cultures in business organizations, the model we propose relies on the principles of ethical culture and ethical community building—an effort similar to the honor code approach used on a number of campuses. Although the honor code tradition has waned on some campuses, we know of several where it remains the backbone of the campus community and governs major aspects of a student's campus life—e.g., Washington and Lee University. We know of some where the honor code is relatively young—e.g., Georgetown University—and others where a modified honor code (tailored to the needs of a larger campus)—e.g., the University of Maryland—has been introduced.

Although we have been asked many times how many campuses actually have honor codes, we have had to answer that we don't know. We have often estimated 100 or so but that is really an educated guess since we find "new" codes (at least new to us) on a fairly regular basis. In addition, getting an accurate count is hindered by the lack of clarity about what constitutes an honor code. When we first started our project in the fall of 1990, we used the principles espoused by Brian Melendez in a study he did at that time for the Faculty of Arts and Sciences at Harvard in 1985. Although Harvard elected not to adopt a code at that time, Melendez identified four characteristics that are often associated with codes—(1) unproctored exams, (2) a student controlled judiciary that would hear allegations of cheating, (3) a pledge which students would have to sign either indicating they will not cheat (often signed annually) or that they had not cheated (typically signed on each piece of work submitted), and (4) by far the most controversial element, a "requirement" or expectation that students will report cheating they observe involving others.

Honor codes that have been proposed to different student bodies in recent years have often failed to gain support if they contain a reporting clause as students are unwilling to accept such an obligation. We rely on a broader approach that does not require the term "honor code" to be used at all. In fact, some of the strongest ethical communities have been built on campuses that don't use the term at all. We're interested in developing cultures of integrity that involve an aspirational ethical culture that strongly encourages students to be honest. This aspirational side is then accompanied by an accountability component that holds community members accountable for their actions. We do not offer a cookie cutter approach. Each institution must work to analyze its own existing culture and develop approaches that fit it such as developing unique campus traditions.

Also critical to our approach is attention to the informal cultural systems (e.g., informal norms on a campus, the people who are held out as heroes, etc.) and formal cultural systems (e.g., the authority structure, the reward systems in place—especially what is rewarded—and the orientation and training that is offered to both students and faculty concerning issues of integrity). Obviously, our approach requires significant attention and ongoing effort and definitely adds cost to the campus budget. But, we view this as an important and worthwhile investment because we believe one of our major objectives is to "create" and educate ethical citizens who will assume key roles in our society in the future.

Q: Many experts say that it is easier to prevent cheating at small institutions where everyone knows everyone. Are there steps you recommend for large universities?

A: Although no campus, large or small, has been able to eliminate cheating, we generally agree that it is easier to "prevent" cheating on smaller campuses that are likely to have a singular or at least simpler culture. So, the level of cheating does seem to correspond to size, with larger schools

Plagiarism & Cheating

experiencing more cheating as students take advantage of the anonymity they experience in larger classes and administrators find it more difficult to create a strong ethical culture in a large and diverse university.

Nevertheless, we do know of some larger campuses that do a reasonably good job in this regard. For example, take Brigham Young University, a large school. Although it has an honor code, it "backs" this up with a system that requires students to take most of their exams in a testing center where they are carefully separated from students taking the same exam— eliminating one common form of cheating on tests (copying from another). While one might expect students to complain about this lack of trust or "opportunity," work we have done on the BYU campus suggests this is not the case. In contrast, a much more common comment talks about why a student at BYU would not cheat because of his/her religious convictions. BYU might be unique in this regard. We tend to hear more often of an honor code preventing cheating because of a reciprocal relationship of trust where students sense some obligation not to cheat because of the many privileges they may obtain under their code—e.g., self-scheduled exams, the ability to take their exam wherever they choose on campus, etc. Both to preserve these privileges and to respond to the sense of trust placed in them, students at code schools seem to refrain from cheating to a greater degree almost independent of size.

Q: Some colleges with honor codes have very strict (single sanction, typically dismissal) punishments for cheating. Do such punishments prevent cheating?

A: We remain ambivalent about the use of strict sanctions to prevent cheating. Discipline for cheating must be part of any academic integrity culture (that's the accountability part). But, we believe that rehabilitation should also be in the mix (to affirm the aspirational message). From a practical perspective, we have yet to find a school, no matter how strong the punishments they use to sanction students (including expulsion), that has no cheating. But, from a more philosophical perspective, as educators, we are not "law and order" supporters. We believe that if we have admitted a student into our campus community we owe that student at least one chance to be rehabilitated after a cheating incident.

A number of codes allow for expulsion, and some even call for expulsion for a first offense. But, we believe the circumstances of the incident must be taken into account. For example, if a first-year student cheats as much through ignorance as intention, we believe a school has an obligation to try to rehabilitate that student rather than expel him or her. In contrast, if a senior who clearly knows the rules cheats, we would evaluate that case more harshly and wonder what impact a failure to punish strongly in that case would have on other students on campus.

So making a blanket statement that we support strong penalties such as expulsion, as a matter of policy, is just not compatible with our views. While strong penalties, up to and including expulsion, are necessary at times, they are not always so. In our opinion, it is better to focus on encouraging honesty than on discouraging cheating. Although accountability is essential, emphasizing punishment is likely to be ineffective and may even prove to be counterproductive (e.g., encouraging cynicism or a backlash from students). We believe that over the long run, fostering a culture of trust, honesty, and integrity helps students internalize values of honesty and integrity and will do more to reduce cheating than creating a climate of fear and retribution.

We should note, however, that the one true single sanction school with which we have worked more than casually—Washington and Lee—may be an exception to this thinking and there may be others. At W&L, incoming and current students are so schooled in the specifics of the honor system on campus that "accidental" or minor violations are not really possible. Indeed, one only needs to spend a few minutes on campus before someone utters the phrase, "Honor knows no measure." Attributed to General Lee, W&L students understand even before they arrive on campus, that honor is such a serious matter at W&L that any violation will lead to an "invitation" for the student to sever his/her relationship with the university. Indeed, the policy is so strongly implemented and discussed on campus that it is almost impossible for a student to claim, "I didn't know." This underscores our stance that the culture of the institution must be taken into account in designing an approach to academic integrity. What works in a military college is unlikely to work somewhere else. That is why we emphasize so strongly the importance of tailoring a comprehensive approach that fits your organization and its broader culture.

Cheating in Academic Institutions: A Decade of Research

Donald L. McCabe, Kenneth D. Butterfield, and Linda K. Treviño

Ethics and Behavior

November 2001

In 2001, Donald L. McCabe of Rutgers University, Kenneth D. Butterfield of Pennsylvania State University, and Linda K. Treviño of Washington State University published an academic study titled "Cheating in Academic Institutions: A Decade of Research." The study affirms research that cheating has increased over the last three decades and attempts to add to the research by accounting for contextual factors such as honor codes, classroom management strategies, and clearly communicated expectations. This piece provides a strong background and contextual basis for approaching the question-and-answer with the authors that is also presented in this chapter.

1. What contextual factors have the greatest influence on whether or not students cheat? Why?

2. What are the benefits and consequences of establishing honor codes and implementing strategies for student accountability?

3. Given the rise of the Internet and advances in digital technology, how do you think results would change if this were a study conducted in the first decade of the twenty-first century?

For the last decade, both collectively and individually, we have studied questions of organizational values and ethics. Although the initial point of departure for each of us was ethics in business organizations, we have expended considerable time trying to understand the ethical inclinations of tomorrow's business leaders—students majoring in business and those majoring in other subjects who intend to pursue a career in business. To understand how the ethics and ethical development of these future businesspeople are similar to, or differ from, those pursuing other career choices, we have also studied the ethical inclinations of college students in general.

With few exceptions, the thrust of this research has centered on one of the most basic ethical decisions faced by college students—to cheat or not to cheat on their academic work. With increasing competition for the most desired positions in the job market and for the few coveted places available at the nation's leading business, law, and medical schools, today's undergraduates experience considerable pressure to do well. Research shows that all too often these pressures lead to decisions to engage in various forms of academic dishonesty (e.g., Bowers, 1964; McCabe, Treviño, & Butterfield, 1999). Research also shows that these transgressions are often overlooked or treated lightly by faculty who do not want to become involved in what they perceive as the bureaucratic procedures designed to adjudicate allegations of academic dishonesty on their campus (e.g., McCabe, 1993; Nuss, 1984; Singhal, 1982). Students who might otherwise complete their work honestly observe this phenomenon and convince themselves they cannot afford to be disadvantaged by students who cheat and go unreported or unpunished. Although many find it distasteful, they too begin cheating to "level the playing field." Fortunately, the picture may not be as bleak as this brief summary suggests. One of the most encouraging aspects of the research we have conducted on academic dishonesty is the many students and faculty who are genuinely concerned about the issue and who are willing to devote time and effort to addressing it on their campuses. In fact, the last decade has actually seen a modest increase in the number of college campuses who have adopted academic honor codes. As we discuss presently, such codes place significant responsibility on students to maintain an environment of academic integrity, and evidence suggests they can be quite successful. Although honor codes are not a panacea and are more difficult to implement on larger campuses, many of the principles on which such codes are built can be implemented on any campus.

Prevalence of Cheating

Understanding student cheating is particularly important given trends that show cheating is widespread and on the rise. In 1964, Bill Bowers published the first large-scale study of cheating in institutions of higher learning. Bowers surveyed more than 5,000 students in a diverse sample of 99 U.S. colleges and universities and found that three-fourths of the respondents had engaged in one or more incidents of academic dishonesty. This study was replicated some 30 years later by McCabe and Treviño (1997) at 9 of the schools who had participated in Bowers's original survey. Although McCabe and Treviño observed only a modest increase in overall cheating, significant increases were found in the most explicit forms of test or exam cheating. Disturbing increases were also found among women and in *collaborative cheating* (unpermitted collaboration among students on written assignments). Although no significant increases were observed in the most explicit forms of cheating on written assignments, this may be due to a changing definition among students of what constitutes plagiarism. In general, student understanding of appropriate citation techniques seems to have changed, and selected behaviors that students may have classified as plagiarism in Bowers's (1964) study do not appear to be considered plagiarism by many students today. For example, although most students understand that quoting someone's work word for word demands a citation, they seem to be less clear on the need to cite the presentation of someone else's ideas when the students present them in their own words.

In spite of Bowers's (1964) conclusions about the powerful influence of institutional context on student decisions to cheat, between the 1960s and 1990 most of the research on student cheating focused on the role of individual factors related to cheating behavior. This stream of research revealed that factors such as gender, grade point average (GPA), work ethic, Type A behavior, competitive achievement striving, and self-esteem can significantly influence the prevalence of cheating (e.g., Baird, 1980; Eisenberger & Shank, 1985; Perry, Kane, Bernesser, & Spicker, 1990; Ward, 1986; Ward & Beck, 1990). Prior to 1990, only a few studies focused on contextual factors that influence cheating behavior. In this research, factors such as faculty responses to cheating, sanction threats, social learning, and honor codes were shown to influence college cheating (e.g., Canning, 1956; Jendrek, 1989; Michaels & Miethe, 1989; Tittle & Rowe, 1973). Although these studies made important contributions, most of them had significant limitations. Perhaps of greatest importance, most of these studies only sampled students at a single institution, obviously limiting our ability to draw meaningful conclusions about contextual influences.

The research agenda we initiated in 1990 attempted to address this shortcoming and led to a course of research that has spanned the past decade. Like Bowers (1964), our distinguishing methodology has been the use of large-scale, multicampus, multivariable studies. The end result has been a series of studies that have advanced our understanding of why college students cheat, provided administrators and faculty with a broader set of tools that can be used to curb cheating on college campuses, and helped foster academic integrity in American colleges and universities (e.g., McCabe, 1992, 1993; McCabe & Treviño, 1993, 1997; McCabe et al., 1996, 1999). Not least among the outcomes of this work was the formation of the Center for Academic Integrity in 1992, a consortium of more than 200 colleges and universities united in a common effort to initiate and maintain a dialogue among students, faculty, and administrators on the issue of academic integrity. As we discuss later, although the Center understands there is no "one size fits all" solution to academic dishonesty, it does indicate that certain fundamental initiatives can yield positive results on almost any campus.

Why Do College Students Cheat? The Role of Contextual Factors

One of the most important studies in our work is McCabe and Treviño's (1993) survey of more than 6,000 students at 31 academic institutions, which was conducted in the 1990–1991 academic year. This project was the first major, multicampus investigation of institution-level variables that influence cheating behavior since Bowers's (1964) seminal work. Major variables investigated in this study included the existence of an honor code, student understanding and acceptance of a school's academic integrity policy, perceived certainty that cheaters will be reported, perceived severity of penalties, and the degree to which students perceive that their peers engage in cheating behavior. This final variable, peer behavior, was found to show the most significant relation with student cheating in this study. Based on social learning theory (Bandura, 1986), McCabe and Treviño hypothesized such a relation, although they were somewhat surprised by its strength. Indeed, they concluded that the strong influence of peers' behavior may suggest that academic dishonesty not only is learned from observing the behavior of peers, but that peers' behavior provides a kind of normative support for cheating. The fact that others are cheating may also suggest that, in such a climate, the non-cheater feels left at a disadvantage. Thus cheating may come to be viewed as an acceptable way of getting and staying ahead. (p. 533)

Perhaps of greatest importance from a practical perspective, their further analysis suggested that an institution's ability to develop a shared understanding and acceptance of its academic integrity policies has a significant and substantive impact on student perceptions of their peers' behavior. ... Thus, programs aimed at distributing, explaining, and gaining student and faculty acceptance of academic integrity policies may be particularly useful. (pp. 533–534)

McCabe and Treviño's (1997) study of almost 1,800 students at nine medium to large-size universities in the 1993–1994 academic year examined the relative influence of contextual and individual factors on cheating behavior, and the results pointed to the primacy of the institutional context in influencing cheating behavior. The contextual factors (peer cheating behavior, peer disapproval of cheating behavior, and perceived severity of penalties for cheating) were significantly more influential than the individual factors (age, gender, GPA, and participation in extracurricular activities). Peer-related factors once again emerged as the most significant correlate of cheating behavior.

McCabe and Treviño (1997) also found in this study that cheating tends to be more prevalent on these larger campuses. This is reflected in Tables 1 and 2, which summarize some of the quantitative data obtained in their 1990–1991 and 1993 studies. The tables also show data obtained in a replication of their 1990–1991 study that was conducted on the same 31 campuses in the 1995–1996 academic year. These data reflect the number of students who admit to the various forms of academic dishonesty. In Table 1, a *serious test cheater* is defined as someone who admits to one or more instances of copying from another student on a test or exam, using unauthorized crib or cheat notes on a test or exam, or helping someone else to cheat on a test or exam. Although other test cheating behaviors were also evaluated (e.g., learning what was on a test from someone who took the test in an earlier class section), the behaviors included in our serious test cheating statistic are behaviors a majority of students agree constitute cheating. The serious cheating on written work statistic was constructed in an identical fashion and includes four behaviors: plagiarism, fabricating or falsifying a bibliography, turning in work done by someone else, and copying a few sentences of material without footnoting them in a paper. As the 1963 versus 1993 comparison suggests, cheating is prevalent and test or exam cheating has increased dramatically over the last three decades.

A distinguishing characteristic of the original McCabe and Treviño (1993) study was its investigation of the influence of academic honor codes on student integrity, an investigation that was extended in McCabe et al. (1999). Earlier work (e.g., Bowers, 1964) suggested that honor codes were associated with lower levels of cheating and the data in Tables 1 and 2 suggest this is still the case. However, there is evidence of a slight deterioration in the relation between honor codes and cheating between 1990–1991 and 1995–1996.

TABLE 1
Self-Admitted Cheating—Summary Statistics

Variable	1963a (%)	1993b (%)	1990–1991 (%)		1995–1996 (%)	
			No Code[c]	Code[d]	No Code[e]	Code[f]
Serious test cheating[g]	39	64	47	24	45	30
Serious cheating on written work[h]	65	66	56	32	58	42
All serious cheating	75	82	71	44	71	54

[a]n = 452. [b]n = 1,793. [c]n = 3,083. [d]n = 3,013. [e]n = 1,970. [f]n = 2,303. [g]Serious test cheating includes students who have engaged in copying on an exam—with or without another student's knowledge—using crib notes on an exam, or helping someone else to cheat on a test or exam. [h]Serious cheating on written work includes students who have engaged in plagiarism, fabricated or falsified a bibliography, turned in work done by someone else, or copied a few sentences of material without footnoting them in a paper.

TABLE 2
Self-Admitted Cheating—Summary Statistics (%)

Variable	1963[a]	1990–1991		1993[b]	1995–1996	
		No Code[c]	Code[d]		No Code[e]	Code[f]
Copied on test or exam	26	30	14	52	32	20
Used unauthorized crib notes	16	21	9	27	17	11
Helped other on test	23	28	9	37	23	11
Plagiarism	30	18	7	26	20	10
Copied one or two sentences without footnoting	49	41	23	54	43	32
Unpermitted collaboration on assignments	11	39	21	49	49	27

[a]$n = 452$. [b]$n = 1,793$. [c]$n = 3,083$. [d]$n = 3,013$. [e]$n = 1,970$. [f]$n = 2,303$.

These data suggest that honor codes are an important phenomenon, and we have studied the relation between honor codes and cheating has been studied in greater depth, along three major themes: (a) implementation of honor codes, (b) faculty views of academic integrity policies including honor codes, and (c) honor codes' effect on students.

Honor Codes Must Be More Than Mere "Window Dressing"

McCabe and Treviño (1993) replicated Bowers's (1964) finding that less cheating occurs in honor code environments. However, McCabe and Treviño were intrigued by an additional finding: One of the lowest levels of cheating occurred at a school that lacked an honor code, and one of the higher levels of cheating occurred at a school that had a long-standing honor code. A closer examination of each of these schools provided an interesting explanation for this apparent paradox. McCabe and Treviño found that although this noncode school did not have a formal honor code, it had

Plagiarism & Cheating

developed a culture that emphasized many of the elements found at code schools and encouraged academic integrity without instituting a formal code. At this school, administrators and faculty clearly conveyed their beliefs about the seriousness of cheating, communicated expectations regarding high standards of integrity, and encouraged students to know and abide by rules of proper conduct. In contrast, the honor code school, although it had a 100-year-old honor code tradition, failed to adequately communicate the essence of its code to students and to indoctrinate them into the campus culture. This finding led to an important insight: It is not the mere existence of an honor code that is important in deterring college cheating. An effective honor code must be more than mere window dressing; a truly effective code must be well implemented and strongly embedded in the student culture. Furthermore, a formal code is not the only way to achieve the desired result. As suggested earlier, a strong culture of academic integrity can exist at an institution that has no formal code but communicates the importance the community places on integrity in other ways.

McCabe, Treviño, and Butterfield's (1996) study of 318 alumni of two private liberal arts colleges suggested honor codes can have long-term effects on behavior. The study focused on alumni who had graduated from their respective colleges between 1962 and 1989, allowing the researchers to test hypotheses about the long-term effects of collegiate honor codes as well as the effect of codes of ethics at their current work organizations. The results supported previous work by showing that dishonest behavior in the workplace can be reduced by an organizational code of ethics. The results also show that dishonest behavior in the workplace varies inversely with the strength of implementation of an organizational code of ethics (i.e., the degree of managerial commitment to the code and the degree to which an organization attempts to communicate its code to employees and to ensure compliance) and the degree to which a code of ethics is deeply embedded in the organization's culture (i.e., the degree to which the code is understood and accepted by employees and guides their day-to-day interactions and activities). The results also indicate that college honor codes can have an enduring effect: Dishonest behavior in the workplace was lowest for participants who had experienced an honor code environment in college and who currently worked in an organization that had a strongly implemented code of ethics. Overall, this work suggests that participation in multiple honor code communities can play a part in reducing dishonest behavior, particularly if the honor codes are well implemented and strongly embedded in the organizational culture.

Faculty Views of Academic Integrity Policies

Faculty members' views of academic integrity policies, and how these views differ across code and noncode schools, was the subject of McCabe's (1993) study of 800 faculty at a geographically diverse sample of 16 U.S. colleges and universities. This study showed that faculty at code schools were more likely to rate their school higher than noncode schools on factors such as students' understanding of academic integrity policies, faculty support of these policies, and the overall effectiveness of the policy. Faculty at code schools were also more likely to believe that students should play a significant part in the judicial process associated with academic cheating. This study also revealed that faculty at both code and noncode schools are reluctant to report cheating and prefer to handle suspected cases of cheating on their own rather than appeal to institutional policies and procedures. Furthermore, this study confirmed student perceptions that many faculty do not treat cases of academic dishonesty very harshly. For example, more than half of the noncode faculty reported that their most likely reaction to an incident of cheating would be failure on the test or assignment involved (39%), a simple warning (9%), various penalties less than test or assignment failure (7%), or nothing (1%). Word seems to travel quickly among students as to who these faculty are, and student comments suggest their courses become particular targets for cheating. As noted earlier, students report that many faculty simply look the other way when they see cheating occur in their courses. When more than a few faculty behave this way, it is hard to convince students that an ethic of integrity exists on campus and cheating can easily become the campus norm.

Effect of Honor Codes on Students

As suggested earlier, some campuses use academic honor codes to combat academic dishonesty. Although Bowers (1964), McCabe and Treviño (1993), and others have documented the powerful effect of such codes, how and why they work when students on code campuses face the same grade pressures as their peers elsewhere is not well understood. Gaining additional insight into this question was the subject of a qualitative study of college cheating reported by McCabe et al. (1999). McCabe et al. analyzed data from more than 1,700 students at 31 U.S. colleges and universities, approximately half of which employed an honor code. Data for this study were collected in the form of open-ended comments made by students at the end of a larger survey on college cheating. At the end of the survey, students were asked to offer "any comments that you care to make or if there is anything else you would like to tell us about the topic of cheating in college." Although this question was added to the survey in a somewhat perfunctory manner, more than 40% of the almost 4,300 respondents offered comments, many of which were quite detailed in nature. We believe this kind of response underscores the importance of the topic of academic cheating to students.

Many of these comments corroborated the importance of the institutional–contextual factors found to be related to academic integrity by McCabe and Treviño (1993, 1997). Contextual influences on cheating that were emphasized by students included the degree to which the code is deeply embedded in a culture of integrity; the degree to which a school has a supportive, trusting atmosphere; competitive pressures; the severity of punishments; the existence of clear rules regarding unacceptable behavior; faculty monitoring; peer pressure to cheat or not to cheat; the likelihood of being caught or reported; and class size.

As expected, the results also revealed important differences between code and noncode campus environments. In particular, the results suggest that students at honor code schools view academic integrity in a very different way from their noncode counterparts. The code students were less likely to cheat, were less likely to rationalize or justify any cheating behavior that they did admit to, and were more likely to talk about the importance of integrity and about how a moral community can minimize cheating. Although students at both types of schools report that they cheat and feel many different sources of pressure to cheat, honor code students apparently do not succumb to these pressures as easily or as often as noncode students. As reported in McCabe et al. (1999), "clearly, code students sense that they are part of a special community that demands compliance with certain standards in exchange for the many privileges associated with honor codes" (p. 230). Such privileges (e.g., unproctored exams, self-scheduled exams, the strong judicial role played by students, etc.) help create a true environment of trust among students and between students and faculty. Students seem to place great value on being part of such an environment in contrast to the environment found on many campaigns where compliance with standards of academic integrity is only pursued through the threat of punishment.

Why Do College Students Cheat? The Role of Individual Factors

Although McCabe and Treviño's primary focus has been on the role of context in influencing academic dishonesty, some of their work also has expanded understanding of the relation between individual influences and academic dishonesty. For example, McCabe (1992) showed that college students use a variety of neutralization techniques (e.g., rationalization, denial, deflecting blame to others, condemning the accusers) to explain away their dishonest behavior.

McCabe and Treviño (1997) also studied some of the more common individual difference factors that have been studied in the literature. Although they found these factors to be less important than contextual factors in their work, they are nonetheless significant correlates of cheating among college students. For example, prior studies (e.g., Anton & Michael, 1983; Haines, Diekhoff, LaBeff, & Clark, 1986) have shown that younger students tend to cheat more than older students and our data supported this result. However, it is not clear how much of this relation is accounted for by age versus class rank. These two variables are strongly correlated, and McCabe and Treviño suggested that many 1st and 2nd-year students who find themselves in large lecture courses, perhaps enrolled in an elective they really do not want to take in the first place, find it very easy to rationalize cheating. They often see a lot of cheating among others in these courses, faculty cannot possibly monitor all of the students in such large classes, and the students often are bored with the material. In contrast, 3rd and 4th-year students seem to be more enthusiastic about their courses and faculty. At smaller schools, these students talk about the personal relationships they have developed with faculty in their major, often making it harder to consider cheating in those courses.

Another individual factor that has received much attention in the literature is gender. The majority of prior studies have reported that men cheat more than women (e.g., Aiken, 1991; Davis, Grover, Becker, & McGregor, 1992; Ward, 1986), but several studies have found no difference between men and women (e.g., Baird, 1980; Haines et al., 1986).

Although McCabe and Treviño (1997) found the more traditional result (i.e., men self-reported more cheating than women), the data suggest that within similar majors, gender differences are often very small. For example, women majoring in engineering, a major one might have considered male-dominated a few decades ago, talk about the need to compete by the "men's rules" to be successful in this major. Thus, generally higher levels of cheating were found among women in engineering compared to women in other majors, and women majoring in engineering reported cheating at rates comparable to men majoring in engineering.

McCabe and Treviño (1997) also examined several other individual-level variables. For example, they found support for the well-documented conclusion that students with lower GPAs report more cheating than students with higher GPAs. They also reported that students engaged in intercollegiate athletics and other extracurricular activities self-reported more cheating, perhaps reflecting the time demands that these activities place on students and their decision to take various "short cuts" to stay up to-date and remain competitive in their coursework.

McCabe et al.'s (1999) qualitative study supported these findings and identified other factors that can influence cheating, including pressure to get high grades, parental pressures, a desire to excel, pressure to get a job, laziness, a lack of responsibility, a lack of character, poor self-image, a lack of pride in a job well done, and a lack of personal integrity.

Preventing Cheating in Academic Institutions

The research discussed here represents one decade of work studying factors that influence cheating among college students. Numerous insights have emerged from this work that faculty, administrators, academics, and students can use to help reduce cheating on their campuses.

The primary implication of this work is that cheating can be most effectively addressed at the institutional level. On many campuses, the fundamental elements of an academic honor code may be a particularly useful tool for colleges and universities who seek to reduce student cheating. However, at an even broader level, academic institutions are advised to consider ways of creating an "ethical community" on their campuses—one that includes clear communication of rules and standards, moral socialization of community members, and mutual respect between students and faculty, and one that extends certain privileges to its students (e.g., unproctored exams, self-scheduled exams, etc.). However, building an ethical community also might involve techniques such as creating a "hidden curriculum" in which students not only receive formal ethics instruction but also learn by actively discussing ethical issues and acting on them. The hidden curriculum might include allowing students to participate in the many opportunities for teaching and learning about ethical issues that arise in the day-to-day operations of an educational institution. In such an environment, messages about ethics and values are implicitly sent to and received by students throughout their college experience, both in and out of the classroom (Treviño & McCabe, 1994).

The research of McCabe et al. (1999) also suggests that cheating behavior can be effectively managed in the classroom. Insights from this qualitative study suggest that faculty members can pursue numerous strategies, including clearly communicating expectations regarding cheating behavior, establishing policies regarding appropriate conduct, and encouraging students to abide by those policies. The more important factors identified in this study are summarized in Table 3.

In addition, McCabe and Pavela (1997) suggested 10 principles of academic integrity for faculty. These principles, shown in Table 4, represent strategies that faculty can employ to minimize cheating in their classrooms. Several of these factors point to the importance of student involvement in reducing cheating behavior. It should not be surprising that many of the factors shown in Table 4 mirror the suggestions offered by students (Table 3). This suggests that faculty and students may not be very far apart in their views on curbing college cheating and further indicates that these groups can work together toward the goal of establishing an ethical community. Indeed, involving both faculty and students in an ongoing dialogue about academic integrity may be one of the most important components of an honor code tradition. Some schools do little more than tell their students where in the student handbook they can find the school's policy on academic integrity. Many honor code schools, in contrast, use orientation sessions, initiation ceremonies, or both to convey to their students the tradition of honor on campus and what will be expected of them as the newest members of the community.

TABLE 3
Managing Cheating in the Classroom: The Student's Perspective

Number	Factor
1	Clearly communicate expectations (e.g., regarding behavior that constitutes appropriate conduct and behavior that constitutes cheating)
2	Establish and communicate cheating policies and encourage students to abide by those policies
3	Consider establishing a classroom honor code—one that places appropriate responsibilities and obligations on the student, not just the faculty member, to prevent cheating
4	Be supportive when dealing with students; this promotes respect, which students will reciprocate by not cheating
5	Be fair—develop fair and consistent grading policies and procedures; punish transgressions in a strict but fair and timely manner
6	When possible, reduce pressure by not grading students on a strict curve
7	Focus on learning, not on grades
8	Encourage the development of good character
9	Provide deterrents to cheating (e.g., harsh penalties)
10	Remove opportunities to cheat (e.g., monitor tests, be sure there is ample space between test takers)
11	Assign interesting and nontrivial assignments
12	Replace incompetent or apathetic teaching assistants

Note. Adapted from student comments in McCabe, Treviño, and Butterfield (1999).

TABLE 4
Managing Cheating in the Classroom: 10 Principles of Academic Integrity for Faculty

Number	Principle
1	Affirm the importance of academic integrity
2	Foster a love of learning
3	Treat students as an end in themselves
4	Foster an environment of trust in the classroom
5	Encourage student responsibility for academic integrity
6	Clarify expectations for students
7	Develop fair and relevant forms of assessment
8	Reduce opportunities to engage in academic dishonesty
9	Challenge academic dishonesty when it occurs
10	Help define and support campus-wide academic integrity standards

Note. From McCabe and Pavela (1997).

Surveys of high school students suggest that most students entering college arrive with some experience with cheating in high school, or at least knowledge of cheating by their peers. Yet, most students come to college expecting it will be different than high school. Many seem to view the primary goal of high school as gaining admission to the college of their choice, and they find their academic work somewhat irrelevant, more of an obstacle to college admission than a true learning experience. Although their view may eventually change, they arrive at college thinking this is where true learning occurs. When they hear the president, a dean, or an orientation leader talk about the scholarly enterprise and the importance of never representing the work of someone else as their own, this is generally what they expected. After all, this is not high school any more. We believe that most new college students, although perhaps a decreasing number, internalize this message to some degree and begin their college experience with a positive attitude about the need for academic integrity, in spite of their experience with cheating in high school. However, if they observe cheating by 2nd-, 3rd-, and 4th-year students and see faculty who seem to ignore what appears to be obvious cheating, their idealistic view is likely to degenerate rather quickly. The reality of the cheating they observe convinces them that college is not that different from high school after all, at least with regard to academic integrity. If they are to survive and be competitive in this new environment, they must play by the same rules as everyone else. On code campuses, however, new students generally will see significantly less cheating than on noncode campuses and most begin to internalize this new community ethic. Although some will eventually engage in academic dishonesty, for most it will only be after they have had an opportunity to think about their new community's ethic and how cheating would be a significant violation of the trust that new community has placed in them. To violate that trust might jeopardize the many privileges they receive as a member of the community. The real power of honor codes may be in the desire of students to belong to such a community, and thus their general willingness to abide by its rules. In our view, schools that do not, at the very least, engage their students in a meaningful dialogue about academic integrity are likely to experience the persistent levels of academic dishonesty identified in virtually all research on cheating in college.

As suggested earlier, however, honor codes are not a panacea and will not work on every campus. Thus, it is important to think about strategies that can, and should, be employed on any campus and foremost among these, in our minds, is dialogue. No campus can assume that its students, incoming or returning, will take the time to familiarize themselves with campus rules about academic integrity on their own. Even if they did, an institution's failure to emphasize for its students the high value it places on academic integrity sends the message that it is not a high priority. Such institutions should not be surprised if they experience above-average levels of academic dishonesty. In the absence of a long-standing tradition of student honor, however, dialogue alone is not likely to be enough. Each campus must send a consistent message to its students that academic integrity is expected and that cheating will result in negative consequences, and more than just a slap on the wrist. To do this, campuses must support faculty who raise allegations of student dishonesty and must be willing to employ sanctions that have both significant educational and deterrence value. In short, the institution must convince students that cheating will be met with strong disapproval and that cheating is the exception on campus, not the rule. To do this, the institution must be prepared to hold students accountable for any cheating in which they engage.

References

Aiken, L. R. (1991). Detecting, understanding, and controlling for cheating on tests. *Research in Higher Education, 32*, 725–736.

Anton, D. L., & Michael, W. B. (1983). Short-term predictive validity of demographic, affective, personal, and cognitive variables in relation to 2 criterion measures of cheating behaviors. *Educational and Psychological Measurement, 43*, 467–483.

Baird, J. S. (1980). Current trends in college cheating. *Psychology in the Schools, 17*, 515–522. Bandura, A. (1986). *Social foundations of thought and action.* Englewood Cliffs, NJ: Prentice Hall. Bowers, W. J. (1964). *Student dishonesty and its control in college.* New York: Bureau of Applied Social Research, Columbia University.

Canning, R. (1956). Does an honor system reduce classroom cheating? An experimental answer. *Journal of Experimental Education, 24*, 292–296.

Davis, S. F., Grover, C. A., Becker, A. H., & McGregor, L. N. (1992). Academic dishonesty: Prevalence, determinants, techniques, and punishments. *Teaching of Psychology, 19*, 16–20.

Eisenberger, R., & Shank, D. M. (1985). Personal work ethic and effort training affect cheating. *Journal of Personality and Social Psychology, 49*, 520–528.

Haines, V. J., Diekhoff, G. M., LaBeff, E. E., & Clark, R. E. (1986). College cheating: Immaturity, lack of commitment and the neutralizing attitude. *Research in Higher Education, 25*, 342–354.

Jendrek, M. P. (1989). Faculty reactions to academic dishonesty. *Journal of College Student Development, 30*, 401–406.

McCabe, D. L. (1992). The influence of situational ethics on cheating among college students. *Sociological Inquiry, 62*, 365–374.

McCabe, D. L. (1993). Faculty responses to academic dishonesty: The influence of student honor codes. *Research in Higher Education, 34*, 647–658.

McCabe, D. L., & Pavela, G. R. (1997). Ten principles of academic integrity. *The Journal of College and University Law, 24*, 117–118.

McCabe, D. L., & Treviño, L. K. (1993). Academic dishonesty: Honor codes and other contextual influences. *Journal of Higher Education, 64*, 522–538.

McCabe, D. L., & Treviño, L. K. (1997). Individual and contextual influences on academic dishonesty: A multicampus investigation. *Research in Higher Education, 38*, 379–396.

McCabe, D. L., Treviño, L. K., & Butterfield, K. D. (1996). The influence of collegiate and corporate codes of conduct on ethics-related behavior in the workplace. *Business Ethics Quarterly, 6*, 461–476.

McCabe, D. L., Treviño, L. K., & Butterfield, K. D. (1999). Academic integrity in honor code and non-honor code environments: A qualitative investigation. *Journal of Higher Education, 70*, 211–234.

Michaels, J. W., & Miethe, T. D. (1989). Applying theories of deviance to academic cheating. *Social Science Quarterly, 70*, 870–885.

Nuss, E. M. (1984). Academic integrity: Comparing faculty and student attitudes. *Improving College and University Teaching, 32*, 140–144.

Perry, A. R., Kane, K. M., Bernesser, K. J., & Spicker, P. T. (1990). Type A behavior, competitive achievement-striving, and cheating among college students. *Psychological Reports, 66*, 459–465.

Singhal, A. C. (1982). Factors in students' dishonesty. *Psychological Reports, 51*, 775–780.

Tittle, C. R., & Rowe, A. R. (1973). Moral appeal, sanction threat, and deviance: An experimental test. *Social Problems, 20*, 488–497.

Treviño, L. K., & McCabe, D. L. (1994). Meta-learning about business ethics: Building honorable business school communities. *Journal of Business Ethics, 13*, 405–416.

Ward, D. A. (1986). Self-esteem and dishonest behavior revisited. *Journal of Social Psychology, 126*, 709–713.

Ward, D. A., & Beck, W. L. (1990). Gender and dishonesty. *Journal of Social Psychology, 130*, 333–339.

Plagiarism & Cheating

Plagiarism and New Technologies

Pew Research Center

pewinternet.org

2011

The images, Plagiarism in Papers Among College Students, and Plagiarism and New Technologies are taken from "The Digital Revolution and Higher Education," a 2011 report conducted by Pew Research Center about online learning. The chart is based on 556 responses by college presidents, and provides staggering visual evidence of the significance computers and the Internet play in plagiarism cases. As always when analyzing graphs of this nature, be sure to practice critical questioning, considering the scope, context, and collection of the data.

1. What aspects of technology (i.e., computers and the Internet) make plagiarism and cheating easy to perform and more difficult to detect?

2. What role does context play in the results of a research study? In other words, what might be some reasons that lead college presidents to think that technology makes plagiarism easier?

3. How do these results measure up to other research that argues that plagiarism is declining with the rise of honor codes?

While technology has shown promise in expanding opportunities for distance learning and for creating less expensive and more interactive learning materials, it may also facilitate certain negative behaviors including plagiarism and cheating. When asked about plagiarism in papers among college students, the majority of college presidents (55%) say that it has increased in the past decade. Another large portion of presidents (40%) believe that it has stayed the same over the past 10 years. Very few college presidents (2%) believe that plagiarism has decreased over the past decade.

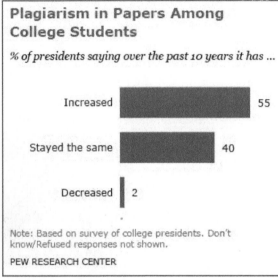

Plagiarism in Papers Among College Students

% of presidents saying over the past 10 years it has ...

Increased	55
Stayed the same	40
Decreased	2

Note: Based on survey of college presidents. Don't know/Refused responses not shown.

PEW RESEARCH CENTER

Plagiarism and Technology

How much of a role have computers and the internet played in the increase in plagiarism? (%)

Major role	89
Minor role	7
No role	1

Note: Based on college presidents who said plagiarism in papers among students has increased over past decade (n=556). Don't know/Refused responses not shown.

PEW RESEARCH CENTER

These findings are similar across different types of colleges and universities, nonprofits and for-profits, four-year and two-year institutions, community colleges, liberal arts colleges and research universities as well as across the spectrum of admissions selectivity.

When asked whether they feel that computers had played a role in the increase in plagiarism, presidents overwhelmingly believe that they have. Roughly nine-in-ten presidents (89%) believe that computers and the internet have played a major role in the increase in plagiarism on papers over the past decade. Just 7% say they have played a minor role, and 1% say they have not played a role in the increase.

Rise in Student Plagiarism Cases Attributed to Blurred Lines of Digital World

Kevin Simpson

Denver Post

February 2012

Kevin Simpson is an education reporter who published "Rise in Student Plagiarism Cases Attributed to Blurred Lines of Digital World" in *The Denver Post* in 2012. The piece explores former professor and director of composition at Colorado State University (CSU) Sarah Sloane's experience with an increase in student plagiarism at CSU. Sloane discusses the recent incorporation of an honor code at CSU and outlines different aspects of plagiarism from intentional plagiarism, to fostering a "culture of integrity," to the importance of understanding how different cultures approach plagiarism. Sloane said in the article "plagiarism always has been community-defined, not only by geography but also by history and culture." As you read, think about how plagiarism is context-driven, and how standards of integrity are determined by the values of a particular community.

1. What strategies mentioned in the piece might be a better approach to student plagiarism than simply using online plagiarism detectors?

2. How have digital tools for detecting plagiarism changed the landscape for cheating in higher education? How effective are websites like turnitin.com?

3. How was the "culture of integrity" lacking in the Atlanta and Harvard scandals? How might these kinds of incidents be avoided in the future?

A rising tide of student plagiarism during her three years as director of composition at Colorado State University left professor Sarah Sloane reeling.

She saw it all: blatant cut-and-paste copying from the Internet; only a word changed here and there, "sort of like Mad Libs"; chunks of material lifted straight from a university-issued brochure.

But why? Last time she counted, CSU's website featured at least five different prohibitions on plagiarism. In recent years, the university instituted an honor code to stem academic dishonesty.

"It's a time of change—we're in flux," says Sloane, noting that plagiarism always has been community-defined, not only by geography but also by history and culture. "Sometimes I think plagiarism rules, as currently codified, haven't caught up."

Teachers see it in high school and college—with varying frequency, but a sense that many students remain unclear about the evolving rules for crediting other people's work. Now, as ever, the teachers see literary scofflaws brazenly claim content under their own name, but most emphasize that the majority of their students try to do the right thing.

In the digital age, though, plagiarism is being re-examined on many fronts through the lens of technology. Today's students—the so-called digital natives—have grown up with concepts such as online file-sharing and rapidly changing notions of intellectual property.

"I don't know how much of that plays into the idea that everything is fair game, and how much is just complete lack of understanding," says Chris Cooper, who teaches English at Douglas County's Castle View High School, where he saw a rash of plagiarism late last year. "When I explain what they did, they break down and cry, like you convicted them of a crime."

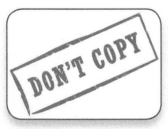

A recent study by the Pew Research Center found that 55 percent of university presidents surveyed thought plagiarism has increased over the past 10 years. Of those presidents, 89 percent said technology had played a major role.

Intentional plagiarism

CSU's Sloane estimates that in the past year she learned of about 100 incidents of intentional plagiarism among 6,800 freshman and advanced composition students—more than in previous years. She became so fascinated by the dynamics that contribute to plagiarism that she designed a graduate-level course called "Writing and Ownership: Plagiarists and Pirates, Forgers and Frauds."

But Teddi Fishman, director of the International Center for Academic Integrity at Clemson University, says other studies have shown incidents of plagiarism to be fairly consistent over time—fluctuating only 3 to 4 percentage points in higher education.

What has changed, she says, are the attention paid to cheating in an era dominated by standardized testing and a greater ability to catch plagiarism using computerized tools.

But she also notes that students tend to be two steps ahead of the technology in finding ways to circumvent the algorithms used by such plagiarism filters as the popular online Turnitin.com.

"I do worry," she says, "that we're teaching people to evade plagiarism detection rather than to cite sources and build upon other people's ideas."

But today's students suffer from an understandable confusion over what constitutes "common knowledge" that requires no attribution or citation, some experts say. Wikipedia—the most popular single online source among high school and college students, according to a Turnitin.com survey—represents a case in point.

"In a vague sense, they know it's written communally and published for anyone to use," Fishman says. "Common knowledge is difficult. There are good reasons students don't know where the boundaries are."

Michael Mazenko, an English teacher at Cherry Creek High School, figures that one of his most important tasks is to help students define those boundaries. He notes that all members of the English department lead discussion on the topic during the first two weeks of school.

"I don't have any feeling that we have a generation of cheaters," he says. "Some might argue that because of technology, they're better at it. I don't think it's any worse these days than it has been in the past—though we might be better at catching them because of technology."

Turnitin.com, a website that scans and archives millions of papers and employs algorithms to scrub them for lifted material, has been a key tool in that effort—serving about 10,000 institutions in 13 languages in 126 countries, according to spokesman Chris Harrick.

In Colorado, it claims to be used by 100 schools—split evenly between secondary and higher education—and more than 200,000 students. Worldwide, the service examines about 40 million papers a year. In December, during final exams, the site processes 400 new submissions per second.

Fishman, who serves on Turnit in.com's board in the United Kingdom, finds no substitute for teachers simply knowing their students, but also recognizes that instructional time amid growing class sizes makes it difficult to give plagiarism the attention it deserves.

"Culture of integrity"

"Concentrating on a culture of integrity, where you actually show students how to make good decisions and how to reason through ethical issues, that's the way to go," Fishman says, "because you don't have to try to out-technology them, which we probably can't, and you also don't have to set up an adversarial system."

Tuned-in teachers often catch plagiarism on their own.

Castle View High's Cooper echoes the experience of many instructors who simply hear a discordant tone in the writer's voice. He might then confirm it with a quick Google search.

"I assume they don't know the rules," he says. "Even if my gut tells me they do, I give them the benefit of the doubt the first time. A zero on the paper, we have a conversation, contact the parents, and it usually doesn't happen again."

Those who do embrace plagiarism-seeking technology sometimes make a point of displaying its capabilities early in the school year to discourage any willful attempts to shortcut the writing process.

"There's a lot of 'scared straight' involved," said Steve Schriener, an English teacher at Cheyenne Mountain High School in Colorado Springs. "I'm kind of old school. There's a running joke in my class where I say, 'If you cheat, remember: It's just your soul.' They come to see that as me being more concerned than sarcastic and biting.

"They want to do the honorable thing."

Some teachers don't try to scare kids straight with technology so much as use it as a tool to help them revise their work.

But as some veteran plagiarism detectives note, students tend to find work-arounds. One method involves running the target material through an online foreign-language translator and then back to English, where it assumes a form that may be sufficiently different from the original to thwart the software algorithms.

At the University of Colorado at Boulder, Will Hauptman, a 20-year-old sophomore, serves as chairman of the Honor Code, a student-run organization that handles cases of academic malfeasance.

Of 461 reported incidents from the spring semester of 2010 through the just-completed fall semester, 33 percent involved plagiarism. That makes it the second-largest category, next to the catch-all "cheating" incidents that account for about 40 percent.

Although the plagiarism stakes tend to be higher in college, Hauptman says that sanctions for first-time offenders aim to educate more than punish. A two-week writing seminar that talks about plagiarism and stresses the importance of citation rules is a common remedy.

"We don't get many repeat offenders," he said. And for good reason: Those students can face suspension or expulsion.

Across the campus, at the Norlin Library, business writing instructor Eric Klinger helps direct the Writing Center, a free service for CU students, faculty, staff, and alumni. He comes across one or two cases of plagiarism every semester—almost always of the inadvertent variety—and draws a stark contrast between academic laziness and students who don't understand attribution rules that have changed and blurred as technology has created new entities such as wikis and blogs.

International setting

"There are differences in how we take in information, how we view and credit information now—it's just inescapable," he says. "Any of these electronic media complicate things. But it doesn't mean there isn't a right or wrong."

Klinger also notes that in an international setting such as a university, culture plays a role—an observation echoed by many experts. For instance, he says, some cultures condone quoting well-known material verbatim without attribution. Those students can face a tough transition.

At the Writing Center—and in his classes—he encourages all students to view writing as a process, not an event, to avoid turning to shortcuts in an eleventh-hour panic.

"I'm encouraged by how much students want to do the right thing," says Klinger, noting that the center's constant capacity crowds speak to students' desire to become better writers.

But there will always be some who try to cut corners and, in the process, produce anecdotes such as the one told by Cheyenne Mountain's Schriener of a poetry assignment turned in by a student early in his career.

It was a beautiful piece. But with a stunning lack of originality, the student titled it "Imagine."

"It was the song by John Lennon," Schriener recalls. "I said, 'Honestly, I was born in 1957; do you think I don't know the Beatles?'

"He just said, 'I was hoping you didn't.'"

Studies Shed Light on How Cheating Impedes Learning

Sarah D. Sparks

Education Week

2006

Sarah Sparks reports on education research, regularly blogging on Inside School Research. In "Studies Shed Light on How Cheating Impedes Learning," Sparks presents studies conducted at Harvard and Duke that show how students deceive themselves as a result of cheating. She explains that cheaters in the studies "lied to themselves." She also discusses the progressive, cumulative effects of plagiarism: cheating in high school leads to cheating in college, and cheating in college in turn leads to dishonesty in the workplace. When reading Sparks' article, consider how you feel about Spark's assertion that when you cheat, the person you hurt the most is yourself.

1. According to the article and previous studies on cheating, what specific measures can teachers and administrators take to encourage cheaters not to cheat?

2. How is the self-deception of cheating habitual and, if started early, how does it create a pattern of learning that follows a student through college into his or her professional career?

3. In what ways does valuing "academic integrity and learning, not just grades," as Sparks mentions, reduce cheating? In what other contexts can the ideas raised by Sparks be applied?

That time-honored anti-cheating mantra, "You're only hurting yourself," may be a literal fact, according to new research.

Emerging evidence suggests students who cheat on a test are more likely to deceive themselves into thinking they earned a high grade on their own merits, setting themselves up for future academic failure.

In four experiments detailed in the March Proceedings of the National Academy of Sciences, researchers from the Harvard Business School and Duke University found that cheaters pay for the short-term benefits of higher scores with inflated expectations for future performance.

The findings come as surveys and studies show a majority of students cheat—whether through cribbing homework, plagiarizing essays from the Internet, or texting test answers to a friend's cellphone—even though overwhelming majorities consider it wrong. The Los Angeles-based Josephson Institute Center for Youth Ethics, which has been tracking student character and academic honesty, has found that while the number of students engaging in specific behaviors has risen and fallen over the years, the number of students who admit to cheating on a test the previous year has not dipped below a majority since the first study in 1992. In the most recent survey, conducted in 2010, the study found that a majority of students cheat sometime during high school, and the likelihood of cheating increases the older students get.

Of a nationally representative sample of more than 40,000 public and private high school students responding to the survey, 59.4 percent admitted to having cheated on a test—including 55 percent of honors students.

In addition, more than 80 percent of the respondents said they had copied homework, more than one-third had plagiarized an Internet document for a class assignment, and 61 percent reported having lied to a teacher about "something important" at least once in the past year. By contrast, only about 20 percent of students surveyed reported having cheated in sports.

"One of the sad phenomena is that, on average, one of the things they are learning in school is how to cheat," John Fremer, the president of consulting services at Caveon LLC, a private test-security company in Midvale, Utah, said of students.

While most academic interest in cheating has focused on how students cheat and how to stop them, the Harvard-Duke study adds to emerging research suggesting that the mental hoops that students must leap through to justify or distance themselves from cheating can cause long-term damage to their professional and academic habits. The findings also point to aspects of school climate and instructional approach that can help break the cycle of cheating and self-deception.

"We see that the effect of cheating is, the more we engage in dishonest acts, the more we develop these cognitive distortions—ways in which we neutralize the act and almost forget how much we are doing it," said Jason M. Stephens, an assistant professor of educational psychology at the University of Connecticut, in Storrs, who studies cheating among secondary school students.

Moreover, the more students learn to focus on grades for their own sake, rather than as a representation of what they have learned, the more comfortable they are with cheating.

Mr. Stephens, who was not involved in the Harvard-Duke study, quoted one high school student, "Jane," who insisted that cheating on a test does nothing to lessen the value of the grade. "It says an A on the paper and you don't go, 'Oh, but I cheated.' You're just kind of like, 'Hey, I got that A,'" she said.

That, said Zoë Chance, the lead author of the Harvard-Duke study, is where cheaters start lying to themselves.

Self-Deception

In the first of the four experiments by the Harvard-Duke team, researchers asked 76 participants on the Massachusetts Institute of Technology campus to take a short test of "math IQ" and score their own sheets. Half the tests had an answer key on the page. After completing the test, all participants were asked

to predict how many questions they would answer correctly on a second, 100-question test without an answer key.

The other related experiments repeated the scenario with 345 students at the University of North Carolina at Chapel Hill, but required the participants to actually take the test after predicting how well they would do. In one variation, the participants were told they would receive money for the second test based on both the number correct and how close the predicted score came to the actual score.

Participants who had access to the test answers tended to use them. In the first rounds of testing in each scenario, mean scores were significantly higher among students who could sneak a peek at the answers. That fits with previous studies showing that, all else being equal, a majority of those who can cheat, do.

The Harvard-Duke research also showed that cheaters lied to themselves.

In a preliminary experiment involving 36 Harvard students, participants were asked simply to imagine cheating on the first test and then taking the second without an opportunity to cheat. Those participants predicted that they would perform worse on the second test, without the opportunity to cheat.

When faced with the real situation, they weren't nearly so objective. Across the board, cheaters tended to predict they would perform equally well on the next, longer test, though they knew they would not have a chance to cheat.

In the experiment involving money rewards for the second test scores, cheaters missed out on getting money because their actual scores were so much lower than the predictions they made based on their first test scores. If participants received a "certificate of recognition" for scoring well on the first test, they became even more likely to be overly optimistic about their success on the second test.

"In our experiments, we find that social recognition reinforces self-deception," said Ms. Chance, a Harvard doctoral student. If a student focuses on the high test score by itself, rather than cheating as the reason for it, she said, then "getting a high grade will lead 'Alex' to feel smart, and being treated as smart by the teacher will lead Alex to feel smarter still.

"Because Alex wasn't conscious of cheating, there's no reason to question the performance evaluation or the social feedback."

That means students may feel they are getting ahead in class, but actually they are falling into a feedback loop in which they fall further and further behind, according to Mr. Fremer of Caveon, the test-security firm. His firm was not part of the Harvard-Duke study.

Moreover, such self-deception can lead to a "death of a thousand cuts" for a student's honesty, Mr. Stephens said.

"Kids start to disengage [from] responsibility habitually; cheating in high school does lead to dishonesty in the workplace as an adult," he said.

Overwhelmed, Unengaged?

Not only does one instance of cheating lead to another, but the school environment can make it easier for students to mentally justify their dishonesty, research shows. Studies by Mr. Stephens and others that show students are more likely to cheat when they are under pressure to get high grades, uncertain about their own ability, unengaged in the material, or some combination of the three. In addition, students are better able to justify cheating in classes where they feel the teacher is unfair or does not attempt to engage them in learning.

Yet the entirety of the studies also suggests that making students more aware of the importance of academic integrity and learning, not just grades, can make them less likely to cheat.

In a previous study, Dan Ariely, a professor of psychology and behavioral economics at Duke and a co-author of the Harvard-Duke study, found test-takers became less likely to cheat when reminded of a school honor code, or if they saw someone they considered an outsider cheating.

Ms. Chance and Mr. Fremer said teachers and administrators should reduce opportunities for students to cheat, help them establish classwide and schoolwide codes for academic integrity, and then stress the importance of that code before every assignment.

Plagiarism & Cheating

"Think about helping cheaters find alternative means to get what they want," Ms. Chance said, "so that they don't react by cheating more or giving up."

Why Is Infographics Plagiarism So Common?

Alberto Cairo

Visualopolis

February 2012

Using eye-catching visuals, Alberto Cairo makes an argument that ethical standards for visual rhetoric ought to be equivalent to other forms of journalism in "Why is Infographics Plagiarism So Common?" Published in February 2012 on his Web site *Visualopolis*, Cairo shows an original layout of a newspaper page and a copy. Through comparing the two, he demonstrates why and how the copy constitutes plagiarism in the field of information graphics. When analyzing Cairo's Web site, consider the way this piece functions as a visual argument. How would the effectiveness of Cairo's text be impacted if it was composed solely of words, not images?

1. What "rules" does Cairo claim get broken in infographics that don't get broken in other genres?

2. Where does the line get drawn between appropriation and plagiarism?

3. What are other examples where work has been closely appropriated to the point where it borders on plagiarism?

It is time to say it loud and clear (again): infographics ethical standards must be equivalent to journalistic ethical standards. What is not acceptable in Journalism must also be unacceptable in information graphics. If this basic rule was respected, quite a lot of people would be immediately and justly fired in many newsrooms: not only infographics designers, but also chief editors and reporters who force them to break basic ethical rules they themselves would never break when writing a story. 'Hey, I've seen this cool illustration in this obscure foreign publication! Let's copy it! After all, it's just a simple drawing! Who is going to care?' Well, some of us do.

Take a very recent accusation of plagiarism: *La Stampa* (Italy) seems to have stolen work by *Estado de São Paulo* (Brazil).

It is obvious that *Estado* got its information about the mine accident from Chilean sources and that, among those, they probably used *La Tercera* and *El Mercurio*, the main newspapers in Santiago. That qualifies as acceptable: you cite a publication from a different country, you get some data from it, and then you design your own illustrations, diagrams, maps, and charts. That's legitimate, as long as you mention who are you getting your stuff from, and that you let your foreign colleagues know.

But a different story is to trace someone else's illustrations and graphics or, even worse, reproduce the originals without getting proper permissions. This was the case in this project, according to *Estado: La Stampa* simply copied a great deal of material. And it is likely that they also got the vector and bitmap drawings from the editable PDF version of the Brazilian newspaper, that can be downloaded from its website if you are a subscriber.

And you know what's even worse? *La Stampa* won a Society for News Design award for this. Below, I am reproducing the three pages of the PDF *Estado de São Paulo* has sent SND to document the case. It seems that there is a lot of work ahead for those of us worried about the state of ethics in journalistic information graphics and visualization, after so many years.

THE ORIGINAL WORK

THE COPY

O ESTADO DE S. PAULO

LA STAMPA

WHAT WAS COPIED

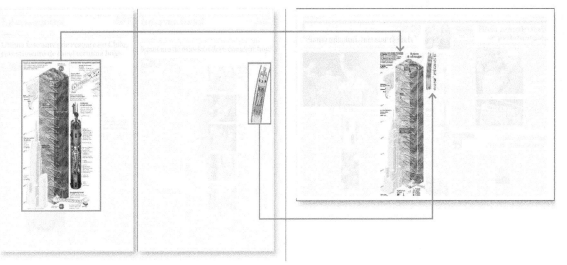

O ESTADO DE S. PAULO

LA STAMPA

IN FACT, OUR STUFF WAS JUST USED

LA STAMPA SENT ITS PDF PAGE FILE. WE OPENED IT ON ILLUSTRATOR AND FOUND OUR VECTOR WORK INSIDE.

WE JUST POSITIONED ITALIAN VECTOR (IN BLUE) WORK ABOVE OUR DRAWING (TIFF IMAGE) AND IS EASY TO SEE THAT OUR VECTOR WAS USED

EVEN THE TERRAIN CROSS SECTION WAS USED

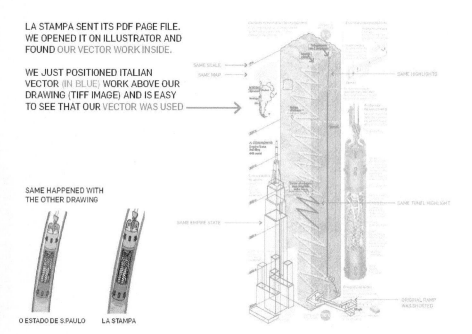

O ESTADO   LA STAMPA
DE S.PAULO

SAME HAPPENED WITH THE OTHER DRAWING

O ESTADO DE S.PAULO   LA STAMPA

Shame Sweepstakes

G.S. Mudur

The Telegraph

October 2012

G.S. Mudur is a reporter for *The Telegraph*, an Indian publication in Calcutta. With "In Plagiarism Too, China Beats India," Mudur presents visual evidence of questionable research practices in India and China. Upon critical reading, it is worth noting that the graphic was published in an Indian newspaper, and presents a comparison in which India comes across in a more positive light.

1. Why did they choose the title "Shame Sweepstakes" to present this information about plagiarism in India and China?

2. How do cultural differences contribute to standards and expectations of academic work and how might the view on plagiarism vary from one culture to the next?

3. What is the purpose of *The Telegraph* publishing an article and graphic such as this one? Within the larger context of cheating and plagiarism in research, what does the information in the graphic suggest?

New Delhi, Oct. 1: India and China appear to lead in plagiarism in life sciences research, but the US, Japan and Germany account for the majority of fraud, scientists reported today after a large analysis of shamed research.

Their study, described as the most comprehensive analysis yet of retracted research papers, also suggests that China accounts for a larger share of plagiarism, duplication and fraud or suspected fraud in life sciences research compared with India.

US scientists who analysed the origins of 2,047 retracted papers said that while scientific misconduct is rare—been retracted—its incidence appears greater than previously assumed.

The study has revealed geographical differences in causes of retractions. Three-fourths of the retractions due to fraud or suspected fraud were by researchers in the US, Germany and Japan, but India and China accounted for most of the retractions due to plagiarism or duplication. The findings appeared today in the US journal Proceedings of the National Academy of Sciences.

Microbiologist Ferric C. Fang at the University of Washington and his colleagues found that 67.4 per cent of the retractions were because of misconduct—fraud, suspected fraud, plagiarism or duplication—while 21.3 per cent were because of errors.

The analysis has shown a sharp increase in the number of retracted papers over the past 15 years. "This may reflect more misconduct and better detection," Fang told *The Telegraph*.

India accounted for 3.4 per cent (30 papers) of the 889 papers retracted for fraud or suspected fraud, 10 per cent (20 papers) of the 200 retracted for plagiarism, and 9 per cent (26 papers) of the 290 retracted because of duplication (see chart). China's count was higher under each head: 6.7 per cent (59 papers), 11.5 per cent (23 papers), and 20 per cent (58 papers), respectively.

Fang, however, has cautioned that the analysis was not designed for country-to-country comparisons, which would ideally also require data of the total number of research papers published by each country.

"The cause of (scientific) fraud is complex," Fang said. American psychiatrist Donald Kornfeld at Columbia University, New York, had published a paper earlier this year that said misconduct depends on both the psychological traits of individual scientists and the specific circumstances in which they work.

Indian scientists tracking academic ethics say the findings raise questions.

"I'm not sure whether the comparatively lower rate of fraud-related retraction from India is because Indians commit less fraud or because the papers aren't important enough to warrant additional scrutiny," said Rahul Siddharthan, a scientist at the Institute of Mathematical Sciences, Chennai.

The detection of fraud typically starts when other scientists try to independently replicate important results reported by one research group, Siddharthan said. Plagiarism and duplication is much easier to detect, he added.

Several cases of plagiarism have emerged in India in recent years, some involving researchers in high-profile institutions such as the IITs, but senior scientists tracking misconduct say there is little institutional response.

Plagiarism & Cheating

"There's little done about this," said Kasturi Lal Chopra, a member of the Society for Scientific Values, a non-government watchdog in India for scientific ethics.

"This contrasts with China, where the government about a year or so ago blacklisted many scientists caught in misconduct."

Fang, lead author of the new study, said the science environment in the US, Japan and Germany was highly competitive and scientists were under pressure to produce high-impact research publications to achieve funding and job advancement.

"Obviously, this is not a justification for fraud, but measures to alleviate stress in the research community would be likely to reduce incentives for misconduct," Fang said.

He said the geographical differences might reflect differences in cultural concepts of intellectual property or in proficiency in the English language.

Some papers might qualify as both plagiarism and fraud, said T.A. Abinandanan, professor of materials engineering at the Indian Institute of Science, Bangalore, who has independently been tracking misconduct in India.

Several papers a scientist in Andhra Pradesh retracted between 2005 and 2010, for instance, had not just plagiarised text but had also changed the names of chemical compounds and reagents. Abinandanan labels it a case of falsification.

Fang collaborated with immunologist Arturo Casadevall at the Albert Einstein College in New York and R. Grant Steen, head of a medical communications consultancy

Chapter 4

Ethical Engagement: Campus Communities

Campus Athletics
Greek Life
Campus Safety

4

Ethical Engagement: Campus Communities

> "We cannot seek achievement for ourselves and forget about progress and prosperity for our community...Our ambitions must be broad enough to include the aspirations and needs of others, for their sakes and for our own."
>
> —Cesar Chavez

Take a walk through a college's student plaza on any given day. You'll hear the thumping of bass music, the chanting of protest, "save the Earth" demonstrations, and a general buzz of excitement. You'll see a single person speaking animatedly while a group of students look and listen—some with an air of disdain, others with intrigue and curiosity. A college is teeming with individuals entertaining various interests and coming from different backgrounds. It is when these individuals interconnect that community can be found. Examples of community are apparent at every turn—student government, club sports, fraternities and sororities, ski club, book club, Student Veterans Organization, the Alpha Center, Pagan Student Alliance, Students for Holocaust Awareness, Students for Study Abroad, and the Zen Club to name a scant few—all expressing their diverse views and missions, reaching out and engaging within a larger campus community.

Diverse views and missions can lead to disagreement about what is right and wrong; in other words, when various communities engage, the ethics that guide those communities must be critically examined and sometimes challenged. While people long to be part of a group, community itself is imperfect and fraught with differences; responsible citizenship means to engage critically and compassionately within the communities in which we play a part. Because every campus hosts hundreds of small communities, this chapter focuses only on campus athletics, Greek life, and campus safety.

Taylor Branch, a noted historian and author of "The Shame of College Sports," writes, "College sports are deeply inscribed in the culture of our nation… [and] college sports has become Very Big Business." This "Very Big Business" of college athletics even has its own association that helps various schools manage and organize their programs, the National Collegiate Athletic Association (NCAA), whose aim is to "protect the well-being of student-athletes." However, the ethical engagements in some areas of this community, as Branch and other sports enthusiasts point out, are currently being scrutinized. In particular, Branch made a bold suggestion that student-athletes should be paid, which ignited a national debate about the treatment and/or exploitation of college athletes. The examination of student-athlete treatment, however, is not new; people like Dr. Krystal Beamon, a Sociology and Anthropology professor at the University of Texas, have been studying the perceived exploitation of athletes for over a decade. This situation begs the question: are student-athletes being treated fairly for the services they provide? Are scholarships and a "free" education proper compensation? Do student-athletes receive preferential treatment when enrolling in classes? Does the NCAA "protect" its student-athletes? These are merely a sampling of issues that arise when considering the ethical engagement within college athletic communities.

Another campus community with a history deeply rooted in U.S. higher education is the Greek system. Nearly 9 million students nationwide, according to the website *Fraternity Advisor*, belong to a fraternity or sorority out of the approximate 21 million undergraduate and graduate students attending colleges nationwide. Since almost half of all college students are members of the Greek community, it is critical to examine the ethical engagements of such organizations, especially when they receive negative media coverage of hazing abuses and binge drinking. Janet Reitman, contributing editor of *Rolling Stone*, wrote an exposé highlighting an egregious case of hazing at Dartmouth. Although Reitman's article casts Dartmouth fraternity members as "entitled booze-hounds," membership in a fraternity could be quite advantageous to its members. The Greek community provides leadership opportunities. Fraternity and sorority members provide countless hours of community service, and make strong social connections that often lead to professional opportunities post-graduation (Asel, Seifert, and Pascarella). In fact, *Oracle*, an academic journal devoted to exploring issues within fraternities and sororities, offers suggestions to change detrimental behavior, like hazing rituals, and highlight the honorable and ethical acts within the fraternal system.

Campus safety is the final area of ethical engagement explored in this chapter. The phrase "campus safety" could refer to a number of significant issues. This section, however, focuses primarily on the ethical engagements of campus safety surrounding sexual assault. Though a difficult issue to discuss, examining issues surrounding sexual assault are critical to establishing a safe campus. The section not only speaks toward keeping students safe, but shows multiple perspectives about sexual assault and the various entities involved. Members of the college community who experience sexual assault often feel they've been victimized twice due to inadequate procedures put in place by their university. This is an ethical concern, and one that demands open channels of conversation to create a safer community.

Campus athletics, Greek life, and campus safety present numerous salient issues of ethical engagement in higher education, but they only represent a handful of the myriad discussions that could, and should, occur within the campus community. As Cesar Chavez's quote above indicates, we do not live in isolation. We must begin to consider our place within a community and *engage*.

Works Cited

"Greek Life Statistics." *The Fraternity Advisor*. 2013. Web. 16 July 2013. <http://thefraternityadvisor.com/greek-life-statistics/>.

Chronology of Enforcement

National Collegiate Athletics Association

ncaa.org

April 2013

One of the biggest "entertainment" engagements on college campuses is sports. The NCAA was created a century ago in order to maintain "fair play" within this popular aspect of student life. In particular, the NCAA strives to "protect the well-being of student athletes." Currently there is a cry for student-athletes to get paid for their athletic performance, which is causing the NCAA to rethink their enforcement policies and mission. As you read their mission statement, consider this controversy about paying student-athletes.

1. From this mission statement, what position does the NCAA currently have on pay-for-play?

2. Consider that the term "fair" (or some variation of the word) is expressed in this short mission statement four times. What audience appeal is being emphasized?

3. In "The Shame of College Sports," Taylor Branch deems the practices of the NCAA unjust. How does Branch's estimation and the NCAA's mission come to such different ends?

Enforcement

Integrity. Fair play. Accountability.

The NCAA enforcement program strives to maintain a level playing field for the more than 400,000 student-athletes. Commitment to fair play is a bedrock principle of the NCAA. The NCAA upholds that principle by enforcing membership-created rules that ensure equitable competition and protect the well-being of student-athletes at all member institutions.

The enforcement program is dedicated to creating positive student-athlete experiences by preserving the integrity of the enterprise. The mission of the NCAA enforcement program is to reduce violations of NCAA legislation and impose appropriate penalties if violations occur. The program is committed to the fairness of procedures and to the timely and equitable resolution of infractions cases.

A fundamental principle of the enforcement program is to ensure that institutions abiding by NCAA legislation are not disadvantaged by complying with the rules.

The Shame of College Sports

Taylor Branch

The Atlantic

April 2013

Taylor Branch is a Pulitzer award-winning author, primarily regarding historical topics from the Civil Rights Movement. However, his 2011 *Atlantic* article (later expanded into an e-book called *The Cartel*) about the hypocrisy and greed of the NCAA and their virtual enslavement of student-athletes sparked a national debate that continues to intensify. As you read this scathing review of the practices of the NCAA, consider how you might define a *student-athlete* and how you might best keep them safe.

1. What does Branch propose as a way to provide "effective checks and balances" to the NCAA?

2. Throughout the article, Branch uses quite a bit of slavery rhetoric. What implications do these suggestions have, and how does this language influence your understanding of the argument?

3. When looking at the mission statement of the NCAA in comparison to Branch's condemnation of the NCAA, who should you believe? Why?

"I'm not hiding," Sonny Vaccaro told a closed hearing at the Willard Hotel in Washington, D.C., in 2001. "We want to put our materials on the bodies of your athlete and the best way to do that is buy your school. Or buy your coach."

Vaccaro's audience, the members of the Knight Commission on Intercollegiate Athletics, bristled. These were eminent reformers—among them the president of the National Collegiate Athletic Association, two former heads of the U.S. Olympic Committee, and several university presidents and chancellors. The Knight Foundation, a nonprofit that takes an interest in college athletics as part of its concern with civic life, had tasked them with saving college sports from runaway commercialism as embodied by the likes of Vaccaro, who, since signing his pioneering shoe contract with Michael Jordan in 1984, had built sponsorship empires successively at Nike, Adidas, and Reebok. Not all the members could hide their scorn for the "sneaker pimp" of schoolyard hustle, who boasted of writing checks for millions to everybody in higher education.

"Why," asked Bryce Jordan, the president emeritus of Penn State, "should a university be an advertising medium for your industry?"

Vaccaro did not blink. "They shouldn't, sir," he replied. "You sold your souls, and you're going to continue selling them. You can be very moral and righteous in asking me that question, sir," Vaccaro added with irrepressible good cheer, "but there's not one of you in this room that's going to turn down any of our money. You're going to take it. I can only offer it."

William Friday, a former president of North Carolina's university system, still winces at the memory. "Boy, the silence that fell in that room," he recalled recently. "I never will forget it." Friday, who founded and co-chaired two of the three Knight Foundation sports initiatives over the past 20 years, called Vaccaro "the worst of all" the witnesses ever to come before the panel.

But what Vaccaro said in 2001 was true then, and it's true now: corporations offer money so they can profit from the glory of college athletes, and the universities grab it. In 2010, despite the faltering economy, a single college athletic league, the football-crazed Southeastern Conference (SEC), became the first to crack the billion-dollar barrier in athletic receipts. The Big Ten pursued closely at $905 million. That money comes from a combination of ticket sales, concession sales, merchandise, licensing fees, and other sources—but the great bulk of it comes from television contracts.

Campus Athletics

Educators are in thrall to their athletic departments because of these television riches and because they respect the  political furies that can burst from a locker room. "There's fear," Friday told me when I visited him on the University of North Carolina campus in Chapel Hill last fall. As we spoke, two giant construction cranes towered nearby over the university's Kenan Stadium, working on the latest $77 million renovation. (The University of Michigan spent almost four times that much to expand its Big House.) Friday insisted that for the networks, paying huge sums to universities was a bargain. "We do every little thing for them," he said. "We furnish the theater, the actors, the lights, the music, and the audience for a drama measured neatly in time slots. They bring the camera and turn it on." Friday, a weathered idealist at 91, laments the control universities have ceded in pursuit of this money. If television wants to broadcast football from here on a Thursday night, he said, "we shut down the university at 3 o'clock to accommodate the crowds." He longed for a campus identity more centered in an academic mission.

The United States is the only country in the world that hosts big-time sports at institutions of higher learning. This should not, in and of itself, be controversial. College athletics are rooted in the classical ideal of *Mens sana in corpore sano*—a sound mind in a sound body—and who would argue with that? College sports are deeply inscribed in the culture of our nation. Half a million young men and women play competitive intercollegiate sports each year. Millions of spectators flock into football stadiums each Saturday in the fall, and tens of millions more watch on television. The March Madness basketball tournament each spring has become a major national event, with upwards of 80 million watching it on television and talking about the games around the office water cooler. ESPN has spawned ESPNU, a channel dedicated to college sports, and Fox Sports and other cable outlets are developing channels exclusively to cover sports from specific regions or divisions.

With so many people paying for tickets and watching on television, college sports has become Very Big Business. According to various reports, the football teams at Texas, Florida, Georgia, Michigan, and Penn State—to name just a few big-revenue football schools—each earn between $40 million and $80 million in profits a year, even after paying coaches multimillion-dollar salaries. When you combine so much money with such high, almost tribal, stakes—football boosters are famously rabid in their zeal to have their alma mater win—corruption is likely to follow.

Scandal after scandal has rocked college sports. In 2010, the NCAA sanctioned the University of Southern California after determining that star running back Reggie Bush and his family had received "improper benefits" while he played for the Trojans. (Among other charges, Bush and members of his family were alleged to have received free airfare and limousine rides, a car, and a rent-free home in San Diego, from sports agents who wanted Bush as a client.) The Bowl Championship Series stripped USC of its 2004 national title, and Bush returned the Heisman Trophy he had won in 2005. Last fall, as Auburn University football stormed its way to an undefeated season and a national championship, the team's star quarterback, Cam Newton, was dogged by allegations that his father had used a recruiter to solicit up to $180,000 from Mississippi State in exchange for his son's matriculation there after junior college in 2010. Jim Tressel, the highly successful head football coach of the Ohio State Buckeyes, resigned last spring after the NCAA alleged he had feigned ignorance of rules violations by players on his team. At least 28 players over the course of the previous nine seasons, according to *Sports Illustrated*, had traded autographs, jerseys, and other team memorabilia in exchange for tattoos or cash at a tattoo parlor in Columbus, in violation of NCAA rules. Late this summer, Yahoo Sports reported that the NCAA was investigating allegations that a University of Miami booster had given millions of dollars in illicit cash and services to more than 70 Hurricanes football players over eight years.

The list of scandals goes on. With each revelation, there is much wringing of hands. Critics scold schools for breaking faith with their educational mission, and for failing to enforce the sanctity of "amateurism." Sportswriters denounce the NCAA for both tyranny and impotence in its quest to "clean up" college sports. Observers on all sides express jumbled emotions about youth and innocence, venting against professional mores or greedy amateurs.

For all the outrage, the real scandal is not that students are getting illegally paid or recruited, it's that two of the noble principles on which the NCAA justifies its existence—"amateurism" and the "student-athlete"—are cynical hoaxes, legalistic confections propagated by the universities so they can exploit the skills and fame of young athletes. The tragedy at the heart of college sports is not that some college athletes are getting paid, but that more of them are not.

Don Curtis, a UNC trustee, told me that impoverished football players cannot afford movie tickets or bus fare home. Curtis is a rarity among those in higher education today, in that he dares to violate the signal taboo: "I think we should pay these guys something."

Fans and educators alike recoil from this proposal as though from original sin. Amateurism is the whole point, they say. Paid athletes would destroy the integrity and appeal of college sports. Many former college athletes object that money would have spoiled the sanctity of the bond they enjoyed with their teammates. I, too, once shuddered instinctively at the notion of paid college athletes.

But after an inquiry that took me into locker rooms and ivory towers across the country, I have come to believe that sentiment blinds us to what's before our eyes. Big-time college sports are fully commercialized. Billions of dollars flow through them each year. The NCAA makes money, and enables universities and corporations to make money, from the unpaid labor of young athletes.

Slavery analogies should be used carefully. College athletes are not slaves. Yet to survey the scene—corporations and universities enriching themselves on the backs of uncompensated young men, whose status as "student-athletes" deprives them of the right to due process guaranteed by the Constitution—is to catch an unmistakable whiff of the plantation. Perhaps a more apt metaphor is colonialism: college sports, as overseen by the NCAA, is a system imposed by well-meaning paternalists and rationalized with hoary sentiments about caring for the well-being of the colonized. But it is, nonetheless, unjust. The NCAA, in its zealous defense of bogus principles, sometimes destroys the dreams of innocent young athletes.

The NCAA today is in many ways a classic cartel. Efforts to reform it—most notably by the three Knight Commissions over the course of 20 years—have, while making changes around the edges, been largely fruitless. The time has come for a major overhaul. And whether the powers that be like it or not, big changes are coming. Threats loom on multiple fronts: in Congress, the courts, breakaway athletic conferences, student rebellion, and public disgust. Swaddled in gauzy clichés, the NCAA presides over a vast, teetering glory.

...

The Myth of the "Student-Athlete"

Today, much of the NCAA's moral authority—indeed much of the justification for its existence—is vested in its claim to protect what it calls the "student-athlete." The term is meant to conjure the nobility of amateurism, and the precedence of scholarship over athletic endeavor. But the origins of the "student-athlete" lie not in a disinterested ideal but in a sophistic formulation designed, as the sports economist Andrew Zimbalist has written, to help the NCAA in its "fight against workmen's compensation insurance claims for injured football players."

"We crafted the term student-athlete," Walter Byers [the first executive director of the NCAA] wrote, "and soon it was embedded in all NCAA rules and interpretations." The term came into play in the 1950s, when the widow of Ray Dennison, who had died from a head injury received while playing football in Colorado for the Fort Lewis A&M Aggies, filed for workmen's-compensation death benefits. Did his football scholarship make the fatal collision a "work-related" accident? Was he a school employee, like his peers who worked part-time as teaching assistants and bookstore cashiers? Or was he a fluke victim of extracurricular pursuits? Given the hundreds of incapacitating injuries to college athletes each year, the answers to these questions had enormous consequences. The Colorado Supreme Court ultimately agreed with the school's contention that he was not eligible for benefits, since the college was "not in the football business."

The term *student-athlete* was deliberately ambiguous. College players were not students at play (which might understate their athletic obligations), nor were they just athletes in college (which might imply they were professionals). That they were high-performance athletes meant they could be forgiven for not meeting the academic standards of their peers; that they were students meant they did not have to be compensated, ever, for anything more than the cost of their studies. *Student-athlete* became the NCAA's signature term, repeated constantly in and out of courtrooms.

Using the "student-athlete" defense, colleges have compiled a string of victories in liability cases. On the afternoon of October 26, 1974, the Texas Christian University Horned Frogs were playing the Alabama Crimson Tide in Birmingham, Alabama. Kent Waldrep, a TCU running back, carried the ball on a "Red Right 28" sweep toward the Crimson Tide's sideline, where he was met by a swarm of tacklers. When Waldrep regained consciousness, Bear Bryant, the storied Crimson Tide coach, was standing over his hospital bed. "It was like talking to God, if you're a young football player," Waldrep recalled.

Waldrep was paralyzed: he had lost all movement and feeling below his neck. After nine months of paying his medical bills, Texas Christian refused to pay any more, so the Waldrep family coped for years on dwindling charity.

Through the 1990s, from his wheelchair, Waldrep pressed a lawsuit for workers' compensation. (He also, through heroic rehabilitation efforts, recovered feeling in his arms, and eventually learned to drive a specially rigged van. "I can brush my teeth," he told me last year, "but I still need help to bathe and dress.") His attorneys haggled with TCU and the state worker-compensation fund over what constituted employment. Clearly, TCU had provided football players with equipment for the job, as a typical employer would—but did the university pay wages, withhold income taxes on his financial aid, or control work conditions and performance? The appeals court finally rejected Waldrep's claim in June of 2000, ruling that he was not an employee because he had not paid taxes on financial aid that he could have kept even if he quit football. (Waldrep told me school officials "said they recruited me as a student, not an athlete," which he says was absurd.)

The long saga vindicated the power of the NCAA's "student-athlete" formulation as a shield, and the organization continues to invoke it as both a legalistic defense and a noble ideal. Indeed, such is the term's rhetorical power that it is increasingly used as a sort of reflexive mantra against charges of rabid hypocrisy.

...

"Whoremasters"

... Last year, CBS Sports and Turner Broadcasting paid $771 million to the NCAA for television rights to the 2011 men's basketball tournament alone. That's three-quarters of a billion dollars built on the backs of amateurs—on unpaid labor. The whole edifice depends on the players' willingness to perform what is effectively volunteer work. The athletes, and the league officials, are acutely aware of this extraordinary arrangement. William Friday, the former North Carolina president, recalls being yanked from one Knight Commission meeting and sworn to secrecy about what might happen if a certain team made the NCAA championship basketball game. "They were going to dress and go out on the floor," Friday told me, "but refuse to play," in a wildcat student strike. Skeptics doubted such a diabolical plot. These were college kids—unlikely to second-guess their coaches, let alone forfeit the dream of a championship. Still, it was unnerving to contemplate what hung on the consent of a few young volunteers: several hundred million dollars in television revenue, countless livelihoods, the NCAA budget, and subsidies for sports at more than 1,000 schools. Friday's informants exhaled when the suspect team lost before the finals.

Cognizant of its precarious financial base, the NCAA has in recent years begun to pursue new sources of revenue. Taking its cue from member schools such as Ohio State (which in 2009 bundled all its promotional rights—souvenirs, stadium ads, shoe deals—and outsourced them to the international sports marketer IMG College for a guaranteed $11 million a year), the NCAA began to exploit its vault of college sports on film. For $29.99 apiece, NCAA On Demand offers DVDs of more than 200 memorable contests in men's ice hockey alone. Video-game technology also allows nostalgic fans to relive and even participate in classic moments of NCAA Basketball. NCAA Football, licensed by the NCAA through IMG College to Electronic Arts, one of the world's largest video-game manufacturers, reportedly sold 2.5 million copies in 2008. Brit Kirwan, the chancellor of the Maryland university system and a former president at Ohio State, says there were "terrible fights" between the third Knight Commission and the NCAA over the ethics of generating this revenue.

All of this money ultimately derives from the college athletes whose likenesses are shown in the films or video games. But none of the profits go to them. Last year, Electronic Arts paid more than $35 million in royalties to the NFL players union for the underlying value of names and images in its pro football series—but neither the NCAA nor its affiliated companies paid former college players a nickel. Naturally, as they have become more of a profit center for the NCAA, some of the vaunted "student-athletes" have begun to clamor that they deserve a share of those profits. You "see everybody getting richer and richer," Desmond Howard, who won the 1991 Heisman Trophy while playing for the Michigan Wolverines, told *USA Today* recently. "And you walk around and you can't put gas in your car? You can't even fly home to see your parents?"

Some athletes have gone beyond talk. A series of lawsuits quietly making their way through the courts cast a harsh light on the absurdity of the system—and threaten to dislodge the foundations on which the NCAA rests. On July 21, 2009, lawyers for Ed O'Bannon filed a class-action antitrust suit against the NCAA at the U.S. District Court in San Francisco. "Once you leave your university," says O'Bannon, who won the John Wooden Award for player of the year in 1995 on UCLA's national-championship basketball team, "one would think your likeness belongs to you." The NCAA and UCLA continue to collect money from the sales of videos of him playing. But by NCAA rules, O'Bannon, who today works at a Toyota dealership near Las Vegas, alleges he is still not allowed to share the revenue the NCAA generates from his own image as a college athlete. His suit quickly gathered co-plaintiffs from basketball and football, ex-players featured in NCAA videos and other products. "The NCAA does not license student-athlete likenesses," NCAA spokesperson Erik Christianson told The New York Times in response to the suit, "or prevent former student-athletes from attempting to do so. Likewise, to claim the NCAA profits off student-athlete likenesses is also pure fiction."

The legal contention centers on Part IV of the NCAA's "Student-Athlete Statement" for Division I, which requires every athlete to authorize use of "your name or picture … to promote NCAA championships or other NCAA events, activities or programs." Does this clause mean that athletes clearly renounce personal interest forever? If so, does it actually undermine the NCAA by implicitly recognizing that athletes have a property right in their own performance? Jon King, a lawyer for the plaintiffs, expects the NCAA's core mission of amateurism to be its "last defense standing."

…

The late Myles Brand, who led the NCAA from 2003 to 2009, defended the economics of college sports by claiming that they were simply the result of a smoothly functioning free market. He and his colleagues deflected criticism about the money saturating big-time college sports by focusing attention on scapegoats; in 2010, outrage targeted sports agents. Last year *Sports Illustrated* published "Confessions of an Agent," a firsthand account of dealing with high-strung future pros whom the agent and his peers courted with flattery, cash, and tawdry favors. Nick Saban, Alabama's head football coach, mobilized his peers to denounce agents as a public scourge. "I hate to say this," he said, "but how are they any better than a pimp? I have no respect for people who do that to young people. None."

Saban's raw condescension contrasts sharply with the lonely penitence from Dale Brown, the retired longtime basketball coach at LSU. "Look at the money we make off predominantly poor black kids," Brown once reflected. "We're the whoremasters."

"Picayune Rules"

NCAA officials have tried to assert their dominion—and distract attention from the larger issues—by chasing frantically after petty violations. Tom McMillen, a former member of the Knight Commission who was an All-American basketball player at the University of Maryland, likens these officials to traffic cops in a speed trap, who could flag down almost any passing motorist for prosecution in kangaroo court under a "maze of picayune rules." The publicized cases have become convoluted soap operas. At the start of the 2010 football season, A. J. Green, a wide receiver at Georgia, confessed that he'd sold his own jersey from the Independence Bowl the year before, to raise cash for a spring-break vacation. The NCAA sentenced Green to a four-game suspension for violating his amateur status with the illicit profit generated by selling the shirt off his own back. While he served the suspension, the Georgia Bulldogs store continued legally selling replicas of Green's No. 8 jersey for $39.95 and up.

A few months later, the NCAA investigated rumors that Ohio State football players had benefited from "hook-ups on tatts"—that is, that they'd gotten free or underpriced tattoos at an Ohio tattoo parlor in exchange for autographs and memorabilia—a violation of the NCAA's rule against discounts linked to athletic personae. The NCAA Committee on Infractions imposed five-game suspensions on Terrelle Pryor, Ohio State's tattooed quarterback, and four other players (some of whom had been found to have sold their Big Ten championship rings and other gear), but did permit them to finish the season and play in the Sugar Bowl. (This summer, in an attempt to satisfy NCAA investigators, Ohio State voluntarily vacated its football wins from last season, as well as its Sugar Bowl victory.) A different NCAA committee promulgated a rule banning symbols and messages in players' eyeblack—reportedly aimed at Pryor's controversial gesture of support for the pro quarterback Michael Vick, and at Bible verses inscribed in the eyeblack of the former Florida quarterback Tim Tebow.

The moral logic is hard to fathom: the NCAA bans personal messages on the bodies of the players, and penalizes players for trading their celebrity status for discounted tattoos—but it codifies precisely how and where commercial insignia from multinational corporations can be displayed on college players, for the financial benefit of the colleges. Last season, while the NCAA investigated him and his father for the recruiting fees they'd allegedly sought, Cam Newton compliantly wore at least 15 corporate logos—one on his jersey, four on his helmet visor, one on each wristband, one on his pants, six on his shoes, and one on the headband he wears under his helmet—as part of Auburn's $10.6 million deal with Under Armour.

. . .

"They Want to Crush These Kids"

Academic performance has always been difficult for the NCAA to address. Any detailed regulation would intrude upon the free choice of widely varying schools, and any academic standard broad enough to fit both MIT and Ole Miss would have little force. From time to time, a scandal will expose extreme lapses. In 1989, Dexter Manley, by then the famous "Secretary of Defense" for the NFL's Washington Redskins, teared up before the U.S. Senate Subcommittee on Education, Arts, and Humanities, when admitting that he had been functionally illiterate in college.

Within big-time college athletic departments, the financial pressure to disregard obvious academic shortcomings and shortcuts is just too strong. In the 1980s, Jan Kemp, an English instructor at the University of Georgia, publicly alleged that university officials had demoted and then fired her because she refused to inflate grades in her remedial English courses. Documents showed that administrators replaced the grades she'd given athletes with higher ones, providing fake passing grades on one notable occasion to nine Bulldog football players who otherwise would have been ineligible to compete in the 1982 Sugar Bowl. (Georgia lost anyway, 24–20, to a University of Pittsburgh team led by the future Hall of Fame quarterback Dan Marino.) When Kemp filed a lawsuit against the university, she was publicly vilified as a troublemaker, but she persisted bravely in her testimony. Once, Kemp said, a supervisor demanding that she fix a grade had bellowed, "Who do you think is more important to this university, you or Dominique Wilkins?" (Wilkins was a star on the basketball team.) Traumatized, Kemp twice attempted suicide.

In trying to defend themselves, Georgia officials portrayed Kemp as naive about sports. "We have to compete on a level playing field," said Fred Davison, the university president. During the Kemp civil trial, in 1986, Hale Almand, Georgia's defense lawyer, explained the university's patronizing aspirations for its typical less-than-scholarly athlete. "We may not make a university student out of him," Almand told the court, "but if we can teach him to read and write, maybe he can work at the post office rather than as a garbage man when he gets through with his athletic career." This argument backfired with the jurors: finding in favor of Kemp, they rejected her polite request for $100,000, and awarded her $2.6 million in damages instead. (This was later reduced to $1.08 million.) Jan Kemp embodied what is ostensibly the NCAA's reason for being—to enforce standards fairly and put studies above sports—but no one from the organization ever spoke up on her behalf.

...

The debates and commissions about reforming college sports nibble around the edges—trying to reduce corruption, to prevent the "contamination" of athletes by lucre, and to maintain at least a pretense of concern for academic integrity. Everything stands on the implicit presumption that preserving amateurism is necessary for the well-being of college athletes.

But while amateurism—and the free labor it provides—may be necessary to the preservation of the NCAA, and perhaps to the profit margins of various interested corporations and educational institutions, what if it doesn't benefit the athletes? What if it hurts them?

"The Plantation Mentality"

"Ninety percent of the NCAA revenue is produced by 1 percent of the athletes," Sonny Vaccaro says. "Go to the skill positions"—the stars. "Ninety percent African Americans." The NCAA made its money off those kids, and so did he. They were not all bad people, the NCAA officials, but they were blind, Vaccaro believes. "Their organization is a fraud."

Vaccaro retired from Reebok in 2007 to make a clean break for a crusade. "The kids and their parents gave me a good life," he says in his peppery staccato. "I want to give something back." Call it redemption, he told me. Call it education or a good cause. "Here's what I preach," said Vaccaro. "This goes beyond race, to human rights. The least educated are the most exploited. I'm probably closer to the kids than anyone else, and I'm 71 years old."

Vaccaro is officially an unpaid consultant to the plaintiffs in O'Bannon v. NCAA. He connected Ed O'Bannon with the attorneys who now represent him, and he talked to some of the additional co-plaintiffs who have joined the suit, among them Oscar Robertson, a basketball Hall of Famer who was incensed that the NCAA was still selling his image on playing cards 50 years after he left the University of Cincinnati.

Jon King, an antitrust lawyer at Hausfeld LLP in San Francisco, told me that Vaccaro "opened our eyes to massive revenue streams hidden in college sports." King and his colleagues have drawn on Vaccaro's vast knowledge of athletic-department finances, which include off-budget accounts for shoe contracts. Sonny Vaccaro and his wife, Pam, "had a mountain of documents," he said. The outcome of the 1984 Regents decision validated an antitrust approach for O'Bannon, King argues, as well as for Joseph Agnew in his continuing case against the one-year scholarship rule. Lawyers for Sam Keller—a former quarterback for the University of Nebraska who is featured in video games—are pursuing a parallel "right of publicity" track based on the First Amendment. ... King thinks claims for the rights of college players may be viable also under laws pertaining to contracts, employment, and civil rights.

Vaccaro had sought a law firm for O'Bannon with pockets deep enough to withstand an expensive war of attrition, fearing that NCAA officials would fight discovery to the end. So far, though, they have been forthcoming. "The numbers are off the wall," Vaccaro says. "The public will see for the first time how all the money is distributed."

Vaccaro has been traveling the after-dinner circuit, proselytizing against what he sees as the NCAA's exploitation of young athletes. Late in 2008, someone who heard his stump speech at Howard University mentioned it to Michael Hausfeld, a prominent antitrust and human-rights lawyer, whose firm had won suits against Exxon for Native Alaskans and against Union Bank of Switzerland for Holocaust victims' families. Someone tracked down Vaccaro on vacation in Athens, Greece, and he flew back directly to meet Hausfeld. The shoe salesman and the white-shoe lawyer made common cause.

Hausfeld LLP has offices in San Francisco, Philadelphia, and London. Its headquarters are on K Street in Washington, D.C., about three blocks from the White House. When I talked with Hausfeld there not long ago, he sat in a cavernous conference room, tidy in pinstripes, hands folded on a spotless table that reflected the skyline. He spoke softly, without pause, condensing the complex fugue of antitrust litigation into simple sentences. "Let's start with the basic question," he said, noting that the NCAA claims that student-athletes have no property rights in their own athletic accomplishments. Yet, in order to be eligible to play, college athletes have to waive their rights to proceeds from any sales based on their athletic performance.

"What right is it that they're waiving?" Hausfeld asked. "You can't waive something you don't have. So they had a right that they gave up in consideration to the principle of amateurism, if there be such." (At an April hearing in a U.S. District Court in California, Gregory Curtner, a representative for the NCAA, stunned O'Bannon's lawyers by saying: "There is no document, there is no substance, that the NCAA ever takes from the student-athletes their rights of publicity or their rights of likeness. They are at all times owned by the student-athlete." Jon King says this is "like telling someone they have the winning lottery ticket, but by the way, it can only be cashed in on Mars." The court denied for a second time an NCAA motion to dismiss the O'Bannon complaint.)

The waiver clause is nestled among the paragraphs of the "Student-Athlete Statement" that NCAA rules require be collected yearly from every college athlete. In signing the statement, the athletes attest that they have amateur status, that their stated SAT scores are valid, that they are willing to disclose any educational documents requested, and so forth. Already, Hausfeld said, the defendants in the Ed O'Bannon case have said in court filings that college athletes thereby transferred their promotional rights forever. He paused. "That's ludicrous," he said. "Nobody assigns rights like that. Nobody can assert rights like that." He said the pattern demonstrated clear abuse by the collective power of the schools and all their conferences under the NCAA umbrella—"a most effective cartel."

The work will be hard, but Hausfeld said he will win in the courts, unless the NCAA folds first. "Why?" Hausfeld asked rhetorically. "We know our clients are foreclosed: neither the NCAA nor its members will permit them to participate in any of that licensing revenue. Under the law, it's up to them [the defendants] to give a pro-competitive justification. They can't. End of story."

...

In 2010 the third Knight Commission, complementing a previous commission's recommendation for published reports on academic progress, called for the finances of college sports to be made transparent and public—television contracts, conference budgets, shoe deals, coaches' salaries, stadium bonds, everything. The recommendation was based on the worthy truism that sunlight is a proven disinfectant. But in practice, it has not been applied at all. Conferences, coaches, and other stakeholders resisted disclosure; college players still have no way of determining their value to the university.

"Money surrounds college sports," says Domonique Foxworth, who is a cornerback for the NFL's Baltimore Ravens and an executive-committee member for the NFL Players Association, and played for the University of Maryland. "And every player knows those millions are floating around only because of the 18-to-22-year-olds." Yes, he told me, even the second-string punter believes a miracle might lift him into the NFL, and why not? In all the many pages of the three voluminous Knight Commission reports, there is but one paragraph that addresses the real-life choices for college athletes. "Approximately 1 percent of NCAA men's basketball players and 2 percent of NCAA football players are drafted by NBA or NFL teams," stated the 2001 report, basing its figures on a review of the previous 10 years, "and just being drafted is no assurance of a successful professional career." Warning that the odds against professional athletic success are "astronomically high," the Knight Commission counsels college athletes to avoid a "rude surprise" and to stick to regular studies. This is sound advice as far as it goes, but it's a bromide that pinches off discussion. Nothing in the typical college curriculum teaches a sweat-stained guard at Clemson or Purdue what his monetary value to the university is. Nothing prods students to think independently about amateurism—because the universities themselves have too much invested in its preservation. Stifling thought, the universities, in league with the NCAA, have failed their own primary mission by providing an empty, cynical education on college sports.

The most basic reform would treat the students as what they are—adults, with rights and reason of their own—and grant them a meaningful voice in NCAA deliberations. A restoration of full citizenship to "student-athletes" would facilitate open governance, making it possible to enforce pledges of transparency in both academic standards and athletic finances. Without that, the NCAA has no effective checks and balances, no way for the students to provide informed consent regarding the way they are governed. A thousand questions lie willfully silenced because the NCAA is naturally afraid of giving "student-athletes" a true voice. Would college players be content with the augmented scholarship or allowance now requested by the National College Players Association? If a player's worth to the university is greater than the value of his scholarship (as it clearly is in some cases), should he be paid a salary? If so, would teammates in revenue sports want to be paid equally, or in salaries stratified according to talent or value on the field? What would the athletes want in Division III, where athletic budgets keep rising without scholarships or substantial sports revenue? Would athletes seek more or less variance in admissions standards? Should non-athletes also have a voice, especially where involuntary student fees support more and more of college sports? Might some schools choose to specialize, paying players only in elite leagues for football, or lacrosse? In athletic councils, how much would high-revenue athletes value a simple thank you from the tennis or field-hockey players for the newly specified subsidies to their facilities?

University administrators, already besieged from all sides, do not want to even think about such questions. Most cringe at the thought of bargaining with athletes as a general manager does in professional sports, with untold effects on the budgets for coaches and every other sports item. "I would not want to be part of it," North Carolina Athletic Director Dick Baddour told me flatly. After 44 years at UNC, he could scarcely contemplate a world without amateur rules. "We would have to think long and hard," Baddour added gravely, "about whether this university would continue those sports at all."

I, too, once reflexively recoiled at the idea of paying college athletes and treating them like employees or professionals. It feels abhorrent—but for reasons having to do more with sentiment than with practicality or law. Not just fans and university presidents but judges have often found cursory, non-statutory excuses to leave amateur traditions intact. "Even in the increasingly commercial modern world," said a federal-court judge in Gaines v. NCAA in 1990, "this Court believes there is still validity to the Athenian concept of a complete education derived from fostering the full growth of both mind and body." The fact that "the NCAA has not distilled amateurism to its purest form," said the Fifth Circuit Court of Appeals in 1988, "does not mean its attempts to maintain a mixture containing some amateur elements are unreasonable."

But one way or another, the smokescreen of amateurism may soon be swept away. For one thing, a victory by the plaintiffs in O'Bannon's case would radically transform college sports. Colleges would likely have to either stop profiting from students or start paying them. The NCAA could also be forced to pay tens, if not hundreds, of millions of dollars in damages. If O'Bannon and Vaccaro and company win, "it will turn college sports on its ear," said Richard Lapchick, the president of the National Consortium for Academics and Sports, in a recent interview with *The New York Times*.

Though the O'Bannon case may take several years yet to reach resolution, developments on other fronts are chipping away at amateurism, and at the NCAA. This past summer, *Sports Illustrated* editorialized in favor of allowing college athletes to be paid by non-university sources without jeopardizing their eligibility. At a press conference last June, Steve Spurrier, the coach of the South Carolina Gamecocks football team (and the winner of the 1966 Heisman Trophy as a Florida Gator), proposed that coaches start paying players $300 a game out of their own pockets. The coaches at six other SEC schools (Alabama, Florida, Ole Miss, Mississippi State, LSU, and Tennessee) all endorsed Spurrier's proposal. And Mark Emmert, the NCAA president, recently conceded that big changes must come. "The integrity of collegiate athletics is seriously challenged today by rapidly growing pressures coming from many directions," Emmert said in July. "We have reached a point where incremental change is not sufficient to meet these challenges. I want us to act more aggressively and in a more comprehensive way than we have in the past. A few new tweaks of the rules won't get the job done."

Threats to NCAA dominion also percolate in Congress. Aggrieved legislators have sponsored numerous bills. Senator Orrin Hatch, citing mistreatment of his Utah Utes, has called witnesses to discuss possible antitrust remedies for the Bowl Championship Series. Congressional committees have already held hearings critical of the NCAA's refusal to follow due process in disciplinary matters; other committees have explored a rise in football concussions. Last January, calls went up to investigate "informal" football workouts at the University of Iowa just after the season-ending bowl games—workouts so grueling that 41 of the 56 amateur student-athletes collapsed, and 13 were hospitalized with rhabdomyolysis, a life-threatening kidney condition often caused by excessive exercise.

The greatest threat to the viability of the NCAA may come from its member universities. Many experts believe that the churning instability within college football will drive the next major change. President Obama himself has endorsed the drumbeat cry for a national playoff in college football. This past spring, the Justice Department questioned the BCS about its adherence to antitrust standards. Jim Delany, the commissioner of the Big Ten, has estimated that a national playoff system could produce three or four times as much money as the existing bowl system does. If a significant band of football schools were to demonstrate that they could orchestrate a true national playoff, without the NCAA's assistance, the association would be terrified—and with good reason. Because if the big sports colleges don't need the NCAA to administer a national playoff in football, then they don't need it to do so in basketball. In which case, they could cut out the middleman in March Madness and run the tournament themselves. Which would deprive the NCAA of close to $1 billion a year, more than 95 percent of its revenue. The organization would be reduced to a rule book without money—an organization aspiring to enforce its rules but without the financial authority to enforce anything.

Thus the playoff dreamed of and hankered for by millions of football fans haunts the NCAA. "There will be some kind of playoff in college football, and it will not be run by the NCAA," says Todd Turner, a former athletic director in four conferences (Big East, ACC, SEC, and Pac-10). "If I'm at the NCAA, I have to worry that the playoff group can get basketball to break away, too."

This danger helps explain why the NCAA steps gingerly in enforcements against powerful colleges. To alienate member colleges would be to jeopardize its own existence. Long gone are television bans and the "death penalty" sentences (commanding season-long shutdowns of offending teams) once meted out to Kentucky (1952), Southwestern Louisiana (1973), and Southern Methodist University (1987). Institutions receive mostly symbolic slaps nowadays. Real punishments fall heavily on players and on scapegoats like literacy tutors.

A deeper reason explains why, in its predicament, the NCAA has no recourse to any principle or law that can justify amateurism. There is no such thing. Scholars and sportswriters yearn for grand juries to ferret out every forbidden bauble that reaches a college athlete, but the NCAA's ersatz courts can only masquerade as public authority. How could any statute impose amateur status on college athletes, or on anyone else? No legal definition of amateur exists, and any attempt to create one in enforceable law would expose its repulsive and unconstitutional nature—a bill of attainder, stripping from college athletes the rights of American citizenship.

For all our queasiness about what would happen if some athletes were to get paid, there is a successful precedent for the professionalization of an amateur sports system: the Olympics. ... Run in high-handed fashion, the AAU [Amateur Athletic Union] had infamously banned Jesse Owens for life in 1936—weeks after his four heroic gold medals punctured the Nazi claim of Aryan supremacy—because instead of using his sudden fame to tour and make money for the AAU at track meets across Europe, he came home early. In the early 1960s, the fights between the NCAA and the AAU over who should manage Olympic athletes became so bitter that President

Kennedy called in General Douglas MacArthur to try to mediate a truce before the Tokyo Olympic Games.

… In November 1978, President Jimmy Carter signed the bipartisan Amateur Sports Act. Amateurism in the Olympics soon dissolved—and the world did not end. Athletes, granted a 20 percent voting stake on every Olympic sport's governing body, tipped balances in the United States and then inexorably around the world. First in marathon races, then in tennis tournaments, players soon were allowed to accept prize money and keep their Olympic eligibility. Athletes profited from sponsorships and endorsements. The International Olympic Committee expunged the word amateur from its charter in 1986. Olympic officials, who had once disdained the NCAA for offering scholarships in exchange for athletic performance, came to welcome millionaire athletes from every quarter, while the NCAA still refused to let the pro Olympian Michael Phelps swim for his college team at Michigan.

This sweeping shift left the Olympic reputation intact, and perhaps improved. Only hardened romantics mourned the amateur code. "Hey, come on," said Anne Audain, a track-and-field star who once held the world record for the 5,000 meters. "It's like losing your virginity. You're a little misty for awhile, but then you realize, Wow, there's a whole new world out there!"

Without logic or practicality or fairness to support amateurism, the NCAA's final retreat is to sentiment. The Knight Commission endorsed its heartfelt cry that to pay college athletes would be "an unacceptable surrender to despair." Many of the people I spoke with while reporting this article felt the same way. "I don't want to pay college players," said Wade Smith, a tough criminal lawyer and former star running back at North Carolina. "I just don't want to do it. We'd lose something precious."

"Scholarship athletes are already paid," declared the Knight Commission members, "in the most meaningful way possible: with a free education." This evasion by prominent educators severed my last reluctant, emotional tie with imposed amateurism. I found it worse than self-serving. It echoes masters who once claimed that heavenly salvation would outweigh earthly injustice to slaves. In the era when our college sports first arose, colonial powers were turning the whole world upside down to define their own interests as all-inclusive and benevolent. Just so, the NCAA calls it heinous exploitation to pay college athletes a fair portion of what they earn.

Should College Athletes be Paid? Why, They Already Are

Seth Davis

Sports Illustrated

April 2013

Seth Davis writes features for *Sports Illustrated* and has a regular column on *SI.com*. He is also a sports analyst with *CBS Sports* and is the host of the show "Courtside with Seth Davis" on the *CBS College Sports Network*. This article appeared in his regular *SI.com* column "Hoop Thoughts" shortly after Branch's *Atlantic* article appeared. As you read this, notice how Davis refutes Branch's argument.

1. Davis suggests, "There is no movement [...] to professionalize college athletes," and contends that student-athletes are already compensated in other ways. In what other ways are student-athletes compensated for their performance?

2. Do you believe, as Davis does, that "there is educational value in competing?" Why or why not?

3. Davis accuses those operating college athletic programs to be "feckless, greedy hypocrites" when it comes to capitalizing on the profits of athletics. And, while Davis admits that the NCAA's enforcement policies are a bit "off the rails," he says, "it's not the NCAA's responsibility to stop schools and athletes from cheating. It's the responsibility of those schools and athletes not to cheat." How does this line of thinking parallel the challenges faced with academic integrity and dishonesty?

A lengthy article in an esteemed national publication criticizes the hypocrisies of college athletics. The author details a multitude of scandals involving seedy recruiting, nefarious boosters and academic fraud. The narrative winds to a damning conclusion: "[T]hanks to the influence of the colleges, there is growing up a class of students tainted with commercialism."

You might think I'm referring to the essay by Taylor Branch that was published last week in *The Atlantic* under the headline "The Shame Of College Sports." But I'm not. I'm actually referring to an article that appeared in the June 1905 edition of *McClure's*, a prestigious monthly academic journal. The two-part series, authored by a former Harvard football player named Henry Beach Needham, makes a compelling case that the enterprise of amateur athletics is doomed. In *The Atlantic*, Branch also writes that "scandal after scandal has rocked college sports," but while that phrase implies this is a recent trend, Needham shows us that it actually extends back more than a century.

I mention this as a counterweight to the prevailing conventional wisdom— namely, that the publication of Branch's article is a landmark event that has skewered the NCAA's bogus amateurism model for good. The piece has certainly spurred much discussion. A post on *The New Yorker*'s website deemed it a "watershed." Jeff MacGregor of ESPN.com suggested "a kind of cultural critical mass has finally been reached." Frank Deford called it "the most important article ever written about college sports." From NPR to MSNBC to *Business Insider* to every sport outlet in between, the story has been hailed as a slam-dunk, once-and-for-all indictment of the NCAA.

To be sure, Branch's article represents a brilliant piece of reporting, which is not surprising considering he won a Pulitzer Prize for his three-volume series on the American civil rights movement. Branch lays out in fascinating detail the structural and legal history of the NCAA that has led us to this point. However, when it comes to analysis, fairness, and context, Branch's work leaves much to be desired. If there is a reasonable counter-argument to be made, Branch ignores it. If there is a fact that contradicts his conclusions, he omits it.

Indeed, the entire article is based on a faulty premise, which is introduced right away in the sub-headline: "[S]tudent-athletes generate billions of dollars for universities and private companies while earning nothing for themselves." This is indisputably untrue. Student-athletes earn free tuition, which over the course of four years can exceed $200,000. They are also provided with housing, textbooks, food, and academic tutoring. When they travel to road games, they are given per diems for meals. They also get coaching, training, game experience, and media exposure they "earn" in their respective crafts. Despite all that, Branch asserts that "[t]he tragedy at the heart of college sports is not that some college athletes are getting paid, but that more of them are not."

If Branch or anyone else wants to argue that college athletes should be paid *more*, let them have at it. But to claim that college athletes earn "nothing?" Pure fiction.

So then: Should college athletes be paid more? As the subject of Branch's most recent bestseller, Bill Clinton, might say, it depends on what the definition of "paid" is. There is a significant and growing gap between the value of a scholarship and what a student-athlete genuinely needs. This is what is referred to as the "cost of attendance" issue. Many people in college sports, from NCAA president Mark Emmert on down, have argued that the scholarship model needs to be updated so this gap can be closed. Part of the challenge is that the gap exists for every athlete in every sport, so the fix must be applied broadly—and expensively. Yes, I'll believe it when I see it, but at least the discourse on this front is moving in the right direction.

However, when Branch and so many others talk about college athletes getting "paid," they are not talking about merely the cost of attendance. They're talking about giving athletes what they're "worth." It's a convincing argument when cast alongside the mind-boggling dollars that are pouring in. Branch points out the SEC recently surpassed the $1 billion mark for football receipts. The Big Ten is close behind at $905 million. He reminds us that the football programs at Texas, Florida, Georgia, Michigan, and Penn State earn between $40 million and $80 million each year in profits. The NCAA received $771 million from CBS and Turner to broadcast last year's basketball tournament, a sum that Branch asserts was "built on the backs of amateurs—unpaid labor. The whole edifice depends on the players' willingness to perform what is effectively volunteer work."

So we learn a lot in this article about how much the schools are making. We learn almost nothing, however, about what they're spending. Branch virtually ignores the basic profit-and-loss structure of college sports. For example, did you know that out of 332 schools currently competing in the NCAA's Division I, fewer than a dozen have athletic departments that are operating in the black? And that of the 120 programs that comprise the Football Bowl Subdivision, just 14 are profitable? That means some 88 percent of the top football programs *lose* money for their universities—and that doesn't even include the reams of cash the schools are spending on the so-called nonrevenue sports. Those are some basic, salient facts, but you won't find them anywhere in Branch's 15,000-word opus.

We might want to believe that the reason schools lose so much money is because of the runaway spending on coaches' salaries, new facilities and frivolous items like private jets. Those are indeed reckless expenditures; Myles Brand, the late NCAA president, frequently railed against them. They don't, however, begin to account for just how expensive it is to operate an athletic program. Branch derides college athletics as "Very Big Business," but the truth is, it's actually a "Very Lousy Business."

People who say that college athletes should be paid as professionals like to invoke the principles of the free market. That's the framework advanced by an entity called the National College Players Association, which recently issued a study that put some dollar figures on this question. The NCPA says those numbers demonstrate what the players would be worth "if allowed access to the fair market like the pros."

Left unsaid is the fact that the players *do* have access to the fair market. If they want to be compensated for their abilities, they can simply turn professional. Yes, the NFL and NBA have draft age minimums, but those rules were put in place by the leagues, not the NCAA. Does that not fall under the rubric of the "fair market"? Since the NFL won't accept a player who is not yet three years removed from his senior year in high school, the "fair market value" for a freshman or sophomore in college is actually zero. Yet, the NCAA is still "compensating" those players with a free education and other expenses, even if they are among the 98 percent who will never make a dime playing football. If anything, most of these guys are overpaid.

The NCPA found that, at the highest end, the fair market value for a football player at the University of Texas is $513,922. Setting aside that this number does not account for the money the university is spending on the athlete (for starters, out-of-state tuition at the school runs north of $45,000 per year), I can't help but wonder what's "fair" about the market the NCPA describes. Clearly the starting quarterback generates much more revenue for Texas than does the third-string safety. Would the NCPA argue those two players should be paid the same? There's nothing fair about that.

If we're going to say that players be paid according to their value, then we should pay them less if their team doesn't make a bowl game. That's only fair. Or maybe the school should enter into individual contracts mandating that in return for access to its training program, practice facilities, game experiences, and television exposure, the players should pay the school a percentage of their future earnings. If the players don't like the deal, they can sign somewhere else. Hey, it's just business, right?

These are just the first small steps down a long and slippery slope. That's why Ben Cohen's assertion last week in *The Wall Street Journal* that the case for paying salaries to college athletes was "gaining momentum" is so wrong. The only place this idea is gaining momentum is in the media. There is no movement—none—within the actual governing structure of the NCAA to professionalize college athletes. It's not just that it would ruin the amateurism ideal. It's that from a business standpoint, it makes no sense.

The other arguments in favor of paying athletes also do not hold up. Some people claim it would serve as a deterrent against the temptation to accept largesse from agents. This insults our intelligence. Does anyone really think that if the schools give athletes another three thousand bucks a year that those kids are going to turn away a fist full of Benjamins proffered by an agent? On what planet?

Then there's the idea, promulgated by Jay Bilas among others, that athletes should have limitless opportunity to pursue ancillary marketing deals. This works much better in theory than it would in practice. Do we really want a bidding war between Under Armour and Nike to determine whether a recruit attends Maryland or Oregon? Do we want Nick Saban going into a kid's living room and saying, "I know Bob Stoops has a car dealership who will pay you $50,000, but I can line you up with a furniture store that will give you $75,000?"

To be sure, there are a lot of legitimate questions about whether many of the NCAA's policies are in line with laws governing trade and copyrights. This terrain is in Taylor Branch's wheelhouse, and his article is at its best when he dissects the various cases that are currently making their way through the courts. The most interesting one is the class action suit being spearheaded by former UCLA basketball player Ed O'Bannon, who claims the NCAA is violating licensing law by continuing to make money off his likeness without compensating him. I'm not a lawyer, but it seems to me O'Bannon has a reasonable argument, and I certainly have no problem with anyone suing the NCAA to address such grievances. But when someone like Branch characterizes these issues as part of a larger civil rights struggle, he loses me. And I suspect he loses a lot of other open-minded people who agree with him that the system needs fixing.

We need look no further than the current conference expansion madness to understand that many of the presidents who are running college sports are feckless, greedy hypocrites. It's also apparent that the NCAA's enforcement process has gone off the rails. Still, in the final analysis it's not the NCAA's responsibility to stop schools and athletes from cheating. It's the responsibility of those schools and athletes not to cheat. Any system is only as good as the people who are in it. You can make all the reforms you want, but at the end of the day, where there's money, there's corruption. It's a problem as old as time.

We spend way too much energy worrying about how the system affects a very small number of elite athletes, young men who are going to be multimillionaires as soon as they leave campus. Thus, it was disappointing to see Branch fall back on the argument that these select young men are being exploited. As the father of three children under the age of eight, I can only pray that someone "exploits" my sons someday by giving them tuition, room and board at one of America's finest universities. Branch also relies on some surprisingly lazy reporting. He reveals without a dollop of skepticism that a basketball team (he doesn't say which one) decided it would not play in the NCAA championship game (he doesn't say which year) out of protest. Thankfully, Armageddon was averted when said team lost in the semifinal (Branch doesn't say to whom, or explain why the players couldn't have boycotted the semifinal). Given that this fantastic scenario has been peddled for decades without ever materializing, it is remarkable that a reporter of Branch's stature would accept the account at whole cloth.

In the end, the greatest flaw of Branch's article is his failure to address the question of why schools operate athletics programs despite having to incur such financial losses. Could it be that maybe—just maybe—they really do believe there is educational value in competing? That they think sports is a worthy investment because it gives tens of thousands of young people the opportunity to learn discipline, teamwork, and time management alongside calculus and English lit? Could it be that the schools really do want to enrich the lives of their "student-athletes" regardless of whether they are turning a profit?

As I read through Branch's essay, I kept waiting for him to acknowledge that the student-athlete gets something of value from all of this. I finally found it in the last paragraph, when Branch quotes a member of the Knight Commission as referring to the "free education" a student-athlete receives. For Branch, this is the final straw. It is, he writes, "worse than self-serving. It echoes masters who once claimed that heavenly salvation would outweigh earthly injustice to slaves."

Giving someone a free college education is akin to enslavement? If that's the great watershed idea of our time, then we are living in a very dry world indeed.

Used Goods: Former African American College Student-Athletes' Perception of Exploitation by Division I Universities

Krystal Beamon

Journal of Negro Education

Fall 2008

Dr. Krystal Beamon is an assistant professor of Sociology and Anthropology at The University of Texas Arlington. Included in the wide range of Sociology courses she teaches are classes such as *Sociology of Sport and Race,* and *Class* and *Sport in the Media.* She has published many articles, mostly focusing on male African American student-athletes. "Used Goods: Former African American College Student-Athletes' Perception of Exploitation by Division I Universities" is an academic article, published in 2008 in the *Journal of Negro Education.* Beamon used ethnographic interviews to illustrate the perception of former African American student-athletes from powerhouse Division I schools; many participants expressed the feeling of being "used" by universities, hence the title of Beamon's article.

1. What is Beamon's thesis? Is this explicit or implicit?

2. Beamon interviews former student-athletes in order to collect her data. How does this ethnographic approach toward research add to the article? What risks, or limitations, does this kind of study have? Do the benefits outweigh the risks? Why or why not?

3. Clearly Dr. Beamon rejects the exploitation of student-athletes. Imagine a conversation between Taylor Branch ("The Shame of College Sports") and Krystal Beamon. What would they agree upon? Where might their positions differ?

Collegiate sports have opened many doors for African American males. However, serious involvement in athletics has hampered the development of the group in several areas such as academic and occupational achievement. It has been alleged that universities exploit athletes, especially African American male athletes in football and basketball. This study uses in-depth ethnographic interviews of former Division I student-athletes who are African American in order to examine the extent to which they feel that universities emphasized their education as opposed to their athletic performance and prepared them for careers off the playing field. The former student-athletes expressed feelings of being "used goods" and recount difficulties in choosing a major.

Sports have become key social institutions in American society that are connected to the economy, education, family, and other spheres of social life. Many scholars have noted that a specific set of difficulties arise for African American males in competitive athletics, especially in high school and collegiate athletics (Benson, 2000; Edwards, 1988, 2000; Harrison, 2000; Hoberman, 2000; Lapchick, 1996; Lomax, 2000; Sellers & Kuperminc, 1997; Siegel, 1996). As a means to upward mobility, educational institutions are thought to prepare students for a future beyond their halls. In terms of African American male student-athletes, there are two opposing perspectives that are employed regarding sports' role in the educational development of the group: (a) athletics may provide educational opportunities to African Americans from underprivileged backgrounds that would not otherwise be available, and (b) sports have exploited the majority of African American athletes (Sellers, 2000).

Although participation in athletics is often considered a golden opportunity for African Americans, compelling evidence to the contrary has been presented for decades (Beamon & Bell 2006; Edwards, 1983, 1988; Lapchick, 1996). In fact, serious involvement in athletics has hampered the development of African American males in several areas, including academic and occupational achievement (Lomax, 2000).

For decades, Edwards (2000) has researched the nexus between sociology and sports, particularly, how sports have affected the African American family and community. He suggested that the overemphasis on sports participation has drained Black talent away from other areas of economic and cultural success and argues that the push toward athletics as seen within Black families is hindering the social and cognitive growth of African American youth (Edwards, 1983, 1988, 2000). Furthermore, the mass media constantly deluges society with images glorifying African American men who are successful by employing avenues connected with sports and reinforces the stereotype of African American males as exclusively athletically talented (Hall 2001).

Collegiate student-athletes, particularly, African American male student-athletes, often have lower career maturity, an impaired aptitude to devise educational and career plans, with self esteem and an identity based on athletics (Baillie & Danish, 1992; Blann, 1985; Harrison & Lawrence, 2003; Kennedy & Dimick, 1987). African American male student-athletes in football and basketball also have lower academic achievement, stronger expectations for a professional sports career, and are socialized more intensely toward sports than their White counterparts (Beamon & Bell, 2002, 2006; Edwards, 2000; Eitle & Eitle, 2002; Hoberman, 2000; Pascarella, Truckenmiller, Nora, Terenzini, Edison, & Hagedorn 1999). Pursuing athletic achievement in an obsessive manner and doing so to the detriment of educational and occupational aspirations is described in an Edwards's study as a triple tragedy for African Americans:

> One, the tragedy of thousands upon thousands of black youths in the obsessive pursuit of sports goals that the overwhelming majority of them will never attain. Two, the tragedy of the personal and cultural underdevelopment that afflicts so many successful and unsuccessful black sports aspirants. Three, the tragedy of cultural and institutional underdevelopment throughout black society as a consequence of the drain in talent potential toward sports and away from other vital areas of occupational and career emphasis such as medicine, law, economics, politics, education, and technical fields (as cited in Harrison, 2000, p. 36).

Due to higher visibility and expectations, these deficiencies are even more pronounced for athletes competing in the revenue-generating sports at Division I institutions. Revenue-generating sports are those that are most likely to yield profits and notoriety. Those sports are defined for the purposes of this study as football and men's basketball. This study uses in-depth ethnographic interviews of former African American Division I student-athletes in order to examine the extent to which they feel that universities emphasized their education as opposed to their athletic performance in order to prepare them for careers off the playing field or court.

Background

No one would have anticipated that on August 3, 1852, when Harvard and Yale met in the first intercollegiate athletic event, a rowing contest, that such a lasting marriage between the universities and athletics would begin (Lewis, 1970). Today, universities use the commercialization of their sports programs to generate revenue, increase visibility, recruit students, and receive alumni support, which creates a pressure to win (Donnor, 2005; Upthegrove, Roscigno, & Charles, 1999). Due to their ability to raise the university's profile and add to the profitability of a school's athletic programs, exceptional athletes are of great financial value to universities. As a result of overrepresentation of African Americans in revenue-generating sports, it is estimated that these student-athletes have earned more than a quarter of a trillion dollars over a 40-year period; and even if 100% of African American athletes earned degrees, the economic value of those degrees would only be 5% of the total value of their athletic contribution (Watkins study as cited in Salome, 2005). The need for superior athletes to maintain team performance and produce revenue may cause institutions to neglect their educational responsibilities to student-athletes by creating contradictory pressures that place the role of student and the role of athlete at odds (Edwards, 2000; Hoberman, 2000; Upthegrove, Roscigno, & Charles, 1999). One of the alleged negative consequences of the relationship between the athletic and educational institutions is the exploitation of student-athletes for their athletic ability (Donnor, 2005). Specifically, the exploitation is especially significant to African Americans in revenue-generating sports because they often create "enough revenue to financially underwrite the non-revenue-producing athletic sports such as crew, swimming, tennis and golf that are overwhelmingly populated by white middle- and upper-class students" (Donnor, 2005, p. 48).

With the clear emphasis placed on the physical capabilities of student-athletes, their academic capacities and role as a student are often overlooked

(Eitzen, 2000, 2003; Hawkins, 1999; Litsky, 2003; Maloney & McCormick, 1993). Sack and Stuarowsky (1998) discussed this emphasis by stating, "Universities are far more concerned with exploiting the athletic talent [of student-athletes] than with nurturing academic potential" (p. 104).

It has been noted that some student-athletes are academically unprepared for college and a gap exists in the graduation rates of African American student-athletes compared to White student-athletes (Benson, 2000; Edwards, 1983; Lapchick, 1996; Washington & Karen, 2001). In 2006, African American football players graduated from Division I institutions at a rate that was 12% lower than that of their White teammates, 62% for Whites and 49% for African Americans (National Collegiate Athletic Association, NCAA, 2006). White male basketball players at Division I institutions graduate at a rate of 51%, while African Americans graduate at a rate of 41% (NCAA, 2006). A more accurate statistic is the graduation success rate which adds in student-athletes who enter mid-year or transfer into an institution and subtracts those with allowable exclusion and those who would otherwise be deemed academically ineligible on returning to an institution (NCAA, 2006). The graduation success rate differentials by race are even more staggering. In football the rate is 77% for Whites and 55% for African Americans and in men's basketball the rate is 76% for Whites and 51% for African Americans (NCAA, 2006). Football and basketball powerhouses are ranked each year by *USA Today*; at eleven of those top twenty football and basketball programs, the graduation differentials between African Americans and Whites were greater than the national average ("African American College Athletes," 2002). While student-athletes often fulfill their obligation to the university by performing athletically and bringing notoriety to the universities, all too often Black students do not see the benefits of their labor by playing professionally or earning a degree. Of those who do graduate, many graduate in less marketable majors "riddled with 'keep 'em eligible' less competitive 'jock courses' of dubious educational value and occupational relevance" (Edwards, 1988, p. 138). Exploitation has been alleged in studies and commentaries (Donnor, 2005; Hawkins, 1999). Meggysey (2000) stated that the NCAA and its member institutions "exploit the talent of Black athletes and deny those same athletes access to a quality education" as well as limiting "employment opportunities of Black athletes after their career ends" (p. 27).

Social Reproduction Theory

The exploitation phenomenon can be examined through the lens of the social reproduction theory, which is based on the concept that social institutions, such as the institution of education, work to reproduce dominant ideology and its structures of knowledge (Giroux, 1983). Proponents of social reproduction theory argue that the function of schools is to recreate the conditions needed to reproduce the social division of labor (Giroux, 1983). According to Giroux, schools impart differing classes and social groups with the skills and knowledge needed to maintain the status quo in the labor force, which is stratified by the variables of class, race, and gender. The interrelationship of the institutions of sport and education has created a situation in which structural components (e.g., the NCAA, athletic departments, economy) and individual actors (e.g., coaches, teammates, family members) work together to reproduce the current stratification seen in the labor force (Singer, 2002). This is certainly the case for African American male student-athletes. By aiding, catering, and nurturing the student's athletic role to the detriment of his or her true academic success and occupational development, educational institutions reproduce students with social inequalities. This phenomenon is illustrated in the sports world where there is an overrepresentation of Black athletes, but the decision-making positions of athletic directors, coaches, owners, and managers are still largely held by White males. African American coaches in the NFL and NBA only make up 17% and 10%, respectively, of the total number of head coaches in these leagues that are largely composed of African American players (Lapchick & Matthews, 2001).

Additionally, some universities do little to endorse an academic lifestyle among student-athletes (Gerdy, 2000). A clear emphasis on the athletic abilities of student-athletes at the high school and university level, reproduce student-athletes with an educational inequality who are not prepared academically or culturally for the transition into the occupational sector. This is especially true of African American male athletes who have been shown to have higher expectations of "going pro" and have been intensively socialized toward sports and embracing the athletic identity (Beamon & Bell, 2002).

The educational attainment of student-athletes is frequently hindered by athletic training and travel; and student-athletes often find it difficult to balance athletics, academics, and social roles. Athletes have less time available for the educational process that "extends beyond going to class every day to socializing with research and study groups, participating with student organizations, and attending campus activities apart from athletics" (Hawkins, 1999, p. 8). Additionally, due to psychological and physical fatigue from sports participation, student-athletes have decreased levels of motivation to study and diminished abilities to benefit from institutional assistance, such as tutorial programs and counseling (Beamon & Bell, 2002; Person, Benson-Quaziena, & Rogers, 2001). African American males are seen as particularly vulnerable to these circumstances since they often enter college with general background disadvantages (e.g., socioeconomic status, academic preparedness) and goal-discrepancy concerning professional sports careers (Roscigno, 1999; Sellers & Kuperminc, 1997).

Student-athletes work under numerous constraints. These constraints include the inability to change majors or drop courses because of eligibility requirements or choose majors that may offer courses during times set aside for sports participation (i.e., majors such as architecture or chemistry with afternoon labs). While students who are not athletes have the freedom to explore courses and majors, spend time on internships, drop and add courses with changing needs, and focus on finding a career that suits their abilities, many student-athletes do not share these liberties. In order to remain eligible, student-athletes are often pushed into choosing majors that are most compatible with athletic participation, even if they are uninterested or unprepared for those majors (Adler & Adler, 1987; Cornelius, 1995).

Procedure

The current literature raises a few questions such as, do African American male student-athletes perceive themselves to be exploited by universities and how does that perception affect their college experience? These questions could be answered by hearing their voices through qualitative research. Several scholars have noted that African American athletes' voices should be heard to truly understand the obsessive pursuit of sports fame and the academic and occupational shortcomings that exist among them (Adler & Adler 1991; Benson, 2000; Winbush 1988). This study presents the viewpoints of former student-athletes concerning the universities' role in the alleged exploitation of athletes. It is based on a sample of 20 African American men who formerly played football or basketball at a Division I university.

Both purposive (selective) and snowball (rare) sampling were used in this research. The criteria for participation were as follows:

- must be African American male,

- must be a former student-athlete from a Division I university and,

- must have played a revenue-generating sport (football or men's basketball).

African Americans were targeted for participation because of their lower levels of academic success (i.e., lower graduation rates) and higher expectations for professional sports careers. The study was exclusive to Division I universities because of their high visibility and perceived profitability. Males from revenue-generating sports were used because of the racial differences and the graduation rates that are lower than those among women and men in non-revenue-generating sports (NCAA, 2006). The twenty participants were from universities all over the country, many of which would be considered "powerhouses". As a former student-athlete and from past research conducted on student-athletes, some personal connections were used for initial contacts. They were contacted by telephone or in person and given (or read) the description of the study. From there, snowballing led to the identification of additional participants.

In-depth semi-standardized interviews were used as the data collection technique. The interviews ranged from one to five hours, with the average interview lasting about two-and-one-half hours. Transcription and analysis were performed by this researcher. The questions were open-ended, non-biased, and designed to elicit candid responses. For example, respondents were asked the following questions: "Talk about your college experiences in sports," "Talk about your collegiate experience with academics," and "How did you choose a major"? These questions produced very similar responses

Campus Athletics

from the majority of participants. The findings presented in this study consist of direct quotes offered in the form of rich narratives articulated by the respondents.

Backgrounds of the Participants

The athletes interviewed ranged from ages 22 to 47. Most were in their twenties, with two who were ages 45 and 47. The two older responders added to the significance of the findings by demonstrating that perceptions seem to remain constant over time, since their responses were similar to the younger participants. Respondents were either playing sports professionally, holding jobs in other professions, training for possible on-the-field sports careers, or unemployed.

Table 1 shows background and demographic information about the participants. Pseudonyms were assigned in order to ensure their confidentiality. According to the table, 17 out of the 20 participants hold degrees (with one choosing not to answer the question) and many (13) of the former student-athletes have careers outside of sports, which is not consistent with the expectations of the researcher. This apparent contradiction of the literature could be attributed to snowball sampling in which the first respondent held a degree and identified additional respondents with degrees. Most (17) were football players; this may be due to the sheer numbers of collegiate football players versus basketball players, since football teams average a little more than 100 players and basketball teams have fewer than 20. Their majors were somewhat varied, with the social sciences being the most popular major.

Findings

During transcription and coding, several themes found in the literature as well as new ideas became apparent. Except for scholarships, many (18 of 20) of these athletes left the universities feeling as if they had given far more than they had gained and were unprepared for careers away from the playing field or court. The findings were organized according to whether

- the respondents felt that their educational development was emphasized,

- the university or student-athletes benefited from collegiate athletic programs, and

- the student-athletes' career preparation was adequate, particularly for choosing a major.

Educational Development

Seventeen of the 20 respondents in this study had undergraduate degrees. However, most of them felt that their attainment was not a reflection of the university's emphasis on the academic success of student-athletes, but through their sheer determination. As Calvin stated, "everybody say you a student-athlete, but coaches, they want you to be a athlete first then a student." Several other respondents felt like "athlete-students." Devin discussed the term "student-athlete":

> They tell you, you a student first and an athlete next, but really you an athlete first and a student second. There is more emphasis on making your practices and meetings. They hit you with the "go to class" and all that stuff, but they don't care. As long as they get them four years out of you they could care less if you get a degree or not.... I think they have to [care about athletes getting degrees] cuz they job depends somewhat on it, but personally, I don't think they care.

Other respondents stated that any reference to education was directly related to eligibility. Oliver stated:

> ... the name of the game is to stay eligible ya know what I'm saying. I guess in the recruitment process, when a coach or whoever is representing that university is sitting in front of your parents uh, academics is stressed highly. However, when you get there, that is not the case.

This sentiment was echoed in Hubert's response:

> I mean they drill on you going to class and making the grade, but that's only because if you don't go to class and make the grade, then you can't be on the field.... Student-athlete, that's not how it is, its athletic-student. It's backwards for college athletics...

Additionally, discussion of graduation or academic achievement was "lip service," as stated by Eddie. Gavin expressed a similar sentiment:

> The coaches I don't think they really care if you do get a degree or not, because ya know they say that but its like they say one thing, but they mean another. They just want you to come and play for them, so ya know you can help their program out.

Adam, who attended a nationally acclaimed football powerhouse, stated that the coaches were very upfront about their emphasis on football over all other priorities, including academics:

> I mean from the time that you get there, they tell ya, "you here for football, you got a scholarship." It's up to you to ya know put yourself in the right classes and to choose the right major. . . . Anything else dealing with academics that was up to you. Ya know what I mean. Whereas with football, they took care of all of that, as long as you was playing football, you was treated like a king or whatever.

Benefits

Kevin summarized his perception of exploitation by the university as he rounded out his four years of eligibility this way: "Okay we've used you up now, so good-bye and good luck to ya and don't come back around here no more." Most (14 of 20) of the respondents actually employed phrases with the word "used" such as "used up," "used goods," and "used and abused" to describe the manner in which they felt they were treated by universities. Many (12 of 20) mentioned the labor exploitation of student-athletes, in that the profits generated by successful sports programs are perceived to be enjoyed primarily by the university. The NCAA maintained that student-athletes should be considered amateur athletes driven by education and the physical, mental, and social benefits that are derived from being student-athletes (Netzely, 1997). Most (15 of 20) of these respondents did not feel that college athletes should be considered amateur athletes. They observed the university's contracts with television and radio networks, merchandising companies, and other corporations, in addition to ticket and concession sales, bowl games, and tournaments, and shared that the university was profiting from their labor.

When asked if athletes and universities were benefiting equally from college athletics, 19 of the 20 respondents noted that athletes and universities do not benefit equally. Adam stated:

> ... the colleges make so much money off of the athletes ...
> those athletes are producing those winning records and those
> winning records are producing millions for that college but
> the athletes don't see any of that, and they get away with it by
> saying "well ok we're giving you a free education."

Several respondents also referred to scholarships as a benefit, but not a
benefit that could be compared to the profits that universities reap from
successful athletic programs. Several respondents discussed scholarships as
an unequal benefit for student-athletes. Oliver stated:

> I'd have to say the university will get more out of it because ...
> their [the athlete's] school is getting paid for [it], so I guess you
> could say they reaping the benefit that way; however, they're
> [colleges] gonna reap a whole lot more than I guess what a
> college education would cost ... from an overall standpoint,
> the university will benefit more because, even if you look at
> bowl games I mean, not even from the financial standpoint of
> them getting money, but however when they're on television
> uh they're gonna advertise the university ... bringing in more
> students.

Nate also felt that universities benefit more than the athletes:

> You and I both know that there are athletes that spend four or
> five years at college or university and don't do nothing and the
> college or university actually just uses them up... uh ya know
> the college athletes are out there working hard ya know they're
> actually running, ya know getting bumps and bruises things of
> that nature.... Okay. And the university is making millions off
> of 18 to 22-year-old kids ya know and all the kids are getting is
> ... maybe an education out of it.

Kevin echoed those feelings and noted a lack of inability to have his basic
necessities met while he was a student-athlete:

> ... even though we had a full ride all your academic and
> everything, books and all that stuff is taken care of but I know
> when I [was] on campus, I lived on campus in the dorms and
> that little whatever thirty dollars a month ... that we got living

on campus was nothing, especially when you coming from a background, a family background where you can't, ya know I wasn't able to call home and be like ya know "mom please send me this, send that" you know I had to gut it out with whatever we was getting at the time was like thirty dollars when you were on campus. So I totally agree with how college athletes are not benefiting from all the money we bring to colleges.

Kevin added in another dimension, which is the fact that many student-athletes do not have money to take care of their day-to-day needs because NCAA rules prohibit athletes from working for pay during the season. For that reason, universities offer a very small stipend to student-athletes who reside on campus and a larger stipend to those who reside off campus. Both amounts were described by the respondents as largely inadequate. Devin summed it up this way, "they make millions of dollars off of athletes, you get that funky (explicative) scholarship check, you supposed to survive off of that." Matt added that he lived on campus without any financial resources stating that "all I could do is ya know go wash clothes and get a combo meal that's it." Fred agreed that the financial needs of student-athletes were not being met:

> I'm not gone say we should get paid to play, but our monthly income that they give the students is definitely not enough to live. Just because they pay for room and board, if you move off campus that check is really not enough to cover expenses to live especially since they always find reasons to take money out of your check instead of putting money in.

Several respondents, like Brad and Hubert, believed that student-athletes should be paid. Brad:

> I mean they make it hard for guys that are student athletes. I mean you can't have a job ... So I mean the athletes don't win, I mean I believe, myself personally, that student-athletes should be paid ... I mean you have no time to make money. I mean you are doing football 24/7, year-round. I mean, you don't have a summer vacation, you have quote-unquote voluntary practice that you have to be at ... So I think they need to set up

programs that can help student-athletes to make money where it won't be illegal.

Hubert proposed that student-athletes were not benefiting enough from the monies made by the universities and should be paid for that reason:

> Overall, I see them (universities) benefiting more than we are because of the money that they make off of us. So, your next question would probably be should we get paid? And yes, we should be paid something more than a little scholarship check because if you look at the revenue that we're bringing in for the university compared to what we get, it is not fair.

Several respondents discussed how other industries profited from student-athletes' hard work. This is yet another way in which the athletes are profitable, but do not profit personally from their labor. Lenny's statement was summarized thusly:

> I feel like we were treated unfairly because we didn't get any money for the proceeds that we brought to the university. And uh, I don't know if you recall, but it was, I think in '92 or '93 was when John Madden first came out with the collegiate Nintendo game or whatever and even had our names and numbers of the players on the jerseys of those players. And we were offended because they were making money with our names ... So I felt like on that aspect we were treated unequally or unfairly because they would not share the money that we were making for the universities ... it's totally lopsided. With Nike he [coach] was getting paid a million dollars for us, for the players to wear Nike products, now I feel like it should have been divided a little bit more equally than that .... And the university was getting money from the ticket proceeds and all the paraphernalia that we were wearing and making popular because we were out there winning ... we were getting at the time I was playing football, I think we were getting $675 a month stipend and that was supposed to get us meals, wash clothes, pay bills, and man that's just not right. They were making millions of dollars off us in a year so I felt like they coulda divided the money a little bit more toward the athlete who was doing the majority of the workload.

The only equalizing factor mentioned by any respondent was if athletes moved on to play in professional leagues. Matt stated that "the athlete would probably benefit if he knew for sure he was going to the league." Jack went into depth on the subject and his statement summarized the sentiments of several of the respondents:

> I think the universities benefit a lot more. I think they use these guys as a meat market and kinda the rules [exploit them] .... They definitely use the athlete .... I think they exploit 'em to a certain degree. They give you the opportunity to get out there and make a name for yourself and you can put yourself up and maybe get drafted into the NBA, but the odds of that are very low . . .

Career Preparation

One of the major consequences of the overemphasis placed on sports by African American young men is a lack of career maturity. The athletes in this study were socialized by family, the community/neighborhood, and the media toward athletic achievement. Most had very salient athletic identities. Athletics had come first during their college careers and their focus, then, was to stay eligible. The following findings concentrated on the respondent's college preparation for careers after sports, particularly choosing a major.

One of the primary sources of career immaturity among college athletes derives from limitations in choosing a major. They cannot choose majors that have required courses held during times set aside for sports participation. (For example, majors such as architecture or sciences often have afternoon labs). Several respondents (9 of 20) mentioned these types of constraints limited their choices for majors. Additionally, most (15 of 20) mentioned choosing majors with courses classified as "easy to pass" or departments that were "athlete-friendly." For these reasons and to remain eligible to play their sport, student-athletes often selected more pragmatic educational goals. Devin, a business major, had a desire to become an engineer. He ended up in a major that was not his first choice:

> My major was something I just kinda wind up getting, I started off wanting to be an engineer, but it's like the labs and stuff would conflict with practice. And cuz I was on scholarship, they figured, uh, my football stuff was more important than going to class or being what I truly wanted to be, so I kinda fell into my degree.

Hubert found himself in the same situation:

> Initially when I first went to college I wanted to major in psychology. But because, the classes for my major were going to conflict with football practice, so I was not allowed to choose those classes ... so instead of psychology I chose journalism.

Perry also had interests that could not be explored due to athletics:

> ... I had an interest in architecture, but the thing about architecture ... the school of architecture classes conflicted with football practice. My friend lost his starting position who went through with it and majored in architecture.

A few respondents felt as if they were lied to during recruiting concerning what they could major in once they came to campus. Oliver recounted what he was told on his recruiting visit:

> I wanted to major in criminal justice and when they were recruiting me I was told that I could major in criminal justice but when I got ya know to [college] there wasn't a criminal justice degree. I found out that all the classes were in sociology and that is different, that is not criminal justice which is what I wanted to major in.

Perry spoke of how his major was chosen for him. He felt that the university had ulterior motives in pushing student-athletes to chose a major before they had explored any options:

> When I first got there, it was about making the university look good ... we meet with counselors ... it was all about making

(the university) look good, you know when you watch the
football games on Saturday, they put your face up there and it
says majoring in whatever. That was the whole purpose of this
counseling part, which I later found this out. . . but basically
you get in there and they try to get you to commit to a major
because the more people we got in business, makes us look
good. ... I committed to business and in that commitment to
business, uh I had to then had to get enrolled in classes to
head me into that direction. Well those classes were absolutely
overwhelming for me . . . so I don't think that they were in our
corner as young folks coming to school. I think they were in the
corner of [the university] making [the university] look good.

With counseling geared more toward the student-athlete's needs, Perry's
interests could have been accommodated with a major in which he could
have experienced success and could have led to more fulfilling career
options. Instead, Perry majored in an area for which he was inadequately
prepared, had no interest, and ultimate had little success. He goes on to
state:

... so in order to get off of probation I had to write an appeal
letter and get a school to accept me which was social work. . .
well I grew up in the system of social work I can relate to this,
so I shouldn't have nothing but success in something that I
could relate to. This is something a counselor working for me
could have found out easy.

Others spoke of academic counselors in the athletic department pushing
them toward majors that were not their choice. Matt discusses being talked
into a major, and then being unable to change his major back to his first
choice:

Actually it was graphic design and I switched it. Me and my
counselor sat down and talked about it, and I told him yeah
I want to work with my hands and these different types of
things. And he said "you might want to try this (fine arts) and
plus you'll graduate faster." So I switched it, then a couple
semesters down the road I decided I wanted to switch back to
graphic design, because I was kinda looking into it and I found
it wasn't nothing in fine arts that really I could do except. . .

work at a museum or something which I didn't want to do.
And at that time it was too late, I was already backed up in that
major so I was stuck with it.

Fred, who actually wanted to be a meteorologist, was also talked into choosing a major that he was not interested in:

Um, its funny, cuz I remember how I got in this major because
I don't like business. I don't like this major, I don't like the one I
got into. And I went in and I said, "Don't know what I want to
major in." and they said, "well you should go into business cuz
. . . it's easy to be successful when you go into this major." I said
okay I'll buy it. So when I got into it, and I didn't like it, but
I had so many hours toward it, it was no choice but for me to
stay into it. I really don't like that.

These athletes' experiences reflect the difficulties they face when choosing a major and, inevitability, these experiences will affect their success in moving out of the world of sports and into the world of work and their ability to identify a career that will be generally rewarding.

Limitations and Implications of the Study

The limitations of this research are those typically associated with qualitative research. The first limitation was the generalizability of the findings. This study focused on twenty participants whose responses were consistent with the issues identified in the literature. However, the findings cannot be generalized to describe experiences or perceptions of all African American student-athletes in revenue-generating sports. Additionally, this study was limited by gender, focusing exclusively on males. In addition to African American males having lower graduation rates than White males, the differential between White female graduation rates and African American female graduation rates is also significant ("African-American College Athletes," 2002). This suggests that future research should include African American females in order to determine if similar influences affect their collegiate experience. Sampling limitations also existed. Although the sample consisted of men of various ages from universities across the nation, snowballing may have led to respondents with similar experiences. This limitation was addressed by assuring that the five initial contacts

Campus Athletics

were varied by occupation, university, age, and region of the country. Another limitation of the sample is its small size (N=20). However, there are recognized obstacles to gaining research access to members of Division I teams and professional athletes (Benson, 2000; Funk, 1991; Winbush, 1988). Interviewing high-profile athletes involves some of the same difficulties as studying elites; similarly, they are rare, and unlikely to participate (Neuman, 1997). For this reason, although small, any sample adds significantly to the current body of knowledge.

This study has implications for institutions of higher education and African American male student-athletes. Universities should foster an atmosphere in which the athletes' roles do not overshadow their roles as students, thus allowing them to choose majors of interest to them that will lead to careers outside of sports.

Discussion and Conclusions

Sports have opened doors both educationally and economically for African Americans. African American student-athletes graduate at a higher rate than non-athlete African American students ("African-American College Athletes," 2002). Although White athletes also graduate at higher rates than White non-athletes, the financial benefit of athletic scholarships seems to be more advantageous for African Americans ("African-American College Athletes," 2002). In fact, 90% (18 of 20) of the participants in this study revealed that they would not have had the opportunity to attend college without the athletic scholarships they received. Many of the respondents had collegiate experiences that they did not consider to be positive because only (20%) reported having an overall good experience on campus. Although most respondents received a degree, none felt that their educational development was emphasized by the universities they attended or that they fully reaped the benefits of receiving a higher education. Furthermore, 90% noted that universities were reaping far greater benefits, financial and otherwise, than student-athletes. Many lacked career maturity, which stemmed, in part, from their choice of majors because they were limited by time constraints, NCAA rules, and inappropriate counseling. In addition to the lack of emphasis placed on academic achievement and career development, most of the respondents felt taken advantage of, or, as Hubert stated, like "used goods." Therefore, universities that provide opportunities to African American males to attend college through athletic scholarships by emphasizing the importance of the athletic role over the academic one, leaving the student-athletes feeling exploited, failing to prepare for careers, and even hindering their choice of majors, contribute to the reproduction of these inequalities. African American student-athletes who come to college with disadvantages and hardships, hold even stronger aspirations for professional sports careers (Beamon & Bell, 2002; Sellers & Kuperminc, 1997; Upthegrove, Roscigno, & Charles, 1999). Some African American male student-athletes are particularly susceptible to the pressures of winning, which creates contradictory pressures to perform on the field and in the classroom. Student-athletes should demand and take responsibility for a well-rounded education. They should value the educational opportunity as much as they value the athletic opportunity. Additionally, the era of the amateur collegiate athlete may be over. As big-time, commercialized college athletics continue to generate revenue, the pursuit to win likely will result in student-athletes being encouraged to neglect their academic development for the sake of their athletic performance, which further increases the perception of exploitation.

References

Adler, P. A., & Adler, P. (1987). Role conflict and identity salience: College athletics and the academic role. Social Science Journal, 24, 443-455.

Adler, P. A., & Adler, P. (1991). Backboards and blackboards: College athletes and role engulfment. New York: Columbia University Press.

African-American college athletes: Debunking the myth of the dumb jock. (2002). The Journal of Blacks in Higher Education, 35, 36-40.

Baillie, P. H., and Danish, S. (1992). Understanding the career transition of athletes. The Sport Psychologist, 6, 77-98.

Beamon, K., & Bell, P. (2002). Going pro: The differential effects of high aspirations for a professional sports career on African-American student-athletes and White student-athletes. Race and Society, 5, 179-191.

Beamon, K., & Bell, P. (2006). Academics versus athletics: An examination of the effects of background and socialization on African-American male student-athletes. The Social Science Journal, 43, 393-403.

Benson, K. F. (2000). Constructing academic inadequacy: African-American athletes' stories of schooling. Journal of Higher Education, 71, 223-246.

Blann, F. W. (1985). Intercollegiate addette competition and student's educational and career paths. Journal of College Student Personnel, 26, 115-118.

Cornelius, A. (1995). The relationship between athletic identity, peer and faculty socialization and college student-development. Journal of College Student Development, 36, 560-573.

Donnor, J. (2005). Toward and interest-convergence in the education of African-American football student-athletes in major college sports. Race, Ethnicity, and Education, 8, 45-67.

Edwards, H. (1983). The exploitation of Black athletes. AGB (Association of Governing Boards of Universities and Colleges) Reports, 28, 37-48.

Edwards, H. (1988). The single-minded pursuit of sports fame and fortune is approaching an institutionalized triple tragedy in Black society. Ebony, 43, 138-140.

Edwards, H. (2000). Crisis of Black athletes on the eve of the 21st century. Society, 37, 9-13.

Eitle, T., & Eitle, D. (2002). Race, cultural capital, and the educational effects of participation in sports. Sociology of Education, 75, 123-146.

Eitzen, D. S. (2000). Racism in big-time college sport: Prospects for the Year 2020 and Proposal for Change. In D. Brooks & R. Althouse (Eds.), Racism in college athletics: The African American athlete's experience (pp. 293-306). Morgantown, WV: Fitness Information Technology.

Eitzen, D. S. (2003). Sports and fairy tales: Upward mobility through sport. In J. Henslin (Ed.), Down to earth sociology: Introductory readings (pp. 405-410). New York: Free Press.

Funk, G. D. (1991). Major violation: The unbalanced priorities in athletics and academics. Champaign, IL: Leisure Press.

Gerdy, J. R. (2000). Sports in school: The future of an institution. New York: Teachers College Press.

Giroux, H. A. (1983). Theories of reproduction and resistance in the new sociology of education: A critical analysis. Harvard Educational Review, 53, 257-293.

Hall, R. (2001). The ball curve: Calculated racism and the stereotype of African- American men. Journal of Black Studies, 32, 104-119.

Harris, O. (1994). Race, sport, and social support. Sociology of Sport Journal, 11, 40-50.

Harrison, K. (2000). Black athletes at the millennium. Society, 37, 35-39.

Harrison, C, & Lawrence, S. (2003). African-American student-athletes' perception of career transition in sport: A qualitative and visual elicitation. Race, Ethnicity and Education, 6, 373394.

Hawkins, B. (1999). Black student athletes at predominantly White, National Collegiate Athletic Association division I institutions and the pattern of oscillating migrant laborers. Western Journal of Black Studies, 23, 1-9.

Hoberman, J. (2000). The price of Black dominance. Society, 37, 49-56.

Kennedy, S., & Dimick, K. (1987). Career maturity and professional expectations of college football and basketball players. Journal of College Student Development, 28, 293-297.

Lapchick, R. (1996). Race and college sports: A long way to go. In R. E. Lapchick (Ed.), Sport in society (pp. 5-18). Thousand Oaks, CA: Sage.

Lapchick, R. (2000). Crime and athletes: New radical stereotypes. Society, 37, 14-20.

Lapchick, R., & Matthews, K. (2001). Racial and gender report card. Boston: Northeastern University, Center for the Study of Sport in Society.

Lewis, G. (1970). The beginning of organized collegiate sport. American Quarterly, 22, 222-229.

Litsky, F. (2003, March 25). Study finds top teams failing in the classroom. New York Times, p. B1.

Lomax, M. E. (2000). Athletics vs. education: Dilemmas of Black youth. Society, 37, 21-23.

Maloney, M., & McCormick, R.E. (1993). An examination of the role that intercollegiate athletic participation plays in academic achievement: Athletes' feats in the classroom. The Journal of Human Resources, 28, 555-570.

Meeker, D., Stankovich, C, & Kays, T. (2000). Positive transitions for student-athletes: life skills for transitions in sport, college, and career. Scottsdale, AZ: Holcomb Hathaway.

Meggysey, D. (2000). Athletes in big-time college sport. Society, 37, 24-29.

National Collegiate Athletic Association. (2006). NCAA report on federal graduation rates data-Division I. Retrieved July 15, 2006, from http://webl.ncaa.org/app_data/ instAggr2006/1_0.pdf

Netzely, D., III. (1997). Endorsements for student-athletes: A novel approach to a controversial idea. Stetson Law Forum. Retrieved March 19, 2003, from http://www.law.stetson.edu/ LawForum/back/fall97/ netzley.htm.

Neuman, W. L. (1997). Social research methods: Qualitative and quantitative approaches (3rd ed.). Needham Heights, MA: Allyn and Bacon.

Parker, K. B. (1994). Has-beens and wanna-bes: Transition experiences of former major college football players. The Sport Psychologist, 8, 287-304.

Pascarella, E., Truckenmiller, R., Nora, A., Terenzini, P., Edison, M., & Hagedorn, L. (1999). Cognitive impacts of intercollegiate athletic participation: Some further evidence. The Journal of Higher Education, 70, 1-26.

Person, D., Benson-Quaziena, M., & Rogers, A. (2001). Female student athletes and student athletes of color. New Direction for Student Services, 93, 55-64.

Roscigno, V. J. (1999). The Black-White achievement gap, family-school links and the importance of place. Sociological Inquiry, 69, 159-186.

Sack, A., & Stuarowsky, E. (1998). College athletes for hire: The evolution and legacy of the NCAA's amateur myth. Westport: Praeger

Salome, K. (2005). Lost wealth: The economic value of Black male college athletes. Network Journal, 13, 32.

Sellers, R. (2000). African-American student-athletes: Opportunity or exploitation. In D. Brooks & R. Althouse (Eds.), Racism in college athletics: The African-American athlete's experience (pp. 133-154). Morgantown, WV: Fitness Information Technology, Inc.

Sellers, R. M., & Kuperminc, G. (1997). Goal discrepancy in African-American male student-athletes' unrealistic expectations for careers in professional sports. Journal of Black Psychology, 23, 6-23.

Siegel, D. (1996). Higher education and the plight of the Black male athlete. In R. Lapchick (Ed.), Sport in society (pp. 19-34). Thousand Oaks, CA: Sage.

Singer, J. N. (2002). "Let Us Make Man": The development of Black male (student) athletes in a big time college sport program. (Doctoral dissertation, The Ohio State University, 2002). Dissertation Abstracts International, 63, 1299.

Upthegrove, T., Roscigno, V., & Charles, C. (1999). Big money collegiate sports: Racial concentration, contradictory pressures, and academic performance. Social Science Quarterly, 80, 718-787.

Washington, R. E., & Karen, D. (2001). Sport and society. Annual Review of Sociology, 27, 187-212.

Winbush, R. A. (1988). The furious passage of the African-American intercollegiate athlete. Journal of Sport and Social Issues, 17, 97-103.

Women's Volleyball Injuries

National Collegiate Athletics Association

ncaa.org

2012

This image from the NCAA's website reflects the number of injuries among women collegiate volleyball players. What is interesting to note about these numbers is the severity of the injuries: while only 14% of student-athletes incur shoulder injuries (which seems like a small number), it is important to think about the amount of time and money spent healing such an injury. When a student-athlete incurs a major injury, like a blown-out shoulder, what are they losing in the process? Does the NCAA really "protect" athletes from such losses?

1. How do the illustrations and charts contribute to your understanding of this report?

2. Why do you suppose the NCAA has chosen to supply this kind of information on its website? How might it boost the organization's ethos?

3. The NCAA's mission statement strongly suggests a desire to protect its student-athletes. How might an incoming volleyball player read the mission statement and this graphic report as competing ideas?

WOMEN'S VOLLEYBALL INJURIES

Data from the 2004/05-2008/09 Seasons

In 2008-09, there were 1,015 NCAA member institution teams and 14,827 participants. The average squad size was 15 players.

Injury Overview

- The overall injury rate in NCAA women's volleyball is 4.3 per 1,000 athlete exposures (games and practices combined).
- There were more than 26,000 injuries and 6.1 million athlete exposures from 2004 to 2009.
- Volleyball players are just as likely to be injured in a game (4.2 injuries per 1,000 athlete exposures) as in practice (4.4 injuries per 1,000 athlete exposures).
- Preseason has the highest overall injury rate (6.5 per 1,000 athlete exposures), while the postseason has the lowest (2.4 per 1,000 athlete exposures) as compared to the in-season injury rate of 3.6 injuries per 1,000 athlete exposures.
- Ligament sprains (28.2 percent), followed by muscle strains (21.7 percent), tendinosis (7.5 percent) and contusions (4.6 percent), are the most common types of injuries.
- Ligament sprains of the lateral ankle (15.6 percent), concussions (4.1 percent), quadriceps (thigh) muscle strains (4.0 percent), and abdominal strains (3.0 percent) are the most common types of injury in women's volleyball.
- The outside hitter suffered the most injuries (38.7 percent) for all positions, followed by middle blocker (27.4 percent), libero (12.0 percent), setter (10.9 percent) and opposite/diagonal player (7.5 percent).

Injuries Unique to Women's Volleyball

Ligament sprains and muscle strains are the most common types of injury in NCAA women's volleyball. In addition, more than 51 percent of the injuries occur to the lower extremity. The explosive, bounding nature of volleyball puts extraordinary amounts of strain on the lower extremity, putting the ligaments and muscles at risk. Conversely, the upper extremity, primarily the shoulder region, is at risk of overuse injuries because of the amount of overhead motion required in the sport.

Catastrophic Injuries*

During this five-year period, there were no fatalities from direct mechanisms and one from indirect mechanisms in college volleyball.* During the 28 years that the National Center for Catastrophic Sports Injury Research (NCCSIR) has collected collegiate volleyball data, there have been no deaths related to direct means (collisions) and two related to indirect mechanisms (exertion). During this same time period, there were no fatalities by either direct or indirect mechanisms in high school volleyball reported by the NCCSIR.

Heat Related Injuries

Heat illness accounted for less than 1 percent of the specific injuries in NCAA women's volleyball during this time period. It is important to remember that heat illness is preventable and coaches, athletic trainers and administrators should work diligently to prevent them, even in an indoor sport.

*National Center for Catastrophic Sports Injury Research

Injury Percentage Breakdown

Concussions
4.1%

Head, face and neck
2.3%

Upper limb
21.3%

Torso and pelvis
13.8%

Lower limb
51.1%

Other
7.4%

NCAA is a trademark of the National Collegiate Athletic Association.

Campus Athletics

Concussions

- A concussion is a brain injury.
- Concussions can occur from blows to the body as well as to the head.
- Concussions can occur without loss of consciousness or other obvious signs.
- Concussions can occur in *any* sport.

- All concussions are serious and change a student-athlete's behavior, thinking or physical functioning.
- Recognition and proper response to concussions when they first occur can help prevent further injury or even death.

Injury Prevention Tips‡

For coaches:

- All on-court personnel should review, practice, and follow their venue emergency plan and be trained in administering first aid, AED use, and cardiopulmonary resuscitation (CPR).
- Athletes with a concussion must be removed from practice or competition, and should not return that day and not until given clearance by an approved medical provider according to the institution's concussion management plan.
- Regarding concussions, if in doubt, sit them out.
- Gradually increase the frequency, intensity and duration of training to avoid overuse injuries.
- Balance cardiovascular, strength, flexibility and skills training.
- Be aware of potentially hazardous environmental conditions such as excessively hot indoor facilities with no air conditioning.
- Consider neuromuscular training programs to prevent common ankle and knee injuries.

For student-athletes:

- Have a preseason physical examination and follow your doctor's recommendations.
- Wear appropriate and properly fitted personal protective gear.
- Hydrate adequately — waiting until you are thirsty is too late to hydrate properly.
- Rest. Take some time away from training both during and between seasons to avoid overuse injury and burnout.
- Consider using external ankle support, such as a brace or taping, to prevent the ankle from rolling over, especially if you have had a prior sprain.
- After a period of inactivity, progress gradually back to volleyball through activities such as aerobic conditioning, strength training and agility training.
- Avoid overuse injuries — more is not always better! Listen to your body and decrease training time and intensity if pain or discomfort develops.
- Minimize the amount of jump training on hard surfaces.
- Participate in adequate and supervised rehabilitation for all injuries. Returning to a sport prematurely is associated with a high risk of re-injury.
- Speak with a sports medicine professional or athletic trainer if you have any concerns about injuries or volleyball injury prevention strategies.

Playing Rules and Safety

- The NCAA requires all players to have a preparticipation medical examination.
- The NCAA mandates institutions have a Concussion Management Plan.
- Referees will suspend the match because of a player injury.
- Medical personnel are allowed to remove a player(s) from the court for a serious injury, bleeding, oozing injuries or blood on the uniform.
- An injured player may be replaced by a substitute.
- A player shall not wear anything that is dangerous to any player.
- A player may not wear jewelry of any type whatsoever unless it is for medical alert purposes.
- Play cannot be conducted on any surface that is wet, slippery or constructed of abrasive material.
- Casts are permissible if they are covered and the referee does not consider them dangerous.
- A soft bandage to cover a wound or protect an injury on the arms or hands is permissible.

More Facts
about Collegiate Women's Volleyball Injuries

- Injury is defined as those that occurred as a result of participation in an organized intercollegiate game or practice, required the attention of an athletic trainer or physician, and resulted in the restriction of participation one or more days beyond the day of injury.

  - Anterior cruciate ligament (ACL) sprains account for 0.6 percent of all injuries.
  - The majority of injuries (35.3 percent) caused three to six days of time loss from participation, while injuries accounting for 21 or more days accounted for 12.1 percent of all injuries.

- The most common activity at the time of injury during competition was general play (26.4 percent), followed by digging (19.9 percent), spiking (18.9 percent), blocking (18.8 percent) and passing (5.8 percent).

- The acute non-contact category was the most common mechanism (39.1 percent) for all injuries, followed by gradual/overuse (17.1 percent) and contact with a teammate (14.0 percent).

  - Injuries were evenly spread between warm-up (16.3 percent), set 1 (17.8 percent), set 2 (18.6 percent) and set 3 (15.8 percent) of competitions.

    - The majority of practice-related injuries occurred during team drills (60.0 percent), followed by individual drills (10.0 percent) and conditioning (6.4 percent).

- Surgery resulted from 2.6 percent of all injuries.

Resources

NCAA Sports Medicine Handbook.
Available at www.NCAA.org.

NCAA Concussion Fact Sheets and Video for Coaches and Student-Athletes.
Available at www.NCAA.org/health-safety.

STOP SPORTS INJURIES
‡ Injury Prevention Tips are provided in collaboration with STOP Sports Injuries.
www.stopsportsinjuries.org

DATALYSCENTER
NCAA Sport Injury fact sheets are produced by the Datalys Center for Sports Injury Research and Prevention in collaboration with the National Collegiate Athletic Association, and STOP Sports Injuries. The Datalys Center manages the NCAA Injury Surveillance Program.
www.datalyscenter.org

The Effects of Fraternity/Sorority Membership on College Experiences and Outcomes: A Portrait of Complexity

Ashley M. Asel, Tricia A. Seifert, and Ernest T. Pascarella

Oracle: The Research Journal of the Association of Fraternity/Sorority Advisors

September 2009

Both Ashley Asel and Ernest Pascarella work at the University of Iowa in the Center for Research on Undergraduate Education; Tricia Seifert is from the University of Toronto and focuses her research efforts on how out-of-class experiences can help students toward their educational goals. *Oracle* is an online academic journal that focuses on issues salient to the Greek system. As you read this article, consider how the authors use the information provided by the study.

Greek Life

1. What were the outcomes of this longitudinal study? To whom do the authors address these results? How do the authors use the information provided in the study to shape the way they address the intended audience?

2. Define the parameters and limitations of the study. Why might knowing the methods of the study be important when evaluating the source?

3. While Asel, Seifert, and Pascarella are not condemning fraternity/sorority culture, they do say, "These findings call into question the culture that fraternities/sororities create in terms of alcohol use and abuse." How does this study support Andrew Lohse's claim about hazing rituals in "Confessions of an Ivy League Frat Boy: Inside Dartmouth's Hazing Abuses"? How does this study contradict Lohse's claim?

This study estimated the effects of fraternity/sorority membership on a wide range of college experiences and outcomes for first-year and senior college students at a large, public, Midwestern university. The findings suggest a complex portrait of the relationships between affiliation, engagement, and learning outcomes. Fraternity/sorority membership appeared to facilitate social involvement during college but may have limited the diversity of relationships. It was associated with higher levels of community service, but also increased the odds of excessive alcohol use. In the presence of controls for important, confounding influences, being a fraternity/sorority member had little consistent influence on grades or perceived impact of college. There was little support for gender differences in the impact of affiliation. Finally, implications for student affairs professionals in their work with undergraduate fraternity/sorority leaders and members were considered.

Most institutions of higher education hold student learning and success as parts of their primary missions (Kuh, Kinzie, Schuh, Whitt, & Associates, 2005; Kuh, Schuh, Whitt, & Associates, 1991). Faculty members, staff members, and administrators have attempted to distinguish between the in-class and out-of-class experiences that foster—as well as inhibit—student learning and success (American Association of Colleges &Universities [AAC&U], 2002).

Developing a thorough understanding of the relationship between fraternity/sorority membership, student engagement, and student learning has important implications for student affairs practice and institutional policy. The apparent lack of congruence between espoused values and fraternity/sorority members' behavior, however, has led to debates on many campuses regarding the educational merits of the fraternity/sorority community (Franklin Square Group, 2003). The present study adds to the body of research by examining the complex relationship between fraternity/sorority affiliation and a wide array of college experiences and learning outcomes in students' first and senior years of college.

Review of the Literature

A body of research has examined the relationship between fraternity/sorority membership, engagement in educationally-purposeful activities, and student learning and development. Some researchers suggest fraternity/sorority affiliation is associated positively with increased levels of volunteerism and civic responsibility, and increased willingness to donate to charitable and/or religious causes, as well as involvement in student organizations, general education gains (Hayek, Carini, O'Day, & Kuh, 2002; Whipple & Sullivan, 1998), and persistence through the senior year (Nelson, Halperin, Wasserman, Smith, & Graham, 2006). Fraternity/ sorority members may also experience greater gains in interpersonal skills than unaffiliated students (Hunt & Rentz, 1994; Pike, 2000). Several other researchers also have reported that fraternity/sorority members tend to be more involved during college (Astin, 1977, 1993; Baier & Whipple, 1990; Pike & Askew, 1990).

Conversely some researchers suggest fraternity/sorority affiliation inhibits student learning and contributes to negative health behaviors. Among the findings, fraternity/sorority members have reported being less open to interacting with diverse peers or being challenged by diverse perspectives than their non-affiliated peers (Antonio, 2001; Milem, 1994; Pascarella, Edison, Nora, Hagedorn, & Terenzini, 1996; Wood & Chesser, 1994). Researchers have also linked affiliation with higher rates of alcohol abuse (Wechsler, 1996; Wechsler, Davenport, Dowdall, Grossman, & Zanakos, 1997; Wechsler, Dowdall, Maenner, Gledhill-Hoyt, & Lee, 1998; Wechsler, Kuh, & Davenport, 1996), and engaging in higher levels of drinking and unsafe sexual practices (Eberhardt, Rice, & Smith, 2003; Tampke, 1990; Wechsler, Kuh, & Davenport, 1996).

Finally, fraternity/sorority members are more likely to admit to academic dishonesty during college than their unaffiliated peers (McCabe & Bowers, 1996; Storch, 2002).

In a major longitudinal study, the report of preliminary results included a negative impact of fraternity membership on men's critical thinking skills after the first year of college (Pascarella et al., 1996), but the first-year deficit in critical thinking skills did not persist through the rest of the mens' college experience (Pascarella, Flowers, and Whitt, 1999). There was no evidence to support the assertion that being a member of a sorority had a significant effect on critical thinking skills.

The impact of fraternity/sorority membership on undergraduate student experiences and outcomes has yielded mixed results. The "significant under-representation of research on fraternities/sororities relative to their prevalence in the campus community," (Molasso, 2005, p. 5), and the fact that "psychosocial, cognitive and identity development issues are as important for this community as they are for the broader campus student body" (Molasso, p. 7), make apparent the need to further study the relationship between fraternity/sorority membership and a myriad of student engagement measures including learning outcomes.

What are some unique effects of fraternity/sorority membership on college first-year and senior students? According to Astin's theory of involvement (1984), if affiliated students were more engaged in their educational experience they should report greater learning outcomes as a consequence of their greater involvement. Unlike previous research, the rigorous analytic method used in the present study took into account both students' levels of precollege out-of-class engagement as well as their inclination to report an influential high school education. This analytic approach provided for a conservative estimate of the relationship between affiliation and a wide range of in- and out-of-class experiences as well as desirable outcomes of college for both first-year and senior students, thus painting a relatively comprehensive picture of the effects of fraternity/sorority membership on a large sample of students at a major state research university where fraternity/sorority life involves thousands of students each year.

Methods

Institution

The site for the present study was a large, Midwestern, public, research university of approximately 20,300 undergraduates. Fraternity/sorority life is one of many—but one of the larger—opportunities for student involvement. Roughly 10% of the undergraduate population at the time of the study were members of 13 organizations affiliated with the Interfraternity Council (IFC) and 14 organizations affiliated with the National Panhellenic Conference (NPC). There were also eight National Pan-Hellenic Council, Inc. (NPHC) organizations primarily serving minority students, but the participant group included no more than 25 students total from these eight organizations. While the present study did not distinguish between IFC, NPC, and NPHC organizations, the overwhelming majority of affiliated students were associated with IFC and NPC organizations. There is a more diverse landscape of fraternities/ sororities than is discussed in this paper (Torgerson & Parks, 2009), but results of this study are generalizable only to historically white fraternities/ sororities.

Sample

The sample for the study consisted of first-year and senior students who completed a 30-minute, web-based survey. Employing questions that have been empirically shown to have the greatest impact on undergraduate student learning and persistence (Pascarella et al., 2006), the survey asked an extensive series of questions about students' high school and college experiences. After two follow-up reminders, completed surveys were received from 3,153 students (1,477 first-year students and 1,676 seniors) for a 36.5% response rate.

Variables

The independent variable in all analyses was fraternity/sorority membership, coded 1 for affiliated and 0 for unaffiliated. Approximately 16.4% of first-year students (N = 242) and about 17.4% of senior students (N = 291) indicated that they were fraternity or sorority members.

The effects of fraternity/sorority affiliation were examined on two types of dependent measures: college engagement and college outcomes. The engagement variables measured both in- and out-of- class engagement. The dichotomous engagement measures asked whether or not students had worked on a research project with a faculty member; participated in a cultural or racial awareness workshop; or had participated in a debate or lecture on current social or political issues. A number of single-item, continuous variables asked students to indicate the typical number of hours per week they spent preparing for class, the hours they participated in cocurricular (extracurricular) activities; hours devoted to community service or volunteer activities; the number of books read, essay exams completed, term papers or written reports completed during the current academic year; and binge drinking frequency during a typical two-week semester period. Finally, students were asked to detail their interactions with faculty, student affairs professionals, and peers. The interaction scales measured the quality of personal relationships with peers (α=.85);

Greek Life

frequency of contact with faculty (α=.80); quality of nonclassroom relationships with faculty (α=.86); frequency of contact with student affairs professionals (α=.87); and experiences and interactions with diverse others (α=.91). Detailed operational definitions and constituent items for the interaction scales are available by contacting the first author.

Four dependent learning outcomes were assessed. The first outcome was student academic performance, defined as semester grade point average, with data provided by the registrar. Student self-reports of the impact of their undergraduate experience on their development in 36 areas formed the basis for the remaining three outcome measures. A factor analysis indicated three underlying factors: development in general/liberal arts competencies (α=.92); development in career/professional preparation (α=.87); and personal/interpersonal development (α=.85). Constituent items and factor loadings for the scales are available by contacting the first author. Since students self-selected to affiliate, analyses attempting to estimate the net effect of fraternity/sorority membership on college engagement and outcomes needed to take important confounding influences into account. As many of these potential confounding influences as possible were taken into account; control variables included retrospectively reported parallel measures for each of the dependent variables with high school as the reference point. Additional controls included sex, race, ACT composite score, high school grades, parental education, graduate degree plans, whether the institution was one's first choice for college, amount of on and off-campus employment, current place of residence during college, and intended or actual academic major. The possible effects of gender on affiliation and outcome variables were analyzed, as well as for those participants who did and did not binge drink in high school.

Data Analyses

Logistic regression analysis was used to estimate the net relationships between affiliation (vs. being unaffiliated) on all dichotomous college engagement variables and ordinary least squares (OLS) regression was used to estimate the same relationships between continuous college engagement and outcome measures.

Results

High school experiences, even when reported retrospectively, tended to have by far the strongest relationships with college engagement, binge drinking behavior, grades, and perceptions of the impact of participants' undergraduate experience. Consequently, without controlling for precollege variables, any comparisons between affiliated students and their unaffiliated peers on any self-reports about college learning would likely be confounded in unknown ways (Pascarella, 2001). Thus, results as reported are conservative estimates of the relationships between fraternity/sorority membership, college engagement, and learning outcomes.

General Relationships

The overall findings suggested affiliated students as a group did not have a discernibly different level of academic engagement than their unaffiliated peers (Table 1, Part A). Accounting for an extensive array of potentially confounding influences, no significant relationship existed between affiliation in both the first and senior years in college and working on a research project with a faculty member, time spent preparing for class, number of books read, number of essay exams completed, and number of term papers/written reports completed. Similarly, fraternity/sorority members in both the first and senior years in college had essentially the same likelihood as their unaffiliated peers of participating in a cultural/social awareness workshop or a debate/lecture on current political or social issues.

A dramatically different picture emerged when the estimated relationships between fraternity/sorority members and binge drinking frequency were considered. Taking into account high school alcohol use (plus other influences), affiliated first-year and senior students were significantly more likely to binge drink in college than their unaffiliated peers. Net of confounding influences, the odds of affiliated, first-year students binge drinking one or more times in a typical two-week period were 1.8 times greater than for their unaffiliated peers. For fraternity/sorority seniors, the odds of binge drinking one or more times in a typical two-week period increased to 2.4 times greater than those of unaffiliated seniors. There was also a tendency for affiliated students to be more likely to binge drink at higher levels than other students. The net odds of first-year fraternity/

sorority members binge drinking between two and five times in a two-week period were about twice as high as the odds for their unaffiliated peers doing the same. Even more dramatically, the net odds of senior fraternity/sorority members binge drinking twice, three to five times, and six or more times in a two-week period were respectively 3.0, 2.6, and 3.5 times greater than the odds of unaffiliated seniors doing so.

Fraternity/sorority members as a group appeared to spend substantially more hours per week participating in co-curricular or extracurricular activities (b=2.359, p<.01 for first-years; b=2.588, p<.01 for seniors) and in community service/volunteer activities (b=1.570, p<.01 for first years; b=1.109, p<.01 for seniors) than other students. One might assume increased levels of participation would be related to increased levels of interaction with peers, faculty, and staff.

However, the relationship between affiliation and the quality and frequency of interactions with peers, faculty, and professional staff during college was unclear. Neither first-year nor senior, affiliated students reported the quality and impact of their nonclassroom relationships with faculty significantly differently than their unaffiliated peers. Yet, for seniors, affiliation was related positively to both the quality and impact of personal relationships with peers (b=.254, p<.01) and the frequency of contact with student affairs professionals (b=.235, p<.01).

Affiliation during the first year of college was related to increased frequency of contact with faculty (b=.142, p<.01) but tended to significantly inhibit experiences and interactions with diverse others (b= -.151, p<.01).

In general, the relationships between affiliation and the learning outcomes analyzed for the purposes of this study tended to be either small and nonsignificant or somewhat contradictory (Table 1, Part B). For first-year students, there was essentially parity between affiliated and unaffiliated students on all four outcome measures. Net of other influences, senior, affiliated students tended to report a significantly stronger contribution of their undergraduate experience to personal/interpersonal development than did their unaffiliated peers (b=1.575, p<.01). At the same time, however, affiliation in the senior year had a modest, but statistically significant negative relationship with academic achievement (b= -.078, p<.01).

Conditional Effects

In general, the relationship between affiliation and outcomes did not differ by student characteristics, with one exception. The positive relationship between affiliation and personal/interpersonal development was significantly stronger for men than for women. In the case of binge drinking, the relationship between affiliation and binge drinking frequency was essentially the same for students who did and did not binge drink in high school.

Discussion

Academic and Social Engagement

Although the findings are limited to a single institution sample, they present a complex portrait of the unique relationships between fraternity/sorority membership and students' level of engagement during college. Net of important confounding influences, no evidence suggested first-year or senior fraternity/sorority members were less academically engaged than their unaffiliated peers. These findings provide empirical evidence to counter assertions that fraternities/sororities promote an anti-intellectual culture (Thelin, 2004). Student affairs professionals who work with fraternities/sororities may draw on these findings in working with scholarship chairs to more fully include all areas of academic engagement, like connecting members to faculty research and organizing a post-event discussion after a campus presentation.

Given fraternities/sororities' roots in the literary and debating societies of the 19th century (Rudolph, 1990) and the effort to align members' behaviors with historic chapter values (Franklin Square Group, 2003), promoting enhanced academic engagement among fraternity/sorority members is well founded.

If fraternity/sorority members and their unaffiliated counterparts were generally equal in academic engagement during college, this was not the case for measures of out-of-class engagement and interacting with members of the university community. The study findings suggested at least some support for the notion that the culture and organizational features of undergraduate fraternity/sorority life tend to facilitate social integration

Greek Life

and enhance the development of close and influential relationships. Fraternity/sorority members have a long history of being highly engaged in the out-of-class life of the campus (Horowitz, 1986; Thelin, 2004). Student affairs professionals who work in fraternity/sorority life can use these findings to share the positive attributes of these organizations with campus stakeholders. Since fraternity/sorority members have a history of organizing in service to their community, campus fraternity/sorority administrators may find it advantageous to collaborate with the community service/volunteer coordinator, as fraternity/sorority members may be natural partners for serving in leadership roles in university-wide service programs. Additionally, investigating the social and organizational processes through which fraternities/sororities foster high levels of out-of-class engagement may provide the building blocks from which student affairs professionals can best promote out-of-class engagement for all students—affiliated or not.

The close and influential interpersonal relationships that fraternities/sororities encourage may limit the heterogeneity and diversity of a member's social involvement and relationships, however, at least in the first year of college. The lack of contact with different others underscores a complex and perhaps even contradictory pattern of influences connected to fraternity/sorority life. On the one hand, fraternities/sororities appear to facilitate social engagement during college, while on the other hand they may place normative social and racial parameters around that engagement. The failure to find significant conditional effects by gender further suggests that this contradictory influence of affiliation holds for women as well as men.

Student affairs professionals who work with fraternities/sororities may choose to highlight these findings in their work with chapter officers, particularly new member educators. In an interdependent, global society in which intercultural effectiveness is a key competency for success (AAC&U, 2004; Thomas & Ely, 1996), it is critical that fraternity/sorority members, especially those in their first year of college, are not hindered in developing meaningful relationships with diverse others. Student affairs professionals can work closely with new member educators to expand the normative social parameters of engagement by providing fraternities/sororities with incentives for collaborating with student organizations with which they do not have a history of collaboration and/or facilitating programs, like intergroup dialogues. These and other efforts are necessary if fraternities/ sororities are ever to silence the criticism that they are exclusionary, racist, sexist, and homophobic (e.g., Kuh, Pascarella, & Wechsler, 1996; Maisel, 1990; Rhoads, 1995; Robinson, Gibson-Beverly, & Schwartz, 2004; Syrett, 2009.

A Culture of Drinking

Consistent with Kuh & Arnold (1993) and DeSimone (2007), evidence from this study strongly suggested that the substantial influence of fraternity/sorority membership on excessive alcohol use was a socialization effect rather than merely a recruitment effect. This influence was discernible as early as the second semester of the first year of college, but was even more pronounced in the senior year. Moreover, the failure to detect significant, conditional relationships between fraternity/

sorority membership, gender, and level of binge drinking in high school suggested the relationship between fraternity/sorority membership and binge drinking was not confined to fraternities, but rather was essentially the same for sorority women as well as for affiliated students who did and did not binge drink in high school.

These findings call into question the culture that fraternities/sororities create in terms of alcohol use and abuse. Student affairs professionals can use this research with chapter alumni(ae) as well as undergraduate chapter leaders in confronting the convenient myths (i.e., fraternities/sororities simply recruit students who binge drank in high school and that the binge drinking problem is confined to fraternities) that may have previously prevented chapters from making necessary changes for the health of their members. Turning the tide of the alcohol culture in fraternity/sorority life requires a coordinated effort (Turning & Thomas, 2008). Rejecting convenient myths and focusing on evidence can aid campus administrators, inter/national organizations, local chapter alumni(ae), and undergraduate members to promote and foster healthy choices.

College Outcomes

Net of an extensive array of confounding influences, little evidence suggested a relationship between affiliation and three of the four learning outcomes, with one exception; affiliated, senior students reported higher levels of personal/interpersonal development than their unaffiliated peers. These findings were inconsistent with previous research in which fraternity/sorority members reported a greater level of self-reported educational gains during college than their unaffiliated peers (Hayek, et al., 2002). This inconsistency in results may be due to the fact that previous research, using self-reported gains, did not introduce a control for students' response inclination on the dependent measures. In the present research, students' inclination to report an influential high school experience acted as a control, and this is likely to have produced a more stringent estimate of the net relationships between fraternity/sorority membership and learning outcomes in both the first and senior years of college.

Finally, while fraternity/sorority membership had only a chance relationship with semester grades in the first year of college, membership had a modest negative relationship with semester grades in the senior year. Even after accounting for binge drinking frequency, the negative relationship between fraternity/sorority membership and grades remained statistically significant and essentially unchanged in magnitude. These findings highlight the need for a four-year academic and developmental model for fraternity/sorority life. Student affairs professionals can use evidence from this study to articulate that focusing scholarship efforts on new members alone is not sufficient. These results suggest a four-year, developmental model and chapter-wide, academic achievement goals may best serve fraternity/sorority chapters.

Conclusion

Our analyses of fraternity/sorority membership, student engagement, and learning outcomes on a single campus suggested more complexity among the variables analyzed than most existing studies. As a developmental influence, fraternity/sorority life appeared to cut both ways, suggesting fraternity/sorority life warrants neither unreserved praise nor blanket condemnation.

Clearly there were areas within fraternity/sorority life where members' behavior aligned closely with espoused values (influential personal relationships; community/civic engagement; and cocurricular participation), but there are important areas where the Call for Values Congruence (Franklin Square Group, 2003) rings true (addressing alcohol abuse; promoting academic achievement; and, fostering interactions with diverse peers). This present study identified these areas and provided suggestions for student affairs professionals to engage fraternity/sorority members and alumni(ae) to create an experience that supports the host institution's educational mission.

Confessions of an Ivy League Frat Boy: Inside Dartmouth's Hazing Abuses

Janet Reitman

Rolling Stone

March 2012

Janet Reitman is a contributing editor to *Rolling Stone*. Several of her articles offer a narrative of a person who has done an unpopular act—Andrew Lohse calling Dartmouth's fraternity system into question, Bradley Manning leaking government documents to the world, and Jeremy Hammond using his computer talent for "cyber-terrorism" with the activist group Anonymous. These high-interest stories fit with *Rolling Stone*'s goal of providing America's youth with bold interviews and commentary about topics they care about. As you read "Confessions of an Ivy League Frat Boy," consider the implications Lohse's "confessions" could have on Greek organizations nationwide.

1. How do authorities address Andrew Lohse's "confession"? What consequences does Lohse face?

2. Reitman relates that when Lohse's former fraternity had been accused of hazing prior to Lohse's whistle-blowing, various brothers "discussed in detail how to respond when questioned by college officials" in order to deny the charges. She writes, "this 'culture of silence'... is both a product of the Greek system's ethos and the shield that enables it to operate with impunity." What are the implications of this "culture of silence" and its double-edged sword?

3. Compare the fraternity's silence with the kind of silence Mark Edmundson accuses administrators of having in "Who Are You? Why are You Here?" How are these ideas of silence similar? How do they differ? In what other ways does a "culture of silence" exist in higher education?

Long before Andrew Lohse became a pariah at Dartmouth College, he was just another scarily accomplished teenager with lofty ambitions. Five feet 10 with large blue eyes and the kind of sweet-faced demeanor that always earned him a pass, he grew up in the not-quite-rural, not-quite-suburban, decidedly middle-class town of Branchburg, New Jersey, and attended a public school where he made mostly A's, scored 2190 on his SATs and compiled an exhaustive list of extracurricular activities that included varsity lacrosse, model U.N. (he was president), National Honor Society, band, orchestra, Spanish club, debate and— on weekends—a special pre-college program at the Manhattan School of Music, where he received a degree in jazz bass. He also wrote songs; gigged semiprofessionally at restaurants throughout New York, New Jersey, and Connecticut; played drums for a rock band; chased, and conquered, numerous girls; and by his high school graduation, in 2008, had reached the pinnacle of adolescent cool by dating "this really hot skanky cheerleader," as he puts it.

That fall, he enrolled at Dartmouth, where he had wanted to go for as long as he could remember. His late grandfather, Austin Lohse, had played football and lacrosse for Big Green, and both Andrew and his older brother, Jon, a Dartmouth junior, idolized him as the embodiment of the high-achieving, hard-drinking, fraternal ethos of the Dartmouth Man, or what Lohse calls a "true bro." A Dartmouth Man is a specific type of creature, and when I ask Lohse what constitutes true bro-ness, he provides an idealized portrait of white-male privilege: "good-looking, preppy, charismatic, excellent at cocktail parties, masculine, intelligent, wealthy (or soon to become so), a little bit rough around the edges"—not, in other words, a "douchey, superpolished Yalie."

A true bro, Lohse adds, can also drink inhuman amounts of beer, vomit profusely and keep on going, and perform a number of other hard-partying feats—Dartmouth provided the real-life inspiration for *Animal*

House—that most people, including virtually all of Lohse's high school friends, would find astounding. This, like the high salaries that Dartmouth graduates command—the sixth-highest in the country, according to the most recent estimates—is a point of pride. "We win," is how one of Lohse's former buddies puts it.

On January 25th, Andrew Lohse took a major detour from the winning streak he'd been on for most of his life when, breaking with the Dartmouth code of *omertà*, he detailed some of the choicest bits of his college experience in an op-ed for the student paper *The Dartmouth*. "I was a member of a fraternity that asked pledges, in order to become a brother, to: swim in a kiddie pool of vomit, urine, fecal matter, semen and rotten food products; eat omelets made of vomit; chug cups of vinegar, which in one case caused a pledge to vomit blood; drink beer poured down fellow pledges' ass cracks... among other abuses," he wrote. He accused Dartmouth's storied Greek system—17 fraternities, 11 sororities, and three coed houses, to which roughly half of the student body belongs—of perpetuating a culture of "pervasive hazing, substance abuse, and sexual assault," as well as an "intoxicating nihilism" that dominates campus social life. "One of the things I've learned at Dartmouth—one thing that sets a psychological precedent for many Dartmouth men—is that good people can do awful things to one another for absolutely no reason," he said. "Fraternity life is at the core of the college's human and cultural dysfunctions." Lohse concluded by recommending that Dartmouth overhaul its Greek system, and perhaps get rid of fraternities entirely.

This did not go over well. At a college where two-thirds of the upperclassmen are members of Greek houses, fraternities essentially control the social life on campus. To criticize Dartmouth's frats, which date back more than 150 years, is tantamount to criticizing Dartmouth itself, the smallest and most insular school in the Ivy League. Nestled on a picturesque campus in tiny Hanover, New Hampshire, the college has produced a long list of celebrated alumni—among them two Treasury secretaries (Timothy Geithner, '83, and Henry Paulson Jr., '68), a Labor secretary (Robert Reich, '68) and a hefty sampling of the one percent (including the CEOs of GE, eBay and Freddie Mac, and the former chairman of the Carlyle Group). Many of these titans of industry are products of the fraternity culture: Billionaire hedge-fund manager Stephen

Mandel, who chairs Dartmouth's board of trustees, was a brother in Psi Upsilon, the oldest fraternity on campus. Jeffery Immelt, the CEO of GE, was a Phi Delt, as were a number of other prominent trustees, among them Morgan Stanley senior adviser R. Bradford Evans, billionaire oilman Trevor Rees-Jones and venture capitalist William W. Helman IV. Hank Paulson belonged to Lohse's fraternity, Sigma Alpha Epsilon, or SAE.

In response to Lohse's op-ed, the Dartmouth community let loose a torrent of vitriol against him on *The Dartmouth*'s website. Lohse, it was decided, was "disgruntled" and a "criminal." His "blanket and bitter portrayal of the Greek system" was not only false, complained one alumnus, "but offensive to tens of thousands of Dartmouth alumni who cherished the memories of their fraternities." Another alumnus put it this way in a mock letter to a human-resources manager: "Dear Hiring Manager, do yourself a favor: Don't hire Andrew Lohse... He will bring disgrace to your institution, just as he did when he embarrassed Dartmouth and SAE." The consensus, as another alum put it: "If you don't want to be initiated, don't pledge."

Though two of Lohse's SAE brothers have confirmed his allegations are generally on the mark, the fraternity has turned on Lohse, portraying him as a calculating fabulist who bought into the Greek system wholeheartedly and then turned against it out of sheer vindictiveness. In a letter to *Rolling Stone*, SAE's lawyer, Harvey Silverglate, labeled some of Lohse's most extreme allegations "demonstrably untrue" and compared Lohse to the stripper who falsely accused a number of Duke lacrosse players of raping her in 2006. "Lohse is... a seemingly unstable individual," Silverglate wrote, "with a very poor reputation for truth-telling and a very big axe to grind."

This is not the first time that SAE has come under fire for hazing abuses, or the first time the house has closed ranks against an attack: In 2009, a member of the Dartmouth faculty accused the fraternity of making pledges chug milk and vinegar until they threw up. According to Lohse and two other SAE alums, the brothers agreed to deny the charges, and discussed in detail how to respond when questioned by college officials. This "culture of silence," as some on campus describe it, is both a product of the Greek system's ethos and the shield that enables it to operate with impunity.

"The fraternities here have a tremendous sense of entitlement—a different entitlement than you find at Harvard or other Ivy League schools," says

Michael Bronski, a Dartmouth professor of women's and gender studies. "Their members are secure that they have bright futures, and they just don't care. I actually see the culture as being predicated on hazing. There's a level of violence at the heart of it that would be completely unacceptable anywhere else, but here, it's just the way things are."

Not so long ago, hazing was viewed at many universities as nothing but pranks, which deans might have privately deplored but nonetheless tolerated. Today, hazing is illegal in 44 states, including New Hampshire— and many colleges have aggressively cracked down on fraternity abuses. Those that failed to do so have increasingly found themselves on the wrong side of the law. Last spring, Yale became the subject of a federal Title IX investigation after a group of 16 current and former students accused the school of creating a "hostile environment" for women, citing a prank in which the pledges of Delta Kappa Epsilon, the same fraternity that boasted both Bush presidents as members, paraded outside the Yale campus chanting, "No means yes! Yes means anal!" Only a few months earlier, in February 2011, a 19-year-old Cornell sophomore died of alcohol poisoning after taking part in an SAE hazing ritual. In response, the boy's mother filed a $25 million lawsuit against SAE, Cornell shuttered its chapter, and the president of the university directed the college's Greek organizations to end the pledging process, effective fall 2012.

Alarmed by the skyrocketing rate of binge drinking, which studies show is nearly twice as high among fraternity residents, a growing number of colleges have opted to kick frats off campus or do away with them altogether. Williams College was the first to shutter its fraternities, in the 1960s, and many others have since followed suit, including Amherst, Bowdoin, Colby, and Middlebury. But Dartmouth, whose unofficial motto is "Lest the Old Traditions Fail," has resisted that transformation, just as it has stood fast against many other movements for social and political progress. Dartmouth was one of the last of the Ivies to admit women, in 1972, and only in the face of fierce resistance from alumni. In 1986, conservative students armed with sledgehammers attacked a village of symbolic shanties erected on campus to protest South African apartheid. More recently, students assailed members of an Occupy vigil at Dartmouth, heckling them with cries of "Faggots! Occupy my asshole!"

Greek Life

"Dartmouth is a very appearance-oriented place," sophomore Becca Rothfeld tells me when I visit the campus in February. "As long as everything is all right superficially, no one is willing to inquire as to the reality of the situation. Everyone knows that hazing goes on, but no one wants to discuss it—just like they don't want to talk about racism, sexism, homophobia, classism." She shrugs, apparently resigned to the situation. "People don't really talk about things at Dartmouth, let alone argue or get outraged about them."

This winter, in the wake of Lohse's op-ed, 105 Dartmouth professors, concerned about this entrenched mindset of avoidance, signed a letter condemning hazing as "moral thuggery" and urged the college to overhaul the Greek system. It was the faculty's third concerted effort to reform the system since the 1990s. Dissent, a signature part of the undergraduate experience at many liberal-arts colleges, is, at Dartmouth, common only to the faculty. "No matter what your actual 'Dartmouth Experience' is, everyone usually falls in line and says, 'Yes, we all love Dartmouth,'" laments English professor Ivy Schweitzer, who has taught at the college for 29 years. "It's really a very corporate way of thinking."

Within the Ivy League, Dartmouth is considered the most "corporate" of the schools, with a reputation for sending graduates to Wall Street and the upper echelons of the corporate world. Statistics show that roughly a quarter of each graduating class find jobs in finance and business—a figure many students consider low, given Dartmouth's prominent ties to its Wall Street alumni, who often come back to campus to recruit. "I've been at our house when a senior partner from a financial-services firm and a chief recruiter from someplace like Bain are standing around drinking with us as we haze our pledges," says senior Nathan Gusdorf. (In the kind of irony rife at Dartmouth, Gusdorf is an organizer of Dartmouth's Occupy movement as well as a brother in Zeta Psi, a house that was "de-recognized" by the college for 10 years after it circulated a newsletter in which some of the brothers promised to reveal "patented date-rape techniques.") "Presumably, you would find a lot of drinking and plenty of frat boys at any university," says Gusdorf, "but here, drunk frat boys are handed so much power right off the bat. People do incredibly bad things to one another here, because they know they're going to get away with it."

That attitude of inherent entitlement often carries over after graduation. "One of the few dependable ways into the one percent is via these elite feeder systems, like Dartmouth," says David Rothkopf, a visiting scholar at the Carnegie Endowment for International Peace and the author of *Power Inc.*, which examines the influence wielded by multinational corporations in the global era. "These schools are about their role as networked conduits to the top as much as they are about education."

Or, as one of Lohse's SAE brothers puts it: "Having a 3.7 and being the president of a hard-guy frat is far more valuable than having a 4.0 and being independent when it comes to going to a place like Goldman Sachs. And that corporate milieu mirrors the fraternity culture."

On a warm February afternoon, I visit Andrew Lohse at his mother's house in Brattleboro, Vermont. Almost 22, he is a handsome kid with tousled brown hair and a polite, almost self-effacing manner. The aggressively preppy look he once favored—ratty Oxford shirts and Nantucket Reds, a style one of Lohse's former friends refers to as "go-fuck-yourself" fashion— has been significantly toned down. In the dining room, his Macbook sits on a table surrounded by legal pads, newspapers, and books by Noam Chomsky, F. Scott Fitzgerald, and Jay McInerney. He's writing a memoir: a "generational tale" that he hopes will be part *Bright Lights, Big City*, part *The Sun Also Rises* and part *This Side of Paradise*, and describes as "a one-way ticket to the secret violence at the heart of the baptismal rites of the new elite." At which point he stops himself. "I bet that sounds incredibly douchey and brash and stupid."

Lohse is a highly self-aware young man who nonetheless came to Dartmouth filled with what he now sees as stupid ideas. His goal, he says, was to raise his station in life as much as his grandfather, a man of humble stock who became a wealthy banker, had done by forging powerful connections. "I read a lot of Fitzgerald before I came to college," Lohse says, "and I guess I wanted to be like that, like a character. I took the idea of creating an identity really seriously. But it wasn't really me. I'm just a regular kid from Nowhere, New Jersey."

In some ways, Dartmouth's own history centers on the concept of identity. Founded in 1769 by a Congregational minister, Eleazar Wheelock, its initial mission was to educate the local Abenaki Indians, a dream that was never realized. Instead, Dartmouth became a college for wealthy white boys who adopted the Indian as their mascot and "Wah-hoo-wah!" as their war cry. They also drank heavily: One cherished facet of the Wheelock myth is that he "tamed" the Indians with New England rum. "It's all a false sense of history," says Lohse. "But it's also very tied into this idea that by going to Dartmouth you're being 'tamed' and civilized and ultimately made into a member of the upper class."

Like most Dartmouth students, Lohse began his journey into this exclusive society just prior to the start of his freshman year, with a five-day wilderness orientation called Trips. This is a Dartmouth tradition, where students hike, kayak, mountain bike, or otherwise explore the White Mountains for few days, winding up at the Dartmouth-owned Moosilauke Ravine Lodge, or the "lodj," where they gather for a communal dinner, followed by song-and-dance routines, and they are even asked to sit on the floor and listen to ghost stories. "Hazed into happiness" is how Gusdorf puts it.

Lohse found the experience both exhilarating and disconcerting. "There is a very specific message you get on Trips," he says, "which is 'We're all your friends, you're part of this awesome new world of Dartmouth, and if you're not having the absolute best time of your life, then there's something really wrong with you.' You are immediately assimilated into this homogeneous way of thinking, where you can't see any of it as uncomfortable or weird, even though it is." One facet of the Trips experience is being served green eggs and ham in the "lodj" and reading Dr. Seuss (a Dartmouth alum, whose real name was Theodor Geisel). "It's like they reduce you to a child in order to remake you," says Lohse. "And then you're in on the joke. You go to one of the best schools in America and you sit on the floor and eat green eggs and ham... and you're going to run the world really soon."

Lohse understood that to enter this privileged class requires one to make the appropriate connections, and he immediately set about trying to forge them. As a freshman, he contributed to *The Dartmouth Review*, the college's staunchly conservative newspaper, founded by a group of young neocons in 1980. He also began to develop his "rush strategy" to prepare for joining a fraternity. "Deciding which fraternity to pledge is the most important political decision a Dartmouth man will make," says Lohse.

It is also, for many, a social necessity. For a college town, Hanover is a fairly boring place to spend four years. Its one main street is lined with cute cafes and high-end shops, but offers virtually no student diversions beyond a movie theater. This leaves the fraternities, whose parties are open to all. Fraternities (unlike sororities, most of which are dry) also happen to be the only campus entities that serve alcohol to minors, which about 70 percent of Dartmouth undergrads happen to be. And the beer is free: Brothers pay for it out of their social dues, with houses sometimes blowing $25,000 per term on beer and other forms of entertainment. Roughly half of Dartmouth's 4,200 students may be affiliated with a Greek organization, but the other half takes part in the system by default.

In high school, Lohse had never been much of a partier. "I never drank before coming to Dartmouth," he says. "I mean, I cut school to go to a John McCain rally." But he knew he'd have to master his aversion to alcohol to gain any kind of traction. According to the National Institute on Alcohol Abuse and Alcoholism, the conventional definition of a "binge" is five drinks in a two-hour period for men. Dartmouth frat boys pride themselves on being able to drink six cups of beer in less than 30 seconds— it's called a "quick six," and requires a person to literally open their gullet and pour the liquid down. There is a YouTube video in which a Dartmouth student does this in less than 10 seconds, but even this feat may not be a record.

All of this binge boozing leads inevitably to binge vomiting. Puking and then continuing to drink—the term is "boot and rally"—is an indelible part of Dartmouth social culture, heralded by successive classes of students. "You're horrified at first, but then you get used to it," says Lohse. "There's a certain way of doing things at Dartmouth, and if you want to succeed, you just have to do it that way."

Lohse had been introduced to the Dartmouth frat culture in high school, while visiting his brother, Jon, a member of Sigma Phi Epsilon. It was in Sig Ep's basement where Andrew, then 16, first encountered pong, Dartmouth's signature drinking game, played with sawed-off paddles and "about five times as much beer as you play with at other colleges." Fraternity basements, legendary for their grottiness, are elevated to a whole new level at Dartmouth. Their precise pungency is hard to describe: urine, vomit, stale beer and sour food, all combined in layers of caked sludge, which emits a noxious odor that can linger on your skin for days. Lohse was grossed out. "I was standing under this dripping pipe, looking at people drinking this watery Keystone Light beer, and I felt cheated," he says.

But Lohse still desperately wanted to pledge. Since Dartmouth students can't formally join a fraternity until their sophomore year, he and his friends cruised a number of frats as freshmen, trying to decide which house to rush. Alpha Delta, the infamous *Animal House* frat, was pretty much out of the question, as were the other elite or "A side" houses on campus, since they recruited jocks and prep-school types who "would have seen right through me," says Lohse. In a way, he was relieved. Rumors about hazing abounded. One fraternity reportedly beat their pledges; another was said to place them in dog crates while the brothers vomited on them. Another frat ordered its new members to crawl between the legs of a line of naked brothers, "with, you know, their ball sacks flapping on their heads." A fourth was rumored to require its pledges to have sex with a frozen turkey.

That left SAE. it had a reputation as a somewhat louche, not particularly athletic fraternity for rich boys, who often wound up "tapped" to join one of Dartmouth's elite senior societies—frats within frats that offer a special inroad to the country's future movers and shakers. Lohse made SAE his first choice.

He wasn't a shoo-in, by any means. "Andrew was a polarizing figure from day one," says a brother. The more conservative members of the house were strongly opposed to Lohse, who had quit *The Dartmouth Review* midway through his freshman year and had gone to write for its rival, the liberal *Dartmouth Free Press*. This was heresy in the eyes of his *Review* colleagues, some of whom were also in SAE. "They came very close to dinging him," recalls an SAE brother. Lohse only received a "bid," or offer to pledge the frat, after several brothers came to his defense, citing his popularity with women. A friend recalls walking into Lohse's room one night to find a girl in his bed, alone, while Lohse was in bed with another girl down the hall.

One night in October 2009, early in his sophomore year, Lohse was studying in his dorm room when he heard someone pounding on his door. A senior stood at the threshold. "You and you," he said, pointing to Lohse and one of his roommates. "Blindfolds. Follow me. Be silent." The boys dutifully did as they were told, grabbing ties to wrap around their eyes and following the older brother down the stairs and into a waiting car. "Shut the fuck up right now!" a brother in the front seat barked, shoving a bottle into Lohse's hands and ordering him to drink. It was MD 20/20, known as Mad Dog, the toxic beverage whose high alcohol content—13 percent— and cheapness has made it popular with homeless men and hard-partying college boys everywhere. Lohse chugged. The stuff tasted like Lysol.

The pledges were driven to a remote spot across the Vermont border, where they were marched up a wooded trail and into a clearing. A group of SAE brothers stood before them, lit by a tiki torch. "Who among you most deserves a bid and why?" they asked. Lohse looked around as 10 sophomores scribbled down on paper why they deserved to be chosen. Then a brother handed each of them a bottle of Boone's Farm Blue Hawaiian—a Windex-colored cohort of Mad Dog—and told them that whoever drank it the fastest got to remain. You go to Dartmouth, Lohse told himself as he pounded the Boone's. You don't lose.

Later that night, Lohse, now very drunk, faced a *Review* brother who had wanted to blackball him. The brother held Lohse's embossed bid card in one hand and a lighter in the other. Ten cups of beer sat on a table. "Do a quick six in the time it takes for this to burn," he told Lohse, setting the bid card on fire. "Go!" Lohse chugged, but was only up to his third cup when time ran out. Seeing his future go up in flames, Lohse vomited all over himself—at which point the brothers told him they were just kidding.

Lohse was given the pledge name "Regina," after the character in *Mean Girls*, in honor of his aggressive social climbing. During his seven-week pledge term, he and his fellow SAE pledges, known as "whale shits," were on call to cater to the whims of the brothers. Most of the formal "hazing" was reserved for meetings and challenges: Pledges would be required to perform endless "quick sixes," recite SAE's creed, "The True Gentleman," while lying in a kiddie pool full of ice, or take shots of mystery alcohol while being quizzed on arcane fraternity lore. (This same ritual, with the addition of tying the pledge's hands and feet with zip ties, led to the death of Cornell sophomore George Desdunes, the SAE pledge who died last February.) There were also "milk meetings," where pledges were asked to chug a gallon of milk in 20 minutes, which always resulted in plentiful booting. "You get points for how many times you booted on other people," says Lohse, who adds that the pledge trainers kept count while they sat on large throne-like chairs in a basement room. One brother recalls the night some of the pledges were served a scramble of vomit and eggs, known as a "vomlet."

"Andrew kicked ass at pledge term, did everything required of him and then some," one SAE brother says. But Lohse also began to complain, quietly at first, to a few sympathetic older SAEs. Why did smart, decent people who were supposed to be "brothers" have to do this to one another? Why did he need to debase himself like this just to belong to a group? Lohse, recalls one brother, "implored some of the guys to tone it down a bit. No one listened to him."

"Sink Night," when new initiates affirm, or "sink," their commitment to a fraternity, was particularly brutal. Lohse recalls the evening in hazy images: lit candles, blacked-out windows, a relentless pounding on the walls of the elegant pool room of the SAE house, where the pledges spent more than an hour standing in a circle around the pool table in total silence, as brothers burst in and out of the room, forcing them to down bottles of Mad Dog. Lohse remembers the intimidating feel of shirtless male bodies standing around him as he was interrogated in a brother's room, where he was ordered to drink three shots and recite SAE's three cardinal rules: What happens in the house stays in the house. Trust the brotherhood. Always protect your pledge brothers.

At last, he and the other whale shits were escorted to the basement, where they were formally baptized as SAE pledges in a kiddie pool filled with a noxious sludge. "By that point you are really, really drunk—which is the point, because if you weren't, you'd never get in it," says Lohse, who was later told that brothers had peed, defecated, vomited and ejaculated into the pool. His account of the kiddie pool has been almost universally contested by others who took part; according to an SAE brother, the pool was actually filled with food products like water, bread, vinegar, soy sauce, salsa and hot dogs. "When you mix all that stuff together, it smells really gross," the ex-brother says. "And when you're in it, you don't know what it is. We let the pledges' imaginations get the best of them." Lohse, for his part, hasn't backed down. "I know this because I watched them make the batch for the 2011 term," he says. "We were told they needed a few more guys to piss and boot in it."

Such rituals were not restricted to SAE. One student tells me that during his pledge term, the brothers in his house set up a tarp in the fraternity basement, covered it in vomit, and made the pledges do a "slip and slide." He loved it. "Everyone peed on it and threw in their chaw," he says. "I thought it was great. I did it 10 times. But I was getting kind of cut up, so the pledge trainer told me I really should stop so I wouldn't get too many infections."

Ritualized vomiting was simply part of brotherly life. SAE has a "boot room," which is essentially a bathroom where brothers in the midst of a rigorous game of pong can stick their finger down their throat—the term is "pulling the trigger"—and then resume the game. At some houses, pledges are not allowed to pull their own triggers, but must get a friend to do it for them. "It's all about the challenge," says one of Lohse's SAE brothers. A game that is played at nearly every Dartmouth fraternity is called Thunderdome, or Dome. The entire goal of the two-man contest is to make the other person drink until he vomits—at which point the winner "claims his right" by throwing up on the loser.

"You don't learn about Doming until you become a brother," says Lohse. "When you realize you're going to have to do this, it's really shocking." SAE, he adds, was never as strict about the "boot on his head" thing as other houses, though it did take place sometimes—"I've been booted on and booted on others," he says. (Another SAE brother confirmed, "Everyone in the house was encouraged to vomit on each other, but the act of actually vomiting on another individual happened only rarely.")

So internalized did these rituals become that even long-graduated brothers reflect on Dome, and other games, with fondness. "Seeing two friends pulling each other's trigger was one of the most glorious things I've ever seen in my life," says Snowden Wright, an SAE brother who graduated in 2004. "It was like two kittens licking each other clean. Pure friendship." I assume Wright is kidding; he assures me he isn't.

By the end of his pledge term, Andrew Lohse had vomited so much that the enamel on his teeth had largely burned away. But he was now a full-fledged brother, and he threw himself into fraternity culture, adopting an attitude that one former friend calls "the frat star who didn't give a fuck."

Greek Life

Throughout his sophomore year, Lohse lived up to every facet of debauchery he could conjure, from hooking up with multiple women to making sure he was the last to leave the basement at 3 or 4 a.m. "There was a nihilistic quality to Andrew," says Aimee Le, a senior who befriended Lohse in his sophomore year. "The difference between Andrew and his fraternity brothers was that most of the other brothers would try to justify their actions to themselves. Andrew wouldn't even bother."

Hazing left its mark on some of Lohse's brothers; one confided to Lohse that he had sought counseling, haunted by traumas like vomlet. Yet that same brother later hazed the next class of pledges. "It's a vicious cycle, but it's how hazing works," says Lohse. "You accepted this was the culture at Dartmouth, and if you wanted to advance in the culture, you got with the program."

Brothers aren't the only ones injured by this unspoken pact around fraternity life. Sexual assault is rampant at Dartmouth; some female students say they circulate the names of men considered "dangerous" and fraternity houses viewed as "unsafe." Between 2008 and 2010, according to the college's official statistics, Dartmouth averaged about 15 reports of sexual assault each year among its 6,000 students. Brown, a school with 8,500 students, averaged eight assaults; Harvard, with 21,000 students, had 21. And those numbers are likely just a fraction of the actual count: One study showed that 95 percent of all sexual assaults among college students are never reported. In 2006, Dartmouth's Sexual Abuse Awareness Program estimated that there were actually 109 incidents on campus.

"It's depressing coming of age here," says Deanna Portero, a senior from New York. While Dartmouth has an equal ratio of men to women, she says, it often feels as though nothing has changed since the 1970s. Today, a girl who wants to play pong at a frat party can do so only if she plays with a brother. Not to play is prudish; to be someone's pong partner, though, "generally means you're going to hook up with him afterwards," says Portero. "And if you don't like it, 'Fuck you—don't drink our beer.'"

Nearly every woman I speak to on campus complains of the predatory nature of the fraternities and the dangers that go beyond drinking. "There are always a few guys in every house who are known to use date-rape drugs," says Stewart Towle, a member of Sigma Nu, who de-pledged in 2011 because of a number of practices he considered dehumanizing. He says some fraternities would remove an intoxicated person from their house before making a "Good Sam" call to campus security to inform them that the person may have alcohol poisoning. Dartmouth's policy states that there will be no repercussions on either the students who made the call, or the student for whom the call was being made. However, whoever gave that student alcohol could still get in trouble with the police—and in the case of a fraternity, this might result in a fine of up to $100,000. As a result, many fraternities tend to make sure the drunken person is well outside the house before calling security.

One senior, who I'll call Lisa, was "curbed" in this manner the second night of her freshman year. She'd been invited to a fraternity by one of its members. Thinking it an honor, Lisa enthusiastically accepted, and once she got there, she had two drinks. The next thing she remembers is waking up in the hospital with an IV in her arm. "Apparently, security found me in front of the house. That was my introduction to the frats: passing out from drinking, waking up in the hospital and not having any idea what happened." What she did notice were bruises that looked like bites on her chest that hadn't been there before. "To be very honest," she says, "I didn't really want to know what actually happened."

Dani Levin is the president of the Sigma Delta sorority, and a peer sexual-assault counselor. "I get calls almost every weekend," she says. During the few days I was in Hanover, she received several, including one from a woman who said she'd been assaulted, and then threatened by her assailant's fraternity brothers not to tell anyone.

Incidents like this are not lost on Dartmouth administrators. Last spring, college president Jim Yong Kim, an anthropologist, medical doctor and the co-founder of the international NGO Partners in Health, established an intercollegiate collaborative known as the National College Health Improvement Project to study high-risk drinking in the same way that Kim approached communicable diseases in Rwanda and Peru. The group is slated to report its findings next year. "We don't expect to have solutions," says Dartmouth spokesman Justin Anderson, "but what we will have is a ton of data and ways to measure the results."

For many in the Dartmouth community, this data-driven approach falls short. "I just don't see that working at all," says Joe Asch, a former Bain consultant and Dartmouth alum who is the lead writer for Dartblog, a site that covers Dartmouth politics. "It all makes for great PR, but this is about a group of college administrators who've all tried different approaches to a serious problem on their campuses, none of which have made a dent." Even more crucially, such initiatives are not directed at fraternity culture itself, which many see as the heart of the problem.

Besides, say many at Dartmouth, the chances that the school will actually change its approach to fraternities seems slim. Kim, whose three-story mansion sits on Fraternity Row, is a strong supporter of the Greek system; he has suggested on several occasions that fraternity membership may have health benefits, citing studies that show that people with long-standing friendships suffer fewer heart attacks. In a strange abdication of authority, Kim even professes to have little influence over the fraternities. "I barely have any power," he told *The Dartmouth* in a recent interview. "I'm a convener."

In reality, Kim is one of the only officials in a position to regulate the fraternities. More than half of Dartmouth's frats are "local"—houses that split off from their national organizations years ago, and are thus unaccountable to any standards other than those set by the college and their boards.

This autonomy, coupled with large endowments—SAE, which retains its ties to the national body, has, by one estimate, more than $1 million in a trust—makes the fraternities a potent power base. Kim's predecessor, James Wright, was appointed Dartmouth's 16th president in 1998 and embarked on a plan to end the Greek system "as we know it" by requiring fraternities to substantially go coed. In response, 1,000 irate students marched on Wright's house and held protest rallies in which they accused the once-popular president, himself a Dartmouth alum, of treason. "Judas, Brutus, Arnold, Wright," read a banner that hung from the window of one fraternity house. Wright declined to elaborate on the conflict, other than to tell me there was "push back" from both alumni and fraternities over his proposal; by July 1999, he had backed off. Instead, he implemented an infinitely softer set of reforms. "It was a whitewash," says Professor Ivy Schweitzer.

Kim—who was recently nominated by the Obama administration to head the World Bank—was initially seen as a potential challenge to the status quo. But instead, he's proven to be just the opposite. Not long after he took office, Kim met with Dartmouth alums and reassured them he had no intention of overhauling the fraternities. "One of the things you learn as an anthropologist," he said, "you don't come in and change the culture."

Throughout his sophomore year, Lohse ran, desperately by his own admission, for a multitude of political offices available at SAE. Yet with the exception of a short stint as a "rush chair," where he "sold the lie" to new pledges, hardly anyone voted for him. "He had a temper and a reputation of being kind of too big for his shoes," says a former brother.

"I guess it started to dawn on me that most of the SAEs didn't really like me," Lohse says. "And then I realized that I had been forcing myself to like them."

Lohse did become close with two popular seniors who openly flouted house rules by bringing cocaine into SAE, which they often snorted with Lohse in their spacious suite on the third floor. As with all fraternities, drugs were by no means uncommon at SAE, but coke had a particular cachet; one of the seniors most fond of the drug would promote it to his brothers as a sign of one's elitism. "He used to say it was the 'white-collar' drug," says Lohse, "where weed was 'blue-collar.'"

Not all members approved of the drug use, though. In May 2010, toward the end of Lohse's sophomore year, a straight-laced ROTC cadet named Phil Aubart caught Lohse and another brother snorting lines off a composite photo of SAE grads, in the house's pool room. Aubart called Dartmouth security, who notified the police. Lohse was charged with cocaine possession and witness tampering—a charge that he incurred for pouring a cup of beer on Aubart's door and allegedly spitting on him in retaliation. Other brothers, who considered Aubart a "snitch," destroyed a table he had built, peed on his socks and sent him threatening e-mails. Aubart ultimately moved out of the fraternity, severing his ties with SAE.

Lohse, who was still a sophomore, pleaded no contest to the charges and received a $750 fine. While the brother busted with Lohse went on to graduate, Lohse was suspended from Dartmouth for a year. "The hypocrisy in that bothered me," Lohse says. "We made bad choices, but I was doing drugs—I wasn't harming other people. There are aspects of Dartmouth's culture that do harm people, that are just corrupt to the core, and nothing happens."

That November, living at home and angry over what he saw as the unfairness of his predicament, Lohse quietly visited the campus to report SAE for hazing. He had been encouraged to make the move by several friends and by his brother, Jon, who had quit his own fraternity during his senior year. Lohse met with Dartmouth's associate dean for campus life, April Thompson, and David Spalding, Kim's chief of staff, who was a brother at Alpha Delta of *Animal House* infamy. He told himself the move was in the fraternity's—and Dartmouth's—best interests. "I saw my role as a reformer," he says. "I would argue that making these issues front and center is a very positive thing to do."

Telling none of his friends or fraternity brothers that he was in Hanover, Lohse presented the school officials with a "dossier of fraternity-hazing and substance-abuse-related information." For well over an hour, he detailed his experiences and even named names; at one point, he showed the administrators a photo of his pledge class standing in front of a table holding more than 550 cups of beer, explaining that evening's mission: to consume all of it. Spalding, Lohse says, "was aghast."

But Lohse "still clung to the idea that things could be different without me having to be truly public"—in part, he says, to protect himself from the kind of retaliation Aubart endured after informing on Lohse and the other SAEs. Both Thompson and Spalding assured Lohse that protecting his anonymity would be "a priority," he says. "I thought I could reform SAE on the inside," he says. "I never saw it as 'narcing' on them."

Two weeks passed without word from anyone at Dartmouth. Just after Thanksgiving, Lohse e-mailed Thompson to follow up. He was told that, acting on the information he had provided about SAE's upcoming "Hell Night," the last and traditionally most intense night of the pledge term, the Hanover police were preparing to stage a sting operation in the hopes of catching the fraternity breaking the law. Lohse responded with a lengthy e-mail, arguing that focusing on one fraternity would do nothing to prompt a sweeping overhaul of the Greek system.

The sting, in fact, proved to be a failure: The cops had tried to bust the brothers in the act of hazing pledges in a public place, but all they saw that night was a bunch of drunken kids near a statue of Robert Frost, reciting the code of the True Gentleman. "We're not idiots," says an SAE brother. "The stuff we do outside can't be seen as hazing." Lohse believed the fraternity had been tipped off—and indeed, Spalding later told The Dartmouth that administrators had discussed plans for Hell Night with the president of SAE to ensure that the event would not violate the college's hazing policy.

Counseled by his brother and his friends, Lohse decided to force the college's hand by going to the media. On the advice of Professor Bronski, who had written for *The Village Voice*, Lohse even tried to set up meetings with reporters from *The Boston Globe* and *The New York Times*. But at the last minute, Lohse backed off. "I wasn't ready," he says. "A part of me still wanted to go back to Dartmouth and return to my fraternity and party." That winter he took off for Asia, where he spent a few months traveling with his brother and working for a small NGO in Nepal. He continued to e-mail Thompson, asking about the status of the investigation, but says she failed to respond. He also says he began getting his act together. "The longer I stayed away, the less I drank," he says, "and the less I felt like the person I was at Dartmouth."

Lohse returned to Hanover last summer, to prepare for his junior year. He also returned to SAE, where he was still a brother, even if one now tainted by a cocaine bust. "He told everyone he'd traveled the world and was a changed person," says a former friend. "But he was still drinking and smoking weed, still actively pursuing all the things that had gotten him in trouble to begin with." To some, Lohse still seemed furious by what had happened to him. "Andrew has the full weight of the law brought down upon him, gets suspended and gets angrier at something he had already been really angry about," says an SAE brother.

Lohse channeled some of his rage by becoming a columnist for *The Dartmouth*, where he took on subjects like Dartmouth's culture of corporate recruiting, describing it in one op-ed as having "siphoned off some of our great minds into a dead-end field that sanitizes the intellect, offers almost nothing to human society and conditions people to act in ways that are decidedly inhuman." At the same time, he clung, albeit tepidly,

Greek Life

to his identity as a "true bro." Last October, right before fall rush, he wrote a column extolling the fraternal experience: "I must concede that, happily or tragically, many of my most poignant experiences here have dealt with fraternity life [and] I've been trying to come to terms with them all—and with how I let those experiences become too tightly entwined with my identity." His advice to those who pledged was to support one another. "Don't forget who you are and don't be consumed by who you think you are becoming," he wrote. "Trust me, the two will never be as distinct as you are led to believe."

But Lohse himself was spiraling downward. After being out in the "real world" and traveling in Asia, which he describes as an "awakening," he now had trouble taking Dartmouth seriously, with its petty fraternity politics and drinking culture. Feeling ostracized by his fellow students, he fell into a depression he calls a "toxic mixture of anxiety and alienation." Some former friends recall Lohse himself as the polarizing force: He would show up drunk at people's doors at 3 a.m., or spend half the night on a desperate search for drugs. "The problem with Andrew is he's always the victim, he doesn't take responsibility for what he does," says one of his former buddies. "But you always want to give him the benefit of the doubt because he's so charismatic. You get high with Andrew Lohse, and all of a sudden he's on a 20-minute tangent about literature and liberal politics, and he's fascinating and exciting to be around, and makes you believe that you can do great things, because he wants to do great things. But one by one, I think a lot of his friends just gave up."

By homecoming weekend, Lohse had descended to the darkest place he'd ever known. "The harder I tried to believe in it all, the more I couldn't, until I just cracked," he says. "I might have drank myself to death there, I just hated it so much."

The Thursday night of homecoming is SAE's annual champagne formal, which Lohse attended, already drunk on red wine. He then proceeded to drink almost two bottles of champagne, followed by lots of bourbon and multiple beers. By 6 a.m., most of the SAE brothers had passed out, and Lohse and some of the pledges took off for breakfast.

In the story he tells of this incident, Lohse was walking across the college green, near a roped-off area where the annual homecoming bonfire would be held the next night. As he cut across the "restricted area," a campus security guard ordered the boys to leave. What followed was, depending on one's reading, a profound expression of drunken entitlement, or "an existential act of rebellion," as Lohse maintains. "I can walk wherever I want to walk," he told the guard. Then he picked up a plastic folding chair and tossed it in her direction.

Lohse was escorted to the college infirmary and given a Breathalyzer, which registered his blood-alcohol level at 0.24—three times the legal limit. Arrested for disorderly conduct, he was handcuffed and taken to the county jail. Sitting on a bench, waiting for his mother, he considered what had become of the overachieving boy who followed his grandfather to the Ivy League. Whatever the true nature of the Dartmouth Man, he had consumed what remained of Andrew Lohse.

The week after his arrest, Lohse withdrew from Dartmouth on "medical leave," an indeterminate timeout often taken by students with eating disorders or drug or alcohol problems. "The day I left, I said goodbye to a guy I thought was one of my best friends, and told him I had a problem," Lohse recalls. "He told me with the way everyone drinks, he had no way to tell who had an alcohol problem." Back at his mother's house, Lohse enrolled in an outpatient rehab program. By Christmas, he'd recovered sufficiently to decide that he was ready to take the action his brother and friends had long advocated. "It didn't feel right until I tried to close my eyes to everything I knew and realized it was impossible," he says. "I just wasn't afraid of the backlash any longer."

The idea of an editorial came slowly; Lohse wrote between 15 and 20 drafts. Finally, one day in January, he sat down and "just crushed it out." After submitting it to his editors, who fact-checked his allegations thoroughly, he phoned his three closest brothers at SAE. One never returned his call. The second was terrified about what his parents and future employer might think—he had just secured a job at a leading Wall Street firm. But the third turned on Lohse. "He launched into a tirade about how I was a traitor," Lohse recalls.

Lohse tried to calm the brother down. "Do you think all the stuff the house did, like the vomlet, was good?" he asked. "Or beneficial?"

The brother became even more enraged. "I ate the vomlet!" he yelled. "I made other pledges eat it! That's brotherhood!"

In the months since he wrote his article, Lohse has virtually lost all of his Dartmouth friends. "I felt like an idiot because I'd defended him," says one brother in a rival fraternity, "and here he was, throwing it back in our face." Even those most sympathetic to Lohse's position wished it had been someone else who had come forward. "The problem is, it's Andrew Lohse who said this," says one Alpha Delta brother, a well-adjusted varsity athlete with a guilty conscience. "Some of the stuff we do is really disturbing and unnecessary, and we do need to put an end to it. But if a less-controversial figure had been the one to stand up and say something, maybe it could actually happen."

But whistle-blowers are almost always complex, often compromised outliers. And while moral outrage surely plays a large part in a whistle-blower's decision to come forward, so may a combination of anger, revenge, hurt feelings, opportunism, or financial benefit. The question, ultimately, is whether their questionable motivations or checkered past make their words any less credible.

"One step toward redemption is making amends," says Bill Sjogren, a 1967 graduate of Dartmouth. Now a financial manager, Sjogren played football and baseball at Dartmouth and was a brother at the now-defunct Phi Gamma Delta fraternity. He is also a recovering alcoholic who says he learned to drink at Dartmouth. Sjogren resides in the Hanover area, where, in his spare time, he counsels students with substance-abuse issues. "No one has physically died at Dartmouth, yet, but the system destroys the souls of hundreds of students every year," he says. "It's just beaten out of you. If you take your academics seriously, you're not one of us. If you complain, you're exiled—like Andrew Lohse. For a Dartmouth kid to do what he did, he had to have been broken and hit bottom before he could break the code of silence."

On February 22nd, his 22nd birthday, Lohse received a call from Dartmouth's office of judicial affairs, informing him that, based on information he'd provided the college, they were pursuing charges against him for hazing. The college has also charged 27 other members of SAE, stemming from events in the 2011 pledge term. While the other students all categorically deny doing anything illegal, the information that Lohse provided to Dartmouth officials may directly implicate him in hazing. As a result, Lohse—the only student to come forward voluntarily—may be the only student who is ultimately punished. Coupled with the chair-throwing incident, the charges could get him expelled from Dartmouth. "I told them the unabridged truth, and they got me to incriminate myself," he says. "I understand that no one is above the rules, but none of this would have even been possible if I hadn't spoken out in the first place."

When I ask Dartmouth's new dean of the college, Charlotte Johnson, about charging a whistle-blower with the crimes he exposed, she rejects the characterization. "That's an inappropriate analogy," she says. "Andrew does not have clean hands. When someone comes forward and admits wrongdoing, it's not an automatic grant of immunity. We investigate, and the investigation goes where it goes. And the outcome will be what it is."

Dartmouth has recently formed a new task force on hazing, the most recent addition to the multiple committees already addressing problems on campus. The question is, given how the school has treated Lohse, will anyone ever come forward and speak truthfully about the culture of abuse and degradation perpetrated by the fraternity system? Lohse doubts it. "The message this sends is, 'Keep your fucking mouth shut.' And that's pathetic," he says. "If someone dies in a hazing incident next year, my saying 'I told you so' is not going to bring that person back. It's not inconceivable that it could happen—people get hurt all the time at Dartmouth. But no one will ever talk again."

Greek Life

Spring Safety on Campus

Public Safety Team

Colorado State University E-mail

March 2013

Colorado State University, like many other universities across the nation, frequently sends important messages to its student body. This email was sent to the CSU community after Spring Break, and urges CSU students to "take care of yourself and others." Taking into consideration the change toward warmer weather and the stress surrounding the end of semester, CSU administrators are demonstrating care and concern for its student population. As you read this, consider the language used to express this concern.

1. What does the author of this email message stress as important safety measures?

2. The author of this email writes, "Unfortunately, there are increases in opportunistic crimes such as theft and sexual assault." Do you agree with the categorization of sexual assault as a crime of opportunity?

3. Compare the university's concern about alcohol consumption to the knowledge about binge drinking revealed in *Oracle's* longitudinal study. Is the emphasis the author places upon consumption of alcohol warranted? Why or why not?

From: **Public Safety Team** <presofc@colostate.edu>
Date: Fri, Mar 29, 2013 at 12:02 PM
Subject: Spring safety on campus
To: Colorado State University Community <RamNOTICE@colostate.edu>

To: CSU students
From: Chief Wendy Rich-Goldschmidt, CSUPD
      Jody Donovan, Interim Dean of Students

Welcome back from Spring Break!

We hope you all enjoyed your break from classes. Each year, spring brings changes on the CSU campus with warmer weather, longer days, and the countdown to summer break. Spring also is a time to consider some specific health and safety concerns on campus.

While for many of you the end of the semester is exciting, it may also be a source of stress and sadness about leaving campus and your friends and studies. As always, we want to remind you to take care of yourself and others. If you are worried and want to talk to someone, or if you're concerned about a friend, it is ok to Tell Someone. Call 970-491-1530 for a confidential referral to resources.

Also, each spring, there is an increase in numbers of bike and pedestrian accidents. If you are riding your bike on campus, remember to obey all traffic laws, just as you would if you're driving a car. If you're driving, please watch for crosswalks and yield to pedestrians—it's the law. And if you're walking, don't assume cars or bikes will stop even when you step into a crosswalk—take responsibility for your own safety and look around before stepping in front of traffic. Finally, if you're riding a skateboard, please use caution and remember that you may only ride on designated walk ways or sidewalks, and not on the road in bike lanes.

When the weather is nicer, the opportunity for getting into a precarious position is sometimes increased, and, unfortunately, there are increases in opportunistic crimes such as theft and sexual assault.

Please keep the following information in mind:

- Be aware of your surroundings. Keep doors and windows locked when away from home or at night. Let a friend know where you are and who you are with at all times.

- Do not walk home alone from dinner out, a party or bar, and do not accept a ride from someone you do not know well and trust.

- It is a crime to engage in sexual acts with a person who is too intoxicated to give consent, whether or not you are both intoxicated. If you initiate or engage in sexual contact with another person it is your responsibility to know that the person is a consenting adult and is capable of giving consent.

- If you choose to drink, don't get so intoxicated that you are not able to take care of yourself. Designate a sober friend to drive and to stay with friends who may have had too much to drink. Don't let drunk friends leave a party or bar with someone they do not know.

- Don't leave your drinks unattended, and don't mix alcohol with medications, illegal drugs or energy drinks. Know the signs of alcohol poisoning and get help immediately if you are worried about someone.

- There is a relationship between alcohol abuse and sexual assault. Alcohol consumption makes it more difficult for people to think clearly, communicate, listen, give consent or assess risk, which can lead to sexual regrets or violation.

We are all happy to be finishing the semester and we hope that your spring is a safe one. Have a great last few weeks of classes before summer—and remember to take care of yourself and each other!

Campus Safety

Sexual Assault on College Campuses

Julia Arielle

Deviantart.com

March 2007

This image appears on the University of Connecticut's website, on a webpage devoted solely to sexual assault. The statistics are disturbing; They show why it is necessity to address such an issue, especially considering the way the numbers have increased since the data was collected in 2006. There are other powerful features of this image to also consider, such as the placement of the statistics.

1. What argument does this image implicitly make?

2. What is significant about the placement of the tape over the young woman's mouth? What does this imply?

3. A "culture of silence" is a common thread throughout many articles in this chapter: fraternity life, administrators, and now campus safety. How might breaking this silence help?

Campus Safety

A Lack of Consequences for Sexual Assault

Kristen Lombardi

The Center for Public Integrity

February 2010

Kristen Lombardi has been an investigative journalist for nearly two decades, six years of which she's spent writing for *The Center for Public Integrity*. Her investigative work into campus rapes won her three prestigious awards, including the Robert F. Kennedy award. *The Center for Public Integrity* is a non-partisan, non-profit news organization established to "reveal abuses of power, corruption, and betrayal of trust... using the tools of investigative journalism" (*Center for Public Integrity*). As you read this article and watch the interviews, consider whether there is an abuse of power at play.

1. What is the difference between the college judicial system and a court of law? Why are acts of sexual assault among students in the realm of the college judicial system?

2. Lombardi relays that Margaux's alleged rapist was suspended for a semester and received other smaller sanctions such as having to enroll in an alcohol class and being banned from the dorms. Indiana University administrators defended this position as a "teachable moment," later expressing that the alleged attacker had a "critical moment in his life" where he turned from being "combative" to remorseful. Do you agree with this assessment? In your opinion, what obligations does a university have in terms of this kind of "teachable moment?"

3. What are the parallels between Margaux's narrative and Andrew Lohse ("Confessions of an Ivy League Frat Boy")? If student-athletes began to break their own "culture of silence" in regards to their perceived exploitation in college sports (see Beamon's "Used Goods"), might they experience a similar administrative response? Why or why not?

"In my opinion ... IU not only harbors rapists, but also completely disregards, ignores, and fails women. . . ."

Indiana University freshman Margaux J. unleashed these fiery words in May 2006 after a campus judicial proceeding on her allegations of rape. It wasn't that the two administrators running the proceeding panel didn't believe her. In fact, they did. The panel found the student she accused was "responsible" for "sexual contact" with another person without consent. School administrators rank the disciplinary charge among the most serious at IU.

It was the penalty that left Margaux sputtering with rage. The panel recommended suspending her alleged assailant only for the following semester—a summer semester, during which he was unlikely to attend school anyway.

Hearing the decision, she rushed back to her dorm to pen a letter to IU deans, back to the scene where, she says, her alleged assailant raped her while she passed in and out of consciousness from intoxication. Livid over the penalty, Margaux fired off a three-page letter to IU deans, urging a review. In it, she painted the 60-day suspension as a sign of just how casually colleges and universities treat cases of alleged sexual assault. She pleaded for harsher punishment.

Margaux (whose last name is withheld at her request) would eventually get her wish—but only after her parents badgered the university to revise its penalty. And only after she left Bloomington, Indiana, for good.

Disappointing Consequences

A year-long investigation by the Center for Public Integrity demonstrates that the outcome in Margaux's case is far from unusual. The Center interviewed 50 experts familiar with the campus disciplinary process, as well as 33 female students who have reported being sexually assaulted by other students. The inquiry included a review of records in select cases; a survey of 152 crisis services programs and clinics on or near college campuses; and an examination of 10 years of complaints filed against institutions with the U.S. Education Department under Title IX and the Clery Act. The probe reveals that students deemed "responsible" for alleged sexual assaults on college campuses can face little or no consequence for their acts. Yet their victims' lives are frequently turned upside down. For them, the trauma of assault can be compounded by a lack of institutional support, and even disciplinary action. Many times, victims drop out of school, while their alleged attackers graduate. Administrators believe the sanctions commonly issued in the college judicial system provide a thoughtful and effective way to hold culpable students accountable, but victims and advocates say the punishment rarely fits the crime.

Additional data suggests that, on many campuses, abusive students face little more than slaps on the wrist. The Center has examined what is apparently the only database on sexual assault proceedings at institutions of higher education nationwide. Maintained by the U.S. Justice Department's Office on Violence Against Women, it includes information on about 130 colleges and universities receiving federal funds to combat sexual violence from 2003-2008, the most recent year available. Though limited in scope, the database offers a window into sanctioning by school administrations. It shows that colleges seldom expel men who are found "responsible" for sexual assault; indeed, these schools permanently kicked out only 10 to 25 percent of such students.

Just more than half the 33 students interviewed by the Center said their alleged assailants were found responsible for sexual assault in school-run proceedings. But only four of those student victims said the findings led to expulsion of their alleged attackers—two of them after repeat sexual offenses. The rest of those victims said discipline amounted to lesser sanctions, ranging from suspension for a year to social probation and academic penalties, leaving them feeling doubly assaulted. An examination of Title IX complaints filed against institutions with the Education Department revealed similar patterns: Eight students whose complaints stem from reported acts of "sexual assault," "rape," and "sexual misconduct" objected to the school's punishment of their alleged perpetrators. All but one of these eight complaints involved lesser sanctions than expulsion and

Campus Safety

three ended in no punishment after responsible students appealed. Survey respondents reinforced the belief that schools fail to hold abusive students accountable. One respondent summed up the sentiment this way:

> *Judicial hearings almost NEVER result in suspension, let alone expulsion. … Alleged perpetrators still remain on campus, in fraternities, and on sports teams.*

By contrast, some students, including Margaux, reported dropping out because of what they considered lenient discipline for their alleged perpetrators, whom they feared seeing on campus. Others said their alleged attackers violated school-imposed sanctions, often with little repercussion.

College administrators stress that the sanctioning in disciplinary matters reflects the mission of higher education. Proceedings aren't meant to punish students, but rather to teach them. "We'd like to think that we can always educate and hold accountable the student," says Pamela Freeman, associate dean of students at Indiana University. IU officials defended suspending Margaux's alleged attacker as, in effect, a teachable moment, according to interviews with the Center and documents from a federal investigation into the school's handling of the case.

But victim advocates question this notion. "There's no evidence to suggest that a college campus can rehabilitate a sex offender," says Brett Sokolow, of the National Center on Higher Education Risk Management, which consults schools on sexual assault policies. "So why are we even taking that chance?"

Margaux's Case

Margaux, a reserved cellist whose black curls frame moon-shaped cheeks, had doubts about the process even as her informal proceeding took place on May 4, 2006. She reported being raped on April 6 by a fellow freshman who lived on her co-ed floor. Within days, she filed a report with IU police; then, a complaint with IU residence staff. Now, she sat in an office with a school advocate, testifying by speaker phone. Nearby, the alleged assailant—a taciturn, stocky athlete who had seen IU's disciplinary process before—faced a two-member panel in a separate conference room, his father beside him.

Three years after the incident, Margaux reflects on the process experienced by victims of sexual assault.

Panel members—a residence coordinator and a judicial affairs administrator—presented the complaint to the accused student, who one of them later described in records from the federal inquiry as "dismissive, stating 'whatever.'" To this day, the student, who spoke with the Center on condition of anonymity, maintains that "Margaux and I had consensual sex."

Over two hours, in testimony before the panel, some details emerged clearly: Margaux and the alleged assailant agreed they encountered each other in the hall after a late night, drinking; she was crying, searching for her keys, when he offered help; he opened her door. But they gave conflicting accounts of what happened next. The accused claimed Margaux invited him into her room and readily "hooked up." She countered he followed her inside and ignored her efforts to resist. "I began passing out," she wrote in her official statement, "and when I would come to again he would still be on top of me."

The proceeding devolved into what IU officials, in the federal documents, called "a shouting match." The student's father interrupted testimony, despite IU rules prohibiting "advisors" to speak, intimating the two had a one-night stand, "saying that kids were being kids."

Ultimately, they agreed on a key detail: Margaux had been intoxicated. That stipulation became the deciding factor for the panel. "That means he knew she was incapable of consent," says Andrew Chadwick, the top administrator on the panel who then worked at IU's Office of Student Ethics and Anti-Harassment, "yet he went ahead and had sex with her."

The student now disputes this fact, telling the Center, "She seemed fine to me, not drunk." His father, who admits speaking out at the proceeding, says alcohol use should have cast doubt on Margaux's credibility.

The proceeding outcome would be muddied by the intermingling of several disparate terms. Panel members found the student responsible for what Chadwick, according to the federal records, described as "sexual assault (power differential)." The so-called differential: she was clearly drunk and essentially powerless; he, while drinking, was not. Yet at the proceeding, as one of the panel members later described it, the finding was "sexual misconduct." Officially, the charge was "sexual contact." Chadwick, now on leave from IU and working as a student affairs consultant, attributes this discrepancy to a lack of evidence that physical violence had occurred. "At IU," he adds, "we considered this charge just as severe as sexual assault."

Margaux saw it differently, referring to legal statutes: "Apparently, at Indiana, it's not rape when you have sex with someone who cannot give consent."

A College Judicial Process, Not a Court

Administrators stress that the college judicial system is, as IU's Freeman, who heads the Office of Student Ethics, says, "not the same thing as a court of law." Unlike criminal courts, which enforce rape statutes, college proceedings enforce "conduct codes" that list prohibited acts like "sexual assault" or "sexual contact." Their hearing boards operate under different procedural rules and evidence standards. Even their mission differs from the criminal justice system: Verdicts are educational, not punitive, opportunities. Alleged student victims may expect punishment from campus proceedings, says Jerry Price, vice chancellor for student affairs at Chapman University, in California, "but there is nothing in our mission about justice."

Critics say the college system is ill-equipped to handle sexual assault cases. Schools may designate an "investigator" to assess a complaint's merit. But they cannot subpoena records and witnesses to sort out conflicting testimony. Many train hearing boards on policies for adjudicating alleged assaults, but those sessions can only begin to address complexities. "Why would we expect university judicial boards to handle [difficult cases] right?" asks David Lisak, of the University of Massachusetts-Boston, who has trained administrators on combating sexual violence.

Many administrators agree they would rather the criminal justice system take on cases involving campus rape allegations—if only it would. Prosecutors often shy away from such cases because they are "he said, she said" disputes absent definitive evidence.

But if determining guilt is difficult, college administrators say, so is the sanctioning process. As much as 75 to 90 percent of total disciplinary actions doled out by schools that report statistics to the Justice

Department's Office on Violence Against Women amounted to minor sanctions, although it's unclear from the data what the nature of the "sexual assault" offenses were. Among those modest sanctions: reprimands, counseling, suspensions, and community service. The most common sanctioning reflected what the data calls "other" restrictions—alcohol treatment, for example, or social probation. Interviews and records in these cases show that other minor penalties include orders that perpetrators write a letter of apology, or make a presentation to a campus advocacy group, or write a research paper on sexual violence. Administrators note that they sometimes issue multiple sanctions. For instance, they may require a no-contact order, a housing ban, and classes on sexual consent. By contrast, the database shows that colleges rarely expel culpable students in these cases—even though the Justice Department encourages its campus grant recipients to train judicial panels to hand down "appropriate sanctions, such as expulsion."

"I find that absolutely outrageous," says Colby Bruno, managing attorney at the Victim Rights Law Center, in Boston, referring to such sanctions. Bruno, who represents alleged victims in these proceedings, has routinely seen responsible students slapped with deferred suspensions, probations, even no penalties at all. "I don't understand in what crazy universe rape or sexual assault doesn't warrant expulsion," she adds.

Administrators say such information can be misleading. Typically, an official considers several factors in sanctioning: the student's disciplinary record, the institutional precedent, and the violation. Yet this last element can cover everything from fondling to forced penetration. Not every sexual offense deserves the harshest penalty, they argue; not every culpable student is a hardened criminal. "There's not a one-size-fits-all in these cases," contends Rick Olshak, associate dean of students at Illinois State University. He says schools are more likely to expel in cases involving penetration without consent, and clear intent. "It's the cases in the middle"—involving miscommunication and mutual intoxication—"that are more difficult and that will result in less than expulsion," Olshak adds.

At times, though, even seemingly stringent sanctions can amount to little. In December 2007, Ariel Brown, then a junior at Bowdoin College, reported being raped by a baseball player in her dorm after an alcohol-soaked party. Two months later, the Bowdoin Sexual Assault and Misconduct Board deemed the student responsible for "the charge of

Sexual Assault," case records show. For Brown, it was little consolation: A school investigation had already dismissed her allegations of forced anal sex, making the finding solely for "an act of oral sex." (Ariel Brown is a pseudonym to protect her identity.)

During her proceeding, Brown requested that the alleged assailant be suspended. Instead, he received "non-academic suspension"—in effect, social probation.Records show he was "removed from campus for all non-academic pursuits"—no housing, no activities. But Brown later learned Tim Foster, Bowdoin's dean of students, had made an exception: The athlete could attend home baseball games. Brown's mother—a Bowdoin alumnae—remembers complaining to Foster, who relayed that the student had been in his office, crying, because of the penalty. He was allowed to march in the May 2008 graduation; according to records, though, his diploma was held for a year. Foster declined to comment on Brown's case, except to stress that "this matter did not involve any finding of rape." The accused did not respond to several e-mails and phone calls seeking comment.

"To allow someone who's been found responsible for sexual assault to continue to attend such an elite school is just awful," seethes Brown, who transferred to Wellesley College.

Leniency in Exchange for Remorse

In Margaux's case, explanations of the sanction by the panel's top administrator, Chadwick, did nothing to temper her outrage. The official, she remembers, painted a contrite portrait of the alleged assailant, relaying that he had, as one official later put it to the federal investigator, "showed remorse and admitted that he had an alcohol problem."

In an e-mail to the IU deans who oversee the judicial process, including Freeman, Chadwick cited this "break" as reason for limiting the suspension to the summer. "Through his self-discovery today," the administrator wrote, "I believe he still has hope." Chadwick and the residence coordinator, Molly Holmes, had intended to suspend the student until January 2007, but lessened the term, as Holmes stated in the federal records, "because of the perpetrator's change in heart."

Holmes, who now works at Northern Illinois University, declined to discuss Margaux's case. Chadwick, though, confirms that the alleged attacker's turnaround from initially combative to a "'what have I done?' moment" gave them pause. "In student affairs parlance, he's had a critical moment in his life," Chadwick says. He defends their sanction as "appropriate," since they also issued a no-contact order, and mandated alcohol classes and counseling. Earlier, the student had been banned from the dorm. "Those are pretty serious sanctions for an 18- or 19-year-old person," he adds.

The alleged perpetrator, for his part, recalls panel members pressuring him to confess to Margaux's account of the incident, "pushing me into a corner." Chadwick, he claims, wanted him to admit to having a drinking problem, though he says he doesn't. He relented because, in his words, "I saw where they were going." He suggests that he was unlikely to go to summer school anyway.

By then, the student was well known to IU disciplinary officials. The university had deemed him responsible for two other previous violations—drinking alcohol in his dorm, and punching another student in a fight also investigated by campus police for criminal battery charges. Meanwhile, another IU dorm resident sent an e-mail to Margaux informally accusing the same alleged perpetrator of sexual assault The woman claimed the accused "has come into my room on two occasions and forced himself upon me" and she offered, in the e-mail to Margaux, to "back you up."

After her proceeding, Margaux sat in her dorm, penning that irate letter to IU deans. Documents show she had objected to Chadwick that the suspension was "not severe enough." That her alleged attacker would be allowed to return in the fall left her feeling "as if my assault had been swept under the rug," Margaux recalls. But in her view, it also seemed to ignore his record—and the alleged attempted assault. The second woman's e-mail message had made its way to Chadwick, who did not factor her claims into sanctioning because, he says, "it hadn't been a formal case."

Hearing the decision, Margaux's parents immediately pressed the university for expulsion. Her father, Michael, repeatedly contacted Richard McKaig, IU's dean of students, and urged the dean to do "the right thing." He forwarded his daughter's letter to IU's board of trustees, along with his own incensed letter. His wife, Eva—an IU alumna, along with nine of her relatives—called the governor's office, as well as state and federal politicians. "That IU would give a slap on the wrist and a suspension is outrageous," Eva says. "People go to jail for these crimes in the real world."

Days later, IU's McKaig informed Margaux that he had extended the suspension for another two semesters. Her alleged assailant could return to campus in May 2007—two years before her scheduled graduation. In the federal records, McKaig, who has recently retired, stated that he did not believe "a one-summer suspension was sufficient in this instance." IU told federal investigators that it did not receive Margaux's letter until after McKaig had made his decision. McKaig did not respond to several calls and e-mails from the Center seeking comment.

By the time Margaux received the news, though, she had already decided to drop out.

Philosophy is 'Not to Expel'

To IU deans—and their colleagues elsewhere—the outcome in Margaux's case shows the college process works; it ended in what Freeman calls "a very strong sanction." Expulsion at many schools, including IU, seems anathema. For instance, IU officials have expelled only one of 12 students found responsible for alleged sexual assaults in the past four years, as compared to seven suspensions and four probations or reprimands. "Our basic philosophy is not to expel," confirms Freeman. The university will kick out a student believed to be a threat, she says, yet "that does not mean that every single person found responsible for sexual assault gets expelled. They're not all predators."

But critics say that attitude fails to recognize a disturbing reality about campus rape: Many incidents go beyond "miscommunication" among two drunk students—a common characterization among school officials—to predatory acts. Lisak, the U-Mass professor, has studied what he terms "undetected rapists" on college campuses. His research suggests that over half of student rapists are likely repeat offenders who rape an average of six times. Yet administrators, Lisak observes, "think of serial rapists as the guy who wears a ski mask and jumps out of the bushes."

"Schools that overlook this paradigm are failing their female students," charges Bruno, of the Victim Rights Law Center, referring to Lisak's research. "Giving someone a deferred suspension is like giving someone carte blanche to do it again."

Some victim advocates argue that anything less than expulsion—or a years-long suspension—violates the Title IX federal law banning sex discrimination in education. Under Title IX, schools must meet three requirements if they find a sexual assault has occurred: end a so-called "hostile environment"; prevent its future occurrence; and restore victims' lives. "None of that says you have to educate the offender," says Sokolow, of the Higher Education Risk Management Center. And when punishment fails to fulfill these obligations, adds Sokolow, who trains schools on the law, "That has the potential to violate Title IX."

Administrators note that the law does not require expulsion in sexual assault cases or specify any punishment. For them, the practice of combining penalties makes for effective and legal sanctioning without jeopardizing the educational mission. But lawyers contend that colleges and universities are missing the broader legal point: By not punishing culpable students, schools are setting up student victims for years of anguish because they have to encounter their alleged assailants over and over.

"It's really a question of entitlement to education," says Diane Rosenfeld, a Harvard law professor who specializes in Title IX. Often, she notes, student victims become deprived of this legal guarantee because they choose to leave school rather than have to face their alleged attackers, even accidentally. "Expulsion should be a given under Title IX," Rosenfeld adds. She, like many critics, wonders how leaving an alleged perpetrator on campus would not perpetuate a hostile environment.

Certainly, the lives of alleged victims are upended. In April 2006, Angela Tezak, a former student at Pennsylvania State University, participated in an informal proceeding after reporting being raped in an off-campus apartment by a fellow student. At the time, she struggled with depression, and lived in fear of seeing her alleged attacker, rarely leaving her apartment. "What he did really devastated me," Tezak confides.

Her proceeding proved equally devastating. Tezak expected the alleged assailant to face serious consequences after Penn State administrators

Campus Safety

found him responsible for "nonconsensual oral sex" and "nonconsensual intercourse." She remembers Joe Puzycki, assistant vice president for student affairs, calling to inform her that the accused had, as records show, "accepted responsibility." But Tezak also learned that the school intended to sanction the student, a senior, simply by delaying his degree for a year, in what Penn State records describe as "temporary expulsion." Days later, Tezak ingested "a big handful" of sleeping pills, landing in the hospital for five days. Penn State records show she never attended a final meeting with Puzycki because of her hospital stay. Tezak says administrators never gave her a chance to request or appeal the sanction. She ended up dropping out, and eventually transferred.

The alleged assailant, for his part, remembers several meetings with Puzycki, who, he says in an e-mail, "coerced me against my will to sign a document accepting sanctions even though I'm 100 percent innocent." The administrator, he claims, explained that he could appeal Tezak's complaint—which he calls "baseless and wholly untrue"—yet portrayed a formal hearing as futile, and virtually guaranteed to end in permanent expulsion. Rather than face such a prospect, the accused says, he chose to "negotiate lesser sanctions." He offered to do counseling, for instance, in exchange for being able to walk in his May 2006 convocation.

"The way I saw it," he relays, "I was between a rock and a hard place and my choice was, 'Which is the two lesser evils?'" Puzycki, he claims, told him the temporary expulsion would appear as "a black mark" on his transcript for up to five years. It has not prevented him from landing several jobs since.

Puzycki declined to discuss Tezak's case, referring a list of questions to Peggy Lorah, director of Penn State's Center for Women Students. Lorah, who served as Tezak's advocate, insists the university followed standard procedures, including that final meeting with alleged victims to approve punishment. Told that records show otherwise, Lorah replied: "The actions that were taken were in accord with what the victim wanted at that time."

An Appeal to the Education Department

Margaux still bristles over what she calls a "false sense of justice." She had been "an emotional wreck," battling nightmares, barely sleeping. Friends of her alleged assailant harassed her in the dorm. "I was having all this trouble," she recalls, "and here he got suspended." Things would get worse when IU officials took disciplinary action against her. Weeks after her proceeding, Holmes, the panel's residence coordinator, sent Margaux a letter charging her with alleged alcohol violations for hosting dorm guests who had been drinking. The accusation turned out to be unwarranted; a roommate had forged Margaux's name on guest passes. By July, IU deans had dismissed the charge.

That summer, in June 2006, Margaux and her parents filed a complaint against IU with the Education Department, alleging violations under Title IX. It centered on the campus punishment. The family argued that IU had "failed to properly discipline" Margaux's alleged attacker and, thus, had "fostered a hostile environment." Later, they filed another complaint saying the university's charge of alcohol violations amounted to "retaliation" against Margaux.

In its official response, according to case records, IU stressed that panel members handed down "sanction recommendations only," and that Dean McKaig had the final say. "Should the Dean decide that the recommendation of his judicial officers is inappropriate for any reason, the Dean will make the final decision," stated IU's response to the department. "That is what happened in this case." Officials dismissed the retaliation claim as an innocent, albeit insensitive, mistake. "I don't think we did anything wrong," replies Freeman today. Last April, the Education Department essentially agreed, concluding there was "insufficient evidence" IU violated Title IX. Asked about sanctioning in sexual assault proceedings, Russlynn Ali, the department's assistant secretary for civil rights, promised the Education Department will issue new guidance for schools, including "remedies ... that comport with the spirit and intent of Title IX."

Margaux and her parents viewed the complaints as their last hope for accountability in her case. Indeed, her alleged assailant has not returned to IU—he calls the year-long suspension "too severe," although he never filed an appeal. But the campus sanction would become the least of his worries. Not long after dropping out, Margaux learned that local prosecutors would not seek criminal charges for her rape report. Instead, they used her allegations as leverage to reach a plea bargain agreement with her alleged perpetrator in the pending felony battery case. He accepted a deal guaranteeing he would not face charges for sexual assault, served six months' house arrest for pleading guilty to misdemeanor battery, and paid restitution to the IU student whose jaw he had broken. His probation expired in January 2009.

In the June 26, 2006, plea agreement, prosecutors promised to "file no charges against the defendant based on any information known to or received by the State," including "allegations by Margaux J. ... of improper sexual activity." He now attends DePaul University, seemingly unimpeded by the "permanent disciplinary record" on his transcript that IU's Freeman says came from the suspension in Margaux's case.

Now, all Margaux has left is that punishment handed down in her IU proceeding—or, as she puts it, the "kangaroo trial with a kangaroo sanction."

97 of Every 100 Rapists
Receive No Punishment

RAINN

Rape Abuse and Incest National Network

May 2009

This graph represents statistics gathered by the Justice Department in 2009 and analyzed by the Rape Abuse & Incest National Network. These statistics are maddening, and, according to RAINN's president and founder Scott Berkowitz, they "send a clear message to offenders that they can commit this horrible crime and get away with it." As you critically read this graph, think about how this relates to the "lack of consequences" seen for alleged rapists on college campuses.

1. What is the implied argument this graph makes?

2. Describe several ways you could paraphrase this information if you were to use it in a paper.

3. Consider Julia Arielle's photo of the woman with tape over her mouth. Why might statistics like the ones reflected in this graph perpetuate a culture of silence among victims of sexual assault?

Campus Safety

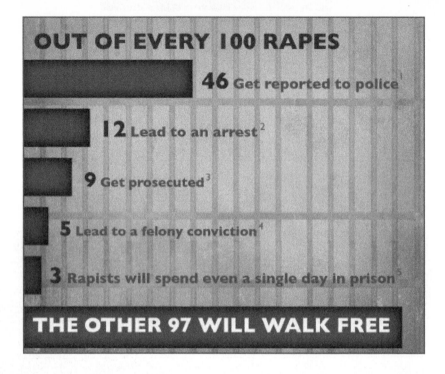

Don't Rape

Think Progress
March 2013

This image comes from a picket sign; the protestor is following the progression of a rape case involving two football players at a Stuebenville, Ohio, high school. This case received national attention in the spring of 2013 after the accused boys' attorney decided to argue that the girl's silence (she was intoxicated and passed out for the majority of the evening in question) was consent. This started a national debate about, among other issues, our society's attitude toward sexual assault and how our society treats sexual assault victims. This sign reflects part of that discussion.

1. How does this picketer's sign reflect the current perception toward sexual assault and a possible change in society's attitude toward sexual assault?

2. Consider the power of language at work in this sign. The original message, "Don't Get Raped," implies the power of circumstances rests solely with the victim. How does the altered argument "Don't Rape" change where the control rests? Why do you suppose the protestor sees more power associated with the changed version?

3. What implications would there be if the emphasis of "keep yourself safe" were shifted toward "don't rape"? Do you think there would be more severe consequences for attackers? Why or why not?

Photo by flickr user cascade_of_rant under Creative Commons 2.0.

Every Student Should Feel Safe on Campus

Prabhdeep Kehal, Cynthia Ledesma, and Carl Nadler

The Daily Californian

February 2013

Kehal, Ledesma, and Nadler are UC Berkeley students attempting to get as many University of California students as possible to participate in a huge, university system-wide survey that will assess the attitudes and perceptions of the campus climate at each of the UC schools. This survey is open to all undergraduate and graduate students, fellows, staff, and faculty, and the goal is to "foster a culture of inclusiveness for an enriched educational and work environment." As you read this article, consider the writing situation within the larger context of the survey.

1. What purpose do Kehal, Ledesma, and Nadler have?

2. What audience appeals do these authors use in order to achieve their purpose? Are they successful? Why or why not?

3. This survey is a concerted effort on the part of administration to improve conditions related to diversity and equity on campuses. Compare this demonstration of care and concern to the actions displayed in other articles, like Kristen Lombardi's "A Lack of Consequences for Sexual Assault," or Janet Reitman's "Confessions of an Ivy League Frat Boy."

Campus Safety

Campuswide surveys from 2008-2012 reveal striking differences in students' experiences at Berkeley. For example, 30 percent of African Americans surveyed over the past five years in the UC Undergraduate Experience Survey (UCUES) felt a gap between the importance of diversity to them as opposed to the importance of diversity to UC Berkeley. On average, one out of every four Chicano or Latino students disagreed that his or her ethnic group was respected on this campus, though importantly over the past five years this sentiment appears to have improved.

For many of you, these statistics, while alarming, come as no surprise. Nevertheless, they raise critical questions for our community: How can we empower our students to be world leaders if we do not cultivate a campus climate of inclusivity and safety? How do we responsibly engage graduate and professional students, faculty and staff? How effective are the existing structures in counteracting these issues? How are our experiences informed by the multiple spaces and places on campus?

Although there is much that remains unclear about the upcoming challenges in our approach to addressing issues regarding campus climate, we urge you to exercise your voice and join us in urging administration to collaborate with students on issues regarding campus climate. Our chance begins February 5. In the largest survey of its kind in the history of higher education, UC Berkeley will join all UC campuses in administering the 2013 Campus Climate Survey.

Please take this survey. Turnout is crucial. Without a large enough number of responses, we will be limited in what we can learn about the groups least represented among us.

You will (or have already) received an email from Chancellor Birgeneau and Vice Chancellor Basri with your personalized "token" or link for taking the survey. If you cannot find that email, you can access the survey through the survey website (http://campusclimate.berkeley.edu).

The Campus Climate Survey is 100 percent confidential. After signing in, your identity is stripped from the data, and you will stop getting official reminders to take the survey. You can take it online or in print. In both situations, your identity remains hidden.

As if improving campus life weren't enough incentive to participate, the university is offering a range of prizes for participation. Systemwide, one lucky undergraduate will get a $10,000 scholarship. Also being offered are two $5,000 post-undergraduate stipends. There are also prizes specific to UC Berkeley students, including 10 $100 Cal 1 Cards. There are prizes specifically for faculty and staff as well. Go to http://campusclimate. berkeley.edu to see a complete list.

At Berkeley, we like to say we take pride in our diversity. This cannot be true if we allow these disparities to persist. To become a true leader in equity and inclusion, we must first be willing to face our limitations. Your answers to this survey will contribute an important first step.

Campus Safety

Women and Gender Advocacy Center Homepage

Colorado State University

www.wgac.colostate.edu

April 2013

It is important to acknowledge that many organizations are working toward making important changes to the way they handle sexual assault, and have begun to offer important resources for victims of sexual assault (and other victimized students). This is Colorado State University's homepage for Women and Gender Advocacy, one such organization making huge strides toward "end[ing] all forms of oppression in our community." Countless universities across the nation have similar resources. As you browse this website, consider how the efforts of such organizations can be beneficial toward campus safety.

1. What services does the WGAC provide to CSU students? What events are sponsored through this organization?

2. The WGAC has an extended history, dating back to the 1960s and the Women's Liberation Movement. Read the "WGAC History" section of the website and consider how the historical context shapes the mission statement and guiding philosophy of the WGAC.

3. Consider the image "Don't Rape" (also in this section). How do the programs, education, and events that the WGAC sponsor support this message? Are there any opportunities to further support campus safety issues?

Works Cited

Chapter 1
Ethical Education: Changes in Mission, People, and Places

Changes in Mission and Vision

Driscoll, Emily. "Higher Education Trends to Watch for in 2013." *Fox Business*. 28 Jan. 2013. Web. 14 July 2013. <http://www.foxbusiness.com/personal-finance/2013/01/28/higher-education-trends-to-watch-for-in-2013/>.

Edmundson, Mark. "Who Are You and What Are You Doing Here?" *Oxford American*. 22 Aug. 22 2011. Web. 6 April 2013. <http://www.oxfordamerican.org/articles/2011/aug/22/who-are-you-and-what-are-you-doing-here/>.

Granholm, Nels H. "Global Imperatives of the 21st Century: The Academy's Response." *Perspectives on Global Development and Technology*. 12.1/2 (2013). 162-178. Print.

"Mission and Purpose." *University of Phoenix*. University of Phoenix, n.d. Web. 12 July 2013. <http://www.phoenix.edu/about_us/about_university_of_phoenix/mission_and_purpose.html>.

"Mission and Strategic Plan." *Front Range Community College*. FRCC, n.d. Web. 13 July 2013. <http://www.frontrange.edu/About-Us/Mission-and-Strategic-Plan/>.

"Mission and Vision Priorities." *Howard University*. Howard University, n.d. Web. 14 July 2013. <http://www.howard.edu/president/vision.htm>.

"MSU Mission Statement." *Michigan State University*. Michigan University. 18 April 2008. Web. 12 July 2013. <http://president.msu.edu/mission/>.

"Vision and Mission Statements." *Wake Forest University*. Wake Forest University, n.d. Web. 12 July 2013. <http://strategicplan.wfu.edu/vision.mission.html>.

Changes in People and Places: The Ethics of Labor and Location in the Academy

"Changing Course: Ten Years of Tracking Online Education in the United States." *The Sloan Consortium.* The Sloan Consortium, n.d. Web. 10 July 2013. <http://sloanconsortium.org/publications/survey/changing_course_2012>.

Gilman, Todd. "Combating Myths About Distance Education." *Chronicle of Higher Education.* 56.24 (26 Feb 2010): A41-A43. Print.

Haynie, Devon. "Veterans Weigh Pros, Cons of Online Education" *US News and World Report.* 7 May 2013. Web. July 5 2013. <http://www.usnews.com/education/online-education/articles/2013/05/07/veterans-weigh-pros-cons-of-online-education>.

Lederman, Doug. "Growth for Online Learning." *Inside Higher Ed.* 8 Jan. 2013. Web. 14 July 2013. <http://www.insidehighered.com/news/2013/01/08/survey-finds-online-enrollments-slow-continue-grow>.

Maistos, Maria and Steve Street. "Confronting Contingency: Faculty Equity and the Goals of Academic Democracy." *Liberal Education.* 97.1 (2011): 6-13. Print.

"Position Statement on the Status and Working Conditions of Contingent Faculty." *National Council of Teachers of English.* NCTE, n.d. Web. 10 April 2013. <http://www.ncte.org/positions/statements/contingent_faculty>.

Thompson, Karen. "Contingent Faculty and Student Learning: Welcome to the Strativersity." *New Directions for Higher Education*. 123 (2003): 17 Sept. 2003: 41. Web. 14 July 2013. <http://onlinelibrary.wiley.com/doi/10.1002/he.119/pdf>.

"Trends in Instructional Staff Employment Status, 1975-2009." Graph. "It's Not Over Yet: The Annual Report on the Economic Status of the Profession." *American Association of University Professors*. March/April (2011): 7. Web. <http://www.aaup.org/sites/default/ files/2010-11-Economic-Status-Report.pdf>.

Weinstien, Adam. "Let's Enroll!" *Mother Jones*. 36.5 (2011): 11-12. Academic Search Premier. Web. 12 July 2013.

Chapter 2
Ethical Values: Economic Costs

Costs and Student Loans

Batchelor, John. "Graduating In Debt." Photo. *The Bagpipe*. 7 Feb. 2013. Web. 10 July 2013. <http://bagpipeonline.com/wp-content/uploads/2013/02/NEWS_Student-Debt-John-Batchelor. jpg>.

Bousquet, Marc. "Students Are Already Workers." *How the University Works: Higher Education and the Low-Wage Nation*. New York: NYU Press, 2008. 125-156. Print.

Brown, Nathan. "Open Letter to Chancellor Linda P.B. Katehi." *UC Davis Bicycle Brigade*. 18 Nov. 2011. Web. 2 Feb. 2013.< http://bicyclebarricade.wordpress.com/2011/11/19/open-letter-to-chancellor-linda-p-b-katehi/>.

"Higher Education: Not What It Used to Be." *The Economist*. 1 Dec. 2012. Web. 2 Feb. 2013. <http://www.economist.com/news/united-states/21567373-american-universities-represent-declining-value-money-their-students-not-what-it>.

Ludden, Jennifer. "College Grads Struggle to Gain Financial Footing." *Morning Edition*. NPR. 10 May 2012. Web. 5 Feb 2013. <http://www.npr.org/2012/05/10/152354154/college-grads-struggle-to-gain-financial-footing>.

"The Path to Student Debt." Infographic. *Collegiate Times*. 2011. Web. 10 July 2013. <http://www.collegiatetimes.com/projects/ student-loan-debt/files/2011/12/debt-graphic.jpg>.

"UC Student Investment Proposal." *Fix UC*. 28 Mar. 2012. Web. 4 Feb. 2013. <http://www.fixuc.org/>.

Woodruff, Mandi. "9 Unbelievable Student Loan Horror Stories." *Yahoo! Finance*. Yahoo! Inc. 26 Nov. 2012. Web. 8 Apr. 2013. <http://finance.yahoo.com/news/9-unbelievable-student-loan- horror-stories-165512874.html?page=all>.

For-Profit Education

"For-Profit Colleges—Are They Only After Your Money?" Infographic. *Visual.ly*. 2011. Web. 10 July 2013. <http://visual. ly/profit-colleges>.

Halperin, David. "Taming the For-Profit College Monster." *Politico*. 24 Aug. 2012. Web. 04 Feb. 2013. <http://www.politico.com/ news/stories/0812/80062.html>.

Kirkham, Chris. "Senate Legislation Targets Aggressive Recruiting of Veterans by For-Profit Colleges." *Huff Post Business*. The Huffington Post. 24 Jan. 2012. Web. 14 June 2013. <http:// www.huffingtonpost.com/2012/01/24/for-profit-colleges- veterans_n_1224407.html>.

Marklein, Mary Beth. "For-Profit Colleges Under Fire Over Value, Accreditation." *USA Today*. 29 Sept. 2010. Web. 04 Feb. 2013. <http://usatoday30.usatoday.com/news/education/2010-09-29- 1Aforprofit29_CV_N.htm>.

"Retention and Graduation Rates for 2011." Infographic. *National Center for Educational Statistics*. 2011. Web. 10 July 2013. <http://nces.ed.gov/programs/coe/analysis/2011-section4.asp>.

Schilling, JoAnna. "What's Money Got to Do With It? The Appeal of the For-Profit Education Model." *Community College Journal of Research and Practice*. 37.3 (2013): 153-159. Academic Search Premier. Web. 22 Mar. 2013.

Chapter 3
Ethical Actions: Academic Integrity

Honor and Integrity

Berlatsky, Noah. "It's Time for a Real Code of Ethics in Teaching." *The Atlantic.* 5 April 2013. Web. 10 April 2013. <http://www.theatlantic.com/national/archive/2013/04/its-time-for-a-real-code-of-ethics-in-teaching/274722/>.

Chace, William M. "A Question of Honor." *The American Scholar.* 81.2 (2012): 20-32. *Academic Search Premier.* Web. 22 Mar. 2013.

Pope, Justin, and Lindsey Anderson. "Harvard Cheating Scandal: Can an Honor Code Prevent Cheating at Harvard?" *Huffington Post.* 12 August 2012. Web. 2 February 2013. <http://www.huffingtonpost.com/2012/09/04/harvard-cheating-scandal-_n_1853663.html>.

Plagiarism and Cheating

Cairo, Alberto. "Why Is Infographics Plagiarism So Common? *Visualopolis.* 7 Feb. 2012. Web. 11 July 2013. <http://visualopolis.com/en/component/content/article/54-featured/121-infographicsplagiarism.html>.

Jaschik, Scott. "Cheating in College." *Inside Higher Ed.* 27 Sept. 2012. Web. 04 Feb. 2013. <http://www.insidehighered.com/news/2012/09/27/authors-discuss-new-book-cheating-college>.

McCabe, Donald L., Linda Kelbe Treviño, and Kenneth D. Butterfield. "Cheating in Academic Institutions: A Decade of Research." *Ethics & Behavior.* 11.2 (2001): 219-232. Print.

"Plagiarism and New Technologies." Image. "The Digital Revolution and Higher Education." *Pew Research Social and Demographic Trends.* Pew Research Center. 28 Aug 2011. Web. 10 Feb 2013. <http://www.pewsocialtrends.org/files/2011/08/online-learning.pdf>.

"Shame Sweepstakes." Graph. "In Plagiarism Too, China Beats India."
    The Telegraph. 2 Oct 2012. Web.12 July 2013. <http://www.
    telegraphindia.com/1121002/jsp/nation/ story_16042659.jsp#.
    UWXXtXBXzjB>.

Simpson, Kevin. "Rise in Student Plagiarism Cases Attributed to
    Blurred Lines of Digital World." *Denver Post*. 7 February
    2012. Web. 4 February 2013. <http://www.denverpost.com/
    news/ci_19907573>.

Sparks, Sarah D. "Studies Shed Light On How Cheating Impedes
    Learning." *Education Week* 30.26 (2011): 1-16. Academic
    Search Premier. Web. 5 June 2013.

Chapter 4
Ethical Engagement: Campus Communities

Campus Athletics

Beamon, Krystal. "Used Goods: Former African American College
    Student-Athletes' Perception of Exploitation by Division I
    Universities." *The Journal of Negro Education*. 77.4 (2008):
    352-364. Print.

Branch, Taylor. "The Shame of College Sports." *The Atlantic*. 7
    Sept. 2011. Web. 13 April 2013. <http://www.theatlantic.
    com/magazine/archive/2011/10/the-shame-of-college-
    sports/308643/>.

"Chronology of Enforcement." *NCAA*. National Collegiate Athletic
    Association. 21 Jan 2013. Web. 13 April 2013. <http://www.
    ncaa.org/wps/wcm/connect/public/NCAA/Enforcement/
    Resources/Chronology+of+Enforcement>.

Davis, Seth. "Should College Athletes be Paid? Why, They Already
    Are." *SI.com*. Sports Illustrated. 21 Sept 2011. Web. 13 April
    2013. <http://sportsillustrated.cnn.com/2011/writers/ seth_
    davis/09/21/Branch.rebuttal/index.html>.

"Women's Volleyball Injuries." Image. *NCAA*. Datalys Center for
    Sports Injury Research and Prevention, n.d. Web. 13 April
    2013.

Greek Life

Asel, Ashley M., Tricia A. Seifert, and Ernest T. Pascarella. "The Effects of Fraternity/Sorority Membership on College Experiences and Outcomes: A Portrait of Complexity." *Oracle: The Research Journal of the Association of Fraternity/Sorority Advisors.* 4.2 (2009): 1-15. Print.

Reitman, Janet. "Confessions of an Ivy League Frat Boy: Inside Dartmouth's Hazing Abuses." *Rolling Stone.* 28 March 2012. Web. 5 March 2013. <http://www.rollingstone.com/ culture/news/ confessions-of-an-ivy-league-frat-boy-inside-dartmouths-hazing-abuses-20120328>.

Campus Safety

"97 of Every 100 Rapists Receive No Punishment, RAINN Analysis Shows." *Rape, Abuse, and Incest National Network* (RAINN). 2009. Web. 10 March 2013. <http://www.rainn.org/news-room/97-of-every-100-rapists-receive-no-punishment>.

Arielle, Julia. "Sexual Assault on College Campuses." Photo. *UConn— Sexual Assault and Violence.* University of Connecticut. 13 Dec. 2008. Web. 13 April 2013. <http://uconncampuscrime. wordpress.com/>.

"Don't Rape." *ThinkProgress.* 19 March 2013. Photo. 13 April 2013. <http://thinkprogress.org/health/2013/03/19/1735451/ university-sexual-assault-policy/?mobile=nc>.

Kehal, Prabhdeep, Cynthia Ledesma, and Carl Nadler. "Every Student Should Feel Safe on Campus." *The Daily Californian.* 5 February 2013. Web. 22 March 2013. <http://www.dailycal. org/2013/02/05/campus-climate/>.

Lombardi, Kristen. "A Lack of Consequences for Sexual Assault." *The Center for Public Integrity.* 24 February 2010. Web. 5 March 2013. < http://www.publicintegrity.org/ 2010/02/24/4360/lack-consequences-sexual-assault>.

Public Safety Team. "Spring Safety on Campus." Message to
        Colorado State University Community. 29 March 2013.
        E-mail.

Women and Gender Advocacy Center. Colorado State University.
        2013. Web. 16 April 2013. <http://www.wgac.colostate.edu/>.